Why We Bite the Invisible Hand

ALSO BY PETER FOSTER

*The Blue-Eyed Sheiks: The Canadian Oil
Establishment* (1979)

*The Sorcerer's Apprentices: Canada's
Superbureaucrats and the Energy Mess* (1982)

*Other People's Money:
The Banks, the Government, and Dome* (1983)

*From Rigs to Riches:
The Story of Bow Valley Industries* (1985)

*The Master Builders:
How the Reichmanns Reached for an Empire* (1986)

*Family Spirits: The Bacardi Saga:
Rum, Riches and Revolution* (1990)

*Self-Serve: How Petrocan
Pumped Canadians Dry* (1992)

*Towers of Debt:
The Rise and Fall of the Reichmanns* (1993)

Why We Bite the Invisible Hand

The Psychology of Anti-Capitalism

Peter Foster

Pleasaunce Press
Toronto

Pleasaunce Press
pleasauncepress@rogers.com

ISBN-13: 978-0992127602
ISBN-10: 0992127602
ISBN 978-0-9921276-1-9 (kindle)
ISBN 978-0-9921276-2-6 (PDF)

For Laurel

About the Author

Peter Foster was born and educated in England. He studied economics at Cambridge and worked for the *Financial Times* of London before immigrating to Canada in 1976 to work for the *Financial Post,* where he became a senior editor.

He has written eight previous books. His first, *The Blue-Eyed Sheiks,* was a number one bestseller. *Self-Serve* won Canada's National Business Book Award. His magazine journalism — which has appeared in *Canadian Business, Toronto Life,* the *Globe and Mail Report on Business* magazine, *Saturday Night* and the *Walrus* — has won awards for subjects as diverse as Moscow McDonald's, oil exploration in the Beaufort Sea and the story behind Toronto's SkyDome. He is a recipient of a Lifetime Achievement Award from the Calgary-based Petroleum History Society.

Since 1998, he has been writing a twice-weekly editorial column for the *Financial Post* section of the *National Post.* In 2011, he received the English-language Economic Education Prize from the Montreal Economic Institute, and his columns have twice been shortlisted for the international Bastiat Prize.

He lives in Toronto.

Contents

Introduction

Dirty Pictures

D ays before the 2012 U.S. presidential election, in early November, a massive storm hit the east coast of the United States, inflicting billions of dollars of damage on New York City and its surrounding areas. A 14-foot storm surge swamped lower Manhattan. Millions lost power in the U.S. northeast. More than a hundred people died.

Democratic president Barack Obama won the election, beating the Republican challenger, Mitt Romney. The media concluded that Superstorm Sandy had helped the president, because it enabled him to look "presidential" when visiting devastated areas and halted any momentum that his opponent might have built. Obama toured parts of New Jersey, accompanied by the state's bulky and charismatic governor, Chris Christie, who had been the keynote speaker at the Republican convention. Christie had previously been sharply critical of Obama, but in the wake of the disaster, he spoke of the president's "extraordinary leadership."

As significant, the storm contributed to Obama's endorsement by New York's billionaire mayor, Michael Bloomberg, who controlled a digital information empire, and in doing so focused on one of the key issues raised by the storm: whether it supported the case for catastrophic man-made global warming, and for draconian policies to confront it. Mayor Bloomberg wrote that one candidate, Obama, "sees climate change as an urgent problem that threatens our planet; one does not."

I

And so Bloomberg was backing the candidate who projected climate catastrophe. Put another way, a capitalist billionaire was acknowledging that the capitalist industrial system posed an existential threat to the world, and was supporting extensive and intrusive government policies to counter it.

Few, if any, regarded this fact as surprising or contradictory. It was widely felt — even by capitalists — that capitalism was an unstable and potentially dangerous system that bred inequality and needed to be regulated and "fettered" for the public good.

Superstorm Sandy pointed to another conundrum about people's — and their representatives' — attitudes toward the system that had made their society so rich. In the storm's wake, both Governor Christie and the Democrat governor of New York State, Andrew Cuomo, hastened to assure their constituents that under no circumstances would they allow free markets to work. The most immediate, obvious and predictable result of their interventions was four-hour lineups at gas stations.

Governor Cuomo managed not merely to disrupt markets but to cause outright panic with the kind of initiative more usually associated with South American dictators. Cuomo promised consumers 10 gallons of free gasoline, which would be distributed from trucks parked at armouries in New York City and Long Island. If price controls cause frustrating waits, the promise of free goods provokes mayhem, and, sure enough, the National Guard had to be called in to deal with the mile-long lineups. The whole ill-conceived scheme quickly had to be scrapped.

Governor Christie meanwhile imposed gas rationing, allowing gas purchases on alternate days, based on whether your licence plate number was odd or even. He had already invoked collectivist solidarity by suggesting that "during emergencies, New Jerseyans should look out for each other — not seek to take advantage of each other." Certainly community spirit was much in evidence in the wake of the storm, but Governor Christie clearly implied that raising prices was the antithesis of such spirit.

When emergencies prevent supplies reaching markets, few take the economist's view that rising prices represent a salutary signal both to suppliers (to provide more) and consumers (to use less). Cries of "gouging" are immediate and reflexive, along with political promises to prosecute all those villainous middlemen attempting to balance supply and demand. Equally predictable are measures to control prices or otherwise "relieve" the situation. What is remarkable about such measures is that they tend to produce far more public hardship than temporary price increases. The sense that "sharing" via rationing is more moral than balancing via the market appears almost immutable. Nobody appears to think it strange that a moral imperative produces perverse results, any more than they think much about where moral imperatives originate.

In fact, many retailers are themselves reluctant to raise prices in emergencies out of quite reasonable fears about the impact on their customers' goodwill. Ironically, by keeping prices unchanged they are harming their customers, or at least some of them. In the presence of panic and in the absence of higher prices, consumers are inclined to hoard, leaving shelves empty for others.

Similarly, "consumer protection" laws often wind up both demonizing retailers and hurting consumers. New Jersey arbitrarily prohibited price hikes of more than 10 percent within 30 days of a declared emergency. New York had made it illegal for retailers to charge an "unconscionably excessive price" for items that were "vital and necessary" for consumers. Naturally, there was, and could be, no reasonable definition of what an "unconscionably excessive price" might be.

Governor Christie's populist statements and actions might have tarnished his reputation but for the fact that other allegedly right-wing politicians in the most allegedly capitalist, free-market nation on earth also tended to abandon any commitment to markets when disaster struck and pump prices rose. Indeed, what would undoubtedly have tarnished the reputation of the Garden State's Republican governor would have been any attempt to awaken the public to the ultimately benign ministrations of markets, or to educate them on the laws of economics. Few politicians in any case want people questioning the notion that governments control and regulate economies to beneficial effect.

At root, the condemnation of markets is a moral one. It has been a perpetual theme of critics since before Marx that money relationships would force out all that is good and kind in traditional family and community relationships, leaving only a "cash nexus" between people, and a relentless rush toward putting a price tag on babies and body parts.

In fact, precisely the opposite seems to be the case. People are relentlessly suspicious of markets and perpetually inclined to believe that they promote harm and inequity, from price gouging through "unconscionably excessive" wealth to environmental destruction.

This book is about the origins of those ways of thinking, which reflect both innate human sympathy and concern for fairness but also severe economic confusion. Those ways of thinking also facilitate political manipulation, with historically disastrous results.

—⁂—

The title of this book — *Why We Bite the Invisible Hand* — combines two metaphors. The first is that of "biting the hand that feeds you," which expresses ingratitude. The "Invisible Hand" is a much more complex and controversial metaphor associated with the great Scottish economist Adam Smith. It refers to the emergent evolutionary processes of commercial markets, which reward competitive innovation and efficiency, promote cooperation and have created unprecedented wealth. The term is often considered a proxy for capitalism.

Smith's great work, *The Wealth of Nations*, was published in 1776. Some might reasonably ask how a book written with a quill pen by a professorial bachelor who wore a powdered wig and ruffles, and who lived in an age of sail and horse power, could still offer insights to a world of globalized mass production, satellite communications, Google and Facebook. The simple answer is that increasing commercial complexity makes Smith's message about markets and economic policy not less relevant but more so.

Smith was not just an incisive analyst of emergent markets and their implications for the role of government, he was an acute observer of human nature, as is clear from his earlier book, *The Theory of Moral Sentiments*. During Smith's lifetime, markets were beginning to evolve at an accelerating pace. Human nature, the subject matter of *Moral Sentiments*, wasn't. That fact stands at the core of my book.

Smith is my constant reference point throughout the voyage of investigation and reflection presented here. It has spanned more than 20 years and has taken me not just to Smith's birth and resting places in Scotland, but to Moscow and Havana, to the sites of the Industrial Revolution in Britain, to Hollywood and into the academic community. The most important place it has taken me is into the human mind, and in particular into the relatively modern field of evolutionary psychology, which is founded on the insights of Charles Darwin (who in turn owed a good deal to Adam Smith).

Let me introduce this perspective via an old joke.

A man goes to a psychiatrist. The psychiatrist shows him a series of Rorschach ink blots — those blobby, random, mirror-image shapes formed by folding a piece of paper with wet ink on it. When asked to describe what he sees, the man interprets each ink blot as some form of sexual act or perversion. At the end of the session, the psychiatrist tells the man, "You have a sex problem."

"Me?" responds the man with indignation. "You're the one who's showing all the dirty pictures."

What we see "right in front of our eyes" is entirely a function of what is behind them. The man who sees the dirty pictures would be routinely considered an example of "abnormal psychology" or psychopathology, but increasingly, the field of psychology has come to realize that "normal" psychology is filled with misinterpretations of the way the world works, and not just when it comes to economics.

We are all subject to optical illusion, but illusions go much deeper than that. The Doobie Brothers sang, "What a fool believes ... he sees," but we all do the same — only now this phenomenon has a fancy name: confirmation bias.

Everybody is familiar with the notion that the mind can play tricks or in some cases entirely deviate from the normal range of perception — or personality — due to some functional deficiency. For example, those with a condition known as prosopagnosia can be perfectly normal except for one rather significant trait: they can't recognize people's faces. "Face blindness" achieved prominence because one of its sufferers, ironically, is a leading neuroscientist: Oliver Sacks.

Again, we are all aware that individuals' personalities incline them to see circumstances and events in different ways. There are numerous metaphors that capture these quirks, such as seeing a glass as half empty rather than half full, or looking at a doughnut and seeing only a hole, or viewing the world through rose-coloured glasses. Extremes of pessimism and optimism are often the source of humour, from Winnie the Pooh's friend Eeyore at one end to Eric Idle singing "Always look on the bright side of life" while being crucified in Monty Python's *Life of Brian* at the other.

One of the spurs to writing this book was that so much that I considered obvious about the benefits of capitalism — benefits that seemed to me to be "right in front of people's eyes" — appeared not to register (although of course I had to be aware that *I* might be the one who was looking through rose-coloured glasses).

The British author Matt Ridley gives an arresting example of my point. In his book *The Rational Optimist*, Ridley points out, "Today, of Americans officially designated as 'poor', 99 per cent have electricity, running water, flush toilets, and a refrigerator; 95 per cent have a television, 88 per cent a telephone, 71 per cent a car and 70 per cent air conditioning." Ridley's killer point was that "Cornelius Vanderbilt had none of these."

Vanderbilt was subsequently dubbed a robber baron. While he certainly participated in the corrupt politics of the time and engaged in business practices that are considered unacceptable today, he revolutionized shipping and rail transportation, hauling down costs and thus greatly benefitting both consumers and businesses (except his direct business rivals). It is significant that the term used to condemn him buries innovation and public benefit beneath implications of political coercion and theft.

What had long intrigued me was that few people appeared to appreciate this lack of appreciation. Put us in a self-drive leather armchair travelling smoothly at 100 kilometres an hour, where we can listen to the best orchestras in the world (or Justin Bieber), and we complain about the price of gas. Fly us in another armchair across a continent in a few hours — a journey that 200 years ago would have taken months — and we moan about airline food.

In fact, far from appreciating advances in human technology, convenience and welfare, many people, including many very bright people, are inclined not merely to condemn the system that has brought about these marvels, but to be profoundly — indeed fashionably — pessimistic about the state of society and the future of the planet. They fret conspicuously about overpopulation, the exhaustion of natural resources, pollution and, in recent decades, impending climate catastrophe, of which Superstorm Sandy was claimed to be a foretaste.

The key to understanding both condemnation and foreboding, I will suggest, requires delving into that ineluctable fact that our perceptions and conceptions are governed by our evolved — or unevolved — assumptions. That in turn involves examining the nature of our minds, how they got that way and how what they see might be a misinterpretation of social processes and relationships that have, in evolutionary terms, appeared in the biological blink of an eye. I will suggest that Smith's hand is not just invisible. For the vast majority of people it is inconceivable. For an influential number, it is a "dirty picture."

Writing this book involved a geographical and intellectual journey, but I can briefly summarize its conclusions without, I hope, spoiling the trip for readers. The first conclusion is that there is much about the market order — and its spectacular results — that is offensive to our moral sentiments, which were designed by natural selection in very different circumstances from those in which we now live. Capitalism is all too easily condemned as being all about greed, exploitation and crass materialism because we are inclined — and encouraged — to view it with moral lenses whose prescription, I suggest, is out of date.

The second is that we not only have no intuitive understanding of economics, but tend to share primitive, erroneous economic beliefs that have been dubbed "do-it-yourself" or "folk" economics. These produce perverse results when embodied in public policy.

The final — most important, but perhaps least examined — element of my conclusions is that those who seek political power tend naturally, indeed subconsciously, to exploit economic misunderstanding and moral confusions, which they might well share themselves.

People's inability to grasp economics is hardly surprising. The Invisible Hand is counterintuitive to a human mind formed predominantly in a hunter-gatherer environment, where there were no extensive markets and no money, technological advance or economic growth. Equally important, we don't have to understand the economic "natural order" to enjoy its benefits any more than we need to understand evolution in order to select a mate, or need to grasp how our own nervous systems work in order to catch a ball.

But ignorance has consequences. Those New Jersey motorists who kvetched in the wake of Superstorm Sandy about gouging, profiteering and rip-offs didn't — and weren't encouraged to — see the connection between their political representatives' strident appeals for economic fairness and the fact that they were stuck eight blocks from a gas station.

In the marketplace of political ideas, the condemnation of greed and selfishness and the promotion of faith in government power tend to beat out appeals to Economics 101 every time. In this regard, I identify a certain "irrational blindness" on the part of some of capitalism's self-proclaimed rationalist champions — such as the Objectivist followers of Ayn Rand — who sometimes seem to imagine that all they need to do to win the battle of ideas is to keep reiterating the supreme logic of their own position. At the other end of the spectrum, I discovered that many experts in the field of evolutionary psychology, which I believe promises profound insights into the nature of anti-capitalism, are themselves steeped in the anti-capitalist assumptions that I imagined they should be examining.

Meanwhile, it's not merely that economics is misunderstood and morally condemned. Professional economics has, from its earliest days, been itself pervaded by moralism and used to justify and serve state power. I examine in particular the assumptions and legacy of John Maynard Keynes, who was dragged from the policy crypt in the wake of the 2008-09 financial crisis despite the fact that his prescriptions had been tried, and had failed, in both theory and practice by the end of the 1970s. I shall also probe an allegedly new branch of the dismal science known as behavioural economics, which claims to be based on the latest psychological insights but misses the elephant in the room.

I will also address the origins of the obsession with corporate "power," which often involves natural confusion about, and/or convenient misrepresentation of, the difference between control of economic resources and political coercion. I touch on two examples of which I have some personal knowledge: the struggles of McDonald's to set up businesses in the collapsing Soviet empire, and the effortless expropriation of the Bacardi rum empire by the revolutionary Cuban regime of Fidel Castro.

I contend that modern corporations are indeed to be criticized — not for single-minded, shareholder-focused profit maximization, but for often hypocritically buying into subversive notions such as corporate social responsibility and sustainable development. These concepts sound unarguable but are, I contend, part of a reformulated anti-capitalist agenda that emerged and expanded after the fall of Communism. The agenda was — and is — rooted in the United Nations and has been promoted by an ever-expanding group of radical non-governmental organizations that have been particularly active in the environmental movement. I highlight one of the most important puppet masters of this agenda, the Canadian Maurice Strong, the most important man of whom most people have never heard.

I profile businessmen who I believe represent the dangerous corporate conceits of our time. The late Georgia-based carpet manufacturer Ray Anderson, perhaps more than any other successful corporate founder, absorbed and promoted the cause of environmental catastrophism while denigrating the markets in which he had thrived. He thought himself exceptional in this regard. Unfortunately he was all too typical of fashionable corporate attitudes.

I also examine the flaws and potential dangers of the concept of "philanthrocapitalism," as promoted by two of the world's most successful businessmen, Bill Gates and Warren Buffett.

I conclude with a summary of why Adam Smith's message is still misunderstood and misreprepresented, but I suggest how the perspective of evolutionary psychology may at least allow proponents of free minds and markets to understand where their opponents are coming from.

This book is not a paean to greed, selfishness or radical individualism. I believe the greatest joys in life come from family, friendship and participation in community, from access to education and the beauty of nature, art and music, and from the satisfaction of providing value, and help, to others. What has long fascinated me is the relentless claims that capitalism destroys these aspects of humanity rather than protecting and promoting them.

— Toronto, November 2013

one

Cardboard Cut-out Capitalism

Everything faded into mist. The past was erased. The erasure was forgotten, the lie became truth.
— George Orwell, *Nineteen Eighty-Four*

Capitalism stands its trial before judges who have the sentence of death in their pockets.
— Joseph Schumpeter, *Capitalism, Socialism and Democracy*

In 2007, as the subprime mortgage crisis was building in the United States, a movie called *American Gangster* was released. It was the true-ish story of a black Harlem drug lord named Frank Lucas. A bright, ruthless and charming country boy, Lucas became temporarily very rich by cutting out the middleman and going straight to the poppy fields of Southeast Asia. During the Vietnam War, he smuggled high-quality heroin in military coffins before cutting and distributing his havoc-wreaking Blue Magic to the black community.

Despite the presence of the Academy Award winners Denzel Washington as Lucas and Russell Crowe as his cop nemesis, Richie Roberts, *American Gangster* was not a great movie. What made it significant, however, was how it equated capitalism with criminality. Even more significant, that take was approvingly regurgitated by reviews in virtually the entire mainstream media.

The film was filled with talk — delivered with an indeterminate amount of irony — about business "principles." Lucas lectured on the importance of "honesty, integrity and hard work." He stressed serving "the consumer," to whom he offered twice the drug quality at half the competitors' price. He was obsessively concerned about his "brand" and with "copyright infringement."

There emerged widespread consensus among reviewers that what Frank Lucas practised was "capitalism," and that capitalism and gangsterism were pretty much joined at the hip. According to the *New Yorker*, Lucas's ascent was presented "as a long-delayed victory of black capitalism." The *Philadelphia Inquirer*'s review suggested that, "like most mob films, [American] Gangster is a study in extreme capitalism." According to the *Dallas Morning News*, "Frank Lucas is a stone killer. He's also a thriving capitalist." The *Santa Fe New Mexican* identified Lucas's success with "operating in the old-fashioned tradition of can-do American capitalism ... You couldn't ask more from Henry Ford."

Henry and Frank. Soul brothers.

Newsweek wrote that the movie "posits the pusher as a triumphant example of black capitalism." *People* magazine suggested that Lucas applied "capitalism's basic principles." The *Chicago Sun-Times* wrote that Lucas "cornered the New York drug trade with admirable capitalist strategies." Its reviewer also opined that "the moral core of the movie ... is a two-pronged look at the corrupting power of capitalism."

Free enterprise made him do it.

A segment on U.S. National Public Radio described the film as "the capitalistic dream run amok." The *New York Sun* called it "the story of organized African-American crime/capitalism." The *Chicago Tribune* dubbed the film "addiction capitalism." The *Detroit News* even sought to put a positive spin on the capitalism/crime connection: "Sure we're shown some of the ugly results of the heroin traffic that Lucas starts," its critic wrote, "but that's balanced by the old entrepreneurial spirit of American capitalism. Lucas is basically a tough competitor in a dirty business, working his way up from the streets."

Heroin. Soap powder. What's the difference?

The British historian Paul Johnson once suggested that capitalism is motivated by a good many of the seven deadly sins (except sloth), but he never suggested that it might be squared with contravention of the sixth and eight commandments. Frank Lucas was a murderer and a thief, albeit a charismatic one. He brought death and destruction to many thousands of individuals and families in and beyond the black community. His self-justification was that, as a black man, he couldn't even have secured a job as a janitor on Wall Street.

Funnily enough, another movie, *The Pursuit of Happyness*, which had been released in 2006, told the more true-ish story of a poor black man, Chris Gardner (played by Will Smith), who not only managed to overcome poverty but wound up founding his own Wall Street brokerage company. The British newspaper the *Daily Telegraph*, a supposedly right-wing organ, described the movie as a "thinly-veiled apologia for rat-race capitalism." Another British newspaper, the *Daily Mail*, which also leans to the right, dumped on the movie's "blind faith in the benevolence of capitalism" as "creepy."

So a successful black gangster is a "capitalist," while a successful black capitalist is just plain "creepy."

Are you beginning to see a little cultural bias here?

—⚇—

Opposite the entrance to the Pump House People's History Museum in Manchester stood a cardboard cut-out. Wearing a top hat, waistcoat and spats, the little cartoon man declared, via a bubble, "I don't approve of this Exhibition at all — but I can't stop you from going in — I would if I could."

Some years before seeing the two-dimensional caricature, I had visited the museum's predecessor, the National Museum of Labour History. A small plaque, part of a temporary exhibit, had declared that, in the 1870s, British cotton workers had toiled "56 and a half hours a day." The claim was presumably a Freudian slip, but how ridiculous would most people consider the reported attitude of the little cardboard capitalist, and his desire to stop people from being exposed to material of which he didn't approve?

In *Nineteen Eighty-Four*, his classic novel of a nightmare totalitarian Britain, George Orwell parodied such caricatures in a "children's history textbook." "In the old days," declared the fictional textbook, "before the Glorious Revolution, London was not the beautiful city that we know today. It was a dark, dirty, miserable place where hardly anybody had enough to eat and where hundreds and thousands of poor people had no boots on their feet and not even a roof to sleep under. Children no older than you had to work twelve hours a day for cruel masters who flogged them with whips if they worked too slowly and fed them on nothing but stale breadcrusts and water. But in among all this poverty there were just a few great big beautiful houses that were lived in by rich men who had as many as thirty servants to look after them. These rich men were called capitalists ... The capitalists owned everything in the world, and everyone else was their slave. They owned all the land, all the houses, all the factories, and all the money. If anyone disobeyed them they could throw them into prison, or they could take his job away and starve him to death."

Today, the case against capitalism — although still occasionally dressed up in a top hat — has morphed toward an assault on giant "faceless" corporations rather than on the bourgeoisie, and toward accusations of destroying the environment rather than (merely) exploiting workers and the state. If individual capitalists hit the headlines, it's likely to be for criminality or the sheer obscenity of their wealth. Meanwhile, Orwell's parody is forgotten. Indeed, Orwell is cited to promote the position he parodied.

—◊—

Simon Schama is a superstar British historian. His 15-part BBC *History of Britain*, originally aired from 2000 to 2002, was as lavishly presented as the three-volume illustrated book of the series. At the time I came across Schama, he was teaching at Columbia University in New York, where he was also art critic for the *New Yorker*. Schama specialized in richly detailed social history, full of witty insights and asides. I had never seen him perform until I caught one of his *History of Britain* programs, which covered the period of the Enlightenment. Schama, on the strength of that one program, seemed guilty of carrying modern sensitivities and assumptions into the past, surely a cardinal sin for any historian.

I probably wouldn't have read his British history, but during a trip to Britain, I spotted an excerpt in the *Sunday Telegraph*. It took me aback. In approaching the Britain of the present, Schama made a good deal of Orwell's insights. He claimed that, in *Nineteen Eighty-Four*, "Orwell had just wanted to … concentrate his mind on what was most important to him: the fate of freedom in the age of the super-power and the super-corporation, which he hybridized in the brutal monstrosity of Big Brother's regime, the Party."

Now *Nineteen Eighty-Four* happens to be one of my favourite books, but nowhere had I ever found any reference to corporations, "super" or otherwise, so I located an email address for Schama and sent off my concern. I received no reply. A couple of months later, I heard that he was coming to Toronto to promote his book. I called his publicist and arranged an interview.

I met Schama at his publisher's office, and after some pleasantries (I was not impolite enough to mention my unanswered email), I read him the offending quote from his book. Then I pointed out that nowhere in *Nineteen Eighty-Four* was there any allusion to corporations of any shape or size.

Schama said, to my surprise, "It's a fair cop. It's true that I slid inaccurately at that point. I was in fact thinking of the way in which bureaucratic corporations work. Orwell does mention such concerns in his correspondence. He was obsessed with 'Fordism,' the kind of streamlining of workers' tasks which took place in the early 1930s. That's what I was thinking of, I now recall. And Fordism is in *Nineteen Eighty-Four*."

Only Fordism really isn't, unless you regard it as synonymous with the mass production of lies, which was the task of the Ministry of Truth, where the novel's hero, Winston Smith, worked. Maybe Schama was thinking of Aldous Huxley's *Brave New World*, which, satirically, deified Henry Ford and gave the invention of the Model T Ford quasi-religious significance in a world where not merely consumer goods but people were mass produced. Then again, there weren't any corporations in *Brave New World* either. Only the state.

I also read Schama the quote about the demonization of capitalism from Orwell's fictional "children's history textbook" and asked him if he remembered it. He admitted he didn't. I asked him what he thought it meant.

"Orwell obviously thinks," said Schama, "that [anti-capitalist historical propaganda] is preposterous. But," he added quickly, "[Orwell] remained a socialist to the end of his days. It's not that he ceased to be a socialist. He certainly thought he died a socialist."

Schama's error about Orwell was hardly an insignificant slip. It raised much larger issues: can history ultimately ever be more than the accumulation of alleged "facts," or sources, to fit the historian's personal prejudices, a rhetorical exercise rather than an objective one? After all, one of the slogans of the totalitarian party in *Nineteen Eighty-Four* is "He who controls the past controls the future."

Not that I'm claiming that Schama was part of some great left-wing conspiracy (at least, not a conscious one). When pressed, Schama claimed that he wasn't an anti-capitalist. When he used terms such as "scoundrel capitalism," he was merely employing qualifying adjectives, not writing off the whole concept. However, he did acknowledge that the term "capitalism" had been "coined by its enemies, and so is saddled with that etymology. If you want to liberate us from that etymology, that's fine."

During our interview, Schama went on to volunteer that he "hated" former British prime minister Margaret Thatcher, which, again, seemed rather a harsh stance for a historian. "I disliked the combination of sanctimoniousness and ferociously Darwinian views," he said, "asking people who were manifestly helpless to help themselves."

I wondered how many of the "manifestly helpless" Schama had ever actually known. Then I asked him if he hadn't gone a little over the top by suggesting that Thatcher had tried to "liquidate what was left of the welfare state."

"All right," he said, "that may be polemical overkill."

Certainly, polemical overkill is far from unusual when it comes to assessing the legacy of Margaret Thatcher, who died early in 2013. There was, around the time I met Schama, a broad left-liberal consensus that the Thatcher era had been a failure. The only requirements for going along with this assessment, or so it seemed to me, were (a) to have no knowledge of, or to apply a particularly rosy filter to, pre-Thatcher Britain, and/or (b) to have no knowledge, or a very selective view, of post-Thatcher Britain.

I had lived in Britain until the mid-1970s and had immigrated to Canada three years before Thatcher came to power. I departed partly because Britain appeared to be circling the toilet bowl of history, beset by bloody-minded unions, low productivity, lousy "macromanagerial" government policies and repeated currency crises. The Britain that Thatcher left when she was ousted in 1990 was a vastly different and,

I would say, vastly improved place. Of course, not everybody would agree. Simon Schama had a great deal of knowledge, so if our interpretations differed, it had to be because of the filters we applied to the information that came our way, or that we sought out. And, as Schama's error indicated, we had to be perpetually on guard against disinformation, albeit unintentional.

—⚬—

The forceful woman in the smart business suit was telling me about her qualifications as a business ethicist: an education in political science, theology and Elizabethan literature. Seated in her office, she suggested parallels between Elizabethan times and the present. One was "a certain degree of rape of other countries. Spices were needed. We do something similar when we say to a small farmer: 'Quit producing soybeans on which you feed your children and produce coffee beans instead, which you cannot feed your children, but which will go into cups of coffee in North America.'"

She leaped to recounting a demonstration in which she had been involved in the early 1970s, against a forestry company that had been dumping mercury into local rivers. The company had refused to meet with the demonstrators.

"We had some Japanese scientists with us. One said to me, 'We just don't understand you Canadians. We thought you were a democracy. We would have driven a bus right through that [company] gate.' And do you know where I heard the CEO of that forestry company went? Love Canal."

The forestry company wasn't doing anything illegal, she stressed, "but they had to make an ethical decision about whether they were going to poison the people in the neighbourhood and ultimately — I don't know much about geography — poison the waters around Toronto."

I asked the name of the company.

"I'm not going to tell you," she said. "*Any* paper company."

She jumped to an account of a fire at a sweatshop in New York in the early years of the 20th century, in which many workers had been killed. "The women were chained to their machines," she said. "Those who could make it away from their machines jumped out of the windows."

But surely, I suggested, chaining workers to machines could hardly have been acceptable behaviour.

"It was a non-issue in 1912," she said. "Chaining, from an employer's position, was a perfectly logical way of seeing that these people didn't wander all over the place, didn't amble off to the washroom. It was a nice organized factory."

"What was the name of this place?" I asked.

"I don't know," she responded, "but another thing, do you know about the blue labels? My mother always insisted on wearing blue labels with an eagle. It was a symbol that these clothes had not been made in a sweatshop. Sweatshops were all over ..."

The woman's wide-ranging anti-corporate tirade was interrupted by an earnest, bearded man who had come by to drop off a publication titled "Citizens for Local Democracy." His name was Darryl. The woman informed Darryl that she was filling me in on the famous sweatshop fire in New York City.

He confirmed that he'd heard of it, although he couldn't remember the name of the factory either. I reasserted my disbelief that chaining workers could have been regarded as acceptable behaviour at the time.

"You regard it as horrifying," said the woman. "I regard it as horrifying. At the time it was not horrifying. Just as dumping mercury into rivers was not regarded as horrifying in 1971."

"No," I persisted, "I think poisoning people was probably regarded as pretty horrifying in 1971."

"But it was legal."

"Was it," I asked, "that the company didn't realize the environmental consequences of its actions, or did they say, 'Poison and be damned'?"

The woman, now becoming visibly annoyed at such picky questions, turned to Darryl: "What was the year of the Minamata poisonings in Japan? Was that 1957, the Fifties?"

Darryl said he thought it was around 1960, but then decided to pitch in directly on my business ethics education: "It's probably more relevant to look at the conditions that prevail in the maquiladora corridor," he said, "the free trade zones along the U.S.-Mexico border. There is a process of de-ruralization going on. Farmers have been forced off their land for reasons of economies of scale as the land has been assembled by transnational food processing corporations who are adopting monoculture. The rural farm people, where before they had lived a subsistence life on the land, are now being forced into industrial working situations. The preferred employee is female, between 15 and 23. There is no housing. They are required to rent tracts of land and erect what hovels they can. There is no potable water. There is no sewage [system]. Working conditions at the factory consist of 12-hour days without any breaks. There is no health insurance. The figures I had for last year are $35 a week, out of which there were deductions. These people are working in virtual chemical cesspools."

Darryl stopped, perhaps puzzled at my lack of outrage.

"Have you *heard* of the maquiladoras?" he asked.

"Oh yes," I said. "Indeed I have."

Darryl had to leave but recommended I further my education via a newsletter put out by something called the Centre for Social Justice. Its title was *Greedwatch*.

—∞—

Third World children deprived of their soybeans; communities poisoned by mercury; charred bodies chained to their workbenches; poor people forced off their lands to work in chemical waste. That some portray capitalism in such uniformly horrendous images has been a fact of life since the start of the Industrial Revolution. I was surprised not so much that such lopsided accounts were still being peddled (and of course some of the stories were true, or had elements of truth) but at the identity of those who were funding the woman who peddled them. Elizabeth Loweth was the executive director of the Canadian Centre for Ethics & Corporate Policy, an organization supported by some of Canada's largest corporations.

"We are here to support the corporation and the business person as they begin to search for another way," she told me. "We don't say, 'You're a good guy or a bad guy.' We just lay out the facts."

The facts.

The Triangle Shirtwaist Company fire was indeed horrendous. It started on the afternoon of Saturday, March 25, 1911, on the eighth floor of a building on Washington Square in Manhattan, and spread to the ninth and tenth floors. The doors to the ninth floor were locked, apparently to prevent employees from stealing. The consequences were truly awful. Inadequate fire escapes collapsed. Over a hundred employees, most of them women, died.

The calamity led to an outpouring of concern. The niece of the great financier J.P. Morgan rented out the Metropolitan Opera House for a meeting on behalf of the Women's Trade Union League. The activist Rose Schneiderman, who had led a strike against the company two years before, declared, "This is not the first time girls have been burned alive in this city ... The life of men and women is so cheap and property is so sacred."

We may be sure that if any worker had been chained to a machine, Rose Schneiderman would have mentioned it, but she did not, nor did the reports of subsequent inquiries record any such occurrence. Thus some of Canada's largest corporations were paying Elizabeth Loweth to denigrate capitalism by peddling monstrous lies.

In *Nineteen Eighty-Four*, Winston Smith had felt a "mute protest" in his bones in the face of assertions that things were better in his bleak, fictional, totalitarian Britain than they had been "before the revolution." I felt a similar — although far from mute — protest when I heard "business ethicists" portray enterprise in unrelievedly negative terms, or when I read historians and journalists declaring that things in (relatively) free enterprise Britain were — primarily due to Margaret Thatcher — worse than in some equally mythical "before."

Thatcher's cardinal sin, it seemed, was her shameless promotion of capitalism, which brings us back to Simon Schama's problematic etymology.

—⁂—

"Capitalism" is one of these words that people throw about but hardly ever define, except by vague negative implication. The *Collins Dictionary of the English Language* describes it as "an economic system based on the private ownership of the means of production, distribution, and exchange, characterized by the freedom of capitalists to operate or manage their property for profit in competitive conditions." One of the dictionary's ancillary definitions of "capitalist" is "Informal, usually derogatory, a rich person."

In fact, both "capitalist" and "capitalism" have always been pejorative terms. Moreover, one might argue with the *Collins Dictionary*'s implication that capitalism is characterized by the freedom only of capitalists.

Seeking the historical roots of aversion to the word and its intellectual trappings, I had turned earlier in my research to a now less frequently consulted, but perhaps more relevant, reference work: the *Great Soviet Encyclopedia*, whose leather-bound heft I had found gathering dust in the Toronto Reference Library.

"CAPITALISM, social and economic structure based on private property in the means of production and the exploitation of wage labour by capital; capitalism replaces feudalism and precedes socialism, the first phase of communism."

Capitalism was doomed, the article claimed, because under it "the working class grows, unites, and organizes; in alliance with the peasantry, at the forefront of all toiling people, it makes up a mighty social force capable of overthrowing the obsolete capitalist system and replacing it by socialism."

Mind you, the vanguard of the proletariat had to stay on its toes. "By means of apologist theories," the article continued, "bourgeois ideologists attempt to prove that contemporary capitalism is a system devoid of class antagonism and that in highly developed capitalist countries factors giving rise to social revolution are generally absent. However, such theories are defeated by reality, which exposes more and more the irreconcilable contradictions of capitalism."

So there you had it: capitalism was a system based on exploitation and doomed to be replaced by socialism under the ineluctable logic of the Communist analysis of history.

The *Encyclopedia* article appeared above the name of a gentleman named Vladimir G. Shemiatenkov and had been penned in the 1970s in a Communist empire long characterized by brutal repression, economic failure, political and personal cynicism, and utter disregard for objective truth — that is, the world of *Nineteen Eighty-Four*.

Since I had first read the entry, I had often wondered what might have happened to the man who wrote it. I thought I might at some point try to track down V.G. Shemiatenkov. I imagined some poor Marxist academic living in straitened circumstances in a cold-water Moscow walk-up, wondering how he could have been so terribly wrong.

But then one day — as accelerating technology overtook the pace of my research — I thought, Why not just Google him? And sure enough, V.G. Shemiatenkov appeared. I discovered that he had been not merely any old Communist hack. He had been at one time Soviet ambassador to the European Union. Now he was principal research fellow and professor of economics at the Institute of Europe in Moscow.

I also found an article by Shemiatenkov in an online journal called *Challenge Europe*, which was sponsored by the British telecommunications giant BT. *Challenge Europe* was published by the European Policy Centre, an "Interface Between Government, Business and Civil Society." The centre's financial supporters included the British retailer Marks & Spencer and the American confectioner Mars. Its "platinum members" included the consulting giant Accenture, BT and Microsoft.

So did the fact that Shemiatenkov was now being given a platform by these corporate giants indicate that he had seen the light about capitalism? Hardly. In the article, dated January 2002, on the subject of 9/11, he peddled the line that the terrorist attacks on the World Trade Center and the Pentagon had been rooted in the "gap" between rich and poor.

"It is only natural that the poor want to be rich," he declared. However, "contemporary social science has no other recipe to offer than market economy and political democracy ... that everybody can make it, provided he accepts capitalist values and works hard."

The results of these "experiments," according to Shemiatenkov, were "at best mixed ... Moreover, if, hypothetically, every wretched individual in those [poor] countries became an avid consumer and a skillful producer *à l'américaine,* the world economy would surely collapse because of the absolute shortage of energy.

"It is the intrinsic schizophrenia of the accepted models of development, which, in the final account, give rise to the ideology and practice of terrorism ... It is the massive disillusionment with Western values which accounts for [the] spectacular rise [of Islam] in the recent decades."

And then of course there was Russia.

"Ten years ago," continued Vladimir, "the country 'voted for capitalism.' However, the new system has so far failed to deliver ... The weaknesses of the market economy and of the nascent civil society allow obnoxious social differentiation and entrenched corruption."

So who was at fault for 9/11? Who was to blame for the parlous state of the former Soviet Union? Was the former rooted in the psychopathology of Islamic failure? Was the latter due to 70 years of Communist repression? Apparently not.

Capitalism did it.

Former ambassador Shemiatenkov obviously hadn't abandoned the ritual hatred of capitalism that would have been required for personal advancement amidst the doctrinaire hypocrisy of the Soviet Union. His views were hardly different from when he had been churning it out for the *Great Soviet Encyclopedia*.

The shocking fact — at least to me — was not that he was under no threat of persecution, sanction or even basic criticism for continuing to misrepresent and castigate capitalism, but that, as with the anti-corporate propaganda being spewed by Elizabeth Loweth, *capitalist corporations* were providing him with a soapbox.

Capitalism thus could hardly be considered to have "triumphed" — as cynics suggested — after the fall of the Berlin Wall and the collapse of the Soviet Union. Indeed, attacks on it had instantly redoubled. For example, let's hear about capitalism's triumph from Robert Heilbroner, the Marxist academic and author of a bestselling book on the history of economics, *The Worldly Philosophers*.

Following the collapse of Communism, wrote Heilbroner, "the Soviet Union, China, and Eastern Europe have given us the clearest possible proof that capitalism organizes the *material* affairs of humankind more satisfactorily than socialism: that *however inequitably or irresponsibly* the marketplace may distribute goods, it does so better than the queues of a planned economy; *however mindless the culture of commercialism*, it is more attractive than state moralism; that *however deceptive the ideology of business civilization*, it is more believable than that of a socialist one" (my italics).

The concept of "damnation with faint praise" hardly begins to do justice to this paragraph, whose underlying message is that the fight must go on against this inequitable, irresponsible, mindless and deceptive system.

For its minority of self-declared fans, capitalism is synonymous with freedom, opportunity, wealth and personal charity, albeit with inevitable glitches, failures and frauds due to the fact that the system thrives on risk and works through (and, significantly, despite) flawed humanity. The system inevitably creates inequality, but that is far from synonymous with inequity.

For its more powerful ideological opponents, "capitalism" is a satanic word, almost invariably attached to derogatory epithets such as brutal, vicious, casino, dog-eat-dog, cowboy, crony, no-holds-barred, unfettered, untrammelled, cold-hearted, hard-hearted, heartless, etc., etc. Rising to the challenge of novel forms of adjectival condemnation, the *New York Times*, in the wake of Superstorm Sandy, coined "Mad Max capitalism" for markets such as those for emergency generators that thrive on (allegedly capitalism-induced) natural disasters.

The intellectual war on capitalism has traditionally been fought on three fronts: its motivations, its processes and its results. In the canon of anti-capitalism, greed channelled through exploitation leads to soulless consumerism, unconscionable power, permanent instability and environmental degradation, not to mention outright war. Capitalism is alleged to be a monolithic ideological system supported by naked self-interest, blind faith and quasi-religious or fundamentalist belief. Exploitation of workers and colonies is a repugnant, but critical, part of its past (and present). Under capitalism, the rich get richer at the expense of the poor. Its orientation is short-term and short-sighted. Its markets are best typified by the "irrational" gyrations of the stock market and the excesses of Wall Street. Its proponents allegedly believe that humans equate to *Homo economicus*, a purely selfish and totally "rational" figment. Capitalism emphasizes competition at the expense of co-operation. It is a system incompatible with altruism, fellow feeling or charity. Its validity depends on theoretical "perfect competition" that has never existed and can never exist. Its markets are inherently prone to failure, monopoly and collapse. It is typified by the production of shoddy, dangerous and superfluous goods. It is destructive of "high" culture and produces entertainment that caters to the lowest common denominator. It is hypocritical — and thus invalid — because businessmen promote laissez-faire when times are good (for them) but then run to the government for bailouts when they are in trouble. With the political reforms of the final quarter of the 20th century and the collapse of Communism, it allegedly became a superhuman and dangerous globalized force that acted somehow independently of the choices and actions of individuals, and for the greater social and environmental harm, in promoting a race to the bottom and threatening our very existence by its impact on the climate. In 2008, it had entered yet another greed-fuelled crisis.

Every one of these endlessly regurgitated allegations is debatable if not downright false, so their pervasiveness and the ardour with which they are disseminated and embraced surely demand examination and explanation. The same series of flawed ideas would not return again and again if capitalism were not an institutional concept that somehow fails to connect with many minds, and/or appears to threaten at least some people's basic psychological needs. It has certainly always threatened a lot of vested political interests, while constantly multiplying the spoils over which those interests can fight.

Friedrich Hayek, the great Austrian economist who spent many years in the intellectual wilderness because his views were unfashionably pro-market and anti-government, admitted to using the term "capitalism" with great reluctance "since with its modern connotations it is itself largely the creation of [the] socialist interpretation of economic history." Or, as another great economist, Joseph Schumpeter, put it, more succinctly and colourfully: "Capitalism stands its trial before judges who have the sentence of death in their pockets."

One profound misrepresentation, or at least misinterpretation, is that capitalism, by analogy to Communism, is a monolithic ideological system. Paul Johnson noted, "[The word "capitalism"] implies a deliberately conceived set of beliefs put together at a specific date to achieve a predetermined purpose. But no such thing ever happened. No one invented the thing ... It is thus a fundamental error to see capitalism and socialism in ideological symmetry; they are quite different phenomena."

And they have produced remarkably different results.

—⁂—

November 9, 2009, was the 20th anniversary of the fall of the Berlin Wall, which had been followed by the collapse of Communism in all but the grim outposts of Cuba and North Korea. It was clear 20 years on that those events had in no way resulted in the "triumph of capitalism." And yet the last decade of the 20th century and the opening decade of the 21st saw an efflorescence of personal freedoms, a surge of economic growth and a corresponding increase in the living standards of literally hundreds of millions of people, particularly in China and India, but also in Indonesia, Brazil and dozens of other countries.

This period was marked by stunning technological innovations, especially related to computers, telecommunications and the internet. "Old" technologies had also been radically improved, along with the range of goods and services available more generally.

The dramatic longer-term improvement of almost all material aspects of life on earth because of capitalism was the subject of a 2007 book by an American economist, Indur Goklany. It was called *The Improving State of the World: Why We're Living Longer, Healthier, More Comfortable Lives on a Cleaner Planet*.

Goklany noted that the U.S. population had multiplied four-fold in the 20th century. Its per capita income had risen by a factor of seven. Life expectancy had increased from 47 to 77 years. Heart disease and cancer rates had shown a sharp decline. Infant mortality had dropped from 100 deaths per 1,000 births in 1913 to just 7 per 1,000.

Such improvements were not confined to "the rich." The proportion of the population in developing countries living in absolute poverty had been halved since 1981, to 20 per cent. People were better educated and more literate than ever before. They were also more politically free and likely to live under the rule of law. Opportunities had never been greater, noted Goklany, "to transcend the bonds of caste, place, gender, and other accidents of birth. People today work fewer hours and have more money and better health to enjoy their leisure time than their ancestors."

In his 2010 book, *The Rational Optimist*, Matt Ridley too pointed to the astonishing increases in human wealth and welfare under capitalism. "Since 1800," he wrote, "the population of the world has multiplied six times, yet average life expectancy has more than doubled and real income has risen more than nine times. Taking a shorter perspective, in 2005, compared with 1955, the average human being on Planet Earth earned three times as much money (corrected for inflation), ate one-third more calories of food, buried one-third as many of her children and could expect to live one-third longer ... She was more likely to be literate and to have finished school. She was more likely to own a telephone, a flush toilet, a refrigerator and a bicycle. All this during a half century when the world population has more than doubled, so that far from being rationed by population pressure, the goods and services available to people of the world have expanded. It is, by any standard, an astonishing human achievement."

The longest-term — and in many ways most dramatic — statistics on the impact of capitalism came from the late Angus Maddison, who had been emeritus professor of economics at the University of Groningen, in the Netherlands. Maddison had painstakingly accumulated figures comparing the past thousand years with the period from the birth of Christ to 1000 AD. In the earlier period, world population and income were essentially stagnant. Between 1000 and 1995, world population increased by a factor of roughly 20, per capita income rose 12-fold, and GDP by a factor of 255. That growth was overwhelmingly concentrated in the period after 1820.

Growth had tended to be universal but far from even, and the gap between advanced capitalist countries — "the West" — and those without good governance or secure legal systems had inevitably widened. Maddison noted that since 1000 AD, per capita income had increased 57-fold in North America and more than 40-fold in Western Europe and Japan. Still "the rest" had experienced a sevenfold increase in per capita income in the past millennium, and the acceleration in Asian growth in the latter half of the 20th century meant that "the West" and "the rest" had similar output at the close of the second millennium. These arresting growth figures did not take into account the stunning improvements in technology and the quality of consumer products, all those things that Matt Ridley noted that Cornelius Vanderbilt didn't have.

The Harvard psychologist Steven Pinker, in his 2011 book, *The Better Angels of Our Nature*, reminded us that before the advent of affluence and technology, our ancestors "were infested with lice and parasites and lived above cellars heaped with their own feces. Food was bland, monotonous, and intermittent.

Health care consisted of the doctor's saw and the dentist's pliers. Both sexes labored from sunrise to sundown, whereupon they were plunged into darkness. Winter meant months of hunger, boredom, and gnawing loneliness in snowbound farmhouses ... Musical recordings, affordable books, instant news of the world, reproductions of great art, and filmed dramas were inconceivable, let alone available in a tool that can fit in a shirt pocket."

Pinker noted that "nostalgia for a peaceable past" was "the biggest delusion of all." He cited in deliciously gruesome detail the results of forensic examination of prehistoric bodies ("CSI Paleolithic," as he called it), and reminded us of the horrors reflected in classical literature and the Bible, which he described as "one long celebration of violence." He cited numerous examples of savagery, from human sacrifice and Roman circuses to the torture of heretics and witches, all of which were witnessed with relish. Shakespeare's work, he noted, is a compendium of rape, murder and cannibalism. The 18th-century wit and dictionary maker Samuel Johnson had recorded the hanging of a seven-year-old girl, whose crime was stealing a petticoat.

That the modern era was a golden age of peace might seem to be patently contradicted by the past century's world wars, and the mass murders committed under fascism and Communism. However, Pinker pointed out that in the great sweep of history, even the horrors of the 20th century had often been surpassed in terms of deaths relative to the size of the global population.

Above all, Pinker acknowledged that one of the central elements in creating both peace and prosperity was what the philosopher Montesquieu had called "gentle commerce," a.k.a. capitalism. That fact, he noted, went remarkably uncelebrated.

—∞—

OK, so capitalism might have promoted peace and prosperity, but what about the environment? Could anybody claim other than that it is under assault on a global scale?

Goklany acknowledged that the picture was more complex there, because economies in the early stages of development tend to put growth above the environment. This remained spectacularly true of pollution in China. But, Goklany noted, this practice had always changed over time, and with increases in wealth and technology. The world's richest economies were also the cleanest.

The issue of modern development and the environment — and in particular the widespread assumption that capitalist growth means environmental destruction — was addressed more broadly by a Danish academic, Bjørn Lomborg, in a controversial 2001 book, *The Skeptical Environmentalist*. Lomborg, himself of leftist bent, had, around 1997, been affronted by the rosy projections made by the economist Julian Simon, who had claimed that — contrary to conventional alarmism — things were actually getting better on both the economic and the environmental fronts.

Lomborg, a professor of statistics at Aarhus University, set his students to an exhaustive examination of the facts on resource depletion and environmental degradation. To his surprise, he discovered that Julian Simon was right and the alarmists wrong. Everywhere he checked out the conventional environmental litany of death and destruction, he found it had been either greatly exaggerated or entirely falsified. Wealth was not bought at the expense of the environment. On the contrary, above a certain level of income, increased wealth tended to go with environmental improvement.

Addressing each of the items of the litany, Lomborg noted that natural resources such as energy were becoming more abundant, that more food was being produced per capita than at any time in history, that species were nowhere becoming extinct on the scale that was claimed, that pollution was in fact abating and that man-made global warming was both based on uncertain science and, insofar as it did exist, not an immediate problem requiring draconian action.

Lomborg's conclusion was that "children born today — in both the industrialized world and developing countries — will live longer and be healthier. They will get more food, a better education, a higher standard of living, more leisure time and far more possibilities — without the global environment being destroyed. And that is a beautiful world." Significantly, as I shall examine later, Lomborg's assessment aroused primal screams from radical environmentalists and their supporters, including some prominent businessmen.

Indur Goklany, meanwhile, concluded, "Man's remarkable progress over the last 100 years is unprecedented in human history. It's also one of the more neglected big-picture stories. Ensuring that our incredible progress continues will require not only recognizing and appreciating the progress itself, but also recognizing and preserving the important ideas and institutions that caused it, and ensuring that they endure."

Given the success of capitalism in creating peace and prosperity, enhancing resources and protecting the environment (save in the alleged case of projected catastrophic man-made climate change, to which we shall return), is it not puzzling that it is still treated with reservations by most, and vehemently rejected by a vociferous and influential intellectual minority?

But what about the financial crisis that started in 2008 and was still with us at the end of 2013? Wasn't that a failure of free-market capitalism, and in particular a condemnation of a system typified by Wall Street "greed"? I shall also return to this issue, but merely note here that the system that teetered in 2008, like the regime underpinning the eurozone, which fell into crisis in 2010, was one pervaded with perverse regulation and burdened with unsustainable government debt.

Why do people appear oblivious to the astonishing record of capitalism? Why do so many powerful and influential people not merely fail to appreciate the achievements of the capitalist system but continually seek to condemn it and recommend a "better way," despite the fact that all better ways tried so far have led to repression, poverty and war?

There is no denying that capitalism has a bad name. The question is, How did it get it, and why does it persist?

A good place to start is with the man often considered the "father" of capitalism: Adam Smith.

two

The Sage of Kirkcaldy

The half-bred and half-witted Scotchman who taught the deliberate blasphemy: "Thou shalt hate the Lord, thy God, damn his law, and covet they neighbour's goods."
— John Ruskin on Adam Smith

In 1993, pondering the conundrum of why capitalism appeared to have been so successful — especially when compared with the alternatives — and yet was so persistently condemned, I set out in search of Adam Smith.

Smith was the 18th-century Scottish professor who wrote *An Inquiry into the Nature and Causes of the Wealth of Nations*, the book considered by many to be the seminal work of both modern economics and capitalism (even though the latter word did not exist in Smith's day).

The specific route I had in mind for that 1993 trip was from Smith's grave in Edinburgh to Karl Marx's tomb in London's Highgate Cemetery, with visits to sites of the Industrial Revolution along the way. It was a route I would travel several more times in the coming two decades.

One immediate inspiration for that first pilgrimage had been a witty article in *Forbes* magazine. Titled "Tale of Two Tombs," it had pointed out the irony of Smith's and Marx's gravesites. "Karl Marx's cemetery is haunted by the spirit of Adam Smith," it noted. "It is privately owned and produces a tidy profit for its owners ... Adam Smith's cemetery in Edinburgh is state-owned, open free of charge to anyone, and is in a terrible state of neglect."

I found the story to be entirely accurate. Smith lay in the desolate graveyard of the Canongate Kirk on Edinburgh's Royal Mile, along with the long-forgotten former cream of Scottish society, their monuments leaning at neglected angles, their very names erased by rain and time. Scattered amid the sad tombs were dirty blankets and an assortment of beer and cheap sherry bottles, the detritus of the homeless people who slept there. *Forbes*'s portrayal of Highgate, too, was spot on. There, the volunteer at the gate charged me two pounds and had pamphlets about Marx for sale.

Marx's monument, topped with its huge, self-righteous, bearded bust, was obviously a far more popular attraction than the tomb of Smith. Tourists stood beaming for the camera beside the call to arms with which *The Communist Manifesto* ends:

"WORKERS OF ALL LANDS UNITE."

They smiled as they had smiled, or would smile, outside Buckingham Palace or in front of the Tower of London, apparently unmindful of the dreadful consequences of the legend carved further down the monument:

"THE PHILOSOPHERS HAVE ONLY INTERPRETED THE WORLD IN VARIOUS WAYS. THE POINT HOWEVER IS TO CHANGE IT."

Marx declared that Smith's "natural order" of liberty and trade, far from offering the prospect of bettering the human condition, meant rather increasing exploitation and poverty, unavoidable revolution and a new collectivist social order. In the Marxian view of the world, Adam Smith's vision was both morally defective and historically doomed.

By any objective measure — or at least so it seemed to me at the time — Adam Smith had been proved stunningly right and Marx spectacularly and murderously wrong. And yet Smith hardly seemed to have as much intellectual — or even popular — support as his nemesis, the man whose theories had caused so much poverty and repression. Indeed, even in his hometown, Smith's celebration was less than wholehearted.

—⁓—

It is still easy to miss the plaque that commemorates the site where Adam Smith wrote most of *The Wealth of Nations*. It is affixed to a wall on the High Street in Kirkcaldy, a little town of solid sandstone villas and faded glory that sits across the grey waters of the Firth of Forth from Edinburgh. Kirkcaldy's claim to industrial fame was that it was once the "home of linoleum."

Since that first trip in 1993, the businesses flanking the plaque have changed numerous times, a fitting indicator of the dynamism and uncertainty of commercial society. The last time I was there, the adjoining establishments represented commerce as Smith knew it, and as he could never have imagined it. On one side was a bakery; on the other, Chickenshop.co.uk, a novelty store with a website. Across the road was a McDonald's restaurant.

On that first visit, I had been shocked at the quotes that had accompanied Smith's little display in the town museum. One, from a work titled *A Hotbed of Genius*, suggested that "Marx regarded Smith as perceptive but heartless, and was more concerned to refute than follow him."

Another, from the "popular economist" John Kenneth Galbraith, read, "With Das Kapital and the Bible, the Wealth of Nations enjoys the distinction of being one of the three books to which people may refer at will without feeling they should read it. There is so much in the book that every reader has full opportunity for exercise of his own preference."

It seemed strange that Smith's reputation should be left in the hands of two men who had specifically rejected his analysis.

Meanwhile a third quote, again from *A Hotbed of Genius,* had declared, "Smith is often misrepresented as an uncritical advocate of a free economy. In fact he believed that the government should be responsible for major public works. He warned against the evils of industrialization."

No indication was given of exactly who might have misrepresented Smith thus. Also, while Smith's reservations about industrialization were stressed, no reference was made — in this government-run institution — to his much greater reservations about government. It also struck me as peculiar to refer to Smith's concerns about the "evils" of nascent industrialization when the actual benefits of advanced modern industrialization were so manifestly present everywhere one looked.

If, that is, one had "eyes to see."

In one way, Galbraith's observation was gallingly correct. Smith continues to be quoted by people with diametrically opposite views, and cited to support causes he might have found problematic, to say the least. In recent years he has been embraced by leftists such as the linguistic philosopher Noam Chomsky and the Nobel laureate economist Amartya Sen, and even by climate alarmists. He has been described in the *New York Times* as "the first action liberal," when in fact Smith's liberalism was arguably the very opposite of that promoted by the *New York Times*.

His memory — at least until quite recently — has been more often buried than buffed, particularly in the land of his birth. Indeed, not long after my first visit to Kirkcaldy, the socialist-dominated local council removed all notices leading into the town that identified it as Smith's birthplace.

—m—

Adam Smith was born in Kirkcaldy — dubbed "the lang toun" for the length of its High Street — in 1723 to a widow, née Margaret

Douglas. His father, Adam Smith Sr., who had died the previous January, had been an important lawyer and government official. His death left his widow comfortably off, which in turn enabled Adam Jr. to have an extended education, even by the standards of our own day.

Kirkcaldy was then a relatively prosperous town in a much less prosperous world, and Smith's mother's house was a substantial property overlooking the firth. (It was demolished in 1844.) Smith clearly enjoyed a comfortable childhood. Its single reported frisson was when he was briefly snatched by gypsies. One of Smith's biographers, John Rae, wryly noted, "He would have made, I fear, a poor gipsy."

Smith went to school in Kirkcaldy, where he received a solid education in the classics. At age 14, he entered the University of Glasgow, which was then in the early throes of the Scottish Enlightenment and experiencing a boom created by colonial trade, which had been boosted by the 1707 Act of Union with England.

Like its French relative, the Scottish Enlightenment stressed the power of human reason to penetrate ignorance and superstition and formulate a "science of man." The intellectual journey of Smith's life would involve probing the fundamentals of human nature, dissecting the mechanics of wealth creation and gauging the characteristics of good — and bad — government. Above all, Smith was interested in analyzing how human institutions and government policies might help or hinder the material — and moral — advancement of individuals and society.

His project required the study of history, science, literature and philosophy, and the observation and analysis of current events. It demanded both extensive reading and going out into the world to talk with merchants, politicians and other philosophers.

Although Smith is sometimes portrayed as an absent-minded boffin, he was never an ivory tower academic. Indeed, he had little but contempt for tenured academics, an attitude he acquired during a six-year scholarship at Balliol College, Oxford, which he attended after leaving his studies at Glasgow.

Smith's time at Oxford fell during a period "when learning lay there under a long and almost total eclipse." Much of his education was thus inevitably self-guided. He admitted in letters to his mother to the occasional "violent fit of laziness," but he was appalled at the much more culpable laziness of Oxford's tenured professors. He concluded that income not linked to performance would tend to produce poor performance.

It was an insight for the ages.

Things were hardly better on the social side. Smith was surrounded at Balliol by wealthy young "hearties" who were primarily interested in sport and drinking, activities for which Smith possessed neither the income nor the inclination. It must have been with considerable relief that he eventually returned to his mother's house in Kirkcaldy. There he continued his studies and travelled frequently across the firth to the vibrant life of Edinburgh, whose intellectual climate shone beneath the fetid pall created by its coal fires, from which it acquired the name "Auld Reekie."

One key influence on Smith's intellectual development was David Hume, the controversial Scottish philosopher and religious skeptic, who would become a close friend. Smith probably first came across Hume's work at Oxford, where it was considered ripe for burning.

Hume's *A Treatise of Human Nature* — which was published to virtually zero acclaim when Hume was still in his 20s, but was "discovered" by another prominent philosopher, Immanuel Kant, almost 50 years later — had many discomforting things to say about how we see the world, and how much we can ever truly know. He also rejected any notion that rationality might ever reign over human affairs, and famously declared that reason was inevitably a slave to passion.

Hume noted that the growth of commerce went hand in hand with the development of both science and moral behaviour. "We cannot reasonably expect," he wrote, "that a piece of woollen cloth will be wrought to perfection in a nation, which is ignorant of astronomy, or where ethics are neglected." He posited the crucial roles of sympathy and a sense of justice in making us sociable creatures, themes on which Smith would elaborate.

Perhaps the most shocking aspect of the science of man project was that it was thoroughly irreligious (although Smith was far less openly anti-religious than Hume). It sought to understand man not in terms of Creation or Biblical revelation, but in terms of a complex human nature and gradually evolving social institutions.

Smith's academic "coming out" after his return from Oxford was a series of lectures delivered in Edinburgh between 1748 and 1751. One set of talks was on rhetoric, the art and science of persuasion; the other was on jurisprudence, the theory of government.

Partly as a result of the Edinburgh lectures, Smith was offered a professorship at the University of Glasgow, where he taught for 13 years. He was remembered there as both an engaging lecturer and an enthusiastic administrator. He participated fully in the life of the town and became friends with prominent merchants. He belonged to a number of important clubs and societies and was reckoned to be convivial company, although prone to wander mentally (one reason why people avoided him as a partner when playing cards).

Although he frequently appeared distracted, his lips moving to some internal dialogue, Smith was an acute observer of human nature. This became clear with the publication in 1759 of *The Theory of Moral Sentiments*. In a review, Edmund Burke, the great conservative thinker and politician, wrote, "It certainly shows the author to have been a man of uncommon observation, not only of his own mental states, but of the life and ways of men about him."

The book so impressed Charles Townshend, another prominent and controversial British politician, that, after several years of trying, he eventually hired Smith away from Glasgow to accompany his stepson, the Duke of Buccleuch, on an educational grand tour of Europe. Such an assignment was attractive because it was not only well paid, it also offered Smith a pension for life, and thus the freedom to think and write.

Smith found the first 18 months of the trip, in Toulouse, excruciatingly boring. To "pass away the time," he began writing another book, which may have been the origin of *The Wealth of Nations*. Smith had planned to write a book on government after *Moral Sentiments* but had realized that he could not write about policy without understanding the workings of commerce.

This is a lesson that has — astonishingly — been persistently neglected ever since. A thorough understanding of economics is not merely an option for politicians and political advisors, it is essential. One problem may be that many politicians and advisors are inclined, by the nature of their activist aspirations, not to like what economics has to tell them.

Beyond Toulouse, Smith made the acquaintance of many prominent French thinkers, including the great iconoclast Voltaire, whom he visited in Geneva. But it was in the salons and theatres of Paris, during the last few months of the trip, that Smith finally found the intellectual stimulation he had been missing. There, *philosophes* enjoyed the celebrity of modern rock stars.

Hume, who had been in Paris as a diplomat just before Smith arrived, wrote of salon life: "I feed on ambrosia, drink nothing but nectar, breathe incense only, and walk on flowers. Every one I meet, and especially every woman, would consider themselves as failing in the most indispensable duty if they did not favour me with a lengthy and ingenious discourse on my celebrity."

Smith spent time with a group of political economists known as the physiocrats, who congregated in the Versailles apartment of the king's physician, François Quesnay. Smith admired Quesnay but disagreed fundamentally with the physiocrats' now strange-seeming view that land and agriculture are the sole source of a nation's wealth. He also rejected Quesnay's view that economics could be turned into an exact mathematical science.

The pension attached to the tutoring job enabled Smith to return once more to his mother's house in Kirkcaldy to work on his magnum opus. He would live there for the next six years, until leaving for London in 1773 to spend another three years preparing his book for publication.

Although commerce had existed for many thousands of years and trade for tens of thousands, Smith was writing as Britain was entering a period of unprecedented growth whose implications would span the globe. The great unfolding political issue as Smith was completing his book was the mounting crisis over the rebellious American colonies. The soon-to-be-independent colonies would be a laboratory of Smith's free-market ideas. America — unlike Britain and other European countries — was constrained by no property-owning nobility with its often self-interested laws. Its citizens enjoyed a freedom not permitted in the Old World. Hence, according to Smith's theories, they should prosper more quickly. He projected in *The Wealth of Nations* that they would create a great power, and indeed they did. He also pointed out that the cost for Britain of maintaining the American colonies was more than it was worth, and that Britain would be far better off with a free trading relationship. Again, history would bear him out.

Smith was a stout anti-imperialist and strongly opposed the privilege and political corruption attached to the giant East India Company, the archetypal symbol of the traditional rancid connection between business and government. Ironically, Britain would thrive in the 19th century through a combination of pro-Smithian free trade and anti-Smithian imperial conquest.

During his three years in London, Smith consorted with, among others, Samuel Johnson, Johnson's biographer James Boswell (who had heard Smith's lectures at Glasgow), Burke, Edward Gibbon (the first volume of whose *Decline and Fall of the Roman Empire* would also be published in 1776) and the great portrait painter Sir Joshua Reynolds.

Dr. Johnson did not get on well with either Smith or Hume. One obvious source of discord was that Smith had critically reviewed Johnson's *Dictionary*. Johnson thought Smith a "dull dog." Smith considered Johnson a "freak." Of Burke, by contrast, Smith said that he was the "only man I ever knew who thinks on economic subjects exactly as I do, without any previous communications having passed between us."

—ɯ—

Smith had been a strong believer in the benefits of free markets under the rule of law and in the counterproductiveness of intrusive government long before he went to Paris. In Glasgow, he had said in a lecture, "Little else is required to carry a state to the highest degree of affluence from the lowest barbarism but peace, easy taxes, and a tolerable administration of justice; all the rest being brought about by the natural course of things. All governments which thwart this natural course, which force things into another channel, or which endeavour to arrest the progress of society at a particular point, are unnatural, and, to support themselves, are obliged to be oppressive and tyrannical."

Smith believed that the desire to "better our condition" was a fundamental fact of human nature, and that nothing broadly facilitated that desire like commercial interaction, which involved a growing network of mutual service, coordinated by the "Invisible Hand" of the market.

"It is not," wrote Smith, in perhaps the most oft-quoted passage from *The Wealth of Nations*, "from the benevolence of the butcher, the brewer, or the baker that we expect our dinner, but from their regard to their own interest. We address ourselves, not to their humanity but to their self-love, and never talk to them of our own necessities but of their advantages."

Smith's meaning was that we satisfy our material wants by a process of exchange in which the participants realize that they can achieve those benefits only by serving others. He wasn't suggesting that butchers, brewers and bakers lacked the milk of human kindness, or a sense of family or community; just that — when it came to commercial relationships — we had to recognize how much systemic good was done by allowing free rein to self-interested voluntary exchange.

Smith certainly never promoted "radical individualism," much less selfishness or greed. For him, the object of moral psychology, moral philosophy, and economic and political inquiry was to determine "wherein consists the happiness and perfection of a man, not only as an individual, but as a member of a family, of a state, and of the great society of mankind."

Smith noted that self-interest was mediated through two forms of commercial interaction to promote economic development: the division of labour, and free trade. People naturally "divide" their labour between trades and professions such as baking, brewing or the law without any need for government guidance because this serves to increase what we now call their "productivity": that is, the amount of goods or services produced in a given period.

The division of labour was hardly a novel insight. The Greek writer Xenophon had recorded it in the fourth century BC. Xenophon observed that the extent of the division depended on the size of the community served. In a small village, he pointed out, a single artisan might make chairs and beds and tables and plows and even build houses. However, in "great cities" such as Athens there would be not merely shoemakers but specialists in men's or women's sandals, and even individuals who specialized in cutting, shaping or stitching leather.

Smith observed that more productive specialists exchanged the more abundant fruits of their labour for the products of other specialists, usually via the intermediary commodity of money. He stressed, however, that real wealth lies not in money but in goods: in factories, machinery, houses, clothing, pots and pans, meat, beer and bread. Money is primarily a facilitating device, a means of exchange and a measure and store of value.

The division of labour *within* enterprises also led to potentially enormous increases in productivity, as Xenophon had implied with the sandal business. Smith used the example of a pin factory. Any individual, working alone, wrote Smith, would have trouble making a single dress pin in a day, but ten individuals coordinating their activities with rudimentary machinery could produce an astonishing 48,000 pins. Widespread and free trade was desirable because — as Xenophon had noted — larger markets spurred specialization and thus further productivity increases.

This whole process was aimed at satisfying the traditional needs and expanding wants of the "consumer," whose interest Smith believed should be paramount. "Consumption," he wrote, "is the sole end and purpose of production; and the interest of the producer ought to be attended to, only so far as it may be necessary for promoting that of the consumer. The maxim is so perfectly self-evident, that it would be absurd to attempt to prove it."

Smith believed that without oppressive legislation, competition to serve the consumer would inevitably lead to more general social welfare. Governments, said Smith, did nothing but harm when they connived with businessmen to "promote" particular industries by restricting imports or subsidizing exports, although the harm was often difficult to see.

Restricting imports and subsidizing exports were all part of the doctrine of mercantilism, which was Smith's primary policy target. Mercantilism favoured big governments, heavy royal expenditures, high taxes, war, imperialism, state monopolies and the maintenance of positive trade balances (that is, the importation and accumulation of gold).

Smith considered it naive to think that governments could promote economic growth or compensate for any alleged shortcomings of the market. Such an authority, he wrote, "would no-where be so dangerous as in the hands of a man who had folly and presumption enough to fancy himself fit to exercise it."

Such folly and presumption would, however, die hard. Indeed, they are very much still with us, most recently in the almost universal embrace by governments of "green industrial strategy" both to combat climate change and to promote "technologies of the future."

Smith was no anarchist. He believed that governments were essential not merely to enforce property and contract laws and to punish the use of force or fraud, but to mount defences against external threats. They were also needed to promote certain public works — what we today call infrastructure — that would not likely be provided privately (although he had little faith in government's ability to do so efficiently). He also believed in the desirability of universal basic education (although provided at the local, parish level, not by central government). Smith's "selling point" for governments was that by interfering less, they would in fact promote economic growth and thus enhance their revenues.

Smith should in no way be considered a mouthpiece for the merchant or manufacturing classes, even if they were the agents of progress in his system. Indeed, Smith was extraordinarily hard on their alleged "rapacity" — despite (or perhaps because of) having socialized with them in Glasgow. While he rightly castigated their attempts to turn legislation to their own advantage, he offered little or no praise for their ingenuity and innovation. Indeed, Smith has been criticized for not emphasizing the central role of the entrepreneur; but then we have to remember that he was writing at the birth of an entrepreneurial explosion.

Smith became an important voice in the political environment that facilitated the Industrial Revolution. By the end of the 18th century, *The Wealth of Nations* had run through nine English editions as well as editions in Ireland and the United States. It would be translated into Danish, Dutch, French, German, Italian and Spanish (although it was suppressed by the Inquisition in Spain for "the lowness of its style and the looseness of its morals"). Its success "for a work of its type," wrote Joseph Schumpeter, was "spectacular" (although Schumpeter was among those who believed that its significance was overrated).

According to Friedrich Hayek, "The nineteenth century enthusiast who claimed that the *Wealth of Nations* was in importance second only to the Bible has often been ridiculed; but he may not have exaggerated so much."

Like the Bible, however, Smith's magnum opus would, as John Kenneth Galbraith suggested, be open to considerable interpretation. Indeed, to grasp the extraordinary range of views about Smith is to recognize his status as part Cassandra, part Zelig, part Rorschach ink blot test and part lightning rod. He has been portrayed as everything from a promoter of starvation for the poor to a gung-ho redistributionist and interventionist. That eminent Victorian aesthete John Ruskin described him as "the half-bred and half-witted Scotchman who taught the deliberate blasphemy: 'Thou shalt hate the Lord, thy God, damn his law, and covet they neighbour's goods.'"

Smith in fact taught nothing of the sort, but Ruskin's remark would be all too typical of the tendency of those who didn't like Smith's economics to heap moral opprobrium upon him.

Smith had no idea of the astonishing burst of technological innovation that would mark the coming centuries, nor of the intellectual and political tumult it would unleash. He did know very well, however, that the "moral sentiments" were complex and troublesome, and that people tended to lose all perspective when it came to matters of religion and politics. A spectacular example occurred not long before my next visit to Edinburgh and Kirkcaldy.

—∞—

Although my research on capitalism continued, I did not return to Scotland until 2002, a few months after the terrorist attacks of 9/11. I was there partly on a mission.

The man who had brought that *Forbes* article to my attention all those years before — the one noting the irony of Smith's tomb being neglected in a government-maintained graveyard while Marx was well cared for in a private one — was a Calgary-based oilman named Bob Lamond. Lamond had been born in Kirkcaldy and educated in Edinburgh before striking out for Canada as a young geologist and becoming a successful petroleum explorer and entrepreneur. I had first met him when I was writing a book about the Canadian oil industry, *The Blue-Eyed Sheiks*. We became friends. Since we were both fans of Adam Smith, the neglected tomb story had often popped up in our conversation. Eventually, Lamond had decided to do something about it. He wrote to the Lord Provost of Edinburgh, contacted local officials, had meetings, heard expressions of support and offered £10,000 to have a sign erected to direct visitors toward Smith's grave. When I told Lamond that I was headed for Edinburgh, he asked me to try to find out why nothing was happening.

The Canongate Kirk graveyard was pretty much as I'd found it nine years before. Although it had been cleaned up a bit, there was still a scattering of empty beer bottles — Beck's, Stella Artois, San Miguel, Grolsch. Also a large plastic container bearing the name "Big Beastie," promising "four shots of vodka." (The unappreciated technological advance on display was not the drink, but the lightweight plastic bottle.)

To one side of the church I noticed a sign on a metal pole. It dealt in some detail with the banning of dogs. At the bottom, as a sensitive and responsible afterthought, was written, "These rules will not apply to guide dogs or police dogs in the performance of their duties." The sign was leaning at an angle because somebody had obviously tried to wrench it out of the ground — possibly empowered by a Big Beastie. Moreover, a ruddy-faced, tweedy-looking woman was walking among the tombs with three small dogs. She did not appear to be either blind or a member of the constabulary.

I also noticed a local feature that I had missed before: Smith's grave was at the edge of the cemetery, its gravestone attached to the back wall of an adjoining structure. This was the old Tollbooth building, which housed The People's Story, a museum offering a social history of Edinburgh, the type of history written by Simon Schama.

Social history is, by definition, a revolt against the Great Man (or Great Woman) view of events, but it also often winds up being synonymous with socialist history: mundane artifacts presented in a context of class struggle; big old walnut-veneered cabinet radios permanently tuned to the left end of the dial.

At the entrance to The People's Story, mannequins representing the contrast between typical families of Smith's time and of our own greeted visitors. The family of the present was obviously much better off, but the only explanation offered was that the head of the current household was a member of the Transport and General Workers' Union. According to a note elsewhere in the museum, "Legislation and Trade Unions have gradually won better working conditions for Edinburgh people." No thanks to free markets, capitalism or Adam Smith.

On the museum's top floor, a continuous-loop film played of old people recounting their days as bricklayers or shop clerks or in domestic service. The important message was that previous generations had it a great deal harder. The pregnant question, again, was how much improvement was due to union pressure and government intervention, and how much to free enterprise and "natural" forces that needed no legislation — or were indeed hindered by it. From the perspective of the Tollbooth, Smith was on the outside both literally and figuratively.

I made calls about my friend Lamond's signage project and arranged to meet one of the cultural officials involved at his office at the Writers' Museum, a quaint former townhouse off the Royal Mile devoted to the Scottish literary giants Sir Walter Scott, Robbie Burns and Robert Louis Stevenson. We repaired to a nearby pub, the famous Deacon Brodie's Tavern.

The official, a slight, affable, red-haired man who rolled his own cigarettes, admitted that he had been put in charge of following up on the Smith signage. He said that he had looked at alternatives and obtained quotes, but claimed that those "higher up" appeared to have lost interest in the project.

He admitted that it was difficult to overcome simple bureaucratic inertia. "You wouldn't believe how much trouble I had to get a light bulb changed in the Scott Monument," he said. "The attendants wouldn't do it because they say it's a technician's job, and it involves climbing a ladder."

Halfway through his pint of Guinness, the official revealed that Smith's neglect might not be entirely a matter of inertia. "Monuments in Edinburgh are intensely political," he said. In fact, they were political throughout Britain. He told me that a bust of Margaret Thatcher had recently been attacked in England. Meanwhile a statue in Glasgow of Donald Dewar, a key figure in the creation of the new Scottish Parliament, had had its spectacles ripped off several times.

Attacks on Dewar's glasses were regarded as the action of morons, but when anybody attempted to smash a statue of Maggie Thatcher, they were generally thought — particularly in Scotland — to be making a valid political statement. The official noted that if Smith's name was linked to that of any modern politician, it was to Britain's first woman prime minister, who remained an object of intense hatred for many Scots.

Smith had indeed been much invoked during both the Thatcher and Reagan revolutions, and his "rediscovery" was declared to be significant in the battle against failed experiments in public ownership, economic planning and excessive regulation. When Thatcher took office in 1979, her ascetic and cerebral secretary of state for industry, Sir Keith Joseph, recommended Smith to his senior bureaucrats. In the first volume of her autobiography, *The Downing Street Years*, Thatcher described Smith as "the greatest exponent of free enterprise economics till Hayek and [Milton] Friedman." During the 1980s,

U.S. president Ronald Reagan's economic advisors frequently sported Adam Smith ties.

The Edinburgh official acknowledged his own socialist family background and the conflicts caused by Thatcherite policies. One of the Iron Lady's most effective initiatives — in her desire to promote a "property-owning democracy" — had been to allow tenants of public housing, known as council houses, to buy their dwellings. "My father wouldn't do it," he said. "He thought that housing should be provided by the state. After he died, we bought the house for my mother."

The official admitted, "If it was politically expedient to put up a memorial to Smith, then it would be done." But it clearly wasn't expedient, at least at that particular moment.

I subsequently discovered that reservations about Smith were far from confined to left-leaning local councils. At the recommendation of my friend Lamond, I went to visit the owner of an antiquarian print shop on the Royal Mile. Lamond had roped this man, a short, stocky figure with a salt and pepper beard, into the scheme to erect a sign pointing to Smith's nearby tomb because he often bought prints from him.

I quickly discovered that the print dealer was no fan of Smith, or rather what he thought Smith stood for. He told me that the attacks on the World Trade Center and the Pentagon were the result of hatred for "the decadent West, a blow against capitalism." He appeared to feel that such blows were not inappropriate. The world's problems, he said, were all based on multinational corporations flaunting their wealth in the Third World, and on the "gap" between rich and poor. His world view seemed astonishingly similar to that of Vladimir Shemiatenkov.

Among the other people I called about the lack of progress on Smith signage was the rector of the Canongate Kirk. His wife returned my call. She acknowledged that the main problem with the church grounds — as highlighted by *Forbes* 12 years before — was that they were owned and maintained by the local council. The council made some effort to keep the place tidy, she said, but the problem was that the cemetery was used by homeless people, many of whom had problems with drugs and alcohol. Vandals also sometimes scaled the wall at the bottom of the cemetery to knock over gravestones.

She told me that the church's immediate bureaucratic struggle was to secure a better notice board than the ramshackle version supplied by the local council. She had never heard of Bob Lamond, but when I mentioned the money he was prepared to spend, she said that perhaps they could combine a spiffy new notice board with Smith signage. I put her in touch with him.

After an initially optimistic exchange of emails, the rector's wife sent a much less hopeful message to Lamond. In it, she pointed out that Smith was "only one of many significant people" in the cemetery. Then came the punch line. "It might also be important to recognize that not everyone shares your admiration for Adam Smith. There are those who see current attitudes to economics and money-management as being a major contributor to the ever-increasing divide between rich and poor; a division which arguably is contributing to the growth of terrorism, as poor or 'failed' countries try to diminish the powers of wealthy ones. This is another reason why I think we do not have much hope of getting simply an 'Adam Smith' sign, or set of signs, through the Planning Department."

Yet again, these sentiments were remarkably similar to those of the man who had written the entry on capitalism in the *Great Soviet Encyclopedia*.

In addition to suggesting that Adam Smith might somehow be to blame for 9/11, the rector's wife put forward a more practical anti-sign argument: that any notices might be carried off. The Big Beastie Brigade might strike again. Best not to provoke them. Or capitalism-hating terrorists. Or leftist local authorities. Not to mention those who believed that Adam Smith's ideas were destroying the planet.

Besides checking on the Edinburgh signage issue, I slipped back over to Kirkcaldy to see how Smith's immortal memory was being handled. I found his low-key exhibit in the local museum pretty much as before. It still featured some aged volumes of *The Wealth of Nations*, along with translations in Japanese and Korean, plus his inkwell and snuff box, and a likeness or two. I noted that John Kenneth Galbraith's words were still on display, but that the citation from Marx had been removed. A museum official seemed disturbed by my suggestion that this might mean that Marx had fallen out of favour.

I contacted the chairwoman of the Kirkcaldy Civic Society to discuss Smith's treatment. The society produced historical pamphlets with titles such as "Kirkcaldy's Famous Folk," where Adam Smith got his fair share of coverage, but the woman — who was also a rare Tory on a Labour-dominated local council — felt that he was still not given sufficient attention.

"A while ago," she said, "we set up a committee to do something more about Smith, but all anybody wanted to do was talk." Reflecting the view of the Edinburgh cultural official, she said that the problem wasn't just bureaucratic inertia. "The council here," she said bluntly, "doesn't like Adam Smith."

During that second visit, it struck me that Smith represented a kind of Ozymandias-in-reverse. In contrast to the shattered statue set in a desolate landscape depicted by Shelley, marked with an ironic claim to glory, Smith went largely unacknowledged amid the "universal opulence" that was at least partly the fruit of his insights. If you wanted to understand those insights, you had to start by looking around at the world of wonders that human ingenuity, private property and (relatively) free enterprise had produced (although clearly not everybody thought it as wonderful as I did).

I reflected that were a reincarnated Smith to stroll the Kirkcaldy High Street pedestrian precinct, he would surely have been stunned. He could acquire everything from fast food or financial services to a cellphone or a "Unisex Tropical Tan." Off the precinct, there were two supermarkets, at either of which Smith would have found a world of merchandise inconceivable in his day: literally tens of thousands of products, many of them fresh, but also frozen, canned, freeze-dried, plastic-bottled or vacuum-packed — all brought to us by largely unacknowledged technological wonders.

What would he have thought of an automobile? How would he have marvelled to be told that a thin line of vapour high in the sky was trailing a vessel bigger than most sailing ships of his own day — only made of metal, carrying hundreds of people and going 50 times faster? We would have to lead Smith as gently as possible into a world of telecommunications, televisions, computers, refrigerators, microwaves and the thousands of other innovations that have made the lives of ordinary people immeasurably more convenient than in his day.

Smith's vision of "opulence" was a mild thing indeed compared with the modern Western world. He looked to the slow and steady advance of society, and with it the gradual amelioration of people's lives. Reflecting on the staple foods of his time, he speculated on whether oatmeal, white bread or potatoes formed the best basic diet for ordinary working people. He came down in favour of potatoes.

This came to my mind as I looked at the McDonald's across from the site of his mother's house. Smith would surely be surprised to learn that any relatively educated person perusing the prospect of a Large Mega Mac Meal — featuring a quadruple-patty burger — would now think more about the meal's health hazards than about its nutritional content. That was surely another measure of how rich society had become.

But here — it seemed to me — was another stunning but insufficiently recognized element of human nature: people took all these stunning technological advances, and the increase in their own wealth and welfare relative to previous generations, *almost completely for granted.* In fact, Smith was among those who noticed this aspect of human nature, but it would surely have seemed far more extraordinary to him were he to be dragged more than 200 years into the future.

Meanwhile, despite the consumer marvels (and cultural shocks) on display, Smith would surely be surprised to learn that Kirkcaldy was a relatively depressed little town, with comparatively high levels of unemployment. Its streets were haunted by industrial relics, particularly derelict buildings that were once the centre of that "home of linoleum" status, which had come with certain environmental problems.

The boiling of linseed oil, a key part of linoleum production, produced a "queer like smell" for which Kirkcaldy became infamous. Still, it was the smell of success. At one time there were half a dozen linoleum manufacturers in the town, the largest of which was the one started in the late 19th century by Michael Nairn, who had donated Kirkcaldy's museum and library. The business had continued to be successful until the 1960s, when superior and cheaper plastic flooring had been developed. Other businesses had come and gone. Before linoleum there had been linen and salt. Whaling fleets had once called Kirkcaldy their home. Pottery had been important. Coal was the most recent industry to die.

There were, however, some signs of revival. Edinburgh's commuter overflow was arriving, partly because of the jobs attached to the new Scottish Parliament. Some might have said that Scotland had more than enough government already. The local council for the county of Fife, in which Kirkcaldy sits, employed 22,000 people, 10 times as many as the largest private-sector employer in the area. And the council represented only one level of government. These governments were all devoted to a concept considered revolutionary in Smith's time: that of income redistribution. They also all dabbled incessantly in the project that Smith had regarded as impossible: "helping" the economy.

I went to visit the head of the Fife Chamber of Commerce at his office in a new business park on the outskirts of Dunfermline. Given Smith's observation that "people of the same trade seldom meet together ... but the conversation ends in a conspiracy against the public," he would undoubtedly have had reservations about the concept of a Chamber of Commerce. However, he would perhaps be surprised — and pleased — to find that the chamber's head thought governments had far too many business handouts on offer, thus creating a "culture of dependence."

He noted that governments' desire to ease transition away from dying smokestack industries had prevented transition. State business grants had caused companies to buy new equipment they didn't need. Rent support resulted in companies going under the first month the support ran out. The (government-promoted) assumption that government would provide jobs had reduced labour mobility. "Europeans are only concerned with the rate of unemployment," said the chamber head, "not the dynamism of the economy." The bitter fruits of that fundamentally misguided approach would become abundantly clear a decade later.

When seeking to attract investment, governments inevitably pursue the strategy of the drunk looking for his car keys under a lamppost, not because he has dropped them there but because that's where the light is. Not knowing where new technological breakthroughs will come, they simply seek to ape success elsewhere. Hence the success of Silicon Valley had led to the attempt to subsidize a "Silicon Glen," with predictably disappointing results.

Apart from the continuation and expansion of such "folly and presumption," what would Smith think of the comprehensive cradle-to-grave welfare state? How would he react to central government-run schooling? What would he think of the vast multiplication of rules and regulations, including even the acceptable amount of froth on beer?

Above all, how shocked would he be to learn that the greater part of humanity had, in the 20th century, come under the rule of totalitarian systems that were based on the refutation — indeed the demonization — of his insights? How horrified would he be that these anti-Smithian systems had cost tens of millions of lives?

We might speculate on all these issues, but ultimately we cannot know what Smith would think. The fact that people seek to recruit him speaks to a central aspect of human nature: its desire for support from "authority."

Smith is an invaluable reference point, even an inspiration, but what is ultimately important is not what Smith thought about how the world works but how the world *actually* works, and how and why we might fail to understand those workings. Interpretations of Smith remain important for such analysis. That was why I trekked off next to Glasgow to meet with one of the world's foremost Smith scholars.

—⚏—

Andrew Skinner, by then retired, had agreed to meet me at the main gate of the University of Glasgow. Grey-bearded and tweedy, he identified himself by holding a copy of *The Theory of Moral Sentiments*, which he presented to me as a gift.

Skinner was a charming and erudite man who described his own writings as being "typically Scottish, written with neither emotion nor speculation." He firmly refuted the view of Smith as a "mouthpiece" for free markets. Over lunch, he recalled a big dinner in Glasgow, in 1976, on the 200th anniversary of the publication of *The Wealth of Nations*, where the American Nobel prizewinning economist George Stigler had made a speech in which he said that Adam Smith was "alive and well and living in [the University of] Chicago." Skinner said, "It became a famous quote and [Milton] Friedman would tend to take that view, but it's wrong. It's a popular facile vision which has been deployed by people in whose interests it is to deploy it, but it's not an accurate description of Smith."

That Skinner was carrying *Moral Sentiments* was significant. There had been a theory — proposed by German academics as "Das Adam Smith Problem" — that Smith's two books indicated a contradiction in his view of human motivations; that he had "swung" between the two books from emphasizing sympathy to highlighting selfishness. I put this issue to Skinner.

"*The Wealth of Nations* and *The Theory of Moral Sentiments* are complementary," he said. "Smith is really pointing out that our psychology is complex, that we are driven by a number of motives. If it's convenient for the purposes of economic analysis to concentrate on self-interest, then that's a useful abstraction, but it doesn't conform to reality. The butcher, brewer and baker all have social contacts and family contacts. Their economic behaviour is not driven by self-interest narrowly defined. They all go home at night. What one has to do is to look at *The Wealth of Nations* through the lens provided by *Moral Sentiments*. Then the complex psychology of economic man becomes apparent. All economic activity for Smith is social activity. He doesn't treat man as an isolated atom."

After a stimulating conversation, I couldn't help thinking that Skinner's self-assessment of writing without "emotion or speculation" was questionable. We all tend to take out of any area of study much of what we bring into it, and it seemed clear to me that Skinner was not only keen to refute the notion that Smith was a champion of free markets, but also critical of Smith for not being more enthusiastic about the possibilities of interventionist government. Skinner spoke approvingly not merely of John Kenneth Galbraith but of Karl Marx and of Sir James Steuart, a mercantilist economist of Smith's time whose ideas Smith rejected.

"If you want to find somebody who is interested in the problems of unemployment and social policy," Skinner told me, "Steuart is the man, not Smith. He's a much more interesting person. From a technical point of view, Steuart is not as advanced, but from a public policy point of view, you should read Steuart. Steuart addressed the questions that Smith was not asking."

But then perhaps Smith was not asking them because he didn't believe that government *could* — or should try to — provide answers. Also, it had already occurred to me that "Das Adam Smith Problem" was perhaps more of a problem than scholars realized. Although Smith might not be guilty of inconsistency, there did indeed seem to be a disconnect between people's moral sentiments and the world of the Invisible Hand. Indeed, I found an example of that disconnect back in Kirkcaldy when I tracked down the modern version of one of Smith's famous supper-providing triumvirate.

—☊—

The William Keith butcher's shop sat in the commercial no man's land between the bustle of Kirkcaldy's High Street and the even bigger supermarkets on the outskirts of town. Darrell Keith, a good-looking man in his 30s, ran the operation started by his grandfather from a horse-drawn cart back in 1932. Darrell was engagingly open but also seemed worried, and with good reason. Business was terrible.

William Keith had once been a thriving operation, one of perhaps two dozen butchers in the town. Now it was one of just four, and they were all under threat. Keith's used to have the contract to supply the canteens of local collieries, but the collieries were gone. Not merely had supermarkets won over traditional customers, but red meat had recently come under siege in Britain as the result of outbreaks of mad cow and foot-and-mouth disease. As if all that weren't enough, outside the shop, local council roadworks were proceeding at a leisurely pace, cutting down the chance of passing trade.

"The supermarkets are the biggest problem," said Darrell. "They've crippled us. We're cheaper, but they offer the convenience of parking and everything else. What with this too" — he gestured toward the roadworks — "I'm black and blue."

Darrell added another colour, red, as in tape. He said that recent health scares had led to yet another round of environmental health regulations. Other bureaucratic burdens included extensive labelling and other requirements laid down by the European Union in Brussels. "The EU regulations are crazy," said Darrell. "Can you imagine regulating the shape of bananas." (Although that regulation wasn't, of course, Darrell's direct problem.)

The back wall of Darrell's little office, which looked out over the shop, was covered with myriad reminders about rules on working conditions and health. Adam Smith wrote that an economy would continue to function despite "a hundred impertinent obstructions with which the folly of human laws too often encumbers its operations." Thanks to the European Union, a hundred impertinent obstructions had become tens of thousands, and yet the private sector continued — as Smith predicted — to prove remarkably resilient. Systemic economic resilience, however, also required that some businesses had to fail. That was the threat now facing William Keith.

The inevitability — indeed necessity — of failure had always been regarded by capitalism's opponents as barbaric. Under Communism in particular, there would be no failure. Everything would be planned rationally, without self-interest or chance being allowed to intrude. Intriguingly, Keith's had a connection to that horrendously flawed experiment.

Some months after our first meeting, Darrell introduced me to his father. I had wanted to meet Bill Keith to get more details of one of the more unusual pieces of provisioning that Darrell had told me about: supplying a huge haggis for a Burns Supper in Soviet-era Moscow.

For a number of years, family members had accompanied the haggis — which weighed some 70 pounds. Darrell had made the trip only once, just before the Communist empire had imploded. "I'm glad I went," Darrell told me. "It was an eye-opener."

I asked Bill about his Soviet trips. He said, seemingly without irony, that Russians celebrated Burns, the poet of universal brotherhood, as one of "the world's greatest Communists." He had done the trip twice. The first problem, he admitted, was getting the haggis, turnips and whisky past Russian immigration. The second was to prevent anyone stealing them. Bill said he'd made friends behind the old Iron Curtain. He had even been invited to their houses "although they told me that they couldn't be seen with me. I had to follow them at a distance."

Bill concluded, "There were some good things about the Soviet Union." I felt that it would be impolite to press him on exactly what they were. It surely couldn't be pervasive bureaucracy, endemic crime or that ordinary people were too scared to talk to foreigners.

Turning to Adam Smith, I mentioned the suggestion, made by the Edinburgh cultural official, that Smith might suffer by association with Margaret Thatcher. Bill said that was plausible: "Remember, she said there was no such thing as society."

Bill Keith conspicuously failed to add: "There were some good things about Maggie Thatcher." Indeed, I was getting the impression that the old Soviet Union would be a good deal easier to defend in Scotland than Mrs. T.

The night I met both Keiths, Darrell, who was deeply tanned, had just returned from a holiday in Egypt and Cyprus, which indicated that for a business to be on the ropes was far from synonymous with its owners going down for the count. Bill Keith revealed he was thinking about retiring to Spain. Capitalism obviously hadn't been too oppressive for the Keiths.

Bill was clearly far more concerned about his son than about the business. It was equally obvious that Darrell felt that if the shop went under, the responsibility of letting a family institution die would be his. Commercial considerations were — as Andrew Skinner had suggested — inevitably very much mixed up with personal and family relationships. Bill said that he had no problem with the business closing; Darrell could easily work for a supermarket. They were crying out for qualified butchers. Darrell looked uncomfortable with the suggestion.

What would Adam Smith have made of the Keiths? He might sympathize with their predicament, but would probably think that supermarkets putting them out of business was entirely a good thing. Indeed, he might point out that it was not the supermarkets that were putting the Keiths out of business, but the Keiths' own former customers. Smith's fundamental rule of the market was that the consumer should be king. But perhaps strangest of all to Smith might be that Bill Keith saw "good things" about the murderous political ideology that had been rooted in rejection of the Smithian system, even though he had had some direct experience of its monumental shortcomings.

—◊—

I sought out one more businessman in Kirkcaldy. He was the franchisee who owned the McDonald's restaurant on the High Street opposite the site of the house where Adam Smith had lived. His name was Jimmy Patrick. Patrick owned not only the McDonald's in the lang toun but three others in the area. I met him at his other Kirkcaldy franchise, which shared a location with a Sainsbury's supermarket.

Jimmy Patrick had grown up in Edinburgh but had studied management at Kirkcaldy College on the way to becoming a mining engineer. "I can remember coming on my first day and seeing the sign saying 'Birthplace of Adam Smith,'" he told me. "I turned to my friend and said, 'Who the heck is Adam Smith?'

"I became a manager in the coal industry just as it went into its strike period and decline. In its heyday there were a million miners and a thousand pits. It was the biggest industry in the U.K."

Patrick said the economics of more efficient fuels, in particular natural gas, had killed the coal industry, but the miners' unions, with whom Margaret Thatcher had her most famous political battles, hadn't helped. "I can't remember Arthur Scargill [the radical union leader] ever agreeing to *anything*," said Patrick. "It was conflict all the time. Scargill used to say there would be no jobs for miners' sons, but I never knew a miner who *wanted* his son to go down a mine."

At the beginning of the 1990s, Patrick took early retirement and decided to try for a McDonald's franchise. "I was turned down the first time," he said, "but I persevered. It's a massively onerous process even to become a candidate. You have five- and six-hour interviews. Then you work at a restaurant for a week, and if you jump through the hoops, you have to go in front of the main board, and they interview you for the right to work for a year for nothing. After that they tell you where to go. They sold me Kirkcaldy High Street. Now I have four restaurants. McDonald's has been a dream come true."

Jimmy Patrick admitted that he didn't give a great deal of thought to concepts such as capitalism or globalization (the term made darkly synonymous with capitalism in the wake of the collapse of Communism). "People get hung up about McDonald's and capitalism," he said, "but it's only a hamburger, for crying out loud."

Jimmy Patrick didn't have to think much about such broader issues. Just as for Smith's classic butcher, brewer and baker, his route to success lay in keeping his customers happy, his staff motivated and his business profitable. Nobody was forced to work at his restaurants or eat there. His success hadn't been achieved at the expense of anybody else. And yet the broad system of private ownership, personal initiative and voluntary relationships of which he was part had come under persistent attack.

But I had to disagree with Jimmy Patrick's assertion that McDonald's was "just a hamburger." As it happened, I had experienced an epiphany about the wider meaning of McDonald's even before I had set out to research the Invisible Hand. Indeed, that experience had been one of the motivating factors for my inquiry. It had taken place in the city to which the Keith family had taken their haggis: Moscow.

three

Fears of a Clown: The Golden Arch-Enemy

*"I've never seen anything more capitalistically
wonderful, more mutually beneficial."*
— Mark Winer, head of Moscow McDonald's (1991)

On the morning of January 31, 1991, I was inside Moscow McDonald's on Pushkin Square as the doors opened for business. Fur-hatted patrons were given an extra-enthusiastic round of applause by the young counter staff because this was the restaurant's first birthday. However, a major celebration had been cancelled. Even the professionally sunny dispositions at McDonald's had been forced to acknowledge that McHappiness might appear out of place given Moscow's grim food supply situation, turmoil in the Baltic republics and the outbreak of the first Gulf War.

McDonald's was operating under nightmare conditions. From the Kremlin, a mile or so down the uncleared black-ice sidewalks of Gorky Street, the winds of a renewed Cold War and anti-business sentiment were blowing. Although McHappy faces had been deemed inappropriate, brave ones were still *de rigueur*. Later that day, two blocks from the restaurant, in converted offices on the eighth floor of the low-rent Minsk Hotel, I sat with Mark Winer, the field commander of this exercise in commercial valour.

Winer was waiting for a call from an Australian radio station. When the call came, he cranked up his enthusiasm for the listeners down under. "Great," he said, "and delighted to have your call ... It's the biggest in the world, the equivalent of 12 or 15 average North American restaurants ... The store looks terrific. We have a tremendous year behind us ... It's the same menu we have everywhere and, God bless 'em, they really love it ... We process two tons of beef, two tons of milk and two tons of potatoes a day ... There's a whole lot of feeding going on." He replaced the receiver, his smile intact.

Mark Winer said "That's great" and "That's terrific" a lot. "We have 1,500 stars in our company," he told me. "We have the capacity to introduce so many people to what McDonald's is ... We know that 40,000 times a day we're doing it right." But there was obviously a lot going on behind the upbeat sound bites.

A New Hampshire–born American with a degree in Russian language and literature from Indiana University, Winer had been hired by McDonald's from Coca-Cola, for whom he'd been making trips to the Soviet Union since 1974, seeking to break Pepsi's hold on the market, such as it was.

Despite his long experience with the Soviets, Winer admitted that he'd had no idea of the difficulties he would face in operating Moscow McDonald's. "Some days," he said, his smile still strapped on, "it's an effort to get up and shave. Doing the simplest things here can be such a struggle. There's no time to think. It's like those cartoons where you see a duck gliding along peacefully above the water, while underneath, it's having to paddle like crazy."

McDonald's liked to keep the paddling out of view, and so far it had done a remarkable job, but it took an awfully complex and skilful organization to appear so effortless. Founded by Ray Kroc, a former jazz musician, radio DJ and milkshake-machine salesman, McDonald's had turned fast food into a corporate art form, built on rigid standards of quality, service, cleanliness and value, or QSC&V. As John Love wrote in his book, *McDonald's: Behind the Arches*, Kroc had evolved a unique blend of conformity and creativity. "In essence," wrote Love, "the history of

McDonald's is a case study on managing entrepreneurs in a corporate setting."

Moscow McDonald's didn't fit this model. It had been the brainchild of George Cohon, the head of the company's Canadian subsidiary. Cohon, so the mythology went, saw in the Soviet Union not 250 million minds perverted by anti-capitalist dogma but 250 million potential consumers yearning for a helping of QSC&V. Cohen's vision meshed with McDonald's larger strategy of diversifying outside the increasingly saturated North American fast-food market. Cohon would later admit that Ray Kroc, who died in 1984, had not been enthusiastic about the proposal. "He had a tough, Cold War attitude toward the Soviets," Cohon would write in his 1997 autobiography, *To Russia with Fries*. "[Kroc felt] they couldn't be trusted."

Ray Kroc had a point.

Cohon, a former lawyer born in Chicago, was a charismatic and publicity-conscious dynamo. His Soviet dream had begun when he had played host to some of the Russian delegation at the Montreal Olympics in 1976. Hopes of sending mobile units to the 1980 Moscow Games had been shattered by the Soviet invasion of Afghanistan and the U.S. Olympic boycott. Then along had come Mikhail Gorbachev.

—m—

I bought a Gorby matryoshka doll at Moscow's open-air market, the Arbat. Matryoshkas are those nests of dolls within dolls. Inside the fat bowling-pin-shaped figure of Gorbachev were contained the complex regressions of Soviet history: inside Gorby, Brezhnev; inside Brezhnev, Khrushchev; inside Khrushchev, Stalin; inside Stalin, Lenin; and inside Lenin, the czars. Each painted doll held something symbolic. Gorby was holding a dossier marked "Perestroika"; Brezhnev was holding a bottle of vodka; Khrushchev clutched an ear of corn. Behind

Stalin's back was a bloody axe. Lenin held only his famous cap; but it was with him, and his embrace of the anti-capitalist teachings of Karl Marx, that the horror had started.

Vladimir Ilyich Lenin was, like so many champions of the proletariat (including Marx), an intellectual from a well-heeled family. He emerged victorious from a factional struggle by being utterly ruthless, seizing power in 1917 amid the domestic confusion following the abdication of the czar.

A Marxist revolution had one major problem: apart from his glib remarks about hunting in the morning, fishing in the afternoon and raising cattle after dinner, Marx had never really indicated what the revolutionaries were meant to do once they were in control. Lenin and his fellow revolutionaries had not the slightest clue about the workings of business or the economy. He seemed to think that business was mostly a matter of bookkeeping.

Within four years, Soviet production had fallen to a fraction of its pre-revolutionary level. Lenin was forced to retreat. Thus was hatched the temporary reversal of the New Economic Policy, under which some private initiative was permitted, while the state retreated to controlling the "commanding heights" of big industry. However, Lenin kept a viselike grip on political power.

Democracy having been squashed, the free press was next. Then, any suggestion that the newly "unchained" workers should actually control factories was rejected outright, as undermining the necessary dictatorial leadership of the "vanguard of the proletariat." Lenin appointed Stalin to repress factions, then crushed resistance in the republics. He attacked Poland as a springboard to the conquest of Central Europe and created the Comintern to spread revolution throughout the rest of the world. Then he was felled by a stroke, leaving Stalin in control.

Mikhail Gorbachev was born during the terror-famine years of the early 1930s, when Stalin used mass starvation to overcome peasant resistance. Gorbachev, studious and earnest, was destined to preside over the collapse of the Soviet empire. He became a devoted functionary, an apparatchik. Like so many of his colleagues, he was apparently shocked when, in 1956, word got out of Nikita Khrushchev's "private" speech to top party officials denouncing Stalin's crimes and "cult of personality." Gorbachev soon persuaded himself, again like most of his colleagues, that Stalin may have been a maniac, but that the system was fine, even as it continued to decline.

The American Marxist economist Robert Heilbroner admitted that "during the Sixties the Soviet Union became the first industrial country in history to suffer a prolonged peacetime fall in average life expectancy, a symptom of a disastrous misallocation of resources." In fact, "disastrous misallocation of resources" was essentially a definition of Communism, and yet Gorbachev kept the faith. His reliability meant that he was permitted in the 1970s to travel abroad, where, in France, Italy and Belgium, he saw how far the standard of living in the Soviet Union lagged behind that of the Western democracies.

Gorbachev became general secretary of the Communist Party after a succession of geriatric leaders, including Leonid Brezhnev, had died in office. There was something stunningly naive about his perspective. "We began a plan," he revealed in his memoirs, "to renew society within the framework of socialist choice." But the whole point about socialism was that there was, and indeed could be, no "choice." Once individual choice meant anything, the Soviet system would inevitably collapse, since personal choice was bound to conflict with any regime planned from the top.

Gorbachev could see that nothing worked: that four times as many people were needed to repair trucks as to make them, that televisions with cardboard components sometimes spontaneously exploded, that shortages and low quality were endemic. But the notion that central planning was the problem was beyond his grasp because it was the core of his Communist faith and — more fundamentally — because most humans reflexively believe in the validity and viability of central planning.

Gorbachev tried exhortation, calling for more inspection and higher standards. Everybody — as in Orwell's *Animal Farm* — was to try harder. Spotting that an extraordinarily large portion of Soviet citizens were killing themselves with alcohol, Gorby upped vodka prices (indicating an intuitive understanding of the laws of economics) and had the lush vineyards of the Republic of Georgia plowed under. The result was a massive budget deficit, since alcohol had accounted for a major chunk of government revenues.

Perestroika, or economic, political and social reform, was his next big idea, but it amounted to mere tinkering. Then came glasnost, or openness, in which Gorbachev invited criticism of the bureaucracy. He introduced a measure of democracy and watched as the republics split off from the empire. Then, in February 1990, the month after Moscow McDonald's opened, he effectively ended Communist rule by agreeing to multi-party politics and announcing the end of opposition to private property, the core of the Marxist system.

My visit to Moscow proved of seminal importance to my project because it gave me an opportunity — at a unique moment in history — to examine the astonishing gap between the realities of capitalist enterprise and its collapsing collectivist alternative. The gap was particularly significant because McDonald's had long been the Golden Arch–enemy for Western elitists, the prime target for distaste of the fatty cravings of the hoi polloi and their plastic-toy-obsessed kids. The giant chain was claimed to be a prime example of the homogenization of the world under "Anglo-Saxon" capitalism, not to mention a promoter of the evils of mass production, animal cruelty, environmental degradation, worker exploitation, dangerous genetic food modifications and the general transformation of the world into a fatter and nastier place.

Moscow provided another perspective on much-derided "fast food." There, the multi-level 700-seat McDonald's restaurant represented not just an attractive, Muzak-filled retreat from the drudgery of imploding Soviet life, a tiny island of organization and quality in a sea of state-sponsored entropy and dross. The venture, and the organization behind it, demonstrated that the Soviet Union had been built upon a demonic vision of capitalism that bore little if any relationship to the reality.

—◊—

Before he presided over the Soviet collapse, Mikhail Gorbachev had already permitted joint ventures between Soviet organizations and foreign companies. That was how, after intense and often frustrating negotiations, McDonald's had entered a 49 per cent/51 per cent partnership with the food service administration of the Moscow city council. The agreement, calling for 20 restaurants supplied by a huge food processing complex, involved two major departures from McDonald's normal practice. "It was not typical for McDonald's to create a franchise without an individual [owner]," acknowledged Mark Winer. "It was a big step to make a franchise through a joint venture with an organization, but that was the only way."

The other, even larger, departure was the processing complex. When the deal was signed, in April 1988, McDonald's had some 2,600 restaurants in 49 countries outside the United States. In all of them it relied on local suppliers. There were, however, no such Soviet entrepreneurs because private property and personal initiative had been crimes for most of the previous 70 years.

When it became clear that it would have to source food locally, McDonald's persuaded some of its largest suppliers to pitch in by coaching selected Soviet farmers and helping build the processing plant. European meat experts introduced new feed programs for Soviet cattle. Potato growers and processors from the Netherlands introduced strains preferred for frozen French fries, and provided the systems for manufacturing them. Bakers from the United States, Canada, Sweden and West Germany developed the bun and pie systems. Dairy experts from Sweden set up a pasteurization process for a country where bacteria levels in milk were often six times those permissible in the West.

"The building of the food complex, the creation of the infrastructure, goes way beyond what we've ever done in another country," Winer told me. "We couldn't have done it without the larger McDonald's family getting involved. I've never seen anything more capitalistically wonderful, more mutually beneficial."

To put up the 10,000-square-metre processing "McComplex," McDonald's called in Teräsbetoni, a Finnish company with long experience in dealing with the Soviets. The man who led the project was Lasse Alanne.

"If you give a project to a Soviet construction company," Alanne told me when I visited him in his Helsinki office, "it will be delayed, over budget and of poor quality. I have *never* seen a development completed on time. The problem is material flow. You just can't plan the job, because you never know when, or if, materials will turn up. The system is such that nobody is to blame. Everybody passes the buck."

McDonald's foray into the Soviet Union was seen by some as an act of hubris, an exercise in what one observer called McDonald's "fatal optimism." Not only was McDonald's taking QSC&V to a place where standards were seen as objects of evasion, small battlegrounds where individuals could get their own back on the system, they were doing it on an unprecedented scale. Moreover, as Winer acknowledged, they were going into an area where the two primary strengths of the McDonald's system — the commitment of franchisees and the quality of suppliers — were non-existent. McDonald's had to rely for its beef, flour, potatoes and vegetables on a farm and food system that was renowned for inefficiency and low quality. To cap it all, McDonald's committed to operate this world-record-sized fast-food joint with rubles, funny money that symbolized the bankruptcy of Communism.

The ruble had always been an Alice-in-Wonderland currency. The Kremlin claimed to be free of the "Western disease" of inflation, but only because prices were rigidly controlled and supplies rationed. (The same reflexive political response to pricing would be adopted by the governors of New York and New Jersey, in the greatest capitalist country on earth, in the wake of Superstorm Sandy.)

The US$40 million that would ultimately be spent on the food processing complex — almost 10 times the cost of the restaurant — would have to be paid in hard cash. The venture thus started with a hefty hard currency debt that it had no hope of servicing in the immediate future. In the meantime, McDonald's had to spin QSC&V gold from the pervasive dross of the Soviet supply system.

—m—

McComplex, situated in the bleak high-rise Moscow suburb of Solntsevo, looked like any other windowless, boxlike factory. The interior, however, once you were past the smiling picture of Ray Kroc above the reception desk, was more reminiscent of a series of glistening operating rooms. It was here, in this elaborately ventilated, temperature-controlled maze of scrubbed floors and gleaming machinery, that the uninspired pick of the state and collective farms was worked into McDonald's demanding shape, ready to be shipped downtown.

The main problem for McComplex was that initiative and enterprise stopped at the plant gate. Even inside the plant, there was something vaguely off-kilter about the Russian workers.

A group of men looked up suspiciously as they hacked away at parts of a bloody carcass. Another cluster peeled and sliced apples by hand, as if huddled together for protection against all this emphasis on quality and productivity. Yet another group gathered protectively around a man opening a large tin of tomato paste. Just how many Russians, I wondered, did it take to open a tin of tomato paste? Meanwhile, perhaps the most impressive part of the plant, the French fry line, stood idle.

McDonald's had always loved to trumpet its corporate vital statistics: "billions and billions served." When it had built its huge potato storage bin at McComplex, it was calculated that its contents would "provide enough French fries to stretch, end-to-end, from Toronto to Vancouver — or from Moscow to Irkutsk." At the time of my visit, its contents couldn't have provided enough French fries to stretch to the guard dogs' kennels at the front gate. The bin was empty. This was not just a crisis; it was one of a *series* of crises with which McDonald's had been forced to cope since before the restaurant opened.

Terry Williams had perhaps the most demanding job in the entire McDonald's empire. He was McComplex's quality assurance manager. "Like everything else here," he told me, "there are raw materials *somewhere*, but there are no Yellow Pages. Quality is always a problem."

Williams also had to deal with the still-Soviet bureaucracy, which not only wanted assurance of standards higher than those in the West but also demanded to be taken, in minute detail, through the formulas for items such as Big Mac sauce, which inevitably didn't crop up in the tomes of Soviet culinary reference.

One bright spot amid all these frustrations was the young Muscovites who clamoured to work at the restaurant. Some 25,000 had applied for just 630 jobs. McDonald's sent the lucky few for training to its Toronto Institute of Hamburgerology, and to Hamburger University at its world headquarters in Oak Brook, Illinois.

From day one, customer lineups stretched around Pushkin Square. After a year, there were Soviet-sized statistics to trumpet. The restaurant had served close to 4 million Big Macs, 4.7 million milkshakes, 5.8 million orders of French fries and 2.7 million apple pies. It had almost doubled its staff, and come rain, shine or Siberian cold fronts, the lineups remained.

This enormous — if unsurprising — demand put more pressure on supplies even as the old command economy was breaking down. The politics of republican separatism threw additional curves. Even the weather conspired against the joint venture. The previous fall's torrential rains had ruined what was meant to be a bumper potato crop, so, whereas McDonald's had arranged to have outside storage because it didn't think its McComplex potato bin would be adequate, the bin wound up, as noted, an echo chamber. The beef supply too was running into problems. Increasingly rapid inflation was eating into margins, forcing the company to raise prices. Meanwhile, McDonald's continued to suffer hard currency costs for items such as sauce mixes, Coca-Cola concentrate and cleaning materials.

McDonald's had managed to develop a local hamburger wrap, but it had proved a long and painful process of buying the paper, then shipping it out to be laminated, then having metal moulds made for rubber stamps, then buying ink, then arranging to have the whole thing printed.

This unaccustomed extra burden highlighted one of the many aspects of capitalism that even corporate managers take for granted: the Invisible Hand, the money-mediated and profit-driven process by which individuals and companies effortlessly come together to innovate and most efficiently meet demand for equipment, supplies and consumer products, thus spontaneously creating a vast system without any central plan.

In North America, or any other capitalist country, McDonald's would merely have put the hamburger wrap out for tender and entrepreneurs would have beaten down the door to gain the business. Said Williams, "If this experience has taught me any-thing, it's a new appreciation of our Western suppliers."

Those suppliers — and the astonishing range of products and services that they fed into the McDonald's system — were a function of a relatively free market where ingenuity, qual-ity, efficiency and reliability were pursued and provided not because they were part of a master plan of statewide control "for the people" but because they were rewarded by financial success, and all that went with it.

McDonald's local partner, by contrast, was still part of a top-down system based on political power. The Moscow city council's inclination was to grab its partnership share of the money and run. That was the Soviet way. Everybody grabbed what they could, as soon as they could, on the basis that if they didn't, somebody else would. Such was the ironic — but inevi-table — fruit of a system based on denigrating and countering the "greed" and "selfishness" of capitalism.

—⁂—

A few days after the restaurant's first birthday, I attended the biweekly managerial staff meeting: 80 or so Russians, plus representatives from McDonald's "global family." In one cor-ner, I noticed a tall, angular young man, a Canadian named Buddy Morin, taking notes. Born in Quebec and educated at the University of Ottawa, Morin had spent a decade working his way up the organization as a manager. When he had heard that the Moscow restaurant was opening, he had decided to take his holidays to coincide with the event, perhaps see if he could lend a hand. He was still there. More than that, he had persuaded his older brother, Majella, an accounting consultant from Edmonton, to join McDonald's too.

"The Soviets have no idea of return on capital," Majella told me later. "They have no idea of what a profit is." He noted that he'd been changed by Moscow. "I've grown much more patient in the past year. I've learned to laugh a lot more. I've also learned to appreciate freedom."

That evening, the McDonald's office staff held a dinner — partly a belated first-birthday celebration — at a private club near the hotel. Majella displayed his new, improved sense of humour. "The Russians wait until the food is on the table," he confided wryly, "then they start making toasts."

Sure enough: the hot food was on the table, and the toasts began. The themes were universal: mutual appreciation; spouses neglected because of work; belonging; achievement. Mark Winer's executive assistant, Marina Tulupnikova, one of the first Russians hired by McDonald's in Moscow, handed out medals. Before she came to McDonald's, Tulupnikova had worked for a Moscow-based United Nations agency that educated Third World countries in food processing.

"When I started," she told me halfway through the evening, "I didn't want to work for Mark Winer. I believed all that stuff about 'capitalist exploiters.' But after I went to Toronto and Chicago, I changed my mind. McDonald's has helped us take our minds off our situation. It has given us some hope for the future."

Around 11 p.m., I walked back to the restaurant with Majella. His brother was sitting at a table in the middle of all the swabbing and disassembling and disinfecting that would go on most of the night. Buddy said it had been a pretty normal evening: a few more thousand customers; a couple of fights. Buddy had spotted a baby outside the restaurant in a locked car and had tried to locate the parents with a bullhorn. When they hadn't appeared, he had the resident militia break the window and bring the baby inside. Just another Friday night a long way from home.

People like Buddy Morin, it seemed to me, were the backbone of the McDonald's system, and of Western business and the Western way of life more generally. Buddy appeared to be without cynicism, the kind of person who looked out for babies stuck in cars, and who gave out Maple Leaf pins to bemused guards at Moscow's Sheremetyevo Airport. He was the type of young man who, in former times, would have gone off without question to die for his country.

Of course, nobody would die for a hamburger, or for McDonald's, but it was during my trip to Moscow that I realized that McDonald's really did represent much more than a hamburger. It seemed ludicrous to see a clown as a danger to any government, but that was what Ronald McDonald was to the dark men still sitting in the Kremlin, who hated the process that Mikhail Gorbachev had started without understanding its implications. Ronald McDonald represented a society where individuals and corporations could come together to provide what people wanted, however mundane or complex that want might be. That made him a natural enemy both to everything for which the old Soviet Union had stood, and to anti-capitalist sentiment in the West.

McDonald's was providing what the Soviet Union most desperately needed: not "Beeg Maks," but organizational infra-structure, technology transfer, managerial talent, agricultural improvement, import substitution and, above all, hope through a vision of the fruits of freedom. But it wasn't doing so out of any bogus collectivism or lust for "corporate power."

The vast majority of those who enjoyed Western capitalism didn't think much about such issues. They didn't have to. They lived under a system that allowed them — mostly — to get on with their own lives. Relatively few Westerners would ever come to Moscow, or study Soviet history or economics, or delve into the nature and meaning of McDonald's.

That trip to Moscow made me realize that it was only by operating in such an environment that McDonald's non-Soviet employees could begin to understand all the things they had taken for granted. That still wouldn't necessarily lead them to understand why they, and the system of which they were part, were so often demonized, and how that demonization had led to the disaster of the society in which they were now struggling to operate. To begin to understand that fact requires some history.

The intellectual historian Jerry Z. Muller suggests that in many ways Adam Smith was the precursor of Victorian values. Smith, wrote Muller, "envisaged a society held together in part by market relations of mutual self-interest, in part by deference, and in part by a culture of respectability which would extend to all social orders ... To a remarkable though often unrecognized degree, this was the path taken by Victorian England."

Critics, however, claimed that Smith's vision came at a terrible price.

four

Dark Satanic Minds

If Marx had one big idea, it was that capitalism was the rule of money — which was itself the expression of greed ... This set of ideas was not the conclusion of his years of inquiry into the capitalist economy: it was the never-abandoned premise of the inquiry.
— Jerry Z. Muller, *The Mind and the Market*

The Industrial Revolution promoted stunning developments in technology and business organization. It also triggered an avalanche of moral condemnation. Much supposed economic analysis in the 19th century turned into a morality play of winners and losers. Given the ugly realities of early industrial development, this is hardly surprising. Political economy — the study of commerce and the state, which would eventually become the more restricted academic pursuit known as economics — did not acquire the name of the "dismal science" for nothing.

Although the stock trader turned economist David Ricardo systematically confirmed and refined Smith's insights about the benefits of free trade, he also posited what looked like a never-ending struggle between "factors of production": land, labour and capital. The "gloomy parson," Thomas Malthus, asserted that the poor were condemned to live perpetually at subsistence level because of the inability of food production to keep up with their own inability to stop breeding. Karl Marx, inspired by his partner Friedrich Engels, a cotton manufacturer, thundered that poverty was due to the depredations of the greedy rich. Above all, critics focused on the conditions of the cotton industry, the sector that led the Industrial Revolution.

In 1776, the year *The Wealth of Nations* was published, Richard Arkwright, the 13th child of a poor family from Preston in Lancashire and a one-time wig maker, had just completed his second water-powered cotton mill at Cromford in Cheshire, in a picturesque gorge close to the River Derwent.

Arkwright had become fascinated by attempts to automate the cotton spinning process; he helped develop the spinning frame. This stout device, which produced stronger thread than was made by hand spinning, was too big to be operated by hand, and so, after trying horses, Arkwright and his partners turned to water power. The completion of Cromford would herald the start of the age of mass production, and Arkwright was dubbed the "father of the factory system." However, the conventional image of "dark satanic mills" (a phrase derived from the poet William Blake, who used it in a different and more complex sense) arose not so much from Arkwright's innovations as from those of a man who had been a very junior colleague of Adam Smith at the University of Glasgow.

Similar statues of James Watt sit in Manchester's Piccadilly Gardens and in Glasgow's George Square. George Square bears many other monuments. Manchester's main square, by contrast, has just two others: one of a shy-faced but voluminously dressed Queen Victoria, looking as if she is concealing a gale under the regal folds of her gown; the other an imposing rendition of Prime Minister Robert Peel, son of a reformist mill owner. These three figures represent the triumvirate of interrelated forces behind Britain's 19th-century greatness: technology, empire and trade.

Watt, who was 13 years Smith's junior, had been sent to Glasgow to study mathematical instrument making. His great breakthrough came when he was asked to repair a Newcomen steam engine, which was used primarily for pumping water from mines. Watt realized that the efficiency of the machine could be greatly improved by installing a separate condenser. He also modified the engine so that it could turn factory machinery. Equally important, he went into partnership with a Birmingham industrialist named Matthew Boulton.

Boulton and Watt were among a group of writers, inventors, entrepreneurs and "scientists" (although that term, like "capitalist," had not yet been invented) who were dubbed the "Lunar Men." They met each month on the Monday nearest the full moon so that they might find their way home in an era before street lighting. Other members of the group included the great pottery manufacturer Josiah Wedgwood, the scientist Joseph Priestley (who discovered oxygen) and the polymath Erasmus Darwin, grandfather of Charles. (There is a small exhibit dedicated to the Lunar Men at Birmingham's science museum, Thinktank. The exhibit devoted to recycling receives much more space and prominence.)

Among the first to see the potential of Boulton & Watt's new engine was Arkwright. The influence of Arkwright's water-driven frames had been dramatic. In 1765, 500,000 pounds of cotton had been spun in England, all by hand. By 1784, the total was 12 million pounds, almost all by water-driven machine. The Boulton & Watt engine led to a further quantum leap. It did not render water-driven mills redundant, but it did enable mills to be built in towns. The introduction of the steam engine to manufacturing, as the British historian Paul Johnson points out, "was the Big Bang of the Industrial Revolution." However, these engines' boilers were all heated by coal, which led to enormous pollution problems.

It was in the shift of steam-driven mills to towns that most of the negative images of the Industrial Revolution were formed: of grimy back-to-back cottages; of dreadful sanitary conditions; of workers as cogs in a faceless and heartless profit-obsessed machine, working for subsistence wages in a world where they had no future.

In fact, the greatest reformers were often themselves businessmen. They included some vehement critics who wanted to overturn capitalism; their theories ranged from the naive to the murderous, yet they are still fondly remembered and celebrated at government-run British museums.

—⚏—

After he built Cromford, Arkwright became involved in the development of another even more spectacular water-driven venture, at New Lanark in Scotland. The fast-flowing river below the beautiful Falls of Clyde made the site ideal. Arkwright's partner there was David Dale, a respected Glasgow merchant. The notoriously prickly Arkwright fell out with Dale, reportedly over a triviality, and withdrew. Dale took control and continued to expand, but the reason New Lanark is so well preserved today is not that it is seen as a monument to capitalism. Quite the contrary. Dale's son-in-law, Robert Owen, turned New Lanark into the promotional centre for a Utopian dream, where he nurtured anti-capitalist sentiment. A fair amount of anti-capitalist sentiment still seems to pervade the site today.

Owen's New Lanark was very far from being an experiment in socialism understood as collective ownership and control. Workers had neither shares in the mill nor much — if any — say in how it was run. Nor was Owen a political revolutionary. What he did share in common with more radical socialists was opposition to religion; belief that human nature was an indeterminate clay (or "blank slate"), there to be moulded by men such as himself; distaste for the "individual selfish" competitive system and private property (even though they enabled him to promote his muddled ideas); demonization of money; and a generally woolly notion of how economies — as opposed to individual businesses — work.

Owen rejected Adam Smith's idea of gradual improvement under a system of "natural liberty." For him, cotton masters, the men who owned and ran the mills, were (except for himself) greedy and selfish, while workers were oppressed sheep to be led, with himself as the Good Shepherd.

Adam Smith had shrewdly noted that people by nature give far more deference to the ideas of the wealthy than they deserve. Of few people was this more true than Robert Owen.

Owen was born on May 14, 1771, in Newtown in Wales, five years before the publication of *The Wealth of Nations*. He received only a rudimentary education before being shipped off by his parents to work in the drapery business. He proved an assiduous employee and developed a keen interest in the then-booming textile industry. He started his own business but soon returned to employment as a mill manager in Manchester. Close to his 20th birthday, he was reportedly managing 500 workers, at the then substantial salary of £300 a year. Owen soon found investors to help him start his own mill. He also became interested in education and social reform (which was the rule rather than the exception for industrialists of the time). However, when he visited New Lanark he saw a place where he might indulge a nascent vision of industrial harmony, a New Jerusalem in which he would be the secular Messiah.

Owen courted David Dale's daughter, Anne Caroline, married her on September 30, 1799, and took over New Lanark early in 1800 on what seemed generous terms, essentially promising to pay Dale out of the mill's future profits. New Lanark was the basis for the fortune and reputation that enabled Robert Owen to indulge his ideas. The scale of New Lanark seems extraordinary even today, but to visitors from the present, if they could travel back to Owen's time, the most arresting feature of the place would be that most of its employees were children, supplied by orphanages in Glasgow and Edinburgh.

Child labour has become one of the great fixed images of the Industrial Revolution, but it is inappropriate to take our modern sensitivities back to earlier times. Child labour was common — as it still is in many poor countries — because it was, and is, necessary for the survival of both the children and their families. It was most necessary for orphans. Indeed, orphanages paid cotton manufacturers to take their charges off their hands. David Dale reportedly treated his young employees well. By 1796 he was employing 16 teachers at the site.

Owen's desire to prevent children under 10 from working appears wholly admirable, until we remember that this might have led them to starve. His desire to educate children and provide an early equivalent of daycare was worthy but ultimately self-interested in business terms, since these measures increased the skills and contentment — and thus productivity — of the workforce, as did his organization of medical insurance, savings opportunities, food and other provisions. There was no conflict between good business and morality. Indeed, Owen himself constantly, at least in the early days, stressed the importance of these measures for *increasing profitability*.

The village shop that Owen set up at New Lanark was reportedly an inspiration for the modern cooperative movement, which was founded in the town of Rochdale in Lancashire. According to a potted history at the New Lanark site, when Owen arrived, there were lots of small traders in the village, "selling poor quality goods at high prices." He was able to buy in bulk, lower the prices and still make a profit. But of course this is exactly what supermarkets and big-box stores do today, even as they are castigated for putting the "little guy"—such as William Keith, the Kirkcaldy butchers — out of business.

Robert Owen put the little guy out of business too. He also made sure that no other traders could survive in the village, by paying his workers with "tickets for wages," which they could spend only at his village shop. Elsewhere such enforced commitment to the company store would be cited as evidence of corporate villainy, but Owen declared that his own motives weren't "selfish." The important thing was not what was good for him, but what was good for mankind, although he clearly expected a little kudos for showing mankind the way.

At New Lanark, Owen in fact displayed more of the enlightened capitalist than of the Utopian dreamer. One might not doubt his good intentions when it came to spreading education and advocating factory reform, but he seemed eager to bury the fact that many other cotton masters, and businessmen of the time more generally, were enlightened and reform-minded.

—◊—

The cemetery of Kirkcaldy's Old Kirk, which sits just up the hill from the site of Adam Smith's mother's house, is in better condition than that of the Canongate. It is filled with memorials to manufacturers, merchants, soldiers, shipowners and harbourmasters. One of the most intriguing memorials is that of Baillie Robert Philp, linen manufacturer and philanthropist, who died on April 14, 1828, at the age of 77.

The inscription reads:

BY ATTENTION TO BUSINESS AND INTEGRITY IN DEALING HE ACCUMULATED WEALTH THE MOST OF WHICH HE DESTINED TO FORM A PERMANENT CAPITAL THE PROCEEDS WHEREOF TO BE APPLIED IN EDUCATING AND CLOTHING POOR CHILDREN AND PROVIDING THEM WITH A SUM OF MONEY. FOR THIS LAUDABLE PURPOSE HIS FUNDS WERE INVESTED ON LANDS IN THE PARISHES OF

STRATHMIGLO	20,000
COLLESSIE	10,200
KINGHORN	39,800
AND IN HERITABLE BONDS	700
	£ 70,700

THE DEAD IN CHRIST SHALL RISE TO GLORY.

Such a bald accounting suggests that Philp and/or his executors were concerned that the Lord might need a little reminder on the Last Day.

Philp's trust fund — sizable in its day — continued to provide for children long after his death. Indeed, it was used to build the Kirkcaldy Philp School, which was opened in 1850. The school building still stands, overlooking the firth. By the time I first visited Kirkcaldy it had been converted into a discotheque, which itself subsequently underwent several identity changes.

Philp was hardly unusual for a successful entrepreneur of his day, or indeed of any day, including his rather too obvious concern that his philanthropic light not be hidden under a bushel. However, we may need reminding that most real-life capitalists, unlike pre-conversion Scrooge or Marxist stereotypes, have always wanted to be loved as much as anybody, and to be respected more than most.

Perhaps Baillie Robert Philp made sure that his benevolence was literally etched in stone because he knew that some were itching to chip away the record. His memorial is surely not too self-congratulatory in suggesting that business success depends on "attention" and "integrity." This was very much Adam Smith's view.

As Owen demonstrated, there was no necessary conflict between humane treatment of employees and profits. Indeed, humane treatment, and its perception as such by the employees, has always been a key factor in increasing productivity and thus profitability. Successful businessmen who contributed to their communities were never the exception.

Go to any town that played a part in the Industrial Revolution and you will find museums, libraries and parks endowed by capitalists. In Kirkcaldy, although the Adam Smith Theatre, the museum, the library and the town parks are all now administered by the local government — part of a comprehensive state takeover of community life — they were all endowed by

industrialists. The library and museum were built by the linoleum manufacturer Michael Nairn. The Adam Smith Theatre
was the contribution of another linoleum laird, Michael
Beveridge. It was opened by one of the greatest industrial phi-
lanthropists of them all, Andrew Carnegie, who was born nearby
in Dunfermline. Beveridge also gave the town a beautiful park,
which still bears his name.

It was Sir Robert Peel, who was among the greatest of the
early cotton magnates — and father of the prime minister whose
statue stands in Manchester's Piccadilly Gardens — who promoted parliamentary legislation in 1802 to protect children in
factories. Peel's act was an acknowledgement that some masters might treat their charges badly, but it was also a reminder
that the spirit of improvement came from *within* the capitalist
"class."

The great reformers Richard Cobden and John Bright —
the most prominent proponents of the abolition of the Corn
Laws, which excluded foreign grain from British markets to
protect British landowners at the expense of consumers —
were both cotton manufacturers. The mill owner John Owens's
bequest formed the basis of the University of Manchester.
John Rylands provided his local community of Stretford, then
a village near Manchester, with a library, baths, a town hall
and even a coffee house. His widow built the John Rylands
Library in his name.

Although he dealt in wool rather than cotton, Titus Salt
was another example of enlightened capitalism. He pioneered
anti-pollution technology in his home town of Bradford,
northeast of Manchester, and went on to build, over 20 years,
the magnificent mill and model community of Saltaire on
Bradford's outskirts, providing his workers with houses featuring running water and gas lighting, and building public
amenities. Nevertheless, Salt — like his colleagues — opposed
trade unions and, significantly, legislation on child labour. He
gave away some £500,000 to good causes during his lifetime, a

massive sum by modern standards. (Saltaire's well-preserved mill is now home to the world's largest collection of works by the local artist David Hockney.)

None of this is to deny that working conditions would be considered extraordinarily harsh by modern observers, but employment in the mills was better than the alternatives. Conditions did, gradually, improve by a process that may have appeared to be led by social agitation and legislation, but in fact had a great deal more to do with the underlying surge of capital investment, productivity and sustained economic growth, which forced mill owners — benevolent or not — to compete for labour by increasing wages and improving conditions. However, it was obviously difficult if not impossible to see this long-term process at work amid the grime and squalor of early mill towns.

As the Napoleonic Wars drew to a close, both mill owners and authorities were disturbed by Luddite riots that resulted in the breaking of new machinery, which was seen as destroying jobs. Robert Owen claimed that what had brought about these awful, and worsening, conditions was economic liberalism and the competitive system, which, he declared, was based on "deception." He came forward with a series of bold proposals for "villages of unity and co-operation," which struck many as workhouses by a more glorified name.

Although the great and the good expressed polite interest in Owen's solutions to what were, after all, pressing problems, many were profoundly skeptical. John Quincy Adams, then U.S. ambassador to Britain, described Owen in his memoirs as "crafty crazy ... a speculative, scheming, mischievous man."

Owen managed to draw the ire of both radical reformers and the political economist heirs of Adam Smith, groups that rarely saw eye to eye. The radicals saw Owen's communities as oppressive, while the economists viewed them as impractical and counterproductive. The reformer William Cobbett described them as "parallelograms of paupers." The political economist Robert Torrens said it was difficult to decide whether Owen was a "knave" or an enthusiast "in whose brain a copulation between vanity and benevolence has engendered madness."

Owen welcomed a steady stream of "philanthropic tourists" at New Lanark. Their number included Grand Duke Nicholas, future czar of Russia. Some — although presumably not the grand duke — found disquieting authoritarian overtones to Owen's operation. After watching Owen's child labourers drill like little soldiers at the mill's Institution for the Formation of Character (which has been lovingly restored with taxpayers' money from the European Union), the poet Robert Southey compared the place to a slave plantation.

Parliament ultimately rejected Owen's scheme. One member suggested that "this visionary plan, if adopted, would destroy the very roots of society." Owen responded to criticism by making his schemes more grandiose. Undaunted, he set off to proselytize in the New World, and not merely to lecture but at last to put into effect his grand plan. He bought an existing cooperative community in Indiana, which he renamed New Harmony.

Owen attracted a large number of settlers, described by one of Owen's sons, Robert Dale Owen, as a "heterogenous collection of radicals, enthusiastic devotees to principle ... and lazy theorists, with a sprinkling of unprincipled sharpers thrown in." Owen Sr. soon went back to Britain to spread the word of his success. Another son, William, confided dolefully to his diary, "The enjoyment of a reformer, I would say, is much more in contemplation, than in reality."

New Harmony soon started to fall apart. Skilled labour did not feel inclined to have its income, under Owen's plan, "equalized" with the unskilled or, worse, with those who did not wish to work at all. A collectivist scheme such as Owen's could in effect work only if powered by either religious conviction or forced labour, a lesson that would not be lost on Owen's more revolutionary successors.

The abolition of money led to a bureaucratic nightmare. When even lettuce had to pass through the company store, it inevitably wilted before it reached the plate. (Moscow McDonald's would encounter analogous problems in trying to get supplies through the collapsing Soviet system almost 200 years later.)

After an absence of two months, Owen returned to New Harmony, arriving by river with intellectual reinforcements dubbed the "boatload of knowledge." He forced the community through numerous reorganizations, all the while churning out portentous exhortations such as the "Declaration of Mental Independence," which promised to free man from the "slavery" of private property, religion and marriage.

One visitor, the Duke of Saxe-Weimar, wrote, "He looks forward to nothing else than to remodel the world entirely; to root out all crime; to abolish punishment; to create similar views and similar wants, and in this manner to abolish all dissension and warfare ... He was too unalterably convinced of the result to admit the slightest room for doubt." Every other member of the community to whom the duke spoke acknowledged that Owen was "deceived in his expectations." The final blow to the community was a falling-out between Owen and William Maclure, a wealthy émigré Scotsman, which led to the two men suing each other over property, the concept New Harmony was meant to transcend.

The one undoubted benefit Owen did bestow upon the former colonies was his children, who turned out to be a good deal more level-headed than their father and who would become prominent in American affairs. Owen then set off on an even more quixotic scheme: to persuade the government of Mexico to grant him a huge swath of land on which to test his theories. He required Mexico first to abandon Catholicism. Mexico demurred.

Owen returned to London and embarked upon expansive new ventures. He became the first president of the Grand National Consolidated Trades Union, an organization that lasted a year. Seeking to trump both the pecuniary root of all evil and "unnecessary" middlemen, he set up "labour exchanges," whereby merchandise was exchanged for "labour notes," whose value was meant to be calculated according to the hours of sweat embodied in each product. The administrators found that they could not possibly calculate values this way and were forced to copy market prices. The labour exchanges collapsed too.

Owen staunchly opposed the "superstition" of religion, and yet his own views were at root profoundly religious, based on a "New Moral World" set up in opposition to a demonic set of greedy capitalists. He founded the Rational Society, complete with Halls of Science instead of churches, and "social hymns." Sample verse:

Outcasts in your native soil,
Doom'd to poverty and toil,
Strangers in your native land;
Come, and join the social band.

Owen's acolytes founded another Utopian community, at an estate called Queenwood in Hampshire, whose collapse Owen hastened by spending it into the ground. One of his more clear-sighted disciples noted that "Mr. Owen was no financier, and had no idea of money." Queenwood, like New Harmony, imploded amid lawsuits, yet again over property.

Robert Owen represented a psychological type that would persist throughout the business world. Although such businessmen have a good grasp of their own business, they fail to understand the nature of markets more generally and believe themselves to be morally exceptional in a world marked by short-sighted greed.

Among the attendees at Owen's Halls of Science was another radical young businessman who despised the alleged crimes of nascent capitalism even more than Owen did, but whose ideas would prove far more influential.

—⁕—

The cotton industry has disappeared from Manchester, but the city still bustles in the rain. Beginning in the 1990s, Manchester underwent an urban renaissance, most spectacularly in the area of Salford Quays, where the old Manchester Ship Canal and its branching docks are now flanked by smart new housing developments, hotels and the arresting architecture of the Lowry art gallery and the Imperial War Museum North. Opposite the Lowry is a huge mall.

The heart of old Manchester has also seen the transition from mills to malls, in particular at the giant Arndale Centre. In the middle of the 19th century, the area to the north of Arndale was choked with grimy alleys, where pigs were raised among people. These conditions were critical in formulating the socialist case against capitalism; they were cited as proof that the greed-driven bourgeoisie was guilty of "social murder."

It is certainly difficult to conjure those images today. The area is now part of Manchester's Millennium Quarter. Its dominant structure is Urbis, a translucent, iceberg-blue, curtain-walled wedge of a museum that, as its name implies, is about cities. I visited the museum on the trail of the man who had come up with that snappy "social murder" line. I had a strong feeling he would be there, and I eventually located him at an exhibit bearing the legend "Gruel and Grind." A disembodied voice with a thick German accent bemoaned the horrors of early industrial Manchester. A written blurb declared, "You don't need a communist agenda to sympathize."

But you do — again — need a little history to provide some context.

The heavily accented words were those of Friedrich Engels, partner in ideology of Karl Marx. In the early 1840s, Engels — a well-heeled young German who had been sent by his father, a mill owner, to work at the Manchester branch of the family business — picked his way through the puddles of the once grim residential labyrinth where Urbis now stands. What he saw fanned a revolutionary passion that would provide intellectual ammunition for his even more uncompromising co-author.

Ironically, one of the reasons Engels's father had sent his son to Manchester was to cure the young man of his revolutionary tendencies. Engels had gone happily because he believed that England was ripe for revolution, and no town was more ripe than Manchester. His first two years there provided much of the literary colour and moral outrage that went into his most significant collaboration with Marx: *The Communist Manifesto*. That brief document, of scriptural importance in the war against capitalism, was in many ways a condemnatory snapshot of the Manchester cotton industry in the "hungry" 1840s. Not only was its analysis flawed, its policy correctives were horrifying.

According to *The Communist Manifesto*, the bourgeoisie's exploitation of the proletariat could be only temporary since the system — whatever its achievements — was racked with internal contradictions. The proletariat would inevitably expand, rise up, overthrow its oppressors, abolish private property and establish Communism. But the actual workings of Communism were spelled out only in the most vague terms. Communist society would — somehow — regulate "general production" and thus make it possible "for me to do one thing today and another tomorrow, to hunt in the morning, fish in the afternoon, rear cattle in the evening, criticize after dinner." As the economic historian Alexander Gray wryly noted, "A short weekend on a farm might have convinced Marx that the cattle themselves might have some objection to being reared in this casual manner, in the evening."

If the *Manifesto* was vague about the specifics of its Brave New World, it was very clear that it would be born in blood. In this it was remarkably prescient, as Lenin, Stalin, Mao and Castro would confirm.

Marx and Engels took Smith's division of labour and his enthusiasm for free trade and turned them into inhumane monstrosities. The complex human nature outlined by Smith in *The Theory of Moral Sentiments* was replaced by two sets of cardboard cut-out "classes": on the one hand a greedy bourgeoisie that controlled the state, and on the other a repressed and exploited proletariat.

Capitalism, according to the *Manifesto*, had replaced "all feudal, patriarchal, idyllic relationships" and "left no other nexus between man and man than naked self-interest, than callous 'cash payment'" and "egotistical calculation." The only value left was economic value; the only freedom, free trade.

While acknowledging the achievements of the industrialist bourgeoisie, the *Manifesto* stated that these achievements came at the price of "constant revolutionizing of production, uninterrupted disturbance of all social conditions, everlasting uncertainty and agitation." National-based industries and local self-sufficiency were being destroyed, claimed the *Manifesto*, by what would now be called multinational corporations. Small business was doomed. Moreover, there appeared to be no escape. "[Capitalism] compels all nations, on pain of extinction, to adopt the bourgeois mode of production ... It creates a world after its own image."

So globalization — and anti-globalization — aren't terribly new ideas.

The system was haunted by the bourgeoisie's lemming-like tendency to "overproduce," which in turn created increasingly large cyclical crises. The growing proletariat, "appendages of the machine," would inevitably revolt, led by a "small section of the ruling class," which had cut itself adrift and joined with the revolutionaries, "in particular, a portion of the bourgeois ideologists, who have raised themselves to the level of comprehending theoretically the historical movements as a whole."

Marx had seen the future, and he — and people like him — would be in charge. All production would be transferred to the state. In the "most advanced countries," the revolutionaries would, on the way to Communism, do away with landlords and rents, squeeze the rich with "a heavy progressive or graduated income tax," and abolish inheritance. They would take over the banking, communications and transport industries, control manufacturing and plan agriculture. Labour would be forced. Education would be free but combined with industrial production.

"The Communists disdain to conceal their views and aims," concluded the *Manifesto*. "They openly declare that their ends can be attained only by the forcible overthrow of all existing social conditions. Let the ruling classes tremble at a Communistic revolution. The proletarians have nothing to lose but their chains. They have a world to win." Then came those stirring words engraved on Marx's tomb at Highgate Cemetery: "Workers of all lands, unite."

In this brief document were contained the seeds of a century of brutality and mass murder. Its intentions were hardly concealed, but its own "internal contradictions" were glaring. For a start, how were the workers of the world to be "unchained" if they were to be simultaneously forced into an "industrial army" and told where to go and what to do?

Marx dealt with criticisms by brushing them off as "not deserving of serious examination." He castigated fellow critics like Owen for wanting peaceful transition and for appealing "to the feelings and purses of the bourgeois."

The philosopher Karl Popper wrote that social upheavals tend to bring forth "prophets" who claim to understand the forces at work, say they can see the future and promise relief if they are given absolute power. Just as Plato's model of the "arrested state" — a dictatorship in which the rulers lived as communists without property, using a specially bred military to control a cattle-like populace — was a response to the first wave of democracy and the Peloponnesian War, so Marx's Communism was a response to the upheavals of the Industrial Revolution. Both appealed for rigid controls to counter the strains of commerce and democracy. Both invoked the threat of anarchy to justify tyranny under the guise of philosopher-kingship.

This all seems a very long way from *The Wealth of Nations*, although some claim that Smith was less at odds with the Marxist interpretation of history than a precursor of it. After all, Smith had criticized the "rapacity" of merchants and the "mental mutilation" of factory work. However, Marx wanted to throw out the market baby with the industrial bathwater. If markets produced problems, what was the alternative? Marx's answer was to impose a dictatorship that would abolish personal choice, private property, the division of labour and free trade — the very wellsprings of the Smithian "natural order."

Smith and other members of the Enlightenment — although they had never foreseen the Industrial Revolution — saw that free commercial society, while not perfect, was superior to its predecessors, and to anything governments might cook up by mercantilist fiddling or grand strategy. Marx portrayed the Industrial Revolution as a seething mass of exploitation doomed to implode and be succeeded by Communism.

The Communist Manifesto was published shortly before the Europe-wide revolutions of 1848, but it had little or no influence upon them. Significantly, there was no revolution in Britain. The real wages of manual workers increased by almost 40 per cent between 1851 and 1881, during the Victorian boom. Downturns did not become more severe. Unions concentrated on winning better pay and conditions rather than on overthrowing the existing order.

Marx dealt with these realities by ignoring or misrepresenting them. He beavered away at the British Museum, poring over one-sided parliamentary factory inquiries, soaking up all the evidence he could find for what he already *knew*: that capitalism was the devil incarnate. (Astonishingly, Marx never actually visited a factory until he was quite old. He derived all his knowledge of industrial conditions from Engels and books.)

Marx and Engels blamed the failure of history to follow their script on the "bourgeoisification" and "narrow-mindedness" of the British working class, who failed to revolt because they had become partners in exploiting the working classes of Britain's overseas colonies. The two men were endlessly able to tailor or ignore inconvenient details because their views about capitalist society were — as Jerry Z. Muller noted — *conclusions* from immutable moral *assumptions*. When they looked at capitalism, they saw only "dirty pictures."

Marxism, once worked over by Lenin and Stalin, opened a Pandora's box of social engineering whose damage would scar the 20th century, from the rusting industrial behemoths of the former Soviet empire, through the killing fields of Kampuchea, to Cuba's island gulag. And yet despite the horrendous practical results of Marxism and the stunning achievements of free enterprise, capitalism still tends to attract the more vehement criticism.

The mass murders of Communist regimes are treated as some unfortunate aberration of a "noble ideal," while the long-past inequities of the Industrial Revolution are eagerly regurgitated in the museums of capitalist countries. The continued astonishing long-term progress of free enterprise is treated as ho-hum, while every hiccup is trumpeted as a "crisis of capitalism," a system that is still allegedly ruled by "plutocrats."

To begin to understand the difficulty of mounting a "moral" defence of capitalism, it's useful to look at the life and work of one of its most uncompromising champions.

five

The Passion of Ayn Rand

"All right, Mr. deMille, I'm ready for my close-up."
— Gloria Swanson as Norma Desmond in *Sunset Boulevard*

The global economic crisis that erupted in 2008 — and governments' response to it — led to a surge in the sales of Ayn Rand's novel *Atlas Shrugged*. The book, which had already sold more than 6 million copies since its publication in 1957, is set in a United States whose economy is collapsing under the dead weight of government edict. The *Economist* noted that sales seemed to spike every time there was a bank bailout.

In 2011, the movie *Atlas Shrugged* (Part I) appeared. Although it had a made-for-TV, daytime-soap feel about it, its slightly off-kilter, futuristic, film noir look did capture — at least to some degree — the wonderful weirdness of the book. Anyone attempting to take Ayn Rand's philosophical doorstop to the big screen faced massive challenges. The problem has never been Randian villains, who are recognizable everywhere; it's her heroes, whose stolid adherence to logical rectitude renders them about as human as marble on a plinth.

Rand's glorification of "rational selfishness" and radical individualism had never been an easy sell, but then reason and radical individualism are by no stretch of the imagination the essence of either human nature or capitalism. It has sometimes seemed that with friends like Ayn Rand, capitalism didn't need any enemies.

Rand, who died in 1982, had long been both an influential and a controversial figure. A joint Library of Congress/Book of the Month Club survey in 1991 had found *Atlas Shrugged* to be second in impact only to the Bible (a claim earlier made, as noted, for *The Wealth of Nations*).

Rand continued to be a lightning rod after her death. Critics were eager to point out that the man considered at least partly responsible for the subprime financial debacle because of his loose monetary policies, former Federal Reserve chairman Alan Greenspan, had once been one of her acolytes. Indeed, the *Financial Times* suggested that the whole crisis was due to the "Randian" philosophy embraced not only by Greenspan but by Margaret Thatcher and Ronald Reagan.

Not quite. Greenspan had indeed been part of Rand's circle as a young man, but his support for macroeconomic manipulation was exactly the kind of government action that Rand had identified as not just conceptually flawed but immoral. Rand's followers had long regarded Greenspan as a sellout.

Rand had always been despised by the left. The linguistic theorist and anti-corporate crusader Noam Chomsky called her "one of the most evil figures of modern intellectual history." The leftist British newspaper the *Guardian* developed something of an obsession with her around the time of the 2008 crisis. One of its writers called *Atlas Shrugged* "an almost unreadable" book, but another admitted, "I hated the thing, but I couldn't put it down." According to yet another *Guardian* writer, "What Rand offers is a sub-Nietzschean world of supermen and super-women, where the brightest and the best effortlessly trample their way to the top."

Again, not quite. Rand regarded Nietzsche as a mystic and an "irrationalist." And the hero of *Atlas Shrugged*, John Galt, and his confreres do their damage primarily by *stopping* their business activities. The novel is about "men of the mind" withdrawing their services from society.

Attacks against Rand seemed to rise to a crescendo ahead of the 2012 U.S. presidential election. One of the most rabid attacks came from the development guru Jeffrey Sachs. During an onstage radio interview to promote a new book, he veered off into an unhinged assault on Rand. "I don't know how many people here have read this awful woman," he said (to much laughter from the sophisticated audience). "Absolutely one of the most pathetic personalities. Really! If you read her biography, she was a sad, sad, lonely, nasty woman, because she preached ... antagonism to compassion."

Sachs declared he had broken out into a "cold sweat" after reading the speech that stands at the heart of *Atlas Shrugged*. "It's so ugly. Ugly, I'm telling you. It says if you as much as give a smile to a poor person, you're degrading yourself, you're making yourself a slave of this person. If you give them the pennies that they want, you're setting the road on the path of destruction."

—⁂—

I had long been fascinated by Ayn Rand and her opponents, and in particular by her desire to put up a "moral" defence of the free market. Dubbing herself a "radical for capitalism," Rand had brilliant insights about the nature of markets and about their enemies. However, while realizing that capitalism needed a moral defence as well as one framed in terms of efficiency, she found both, problematically, in the elevation of "selfishness." She chose to define this not in the commonly accepted pejorative sense of indulging oneself at the expense of others, but simply as the unembarrassed pursuit of one's own interests. It was almost as if, to fight what she saw as the evil of Communism, she had deliberately donned the poisoned mantle that Marx had created for his nemesis.

Seeing altruism as the great problem, Rand had responded with individualism so radical that she once declared, "All that which proceeds from man's dependence upon men is evil."

Rand called her philosophy Objectivism because it was meant to be based on the unquestionable existence of an objectively "real" world and the ability to discover moral values through rational evaluation. Just think hard enough, she said, and you can't avoid becoming a capitalist.

I had first discovered Ayn Rand through *Atlas Shrugged*. Part soap opera, part sci-fi/mystery/adventure, part philosophical treatise, the book is the underappreciated free-market capitalist entrepreneur's wet dream. Set in some indeterminate but not too distant future of the American 1950s, it tells of a society that is crumbling under the slow rot of creeping statism.

For Rand, the modern mixed economy in which private enterprise jostled with, and took advantage of, government interventionism was fundamentally immoral. It could function only through rancid compromise. Rand's heroic men of the mind, who came up with all the productive ideas, sold those ideas to investors, built the factories and ultimately supplied all the jobs, nevertheless went along with the fraud that wealth was somehow a tribal effort in which everybody had pitched in and thus deserved "fair shares." A mixed economy, she wrote, "is a country in the process of disintegration, a civil war of pressure groups looting and devouring one another."

Having myself studied Russian history, experienced pre-Thatcher British politics and immigrated to the interventionist pretensions of Pierre Trudeau's Canada, I found Rand's insights penetrating. I read her other works and was impressed by her often devastating analyses of the semantic obfuscations of social democratic politics, the fallacies of conventional economic wisdom and the misrepresentations of history.

Atlas Shrugged, it seemed to me, was a peculiarly American variant of Orwell's *Nineteen Eighty-Four*. Both presented futuristic political nightmares, but while Orwell's was totalitarian, Rand's foreshadowed a breakdown under a democratic system.

Another key difference was that Rand's heroes prevailed, and then some. Orwell's Winston Smith and Rand's John Galt both wind up in torture chambers, but whereas Smith whimpers before the rats-in-the-face of Room 101, Galt suggests that his inquisitors turn *up* the electricity. The heroes in *Atlas Shrugged* also prevail in a more comprehensive way, by withdrawing from society, which they leave to stew in its envious and ignorant juices as they go off to found a capitalist Utopia — Galt's Gulch — in the mountains.

That denouement, however, represented both the novel's fictional acme and one of Objectivism's fatal weaknesses: it offered no realistic political program for correcting the wrongs that it claimed to see because it refused to compromise, which not merely cut it off from mainstream politics but helped turn it into a closed cult.

Randian heroes were idealistic caricatures. Intended to portray man "not as he is but as he ought to be," they took individualism to sometimes ludicrous extremes. Then there was all that rough sex, with the suggestion, especially in Rand's other big novel, *The Fountainhead*, that "No" means "Please."

—⚭—

In pursuit of a better understanding of Rand and her Objectivism, and of the moral problems of capitalism, I attended a conference about her in Hollywood in 2002. It was held at the Harmony Gold Theatre on a slightly seedy stretch of Sunset Boulevard. On the first evening, and despite Rand's allegedly enormous popularity, there were only around 50 people present to see the documentary *Ayn Rand: A Sense of Life*. Although the film, which had been nominated for an Academy Award, was intended as a celebration, Rand came across as a sad and tragic figure. But then perhaps that was a conclusion that I had brought with me.

Born Alice Rosenbaum in St. Petersburg in 1905, Rand saw the Russian revolution up close. She had an overbearing "intellectual" mother who instilled the notion that children were a huge burden. An extraordinarily independent little girl, she decided that she wanted to be a writer at the age of nine. After attending university, she was sent to relatives in America, who helped her secure her dream: to live and work in Hollywood. She changed her name (although it is apparently a myth that she took her surname from her typewriter).

She played bit parts and became a protégé of Cecil B. deMille (who referred to her as his "little caviar"). She married another bit player, Frank O'Connor, and between work as an extra and in the costume department, she wrote and eventually sold several screenplays. Despite initial lack of interest from publishers, she achieved success with *The Fountainhead*. She moved with Frank to a modernistic house in the desert, where they grew flowers and vegetables commercially, and then to New York, where she completed her magnum opus.

There were clips throughout *A Sense of Life* of her interviews with leading American television journalists and talk-show hosts: Phil Donahue, Mike Wallace and Tom Snyder. Rand appeared to give better than she got, but the physical sense of her in the film was depressing. She had a certain gamine quality when she was young, and had an undoubted intellectual attraction well into middle age, but her teeth were bad (she smoked like a chimney) and her swollen ankles in a famous photograph of her in a cape reminded me of my late grandmother (a later version of the picture had the ankles airbrushed to be more shapely).

These were not mere details. Physical attractiveness and age would prove important issues not just for her but for her movement and her philosophy. The most significant aspect of her life airbrushed out of the film was her 14-year affair with her acolyte Nathaniel Branden, which received only a peripheral reference. Apparently one of the conditions for the filmmaker Michael Paxton to get access to the Ayn Rand Archives had been that he would not interview Branden. This was hardly the stuff of free and fearless rational inquiry.

Rand had an extraordinarily idealistic view of love and romance. "For a woman *qua* woman," she wrote, in a statement designed to make feminists everywhere blanch, "the essence of femininity is hero-worship — the desire to look up to man. 'To look up,'" she added, "does not mean dependence, obedience or anything implying inferiority. It means an intense kind of admiration ... The object of her worship is specifically his *masculinity*."

However, before any macho cheers of approval ring out, we should perhaps also hear what Rand had to say on romantic love: "Romantic love, in the full sense of the term, is an emotion possible only to the man (or woman) of unbreached self-esteem; it is his response to his own highest values in the person of another — an integrated response of mind and body, of love and sexual desire. Such a man (or woman) is incapable of experiencing sexual desire divorced from spiritual values."

Sounds like trouble, doesn't it?

And it was.

—⚏—

As a young psychology student, Nathan Blumenthal was so inspired by *The Fountainhead* that he changed his name to Nathaniel Branden (apparently because it contained the letters R-A-N-D). In 1953 he married Barbara Weidman at a ceremony at which Rand and hubby Frank were matron of honour and best man. Soon afterwards, Rand and Branden began expressing their unbreached self-esteem in each other's arms.

Rand never doubted that her husband and Branden's wife would fall in with this tangled set of "spiritual values." She reportedly told the cuckolded spouses, "Whatever the two of you may be feeling I know your intelligence. I know you recognize the rationality of what we feel for each other, and that you hold no value higher than reason."

One big bonus for Branden was that, as Rand's love interest, his name went on Objectivism's official think tank: it started out as the Nathaniel Branden Institute. However, when Branden found his fancy taken by a woman 35 years Rand's junior, Rand had some problem spotting the spiritual values involved. Sauce for the gander, it seemed, was not sauce for the goose.

"Get that bastard down here, or I'll drag him myself," Rand reportedly screamed on being told of Branden's infidelity (although the word "infidelity" seems singularly inappropriate in the circumstances). After elaborating at some length on how she was going to destroy him, she declared, "If you have an ounce of morality left in you, an ounce of psychological health — you'll be impotent for the next 20 years."

Rand subsequently wrote an open letter to her movement repudiating Branden and quoting "certain ugly actions and irrational behaviour in his private life."

That the symposium I was attending was taking place on Sunset Boulevard thus acquired an additional, ironic dimension. Rand wound up looking and sounding like Norma Desmond, the aging silent-movie star from Billy Wilder's classic — named for that famous thoroughfare — who "buys" an out-of-work scriptwriter, played by William Holden, to help flesh out her delusions.

Instead of shooting her young lover when he tried to depart, as Norma Desmond had done, Rand vilified her Holden look-alike, attempted to destroy his career and left it to her acolytes to airbrush him from history. One of the faithful reportedly asked whether it might be morally appropriate to assassinate him.

Rand might not have slipped into madness, as Norma Desmond had done — "All right, Mr. deMille, I'm ready for my close-up" — but her movement henceforth became slightly unhinged. Perhaps Rand's greatest fictional creation had been herself. The trouble was that no human was capable of playing the part.

The Branden affair, with its messy end, represented more than merely salacious detail; it fundamentally undermined Rand's claims that man (and presumably woman) was a creature capable of controlling his emotions and acting "rationally." Adam Smith's friend and mentor David Hume had pointed out that our reason is always slave to our passions. Nobody appeared to exemplify that fact better than Rand, but since her defence of capitalism was built on the same rationalistic foundations, she was inevitably a problematic champion. Her philosophy was undermined by her apparent failure to obey philosophy's first commandment: "Know thyself." And yet she was undoubtedly a brilliant and incisive thinker, and it should be recognized that flaws in her defence of capitalism are not synonymous with flaws in capitalism itself.

Rand realized — as Adam Smith had done — that any defence of minimal government and free enterprise as not merely efficient but good had to lie in its fit with human nature. However, seeing altruism — which she defined as irrational self-sacrifice — and mysticism as the great enemies of free markets and free societies, Rand took an ultra-rational approach, rejoicing in that supposed "virtue of selfishness."

For Smith, by contrast, moral perfection was the cultivation of benevolence, when we "feel much for others and little for ourselves." Such a sentiment would have caused Rand to have a conniption. She did not regard charity as either a moral duty or even a primary virtue, and yet both these thinkers were promoting free enterprise. How could their approaches and conclusions have been so different? Partly because they started from quite different philosophical premises, and partly because they lived in very different times.

Rand's reliance on the supremacy of rationality would have seemed naive to Smith, who, like Hume, noted the limits of reason and the power of emotion. However, Smith and Rand were also asserting the value of freedom and free enterprise against very different opponents. Smith's foe was mercantilism, a doctrine that while power-oriented was essentially pragmatic and thus open to modification. Rand's enemy was Communism, a quasi-religion that demanded adherence and sacrifice for ends that could not be questioned.

Ironically, it was the misunderstood and indeed demonized success of the Smithian system that spawned modern socialism and its champions. Marxism had been seized upon by Lenin as the justification for grabbing revolutionary power. Socialist principles had also permeated the entire Western democratic world, feeding off capitalist wealth. Rand was fighting an intellectual enemy that simply had not existed in Smith's day, except in embryo in the French Revolution.

Rand's background and personal experience were also crucial to the development of her thought, as Smith's was to his. She was, as one biographer claimed, "the Russian radical." She came from the city in which Lenin had seized power. She saw her father's pharmacy business grabbed by Communists as the "property of the people." She witnessed university professors and fellow students being hauled off, never to return.

She had headed for what she thought was the land of freedom but found U.S. authorities in the 1930s describing the Soviet Union as a "noble experiment." During the Great Depression, President Franklin D. Roosevelt had declared capitalism to be "over" and introduced a slew of interventions, which were cheered on by the intellectual and artistic establishment, and which passed into conventional leftish history as an exercise in "saving capitalism from itself."

It was against this conventional wisdom — and in opposition to the traditional mysticism of her native Russia — that Rand formed her uncompromising world view. However, the shortcomings of its emphasis on rationality were obvious not merely from the Branden affair but also from what her movement did to her followers. As Barbara Branden wrote in a tell-all book, *The Passion of Ayn Rand*, Rand damaged many of those who worshipped her: "Those who accepted the package were on their way to becoming true believers, growing self-alienated and alienated from others, intellectually rigid, guilty over their failures, quick to judge and accuse others."

Rand was as harsh on prominent right-wing intellectuals as she was on the left. She described Hayek as "an example of our most pernicious enemy." When two other great economists, Milton Friedman and George Stigler, wrote a postwar pamphlet arguing that rent controls were counterproductive, Rand — who of course didn't support rent controls either — castigated them because they made their arguments on "practical, humanitarian grounds" instead of "the inalienable right of landlords and property owners." Rand labelled their pamphlet "collectivist propaganda."

—⁂—

One of the Hollywood symposium's sessions — on Ayn Rand's philosophy — was conducted by a man named Harry Binswanger. He was introduced by Yaron Brook, the president of the Ayn Rand Institute, who told us that Binswanger had written a book on the "biological origins of teleological concepts," and was now working on a tome about "the causal nature of consciousness."

Binswanger started off by asserting that reason was the central factor of Rand's philosophy. Reason, he said, is what sets us apart from the animal world. It is what identifies and integrates the material provided by the senses. Reason, according to Aristotle (of whom Rand was a great fan), is the senses plus logic. Reason is the main tool of man's survival, the means by which he plants crops, avoids toxic plants and builds shelter.

Binswanger quickly swept away the problem of mind/body dualism. Objectivists, he declared, believe that body and mind are one. Then he declared that humans had no innate emotions. Emotions, he said, are a "rational response."

By now I was beginning to have severe problems with Binswanger's presentation. I had no difficulty with rejection of the mind/body dichotomy, or with accepting (a measure of) reason as man's defining characteristic, but emotions as a "rational response"? See Branden, Nathaniel, not to mention the writings of Hume, David, and Smith, Adam. Then there was the claim that apparently you needed reason to farm, avoid poison and build a home. But termites farmed, birds avoided toxic plants, and beavers built homes.

"Man is a self-made soul," Binswanger plowed on. "You are not a social product." But that was surely a moot point too, even if you didn't believe in Marxist determinism. Seen from the perspective of 18th-century Enlightenment Edinburgh, Binswanger's take seemed astonishingly crude. Asked a question about love, he declared that it amounted to a "rational" judgment.

Love, I thought, at first rational evaluation.

Binswanger's performance fed my simmering belief that Objectivism had in fact taken many of the great questions of philosophy and simply thrown them out the window, which could hardly be a good foundation on which to mount a stout philosophical/moral defence of capitalism.

The weekend's big event, an *American Writers* segment broadcast on C-SPAN, was telecast live from the roof of the Harmony Gold, which offered spectacular views of Hollywood. The show interspersed clips of Rand with live interviews, featuring, among others, Rand's "heir," Leonard Peikoff, and the Ayn Rand Institute film archivist, Jeff Britting. When a caller noted that the Branden affair hadn't figured too prominently in the "approved" film that we'd seen the first night, Britting said that the affair "wasn't very interesting."

I had the sudden urge to look up a section about "evasion" that I remembered from the hero John Galt's 60-page speech in *Atlas Shrugged* (the speech that made Jeffrey Sachs ill). I found it later. Evasion, it claimed, "is the act of unfocusing your mind and inducing an inner fog to escape the responsibility of judgment — on the unstated premise that a thing will not exist if only you refuse to identify it."

Sounded pretty much like the Ayn Rand Institute's attitude to the Branden affair. The guardian of that defining piece of self-deception was Leonard Peikoff. Looking at Peikoff, it was still possible to see the cocky, gangly, high-IQ pre-med student who had fallen under Rand's spell, only now he came across as an arrogant senior citizen with a major dye job, a hefty income from Rand's book royalties and automobile licence plates that read "AYN RAND."

Asked about Alan Greenspan, who was then still chairman of the Federal Reserve, Peikoff castigated him for selling out to the establishment. Asked about the United Way, he deigned to admit that "voluntary charity is acceptable." Questioned on affirmative action, he said, "If we could treat each other as individuals, the whole civil rights problem would be solved."

But while affirmative action might be profoundly flawed, what Peikoff said amounted to a cop-out. People *don't* treat each other as individuals. Them-and-us "groupishness" appears to be a fundamental human trait.

Just look at the followers of Ayn Rand.

—⚍—

That evening, I wound up in a pub called the Fox and Hounds on Ventura Boulevard with my ex-brother-in-law. He used to be an

NFL linebacker but is a gentle soul. He brought along a buddy named Kevin, who wanted to meet me because I had grown up in London. This young man, a brilliant graphic designer, and his brother had just been given $20 million to make a movie. Gwyneth Paltrow and Jude Law had been lined up as the leads. Jude Law had apparently agreed to do the film only if it was made in England, so they were going to make it at the Elstree Studios, where *Star Wars* had been shot.

Kevin had never been outside the United States. He had never made a movie. Now somebody was offering him and his brother $20 million to back a vision (which would indeed be realized, as *Sky Captain and the World of Tomorrow*).

Only in Hollywood.

Which brings us to another of the many paradoxes about Ayn Rand: how could this supposed doyenne of rational Objectivism be so drawn to a world of fantasy and make-believe? Movies raise deeper questions about human rationality and emotional control. By bringing back the same film stars time and time again in different roles, and by having us believe in their characters and react emotionally to their staged dilemmas, movies reveal surely astonishing features about our mental makeup and seem to mock our "reason," even if we do try to explain it away by concepts such as "suspension of disbelief."

The next morning I went to see the Ayn Rand Institute's head, Yaron Brook, at his office in Marina del Rey. The place was in some disarray since the institute was in the process of moving, but Brook, a friendly man with a Barbara Walters–type lisp, saw me in a conference room overlooking the sailboats bobbing in the harbour.

Despite my slight hangover, I got straight to the deep stuff: Where did Objectivists think the mind came from?

"I don't think where the mind came from is an important philosophical question," Brook responded. "Evolution made one big giant leap with human consciousness. The fact that we have free will takes a lot of the evolutionary mechanism out of the picture. There was at some point a leap, at which we went from a being with instincts to a being with a free will ... All the other semi-human beings that didn't have free will fell away because free will is so much better of a survival mechanism than anything else. The question of a leap, or of gradual development, is a biological issue. I'm not a biologist. I'm not a scientist ... What's important is what we landed up being, not where we came from."

"But how," I responded, "can you understand what we are unless you understand where we came from?"

"By observation," said Brook. "You can look at human history. You have thousands of years of historical documentation that tell us who we are. We don't need to understand what we were before we were human to understand what we as human beings are."

This suggestion seemed to me an almost bizarre recommendation to block off huge areas of scientific inquiry. Moving on, however, I suggested that one thing that most people didn't seem to be was radical individualists.

"People are not by nature anything, in my view," said Brook. "There are lots of people in society who will always follow trends: 'second-handers.' [Rand] believed that everything came down to one basic choice in life: to focus your mind, to use your mind. A certain percentage of the population will always choose not to use their mind. I don't know why; they just won't."

But didn't that indicate, I suggested, that human nature isn't inclined to original thought, that most people reflexively say, "What attitude should I adopt? What do others think?"

"To us that is the opposite of human nature," replied Brook; "that is animal nature. Not everybody jumps into groups. For every rule that evolution would tend to dictate, there are exceptions. Those exceptions indicate that we don't have instincts, that we don't have preprogrammed notions, that people can make choices. If you were right, then people's choice would either be to be first-handers and think for themselves, or rely on their instincts."

I disagreed, suggesting that it was a combination of the two. What about intuition?

"I regard intuition as an automatized, very fast, reflex-like integration of the facts," said Brook. "So I can look at somebody and have an intuition about whether he's a good person or a bad person, but that intuition is based on certain automatized observations I've made across many people and how they behave in certain circumstances. All intuitions are based on previous conclusions we've made about certain phenomena ... It's like a computer. There is a search and integration mechanism going on in my subconscious continuously while I'm talking with you ... The more brilliant you are, the more the connections in your brain are integrated. Sure, rationality is not just a matter of saying A, B, C, etc. We do a lot of stuff automatically. Where rationality comes in is: how do we treat that stuff? I think you have to admit that there is a lot going on in the background without our knowing, and sometimes we have emotions that we can't explain, and that's when we go to therapy."

"But doesn't that cast doubt on the power of reason?" I asked.

"Not at all," replied Brook, "because it's still in our power to control those emotions, to evaluate whether those emotions are good for us or bad for us, and that is the power of reason. We can control our emotions. It might take psychotherapy, but there's a science yet to be discovered of psychology, which is in its infancy, that will one day make us better able to examine and evaluate our subconscious and better understand our emotions."

Which brought us to the Big Issue.

"Rand's reaction to the Branden affair looks typically emotional," I said. "She was pissed off, lashed out, and then rationalized that she was right to be pissed off."

"I think that one day the evidence to show that that is not true will come out," responded Brook.

"Why is the evidence not released?" I asked.

"It will be," said Brook. "Part of the problem is that we have been trying to find a biographer for Ayn Rand and it's been a challenge, but we'll find one at some point who will write the definitive biography of Ayn Rand, and that issue will be dealt with in that biography."

When I left Brook, my head was spinning, and it wasn't the influence of the previous night's session in the Fox and Hounds. I liked Brook as a person. I certainly found him more sympathetic than Leonard Peikoff, but seldom had I heard — to use Randian terms — so many "evasions," so many "blank-outs" and so much half-baked philosophy and psychology.

—⚋—

One of the great issues of philosophy — and hence of undergraduate bull sessions — has always been whether we are in fact capable of comprehending the "external" world as it really is. Do we see the same things as others see? Is your blue my red? That issue is at the heart of the "dirty picture" joke. Ayn Rand believed that even to ask such a question was to begin down a slippery slope to mysticism and muddle-headedness.

Rand believed there was an "objective" world accessible to us all through the use of our minds. That is certainly what most people believe, at least implicitly, except that Rand and her followers seemed also to believe that the mind was a tabula rasa, a blank slate with no innate mental structure. By some unexplained process, however, this formless mass called "mind" could allegedly come to an "objective" understanding simply by thinking "rationally" about sensory input.

Emotions for Rand — and thus for her loyal followers such as Yaron Brook — represented "automatic subconscious evaluations," a black box that we had no need to unlock. The subconscious wasn't the roiling cerebral snake pit suggested by Freud (whom Objectivists despised). It was another black box, an "integrating mechanism." Brook had repeated Rand's claim that the subconscious was, like a computer, "programmed" by the conscious mind. "Man's conscious mind observes and establishes connections among his experiences," she wrote; "the subconscious integrates the connections and makes them become automatic ... A mind's cognitive development involves a continual process of automatization."

But while this appeared plausible, where did all this automatizing equipment come from? What were its design features? What were its potential shortcomings? Indeed, elsewhere Rand admitted — as had Brook — that psychology, as a science, was "barely making its first steps." "Psychology," she wrote, "has not yet found a Plato, let alone an Aristotle, to organize its material, systematize its problems and define its fundamental principles."

But how then could she make categorical statements about philosophy without understanding the machine that was doing the categorizing, and, in particular, that machine's limitations? In fact, I had been struggling with this issue for many years by the time I visited Sunset Boulevard, and I had come to conclusions radically different from those of Objectivism.

six

Tuesdays with Mandeville

One of the greatest Reasons why so few People understand themselves is, that most Writers are always teaching Men what they should be, and hardly ever trouble their heads with telling them what they really are.
— Bernard Mandeville, *The Fable of the Bees*

The scientific investigation of human nature runs against the grain of human nature itself.
— David Livingstone Smith, *Why We Lie*

In retrospect, one of the most important parts of my first trip to Britain in search of Smith and his meaning, although I did not realize it at the time, occurred en route between the graves of Smith and Marx. One beautiful afternoon, I was sitting on a garden terrace in the Lake District. The sun was picking out the contours of hills where sheep grazed. I could see Lake Windermere in the distance through the trees. The air was filled with the trill of birds, the bleat of lambs and the soft hum of traffic on the road below.

I found myself thinking about the "Adam Smith Problem." I hadn't planned to think about it; it had just popped into my mind. The problem, as I understood it, was that Smith's first book, *The Theory of Moral Sentiments*, had suggested that moral judgments were based on a broadly defined sympathy, or "fellow feeling," combined with a desire to be thought praiseworthy in the eyes of others. *The Wealth of Nations*, by contrast, was essentially about the beneficial effects of what Smith regarded as inevitably self-interested behaviour. A Teutonic academic had suggested that there was a contradiction, and that between the two books Smith had swung from a belief that man was motivated by fellow feeling to one in which he was driven by self-interest.

I hadn't made any study of the issue at the time. Indeed, I hadn't even read *Moral Sentiments*. Nevertheless, I found myself reflecting on the conundrum of human motivation through a "thought experiment." I was then writing for a magazine whose editor was a good friend. Whenever I sold him an article, I obviously tried to get as high a fee as possible. He, by contrast, was interested in securing good articles for as little as he had to pay. This was a commercial transaction, although it was complicated by our friendship. But what, I thought, if my friend the editor needed a kidney and I was the only suitable donor? Although thought experiments are considerably less complex than real-world choices, I decided that if his life depended upon it, then I would give him one. Obviously I wouldn't ask for payment (although why I should regard this as obvious required further explanation). So the answer to whether I was motivated by self-interest or fellow feeling appeared to be that it depends on the circumstances. But I also reflected that donating a kidney would make me something of a hero, which had an undeniable self-interested attraction. So not only do we act from different motives in different circumstances, we act from a variety of motives in any particular circumstance. Acting "selflessly" obviously has its benefits, which makes the term "selfless" contradictory. Not only would I receive the gratitude of the editor, but my reputation would be burnished. Indeed, could there *be* such a thing as truly selfless behaviour if others knew about it?

Then, in the midst of these weighty ponderings, something quite unexpected happened: tears came to my eyes. It had nothing to do with being overcome by the scenario of my own generosity in donating a body part. It was because I suddenly found myself — in the midst of all the other streams of thought I was trying to negotiate — thinking of a woman named Dora, whose parents had planted a field of daffodils in the garden below me.

The mental kidney departed and was replaced by another puzzle. Dora Wordsworth had died in 1847. Why, exactly, were tears beginning to run down my cheeks? (And I was looking for a deeper answer than "It's because you're such a sensitive soul.")

Dora's father, the poet William, was a leading light of the Romantic movement, representative of sensitive aversion to the conspicuous squalor and hardship of the nascent factory system and to commercial society's allegedly relentless "getting and spending." (Neither was Wordsworth a fan of Scottish Enlightenment philosophers. He called Smith "the worst critic, David Hume excepted, that Scotland, a soil to which this sort of weed seems natural, has produced.")

It was partly to understand the Romantic perspective that my itinerary had included Rydal Mount, one of the two places where Wordsworth had lived in the Lake District. However, I was surprised to find myself sharing his long-passed grief for the loss of his daughter, about which I had only just learned. It wasn't that I had never had similar emotions before, or that such emotions are unusual; it was that I had never before thought much about their origins. Why do we *have* emotions? What purpose do they serve? And why was I embarrassed at an emotional display over which I had little or no control? And come to think about it, why and how did things "pop" into my mind unbidden? How could I say that I "found myself" thinking involuntarily about some issue? Just how much access did I have to what was going on in my mind? And what was my mind anyway?

These questions came flooding in because they seemed somehow profoundly related to the broader issue I had just started pursuing: why capitalism was difficult to appreciate and so often caricatured and denigrated. Why did it arouse such passions? What persuaded people that it was a harsh and heartless system motivated by greed and selfishness; that its past was a catalogue of crime; that it created poverty instead of alleviating it; and that it was a dangerous, disruptive, inherently unstable and perhaps evil force? Above all, what made people believe some or all of these things while the system's enormous benefits — or so it seemed to me — were right in front of their eyes?

It began to dawn on me that the notion that anything can be "right in front of our eyes" in some universally agreed objective sense was naive. Optical illusions demonstrate that our minds make assumptions about the physical world that may not always be true. Might that be the case for the social world too?

Further questions on that issue arose as a result of reflection on another "artistic" source, although it was a long way from Wordsworth.

—⚭—

A year before the fall of the Berlin Wall, the film director John Carpenter, who is famous for horror films such as *The Thing*, had released a cinematic bomb of epic proportions. Titled *They Live*, it starred the professional wrestler Roddy Piper, an extraordinarily bad actor. Its plot was that aliens had secretly invaded the earth and were using subliminal messages to turn human beings into mindless consumers.

It has long been a mainstay of leftism that consumers are in thrall to brilliantly manipulative corporate advertisers and marketers, who can foist any shoddy nonsense upon them. In his 1957 book, *The Hidden Persuaders*, Vance Packard had revealed how big companies hired psychologists to probe for the soft spots in consumers' mental defences, so they might pour frivolous or more expensive products through the breach. Packard noted that psychologists had discovered that women would pay 25 cents for a bar of soap that would make their hands clean but $2.50 for a bar that promised to make their hands more beautiful. But this was surely an indictment of human vanity, not soap marketers.

One of Packard's examples of manipulation — apocryphal, as it turned out — was the flashing of subliminal messages onto television and/or cinema screens. The subliminal manipulation theme was taken up in *They Live*. Where people saw a billboard with a bikini-clad girl in the surf, bearing the message "Come to the Caribbean," beneath lurked the subliminal command "Marry and Reproduce." Hidden elsewhere were commands to "Consume" and "Obey." The blurb for the film ran: "They influence our decisions without us knowing it. They numb our senses without us feeling it. They control our lives without us realizing it."

The Roddy Piper character became able to "see through" the wiles of the aliens with the help of a pair of magic spectacles. These allowed him not merely to penetrate the subliminal messages but also to spot the aliens for what they really were: "Capitalists!"

Most people are familiar with the notion of looking at the world through rose-coloured glasses. The bleak optical prescription of the magic specs in *They Live* enabled wearers to see through to the black commercial heart of a society penetrated by allegedly non-human values. It was certainly a novel take on the origins — if not the supposed nature — of capitalism, but this terrible film raised a profoundly important question about how we see capitalism.

Could it be that something about the capitalist system does not fit our "mind's eye"? Could it be that we look at it through mental spectacles with an outdated prescription, a prescription that prevents us from appreciating its benefits and inclines us to believe those who tell us that it is fundamentally immoral, or even downright evil? That was the issue that came alive for me at Dora's Field, and echoed through my subsequent research.

One could understand Wordsworth's concern at the sight of early factories, and his failure to understand the long-term systemic forces at work, but how could people still think the same way after everything that had happened in the intervening 200 years? And how might that way of thinking be related to my sniffling at Wordsworth's Cottage?

When I read Smith's *Moral Sentiments,* I came to understand why Smith gave sentiment such importance, and I also began to realize how strange it was that the book's central topic, human nature, and in particular the nature of morality, seemed to have been so neglected. I would also eventually come to believe that there really was an Adam Smith "problem," but it was not about Smith being contradictory on human motivation; it was how our "moral sentiments," which had emerged over countless millennia, reacted to the unprecedented and accelerating social developments related in *The Wealth of Nations.*

In fact, I would discover that this problem had already been highlighted a generation before Smith, by a cynical but extraordinarily insightful Dutchman.

—⚏—

Bernard Mandeville was born in Rotterdam in 1670 and studied philosophy and medicine at the University of Leyden. In 1691 he received a doctor's degree, moved to London and became a respected physician. He also pursued a second career, as a writer. His most famous and controversial work was *The Fable of the Bees: Or, Private Vices, Public Benefits.* There was, wrote Mandeville, not merely an enormous gap between the beneficial realities of commercial life and people's appreciation of them; there was a similar chasm between what people practised and what they preached.

Mandeville was fascinated by people's lack of introspection, and by moralists' lack of interest in human nature. "One of the greatest Reasons why so few People understand themselves," he wrote, "is, that most Writers are always teaching Men what they should be, and hardly ever trouble their heads with telling them what they really are."

He raised uncomfortable questions about the central role of self-deceit in social life. "It is impossible," wrote Mandeville, "we could be sociable Creatures without Hypocrisy." He also wrote of "that strong habit of Hypocrisy, by the Help of which, we have learned from our Cradle to hide even from ourselves the vast Extent of Self Love."

Mandeville spotted — although imperfectly — the counterintuitive fact on which Smith would elaborate: that pursuing self-love through commercial markets unavoidably meant helping others who were pursuing their own self-love. Mandeville also pointed out that if people really pursued the virtuous life they claimed to admire, rather than indulging "Pride and Luxury," the economy would grind to a halt. Decrying luxury might be fashionable, but spending on luxuries created jobs. Men might be driven to produce and consume by "Envy and Emulation," but at least Mandeville grasped that all these allegedly "vicious" inclinations produced beneficial results. Or, as he put it:

Thus Vice nursed Ingenuity,
Which join'd with Time, and Industry
Had carry'd Life's Conveniencies,
It's real Pleasures, Comforts, Ease,
To such a Height, the very Poor
Lived better than the Rich before;
And nothing could be added more.

Nothing except (to name but a few post-Mandevillean materialistic baubles) an ongoing revolution in agricultural production, mass-produced cotton clothing, railways, the telegraph, electric light, indoor plumbing, a phalanx of domestic appliances, flushing toilets, sewage systems, the telephone, radio, television, automobiles, 100-storey buildings, stunning advances in pharmaceuticals and medical technology, plastics, refrigeration, air travel, air conditioning, space flight, supermarkets with 50,000 products, computers, pre-finished hardwood flooring, the internet, the BlackBerry, the iPod, the iPad, Google, Facebook, etc., etc.

The cynical doctor inevitably had an imperfect grasp of the economic processes of nascent commercial society (although he wrote eloquently on the importance of the division of labour). He concentrated on the usefulness of the expenditures of the idle rich, and suggested that "the Prodigal is a Blessing to the whole Society, and injures no body but himself." But Mandeville never stopped to ask where the unproductive prodigal's wealth originated — which in his day was almost certainly from hereditary entitlement to revenues from productive agricultural land, which somebody had to "work" — nor whether a less "prodigal" person might have produced greater good by investment rather than consumption.

In fact, the prudent diversion of capital toward the new processes and technologies of the Industrial Revolution would be one of the key factors that helped the revolution take off, not "prodigal" expenditures.

Mandeville the contrarian cynic was so keen on the beneficial aspects of vice that he even spoke up for theft, as providing work for locksmiths, and fraud, for employing lawyers, although he was hardly charitable about the latter profession. He wrote:

> The Lawyers, of whose Art the Basis
> Was raising Feuds and splitting Cases ...
> They kept off Hearings wilfully,
> To finger the refreshing Fee;
> And to defend a wicked Cause,
> Examin'd and survey'd the Laws;

As Burglars Shops and Houses do;
To find out where they'd best break through.

Mandeville's most outrageously misguided suggestion was that the Great Fire of London had been an economic boon. After all, look at all the construction activity that had followed. He was thus exhibiting what the great 19th-century French economic journalist and satirist Frédéric Bastiat would later dub the "broken window fallacy." People might imagine that a broken window is an economic benefit because it provides work for the glazier. They ignore the cost to the owner of the window, who would otherwise have spent elsewhere the funds he used to replace the window.

Although his grasp of how markets worked was flawed, Mandeville's cynical take would prove both highly influential and politically useful. He would be effusively praised by Marx. His upside-down notion that it is consumption rather than production that creates wealth would be reborn with Keynesianism and its support for prodigal government expenditure. His summary of commercial society as a process by which "private vice becomes public virtue" would be eagerly regurgitated by moralists masquerading as economists, such as John Kenneth Galbraith. Nevertheless, Mandeville did not so much criticize commercial society as target those hypocrites who pretended not to be interested in its benefits or who condemned them.

He made many insightful and often discomforting observations about human nature. He noted that humans were creatures of habit rather than reflection: "In what concerns the Fashions and Manners of the Ages Men live in they never examine the real Worth or Merit of the Cause, and generally judge of Things not as their Reason, but Custom directs them."

Mandeville presented a devastating critique of humanity. All, he suggested, was self-deception, expedience, herd-following and hypocrisy. The price of society, he claimed, was the suppression of self-awareness, a take that was positively proto-Freudian.

In Mandeville's day, Britain was beginning to evolve from an economic system dominated by a land-owning aristocracy to one where manufacturing — and meritocracy — would assume increasing importance. That would certainly prove disruptive, but it would also open unimagined possibilities for ordinary people to better their condition.

Adam Smith was the bard of that developing system. He was also among those who felt they had to respond to Mandeville's thoroughgoing skepticism. *The Theory of Moral Sentiments* was at least partly a response to *The Fable of the Bees*.

Mandeville's economics was easier to refute than his psychology. Smith's teacher at Glasgow, Francis Hutcheson, had rejected the notion of benign profligacy and foreshadowed the broken window fallacy by pointing out that "income not spent in one way will be spent in another and if not wasted in luxury will be devoted to useful prudent purposes."

However, that didn't deal with Mandeville's assault on the prevalence of hypocrisy and self-deceit. Mandeville had suggested that "most Writers" were keen on lecturing people on what they should do, but didn't pay enough attention to the way people actually thought and acted. There were far too many moral philosophers and not enough moral psychologists.

In *Moral Sentiments* Smith took up Mandeville's challenge to tell people "what they really are." Its opening sentence expressed a more fundamentally positive view of human nature, albeit a qualified one. "How selfish soever man may be supposed," wrote Smith, "there are evidently some principles in his nature, which interest him in the fortune of others, and render their happiness necessary to him, though he derives nothing from it except the pleasure of seeing it."

Like Hume, Smith believed that morality was based ultimately on feelings rather than reason. "General rules" of morality were rooted in certain "natural" sentiments — such as sympathy and aversion to violence — and refined by absorbing others' attitudes toward our actions and modifying them so as to make them more socially acceptable. Smith saw that social mores evolve. For example, the harming of infants was considered barbarous in his own time, but infanticide was common in ancient Greece and still existed among "savage" nations.

At the heart of Smith's moral psychology and philosophy was a problematic presence called the "Impartial Spectator," who was part conscience, part internal cheering section. This inner voice could promote great heroism. "Men," Smith wrote, "have voluntarily thrown away life to acquire after death a renown which they could no longer enjoy. Their imagination, in the mean time, anticipated that fame which was in future times to be bestowed upon them."

Unfortunately, this is a perfect description of suicide bombers, whose internal spectators could not be farther from impartiality. Smith indeed realized there were obvious problems with the notion that any aspect of man could be truly impartial. He acknowledged that the Impartial Spectator is soon shown the psychic door when it comes to matters of religion, politics or international relations. "Truth and fair dealing," wrote Smith, "are regarded in these circumstances as foolish or idiotic. The animosity of hostile factions, whether civil or ecclesiastical, is often still more furious than that of hostile nations; and their conduct towards one another is often still more atrocious."

The problem is that those in the grip of "faction and fanaticism" inevitably regard themselves as "morally" motivated, while condemning their opponents as wicked or evil. Indeed, it is "moral conviction" that *leads* to faction and fanaticism.

Jonathan Swift had described satirically in *Gulliver's Travels* how rival factions would battle over the most trivial issues. His example was internecine conflict over which end of a soft-boiled egg should be cracked open. Hence the struggle between the "Big-Enders" and the "Little-Enders."

Smith noted that political factions even tended to recruit God to their cause. "Even to the great Judge of the universe, they impute all their own prejudices, and often view that Divine Being as animated by all their own vindictive and implacable passions. Of all the corrupters of moral sentiments, therefore, faction and fanaticism have always been by far the greatest."

Smith also acknowledged that any truly reflective internalized moral arbiter could easily be shaken by public opinion, even the opinions of the "ignorant and weak." Moreover, we are even at the best of times inclined to judge ourselves far too easily and justify whatever pleases us. "This self-deceit," noted Smith, "this fatal weakness of mankind, is the source of half the disorders of human life. If we saw ourselves in the light in which others see us, or in which they would see us if they knew all, a reformation would generally be unavoidable. We could not otherwise endure the sight." The portrait Smith drew may thus have avoided Mandeville's utter cynicism, but it still presented human nature as complex, often conflicted and not simply prone to irrationality but almost entirely based on it, particularly when it came to demonizing enemies.

Smith's theories of morality were — like those of Hume — already highly controversial, since they suggested that moral sentiments might be innate and "tuned" by social circumstances, rather than guided by divine revelation. He left room for the Creator, however, by suggesting that he had effectively "designed" the moral sentiments to make men sociable.

Smith had spotted the essentially utilitarian nature of morality. It existed to help us live together in society, but it had not been deliberately designed by humans, although people were inclined to believe this because morality — or at least its benign aspects — seemed eminently rational and reasonable. Still, there appeared good reason to be skeptical — if not too publicly so — about the Designer, because morality also helped us justify our hatreds and prejudices.

In the end, the psychological significance of Smith's Impartial Spectator lay far more in the circumstances of his *absence* than in his presence. It is not, it seems, the reflective man of virtue who is likely to be prominent in public affairs but the activist who has no problem in persuading himself that he is motivated by the highest principles. That fact would become horribly apparent soon after Smith's death with the French Revolution and the Reign of Terror. Ironically, over the coming two and a half centuries, one of the prime targets of moralists' activism would be the system that *The Wealth of Nations* helped create: capitalism.

Unlike Mandeville, Smith did not regard the pursuit of self-interest as vicious. Indeed, he recognized that sympathy was not only the essence of sociability but a key aspect of commerce. To provide profitably what people in commercial markets want, you have to do much more than calculate costs and prices: you have to put yourself in their minds. As the satirist P.J. O'Rourke noted in his (relatively serious) book *On the Wealth of Nations*, imagination "links the moral sympathy central to *The Theory of Moral Sentiments* with the material cooperation central to *The Wealth of Nations.*"

The universality of human nature would be at the root of the "mass market" that was beginning to stir in Smith's day. Stunning success awaited those who could improve existing goods and/or produce them more cheaply, or who could concoct appealing new products that people had never imagined, opening up a commercial world that satisfied expanding wants rather than merely basic needs. Yet moral condemnation of commercial society has not declined with the multiplication of that society's wonders. Indeed, anti-materialist hypocrisy is celebrated and even lavishly rewarded by the very capitalist system it condemns.

—⁂—

I didn't meet Morrie in the best of circumstances. It was the second day of a post-Christmas holiday with my daughter, eight years old at the time, in Orlando, Florida. I had the flu. While bending over to clean my teeth that morning, I had put my back out. That put a visit to Universal Studios out too. It was all I could do to drag myself to the hotel pool and ease myself painfully onto a lounger. My daughter was, if not entirely understanding, at least resourceful. I plied her with money to use in the hotel's games room. She also hunted for frogs around the pool and would return at regular intervals to berate me for my culpable incapacity.

I settled down to the only piece of non-fiction I could find at the hotel store, *Tuesdays with Morrie*, by Mitch Albom, although I had misgivings about any book whose dust jacket threatened "an old man, a young man, and life's greatest lesson." *Tuesdays* is a reputedly heartwarming story set during the final months of a former university professor, Morrie Schwartz. At a series of Tuesday meetings, the professor passes on pearls of wisdom to Albom, a former pupil and now a star sports reporter and broadcaster.

The opening pages of the book were filled with blurbs from well-known self-help writers and testimonials from those who claimed the book had "changed their lives."

"Captures the simplicity beyond life's complexities," claimed M. Scott Peck, MD, author of *The Road Less Travelled*.

"It has a stubborn honesty that nourishes the living," wrote Robert Bly, who wrote *Iron John*.

"Only a man — no, a saint — like Morrie Schwartz could take his own impending death and teach us how to live," declared Jeff Daniels, who co-starred in *Dumb and Dumber*.

The changed-my-life crowd included a rabbi who claimed that this was "'must reading' for anyone who is a seeker of truth." A Unitarian minister called the book "a wise and loving story that teaches us those things we ought to know already, but have somehow forgotten."

I would discover later that the book was not just a bestseller, it was a 5-million-plus mega-seller. Oprah Winfrey had turned it into a made-for-TV movie, which had won an Emmy.

My own condition — although not terminal — undoubtedly rendered me even less tolerant than usual, and I soon ran into severe problems with both Morrie and Mitch.

On their third Tuesday, Mitch turned up with a tape recorder. "I want to remember what we talk about, I told Morrie, I want to have your voice so I can listen to it later." Oh, and also maybe use the transcript to write a blockbuster.

It never seemed to occur to Mitch that he might be in the process of writing a bestseller, or that money might be a motivation. This was particularly relevant because Morrie spent a good deal of time berating materialism and people obsessed with filthy lucre. Moreover, Mitch eventually revealed in the book that *Tuesdays* had been *Morrie's* idea, and that the professor had been cut in on the advance.

This in turn shed a somewhat different light on Morrie's wisdom, forbearance and courage. While these may all have been features of his character, wouldn't knowing that you are participating in a book that will be your memorial incline you to put your best foot forward? As Samuel Johnson wryly noted, "Almost no man dies in public but with apparent resolution; from that desire of praise which never quits us."

The much bigger problem was that Morrie's philosophy ranked in profundity with that of Hallmark Cards. Indeed, at times the greatest threat to his life appeared that he might drown in his own clichés.

Morrie's main beef was with American capitalist culture. "We are too involved in materialistic things, and they don't satisfy us," he declared. But wasn't it rather presumptuous to be speaking for the satisfactions of others? Apparently not, because Morrie — just like the Roddie Piper character in *They Live* — had seen through the fact that society was being "brainwashed" along these lines: "Owning things is good. More money is good.

More property is good." This meant, lectured Morrie, that "the average person is so fogged up by all this, he has no perspective on what's really important anymore."

According to Morrie, "There's a big confusion in this country over what we want versus what we need ... You need food, you *want* a chocolate sundae. You have to be honest with yourself. You don't *need* the latest sports car, you don't *need* the biggest house."

"So," explained Albom sombrely, "the TV was the same old model, the car [that Morrie's wife drove] was the same old model, the dishes and the silverware and the towels — all the same."

But wasn't it worth reflecting that Morrie actually *had* a TV and a car and a house? And who, exactly, was meant to mandate the acceptable level of automobile features or square footage that people "need"? Morrie was dying, and thus hardly likely to be cruising the auto dealerships or flipping real estate. And it wasn't as if he lived, like the Greek cynic philosopher Diogenes, in a tub. He had splashed out on lots of medical equipment that he wouldn't have been able to afford without the book advance, and that wouldn't have been available outside a rich, technologically advanced "materialist" society (and don't forget that tape recorder).

Morrie's condition also required the attention of lots of doctors, nurses and helpers. While he was berating commercial society, did it occur to him where and how all these wonderfully qualified men and women had been trained? Finally, did Morrie or Mitch ever stop to consider what might happen if everybody decided — or was forced (or "brainwashed") — not to make or buy anything new?

Morrie blithely declared, "The culture we have does not make people feel good about themselves. And you have to be strong enough to say if the culture doesn't work, don't buy it." Thus, according to Albom, Morrie "wasted no time in front of TV sitcoms or 'Movies of the Week.'" He decried "meaningless" lives. But who the Hades was he to be telling people that their lives were meaningless? Also, Morrie loved music. Where did he think his sound system came from? And did he really *need* music? Meanwhile, how could Morrie recommend being content with less while his wife, Charlotte, as we had been told on page 8, was worrying about how to pay his medical bills?

When it came to kindness and compassion, according to Morrie, "our culture tells us we should be ashamed if we can't wipe our own behind." Now I'm not sure where this cultural commandment is expressed, but from my experience with care for the aged in the decadent West — which had included watching the deaths of my own parents in Britain — nursing and auxiliary staff are extraordinarily kind. Moreover, although my knowledge of anthropology is a bit spotty, I'm prepared to venture that cultures where wiping old people's bottoms is considered an honour and a privilege are pretty rare (unless the old people happen to be kings or emperors).

Morrie recalled that as a child he had narrowly avoided working in a "sweatshop." He vowed after seeing the place that he would "never do any work that exploited somebody else, and he would never allow himself to make money off the sweat of others." He had thus eventually headed for academic research "where he could contribute without exploiting others."

But where had his university income arisen from if not from taxes on both the "exploiters" and the "exploited," or from exploiters' endowments? And is academic research a career available to everybody? Above all, what alternatives are there to this sorry system? Admittedly, there isn't much political economy in Hallmark World.

Morrie declared that people were mean only when they were "threatened." Where did the threat come from? "Even people who have jobs in our economy are threatened, because they worry about losing them. And when you get threatened, you start looking out only for yourself." But again, giving tenure to ordinary workers isn't quite as easy as giving it to social science professors. And the whole notion of academic tenure, as Adam Smith noted, is far from conducive to the best education.

Morrie subscribed to the stock Rousseauian nature-versus-nurture view that we are all corrupted by a society that has somehow emerged despite us, or has been inflicted upon us. The notion that men might want to be rich, or women slim, was apparently all due to perverted cultural conditioning. Otherwise, presumably, men would be delighted to be poor and women would eschew makeup.

When faced with the real problems of the world, such as a labour strike, Morrie professed that he "couldn't understand why both sides didn't simply communicate with each other and solve their problems." Instead of being treated as facile, this remark was patronizingly buffed as brilliant insight. "I told him," wrote Albom, "not everyone was as smart as he was."

The biggest question that occurred to me by the pool in Florida was that if Morrie's philosophy was so refined, so against crass conventional wisdom, so at odds with American culture and society, why did *Tuesdays* fly off the shelves by the millions?

The simple answer seems to be because human nature hasn't changed one whit since Mandeville's *Fable of the Bees* was published. Hypocrisy is, if anything, even more rampant than in Mandeville's day because there are so many more commercial wonders to fail to appreciate, to pretend not to be interested in, and so many more producers of those commercial wonders to scorn. The puzzle is not merely why people have such trouble grasping the benefits bestowed by the Invisible Hand, but why they are inclined to condemn it in moral terms. This is the true "Adam Smith Problem." The key to understanding it appeared exactly 100 years after *The Theory of Moral Sentiments* with the publication of a far more controversial work: *The Origin of Species*.

seven

Darwin's Dangerous Idea

*Our ancestor was an animal which breathed water, had a swim
bladder, a great swimming tail, an imperfect skull &
undoubtedly was hermaphrodite! Here is a
pleasant genealogy for mankind.*
— Charles Darwin, letter to Charles Lyell

We do not see things as they are. We see them as we are.
—The Talmud

Our brains were shaped for fitness, not for truth.
— Steven Pinker, *How the Mind Works*

Charles Darwin was the son of a well-to-do medical family
from Shrewsbury. His grandfather was the larger-than-life
physician, naturalist, poet and inventor Erasmus Darwin, one of
the Lunar Men who met at the house of James Watt's business
partner, Matthew Boulton, outside Birmingham.

Erasmus lived in the beautiful cathedral town of Lichfield,
which was also the early home of Adam Smith's sometime sparring partner Samuel Johnson. The ever-abrasive Johnson had
declared to Boswell, "We are a city of philosophers; we work
with our heads, and make the boobies of Birmingham work for
us with their hands." However, the Lunar Men demonstrated
that there was no clear distinction between industry, science

and philosophy. Indeed, the three were inextricably intertwined. As David Hume had suggested, you were unlikely to find sophisticated manufacturing in a place without science and moral philosophy.

Erasmus was a fossil hunter, a botanist and a believer in evolution. He suggested that "man and ape have had a common ancestor like the horse and the ass." He also wrote about evolution in verse:

First, forms minute, unseen in spheric glass,
Move on the mud, or pierce the watery mass.
These, as successive generations bloom
New powers acquire and larger limbs assume.

Born in 1809, toward the end of the Napoleonic Wars, Charles Darwin was well acquainted with the thoughts and activities of his grandfather because he wrote his biography.

Charles proved something of a disappointment to his father, who had hoped that he, too, would become a doctor. But as a student at Edinburgh, Charles reportedly fled in horror at the sight of a bloody operation. He was subsequently sent to Christ's College, Cambridge (my own alma mater), en route to a likely career in the church. At Christ's, he cultivated an interest in the natural world, encouraged by his friendship with J.S. Henslow, a professor of botany.

Darwin might have become just another gentleman naturalist had fate not exposed him to much more of the natural world than was seen by most gentlemen scholars of his day. The turning point of Darwin's life came when Henslow recommended him for the post of naturalist aboard HMS *Beagle*, which was headed on a five-year voyage to survey the southern hemisphere.

Darwin journeyed to South Africa, Australia and the South Seas. He probed the jungles of South America, climbed the Andes and, most famously, visited the Galapagos Islands. His acute observations and meticulous collection of samples would eventually guide him toward an explanation for the diversity of life. The road would be long, and he would tread it at times reluctantly, increasingly aware of the shock to man's self-esteem that lay at its end.

Darwin returned to Cambridge, wrote an account of the *Beagle* voyage and became an expert on coral reefs. Then he married and retired to a big, rambling house at the village of Down in Kent, to have a large family, study barnacles, orchids and earthworms, play snooker with his butler and ponder the mysterious workings of nature.

The study of natural history was hardly meant to be the route to intellectual upheaval. Indeed, it was an approved pastime for the clergy, whose number Darwin had almost joined. Everywhere naturalists looked, they saw evidence of a marvellously complex "intelligent design." God was sought in ponds and hedges, just as, at the cosmic level, Sir Isaac Newton had revealed the deity as a clockmaker of unbounded scope and precision.

The most influential book on "natural theology," and the primer on intelligent design, had been written by another member of Christ's College, William Paley (whose portrait still hangs beside that of Darwin in the college dining hall). Published in 1802, its full title was *Natural Theology: or Evidence of the Existence and Attributes of the Deity*. In every aspect of the human body — from the tear ducts and stomach juices to the cartilages of the joints — Paley saw "intelligence and intention."

Evolutionary theory was "in the air" when Darwin made his breakthrough. The idea that humans had somehow evolved from the primeval slime (as suggested by grandfather Erasmus) was as old as the Greek philosophers, although hardly popular with the church since it clashed head-on with Biblical accounts of Creation.

David Hume was among those who had proposed a protoevolutionary theory. "No form," he wrote more than a century before *The Origin of Species*, "can persist unless it possesses those powers and organs necessary for its subsistence: some new order or economy must be tried and so on, without intermission; till at last some order which can support and maintain itself, is fallen upon." Like Erasmus Darwin, however, Hume had no idea how this process might work.

Behind much of the more recent speculation on evolution lay advances in geology and paleontology. The study of fossils, a booming area of inquiry since the previous century, suggested that entire species had been wiped out in the course of the earth's history. One massive problem for theories of biological evolution was the belief that there just hadn't been enough time for minutely gradual changes to take place. Eventually, however, it became clear that geological time was far more immense than anybody had imagined.

In 1844, *Vestiges of the Natural History of Creation*, by an anonymous author (Robert Chambers, a successful Edinburgh publisher), caused a sensation, not least because it broached the issue of evolution. Chambers was not a scientist, and his book was wildly ambitious and often inaccurate, but it confirmed public interest in human development and gave Darwin a hint of the controversy that his own work would provoke.

Darwin had been influenced by Adam Smith, whom he had studied at Cambridge, and whose view of an emergent commercial "natural order" was profoundly evolutionary. Other philosophers had suggested a division of labour within bodies and ecosystems. Another key inspiration from the political economists was Thomas Malthus's *Essay on Population*, which presented a grim view of humanity doomed to live at the margins of subsistence because of inability to control its breeding. Malthus would turn out to be both wrong and enormously influential down to the present day. His insight certainly had validity when it came to *non*-human life forms. The tendency of creatures to breed beyond the bounds of available resources meant inevitable and perpetual scarcity and competition, a struggle for survival. In such a struggle, Darwin realized, muta-tion might lead to an advantage that could mean the difference between life and death, between procreating and being the end of the biological line.

That species could be deliberately modified was clear from the selective breeding of dogs and other animals, as well as plants, that had been carried on for thousands of years. Promise of an evolutionary theory was also seen in the common embry-onic forms of many species. There were also vestigial features, such as male nipples, which suggested a biological purpose made redundant over time. To these observations were added, thanks to Darwin's travels, questions about the geographical distribution of, and environmental influence on, species: that is, how similar species appeared in similar environments in far distant parts of the world.

Darwin spent more than 20 years mulling over these issues in the bucolic surroundings of his Kent estate, going for thrice-daily walks along his "thinking path." Then, in 1859, he was shocked when another naturalist, the self-taught Alfred Russel Wallace, sent him a letter outlining a theory almost identical to his own. Darwin was forced to produce *The Origin of Species* in a relatively short time, and to present it beside that of Wallace, who generously deferred to Darwin's superior scientific status.

Darwin's theory of natural selection states that life forms evolve — and split into different species — by a process of muta-tion between generations. Those mutations that make a life form more "fit" to survive and procreate within its relevant environment are more likely to be passed on, further mutated, tested once more for fitness and on and on. The creation of new species occurs when life forms branch off via mutation and can no longer interbreed with those on the home branch. Darwin noted how, in such a process of evolution and speciation, the natural selection of adaptive random variations could give the appearance of intentional design.

One of the reasons Darwin had hesitated so long over his theory was that he realized how controversial it would be. He steered clear of human evolution in *Origin*, making just a brief reference to it toward the end of the book, but the implications were clear. Darwin immediately came under fierce assault for his "monkey theory," which was still far from complete. The most important gap was an explanation for how reproductive variation occurred. The answer lay in genetics. A Moravian monk, Gregor Mendel, was in fact laying the groundwork for genetic theory at the time of Darwin, but it wasn't until the 1930s that Mendelian genetics and Darwinian natural selection were put together in a "grand synthesis."

Genes, we now know, carry the design specifications for living creatures. Genes split during reproduction. Mutation comes via a "transcription error." Most mutations are maladaptive, but occasionally one increases its organism's chance of reproduction. Hence "useful" adaptations — which marginally increase speed or strength or reaction times or smell or eyesight, or any of a multiplicity of interrelated characteristics or tendencies — are more likely to be passed on.

—⁂—

In November 2004, *National Geographic* carried a cover story titled "Was Darwin Wrong?" The piece concluded that no, Darwin was right, and that the evidence was overwhelming, and becoming ever more conclusive. The article reported, however, that Darwinism was still vehemently resisted by fundamentalist Christians, Jews and Muslims and discounted by what appeared an astonishing number of people. According to a 2001 Gallup poll, 45 per cent of responding Americans agreed that "God created human beings pretty much in their present form at one time within the last 10,000 years or so." Thirty-seven per cent could find room for God to work *through* evolution, but a mere 12 per cent believed that humans evolved from other life forms without any involvement by "God."

Perhaps as arresting as these figures was the fact that not once did *National Geographic* refer to the area of evolution to which one would ultimately have to turn to begin to explain such belief patterns: that of the mind itself.

The notion of an evolved — and thus limited and potentially biased — mind tends to be inconceivable, even anathema, to that very mind. Alfred Russel Wallace, for example, the man who had come up with a theory similar to that of Darwin, couldn't bring himself to countenance the mind as merely the function of an evolved organ. As the philosopher David Livingstone Smith wrote in his book *Why We Lie*: "The scientific investigation of human nature runs against the grain of human nature itself. It is triply paradoxical that although we are the only animal that has evolved a mind with the remarkable power to scientifically analyze its own nature, this same mind has been configured by the forces of natural selection to oppose and dismiss the outcome of this investigation."

To ask what kind of thing the mind is, we have to start by asking how, and in response to what particular challenges, it evolved. Our mental apparatus evolved to help us survive in our immediate environment, but it wasn't just a physical world of colours, odours, shapes, masses, distances, velocities, trajectories, poisons and predators; it was also a social world. Man formed society, and society formed man. The key issue was the nature of that chicken-and-egg relationship.

Humans are unique — as far as we know — in evolving complex problem-solving intelligence and self-awareness. However, it is a severely constrained intelligence and self-awareness. For example, one piece of information we continue to resist is that our very distant ancestors were unaware. They were, as Darwin noted, primates, and, before that, shrew-like creatures, and before that things that swam and slithered. Recent advances in the brain sciences offer remarkable insights into how the mind evolved, and thus what kind of minds we have. Above all, neo-Darwinian studies of the mind can help us understand why we get so many things wrong, and why some of us — consciously or unconsciously — seek to exploit those errors in others for our own ends.

Our minds — defined as what our brains do — developed along with, and as a computing and guiding mechanism for, our physical and social interactions. The key insight of evolutionary psychology is that as much as 99 per cent of that evolution may have taken place while we were hunter-gatherers. Thus our brains and minds were overwhelmingly formed when we lived in small, closely related tribal groups, whose existence revolved around hunting, food gathering, sex, fighting and "local politics."

Many thinkers, including Smith and Marx, had posited a version of history in which *societies* evolved in stages, from hunter-gatherer through nomadic pastoralist and settled farmer to full-blown commerce. What none of them grasped was just how dominant the hunter-gatherer period had been in human evolution. This age — known as the Pleistocene — lasted from perhaps 1.6 million years ago until the invention of agriculture and the creation of larger settlements some 10,000 years ago. Thus proto-humans and humans lived as hunter-gatherers for tens of thousands of generations, compared with the mere 500 or so since the invention of agriculture, and the smaller number since humans began to record their history.

Evolutionary psychology is based on reverse-engineering mental traits to see how they made people more fit to survive in this "ancestral environment." Some critics claim that this makes its theories like Kipling's "Just So" stories, which offered fanciful explanations for animal characteristics such as the elephant's trunk (it was pulled out in a struggle with a crocodile). However, Adam Smith had written of the necessity of "conjectural history" when direct knowledge was unavailable. One of his biographers, Dugald Stewart, described it as reconstructing the past by "considering in what manner [humans] are likely to have proceeded, from the principles of their nature, and the circumstances of their external situation."

Evolutionary psychology follows a similar course but is concerned with determining how the circumstances of the ancestral environment, in particular social interaction, formed the basic principles of human nature. The resulting mind, although in some respects remarkably neuroplastic — having the ability to adapt and even heal itself — is far from a blank slate, and thus far from endlessly malleable.

The work of evolutionary psychologists has thoroughly undermined the notion of any kind of "domain-general" rationality, in which the brain is a problem-solving black-box supercomputer. We have "modular" minds, in which different bits evolved to deal with different problems, the most complex of which involved dealing with other people on issues from food sharing and incest avoidance to political coalition building. Those bits don't always fit perfectly — or comfortably — together. This fact was brilliantly expressed by the evolutionary biologist William Hamilton, who wrote in the first volume of his collected papers, *Narrow Roads of Gene Land*, in 1996, of his sudden realization that the genome, the genetic master plan for human life, "wasn't the monolithic data bank plus executive team devoted to one project — keeping oneself alive, having babies — that I had hitherto imagined it to be. Instead, it was beginning to seem more a company boardroom, a theatre for a power struggle of egotists and factions ... I was an ambassador ordered abroad by some fragile coalition, a bearer of conflicting orders from the uneasy masters of a divided empire."

Human nature, seen as a set of universal and sometimes conflicting characteristics, is being rediscovered, and with it a new appreciation of man's uniqueness as a specializer, trader, sympathizer and cooperator: the very fundamentals of capitalism. However, we have also evolved more problematic traits and tendencies, such as aggression, an urge for power and status, a tendency to moralize and toward self-deception. These latter characteristics, although they are "adaptive" — that is, they have helped us pass on our genes — form a much more problematic fit with peaceful commercial society. Indeed, I believe that is where the real "Adam Smith problem" lies.

—ɯ—

Evolutionary psychology confirms that human nature is far from comprehensively malleable. The anthropologist Donald E. Brown has compiled a lengthy list of human "universals." Here is a brief selection, which I have arranged in alphabetical triads:

abstraction, affection and anthropomorphization
coalitions, collective identities and crying
dance, death rituals and dreams
envy, ethnocentrism and etiquette
gossip, government and grammar
hairstyles, healing and hospitality
language, law and logic
magic, metaphor and music
narrative, nouns and numerals
planning, play and poetry
reciprocity, revenge and rhythm
semantics, sexuality and shelter
taboos, territoriality and trade
verbs, violence and visiting

This limited list demonstrates how human characteristics span all the way from the fundamentally psychological, such as envy or sexuality, to the elaborately cultural, such as law or poetry. The universals stretch along a continuum, which suggests that there is no clear dichotomy between "nature" and "nurture." One challenge is to plumb the feedback relationship between the biological and the cultural and analyze just how malleable human nature really is: how far the genes, as the biologist E.O. Wilson put it, hold culture "on a leash." Another is to seek to understand why we can collectively and unconsciously create social institutions that are "beyond" the intentions or designs of any individual, then misunderstand and condemn them.

A few years ago, I went with my daughter to see the "world's most advanced lifelike robot." Named Asimo (after the science fiction writer Isaac Asimov) and built by the Japanese auto giant Honda, it was a truly thought-provoking little android. The main thought that it provoked was how astonishingly *little* it could do. Its chief party trick was to laboriously negotiate a set of stairs.

We have tended to overestimate the potential of robots because we underestimate ourselves, taking our quite remarkable abilities — and peculiarities — for granted. We have evolved enormously complex sensory and motor tools to deal with the physical challenges of our environment. Our brains evolved to evaluate the external physical world as it affects our survival and procreation in terms of masses and distances, velocities and trajectories, potability and edibility, and the likelihood of disease. It was only when man went to the moon that scientists began fully to grasp the stunning computational — not to mention physical — achievement of running to catch a ball. Throwing a spear at a target zigzagging through the undergrowth involves an additional set of unconscious calculations that would clog any supercomputer, as would the program for *avoiding* a spear.

We take such abilities entirely for granted, as we do others, such as the ability to learn language and express ourselves. Robotics and the field of artificial intelligence have highlighted how little we think about thinking.

In the classic Stanley Kubrick movie *2001: A Space Odyssey*, the spaceship's supercomputer, HAL, "decides" to kill the astronauts, who have become suspicious of "him." To humans,

acutely, if unconsciously, sensitive to Machiavellian devious-
ness and the primacy of self-preservation, this seems entirely
comprehensible. It also seems natural that HAL should be able
to converse with his potential victims, including the astronaut
who eventually disables him. However, in recent decades,
research into speech recognition has made researchers realize
how astoundingly complex and subtle such a faculty is.

Artificial intelligence buffs thought it was just a matter of
time before they could make a machine that could hear, understand and respond to a human, thus passing the "Turing test"
(invented by the British mathematician Alan Turing) of being
able to fool a human into thinking he was interacting with
another human. Decades of research, however, have established
that this is much more difficult than originally imagined.

In 2011, Watson, a supercomputer developed by IBM, beat
the previous top two champions of the TV quiz show *Jeopardy!*
The main achievement of Watson's programming was less in
providing the answers than in recognizing the questions. But
the machine, which weighed several tons, had absolutely no
capacity to catch balls, climb stairs or chat at cocktail parties,
three of the many, many categories of activity its *Jeopardy!*
opponents could have handled quite effortlessly.

This should make us wonder what else we take for granted,
particularly since, despite their complexity and sophistication,
our perception and computational systems can easily be fooled.
Steven Pinker provided an arresting case from everyday life in
his book *How the Mind Works*. "When we watch TV," he wrote
in 1997, "we stare at a shimmering piece of glass, but our sur-
face-perception module tells the rest of our brain that we are
seeing real people and places ... Even in a lifelong couch potato,
the visual system never 'learns' that television is a pane of glow-
ing phosphor dots, and the person never loses the illusion that
there is a world behind the pane."

More profound illusions and delusions are built into the
brain's circuitry. Sexual, emotional and other needs are not

necessarily best served by objectivity, logic or even self-awareness. Wooing a mate is quite different from spearing an animal (despite the claims of certain radical feminists), but also requires complex *implicit* calculations.

There is a huge and growing literature on humans' often unconscious sexual attitudes, preferences and strategies, and how they differ between men and women. For example, males tend to be more concerned about sexual infidelity, women about emotional infidelity. That's because it is more adaptive for males to be concerned with paternity (whether a child is likely to have their genes), while women tend to be more concerned about male "commitment," which goes with protection and access to resources for their children (whether those children are the progeny of the committed man or not).

The fact that contraceptive technology has made men's jealousy "rationally" redundant doesn't make much difference to our moral sentiments. As the journalist Robert Wright wryly points out in his book *The Moral Animal*, "For the average husband, the fact that his wife inserted a diaphragm before copulating with her tennis instructor will not be a major source of consolation." Similarly, Ayn Rand's reaction to Nathaniel Branden's emotional desertion was certainly not related to any concerns that he wasn't going to be around to look after the babies that she was never going to have. Both these examples indicate how emotions evolved to serve *genetically* "rational" ends, while driving us, their vehicles, crazy.

One of man's unique characteristics may be that he can, as Smith noted, stand outside himself and examine his own thoughts and actions (although Smith acknowledged that this faculty tended to be honoured more in the breach than in the observance). However, probing our self-*un*awareness is arguably more fascinating; and it is more important, not merely for grasping such metaphorical truisms as the blindness of love or the "thickness" of "blood" but also for understanding why our assumptions about capitalist wealth and corporate "power" might be misguided, at least if we are truly concerned that people should be able to better their condition.

In a rational world — the world, say, of *Star Trek*'s Mr. Spock or Jonathan Swift's noble Houyhnhnms — all that would matter about ideas would be their objective validity: whether they appear to explain how things work, and what objective evidence can be brought forth to support them. But that's why Mr. Spock comes from another planet and Swift made the only rational creatures in *Gulliver's Travels* horse-like, to emphasize that humans are anything but rational.

The insight that we still think like hunter-gatherers can be viewed from two perspectives: that our brains are "primitive," or that our human ancestors had evolved, before the earliest stages of recorded history, mental equipment with an astonishing ability to learn, adapt, imitate, invent and plot. In fact, yet again, both these perspectives are true. However, as Pinker explains, our basic cognitive faculties and "core intuitions" are "suitable for the life-style of small groups of illiterate, stateless people who live off the land, survive by their wits, and depend on what they can carry. Our ancestors left this life-style for a settled existence only a few millennia ago ... [Thus] for many domains of knowledge ... people show no spontaneous intuitive understanding."

We also project our own perspectives onto the world around us and into theories about the way the world works. We read spirit into inanimate objects, imagine that animals think like us, and misunderstand evolution as "purposive."

A while ago I came across an attempt to rehabilitate the dodo — perhaps the most oft-cited example of extinction in modern times — as by no means "stupid" but just "friendly." It was neither. The dodo was simply a creature that came under assault from other creatures that had played no part in its evolutionary environment. Humans brought a new environment for which dodos were no longer fit. Dodos weren't stupid or friendly. Those are *human* characteristics. Dodos were just dodo-ing what came naturally, without emotion or reflection.

Antelopes that live on the Serengeti do not flee from lions because they are smarter than the dodo. Nor do they flee because they can anticipate the adverse consequences of being tripped up by a lioness, as a human almost certainly would. They have no foresight — nor do they need any. Their brains have evolved in a lion environment with a mutated genetic disposition to run when they see a lion shape moving toward them. Any mental algorithm that announced, effectively, "If you see a lion shape, run toward it" would soon have disappeared from the gene pool.

It is hard for us to understand that living creatures did not evolve characteristics *in order to* achieve particular results. However, assumptions of deliberate agency, and cause and effect, are built into our genetic makeup. We say, "That animal is running *for its life*," or "The squid squirts ink *to* fool its predators," or "Anteaters have evolved long snouts *in order to* penetrate termite mounds," but this way of articulating supposed facts indicates a purpose that is simply not there. Speed and squid ink and snouts stuck around as evolved characteristics because they *happened* to increase fitness; they did not evolve *in order to* increase fitness. Our assumptions of purpose tell us much more about the nature of the evolved brain than about the process that created it. They also raise profound questions about our own assumptions of rationality and free will.

We see purposive behaviour in animals because our minds evolved to read purpose in the behaviour of humans. This is highly adaptive because *mis*reading intentions can be fatal. Humans are unique in being concerned about, and able to reflect upon, why people do things and what is likely to happen next. Humans really *do* have purposes. We have apparently transferred a mental trait that is adaptively useful when dealing with humans to other living things, and sometimes even inanimate ones.

Humans are unlike antelopes in that they can conceive and articulate the idea "That lion wants to eat me." Both are inclined to flee, but only humans believe that the lion has "desires," which it is unlikely to do in any way that we might comprehend. As the philosopher Ludwig Wittgenstein noted, with an indeterminate amount of humour, "If a lion could speak, we would not understand what it said."

Similarly, it appears to us that when dogs bury bones or squirrels gather nuts, they are displaying foresight, but they are not; they are merely displaying randomly generated adaptive behaviour. They have no "idea" what they are doing. Moreover, some actions of animals, if they were intentional, would have to be characterized as examples of monumental stupidity.

In *The Moral Animal*, Wright gives an example of mental programming in turkeys. Male turkeys will "avidly court a stuffed replica of a female turkey. In fact, a replica of a female turkey's head suspended fifteen inches from the ground will generally do the trick. The male circles the head, does its ritual displays, and then (confident, presumably, that its performance has been impressive) rises into the air and comes down in the proximity of the backside, which turns out not to exist. The more virile males will show such interest even when a wooden head is used, and a few can summon lust for a wooden head without eyes or beak."

Silly turkeys, you might think, until you reflect on the stimulative impact of two-dimensional pornography. Human males might persuade themselves that they are merely "choosing" to stimulate their imaginations, but it's really, as it were, out of their hands.

It's interesting to note how much anthropomorphic language Wright uses. Turkeys know no "confidence." Nor do they "summon lust." Presumably Wright is writing for comic effect, but he is also writing for a human audience, and that is the way we look at things. We project human characteristics onto everything.

We imagine ourselves to be much smarter than dodos, antelopes and turkeys, but in many ways our brains work similarly. We respond "automatically" to many stimuli, even when the rational part of the brain "knows" that they are manufactured, just as we imagine many actions are deliberate when in fact they are programmed.

Pinker gave the example of how our brains are fooled by television. But the illusions — and delusions — run much deeper. The couch potato, or the visitor to the movies, becomes unavoidably *emotionally* engaged with this unreal world, which brings us back to the primacy of Adam Smith's concept of sympathy.

The suspension of disbelief is no great effort at the cinema because we have trouble *not* responding to emotional stimuli. (I have seen the Christmas classic *It's a Wonderful Life* dozens of times, but I still have to get out the Kleenex.) No completely rational creature could ever enjoy a movie once she had been told what it was and how it had been made. She would never need to take another box of tissues, because her tears would be incapable of being "jerked." She would simply know that what she was seeing was not real. But she also wouldn't be human.

Even the ever-perceptive Adam Smith — although he referred several times to emotional responses at dramatic presentations — never commented on the fact, which would surely be astonishing to the proverbial clear-eyed Martian, that we become unavoidably emotionally engaged in situations that, viewed rationally, could not be more obviously unreal.

We are programmed to respond to a range of visual and mental stimuli, and we often have great difficulty overriding these tendencies. We have as much trouble controlling our belief in what's going on on the silver screen as we do in conquering jealousy or road rage. That's why tears were running down my cheek in Wordsworth's garden, even though the image to which I was responding was purely mental.

So what — at least superficially — is evolutionary psychology's answer to my sorrow at Dora's Field? What lies behind Adam Smith's "sympathy"? Sympathy, it seems, is a powerful evolved emotion that has an adaptive benefit because personal survival depends on the assistance of other humans, and fellow feeling helps promote cooperation and the evolution and acceptance of cultural or moral values.

My sudden mushiness in the Lake District indicated an evolved, pan-human feeling about the preciousness of children (even though Dora Wordsworth was quite old when she died). Concern about, protection of and emotional attachment to children is obviously highly adaptive from a genes'-eye view: children are the vehicles that carry our genes into the future, but we don't love them for that reason. All our genes have to do is design us to love them. (There's another sentence filled with anthropomorphism.)

Yet again, Smith spotted the centrality and utility of the child-nurturing aspect of human nature without understanding its origins. Nevertheless, he shrewdly observed the disproportion between parents' love for their children and children's love for their parents. The former, he noted, is much stronger because it serves nature's "design" for the propagation of the species. Affection, as we now understand, evolved to be skewed toward future generations rather than previous ones, because such skewed affections were obviously likely to protect offspring and thus make them more likely to procreate and spread those future-affectionate genes. As evidence, Smith points out that the Ten Commandments contain no edict to look after our children. In the vast majority of cases they don't have to. However, we often need to be reminded to honour our parents.

Smith wrote, "The weakness of childhood interests the affections of the most brutal and hard-hearted ... Scarce a child can die without rendering asunder the heart of somebody." He might have said "the heart of almost everybody." Humans are programmed to grieve for the loss of precious children, even those who are not their own.

There are, however, limits to such emotionally based moral values, and they kick in when it comes to children who might be a threat to our own survival or successful procreation. Poor societies, and/or those subject to particular types of social engineering, have tolerated infanticide and still do. Stepchildren have also been shown to be in danger of neglect, or worse. The story of Cinderella has its basis in evolved psychology. The ugly sisters were programmed to look primarily after their own or their father's genes, not those of Cinderella, which represented rivalry for their father's resources.

One arresting point of subsequent reflection for me about my epiphany at Dora's Field was that at the time I had no children. That, however, may have strengthened my emotions because I realized that — or perhaps, more accurately, was programmed by my genes to be concerned that — I was running out of time to have my own offspring. But perhaps my attitude was "adaptive" even without children of my own because, in the ancestral environment, nearby children were much more likely to be related to me: that is, to carry my genes.

Thus an adaptive genetic trait became a more general human disposition. That is why most of us tend to respond automatically to the distress of any child, even to one of a clearly different race who lives a long way away. That's why organizations such as World Vision receive such enormous donations. They show pictures on television of distressed children, and our emotions don't distinguish between the phosphor dots (or whatever the latest technology is) and the real thing. But "sharing the wealth" with people half a world away is much more difficult than we imagine. It is also practically — and even potentially morally — problematic.

The observation that those who like laws and sausages would best not see how they are made is attributed to Bismarck. Not only are the moral sentiments infinitely messy in construction, but people appear designed to vehemently reject the notion that the recipe for their own sentiments might be a trick of evolution, or that certain moral assumptions might have been rendered inappropriate by rapid social evolution. That applies even to students of Darwin and moral psychology, whose attitudes, like the majority of those in the academic community, tend toward Morrie more than Mandeville.

eight

Do-It-Yourself Economics

The price of metaphor is eternal vigilance.
— Arturo Rosenblueth and Norbert Wiener

*The principle of order that economics teaches is in no way
"natural" to the human mind which, in its innocence,
is biased towards simplistic collectivism.*
— James Buchanan, *What Should Economists Do?*

Since at least the time of Marx, metaphors for business and businessmen have tended to be wildly negative. Marx compared capitalists to vampires, werewolves and cannibals. Engels declared that economic competition transformed mankind into a "horde of ravenous beasts ... who devour one another." One of the most oft-repeated negative metaphors suggests that market competition is analogous to the "law of the jungle."

The media is full of reports of companies "battling" for, or "stealing," market share; of "predators" whose potential acquisition targets try to "fight them off" or resist being "gobbled up." Speculators seek to "make a killing." Competition is "cutthroat."

Since people naturally regard life as precious, indeed beyond price, they are reluctant for companies to be "killed off" or for employees to be "sacrificed to the bottom line." When business failures or rationalizations occur, their human consequences are often dubbed "brutal," as if employees were being slaughtered rather than merely required to find other jobs.

Another set of misleading metaphors describe economic forces as being like natural disasters: mighty storms blowing winds of unwanted change — "headwinds" against which governments must stand firm; or firestorms against which governments must build "firewalls." Policy solutions are often associated with metaphors of force. In the wake of the 2008-09 and eurozone crises, the need for a policy "bazooka" was invoked, as if governments might blast their way to stability.

Following the collapse of Communism and the myriad failures of government ownership, planning and control in the 20th century, policy-makers claimed that they now appreciated the positive power of markets. However, they said, we couldn't possibly have "unfettered" markets. But markets represent the coordination of the highly dispersed, money-mediated wants, skills and innovations of vast numbers of people. So why would people equate this complex and overwhelmingly benign system with wild animals, or unruly domesticated ones? Why would they imagine that it needs to be "fettered" or "bridled"?

Metaphors are essential in our attempts to explain the world, and in particular to grasp and explain novelty by analogy to things we already think we understand. A metaphor is meant to suggest an enlightening comparison, but economic metaphors are often more effective at revealing our outdated assumptions than they are at explaining modern events. In his book *The Stuff of Thought: Language as a Window into Human Nature*, Steven Pinker points out that metaphors offer profound insights into how our minds deal with language, and he explains how those workings reveal what assumptions we hold about how the world works. This field of study is called conceptual semantics.

Our brains are equipped to learn language, Pinker says, and the equipment already embodies theories of space, time and causality. We are born into a world that, in many respects, we already "know," because our brains evolved to operate in such a world. However, Pinker explains that our embodied assumptions differ "in major ways from the objective understanding of reality eked out by our best science and logic." We have, for example, "eccentric" conceptions in which space and time are often conflated: we speak of "looking forward" to the future and "looking back" on the past.

Pinker notes that we can "see through" metaphors (which is, of course, itself a metaphor). "Like other generalizations," he writes, "metaphors can be tested on their predictions and scrutinized on their merits, including their fidelity to the structure of the world." The problem is that when it comes to economics, not only are the fundamental concepts involved novel and complex but the subject matter is profoundly intertwined with moral assumptions about human relationships. Inappropriate metaphors might be fondly embraced and propagated not only because they are morally satisfying but because they are politically useful.

Markets are in no way analogous to physical combat. Business "aggression" does not mean killing your competitors or blowing up their plants. The prevalent characteristic of commercial society is not "brutal competition" but the stunning amount of peaceful cooperation involved, both within and between business organizations, and systemically via the price mechanism.

It's not just that we are inclined to misinterpret commercial relationships, it's that we all tend to get them wrong *in the same way*. I believe that this common way of misunderstanding supports the thesis that we often still think — or, more precisely, fail to think — on the basis of hunter-gatherer assumptions.

—⚏—

In the late 1980s, just before the collapse of the Berlin Wall, I was introduced to a Cuban exile couple, Ignacio and Iliana, who were living in Toronto. Ignacio explained that he had escaped Cuba by appearing to be an exemplary Communist. He knew that one of the rewards for exemplary Communism was a trip to Lenin's tomb. He had told party officials that he wanted to share this thrill of a lifetime with his wife. When their plane stopped to refuel at Gander, Newfoundland, on the way to Moscow, the couple walked to freedom.

The summer I met them, Toronto was blisteringly hot. One evening I visited the couple after they had spent the day looking for an air conditioning unit. Although they had found one, Ignacio was annoyed at how long it had taken. "Things should be better organized," he said. "There should be more planning."

I was stunned. Here was a man who came from an island whose economy had been ruined by central planning, yet because he hadn't immediately been able to find an air conditioner — which wouldn't have been available in Cuba except through political connections, and even then not the same day (unless your name was Fidel Castro) — he wanted to turn the Canadian economy over to the Cuban system.

Ignacio had at least some excuse for his attitude: he had grown up in a country in which private property, personal initiative and commercial markets had been demonized and outlawed. There was another reason why Ignacio might have been friendlier to state planning than the average Cuban: he had been a state planner himself. However, Ignacio's preference for planning over markets wasn't that different from that of most people living within relatively free economic systems.

John Maynard Keynes, the most influential economist of the past century, claimed that "practical men, who believe themselves to be quite exempt from any intellectual influence, are usually the slaves of some defunct economist." Another British economist, David Henderson, suggested that Keynes couldn't have been more wrong. Most people — including not merely "practical men" but policy-makers — don't derive their ideas about economics from economists at all. Those ideas are intuitive, and mostly erroneous.

Henderson, who had been chief economist for the Organisation for Economic Co-operation and Development, called this phenomenon do-it-yourself economics, or DIYE. He suggested that DIYE beliefs were — like Donald Brown's gossip, government and grammar — universal. "They can be seen across national frontiers and down the centuries. They are unchanging, timeless, and often deeply held. They are the economics of Everyman."

DIYE is pervaded by what Henderson called "unreflecting centralism" — a belief that economic outcomes need to be planned by governments and that self-sufficiency is an unquestionable good. Among the other leading principles of DIYE are that domestic manufacturing should be "encouraged" by government, and that exports are better than imports, but that it is wrong to export raw materials, which should be domestically "upgraded." DIYE also tends to assume that economic output is fixed, and that "labour-saving" technologies reduce long-term employment.

"Public opinion ... is in general suspicious of the idea that markets should be allowed to operate freely," wrote Henderson. This mindset inevitably fed support for interventionism. Henderson suggested that the biggest gap in thinking occurred in trade policy, the guiding principle of which tended to be "opportunist mercantilism." Two hundred years after *The Wealth of Nations*, exports were subsidized, or preferentially financed, or promoted by politicians who sallied abroad as national "salesmen." Imports were restricted either directly or through "Buy National" exhortations.

Henderson noted that from the "mutually supporting notions" of do-it-yourself economics "comes a view of market processes as anarchic, amoral, ineffective and biased against the weak. This view does not involve a conscious rejection of the orthodox economist's vision of reality, but rather a lack of awareness of what this vision comprises." In other words, so reflexive are these largely spurious ideas that it simply does not occur to people that they might be both wrong and dangerous, and that there might be an alternative way of thinking.

I found Henderson's observations, which I read in his book *Innocence and Design*, fascinating, but what intrigued me was the psychological origins of such widespread fallacy. Why would people almost universally embrace erroneous ideas, and — like Ignacio — be impervious to their adverse consequences?

It seemed to me that many of the fallacies identified by Henderson could be explained by the perspective of evolutionary psychology: that is, by reference to the assumptions of a mind formed in a much simpler environment of xenophobic intertribal hostility, where self-sufficiency was the default and from which extensive economies, voluntary employment, technological advance, money and economic growth were entirely absent.

The broader workings of modern commercial society — which has evolved in the biological blink of an eye — are just one area of knowledge for which people have little or no intuitive appreciation. The fact that more people might believe in astrology than have any knowledge of astrophysics is not generally dangerous. The same, however, cannot be said about economics because ignorance and moralistic rejection of markets have had — and continue to have — profound implications for wealth and freedom.

The phenomenon of DIYE takes us to the crucial area of what we see when we think about the workings of society beyond our direct experience. We obviously don't see organizational complexity in any physical sense. Here "seeing" means our assumptions and the views we adopt from our peers and "thought leaders," those we regard as "authorities."

The mind, as Adam Smith noted in an early essay on astronomy, has a craving for explanations. Evolutionary psychology suggests that it might like certain explanations better than others, even if they are erroneous and hypocritical. Mandeville spotted the hypocrisy, but was himself prone to economic error (especially the notion that the Great Fire of London had been — to link it to a related modern policy conceit — a valuable economic "stimulus").

Almost everything about economics as the study of broad, impersonal, commercial relationships is counterintuitive precisely *because* it is impersonal. Our intuition is based on reading character and motives, and being wary of the selfish and those who wish to control or cheat us. It is not designed to appreciate systemic "unintended consequences" because such consequences simply did not exist during that long period when our brains and minds were evolving. There was no economic system. Indeed, the very phrase "unintended consequences" implies that we now operate in an economic environment whose workings do not fit our intuitions. Today, *negative* unintended consequences come about from policies that fail to take into account the workings of the Invisible Hand. By contrast, Smith noted, the hand guides the commercial actor, in pursuit of his own interests, to bring about a good that is "no part of his intention."

Mandeville's highlighting of hypocrisy, and Smith's of self-deceit, had already pointed to a mind that was built for evolutionary success rather than the pursuit of truth or objectivity. Moreover, Smith's two books suggested the potential discord between the moral sentiments, which were in many respects "fixed," and the emergent world of the market, to which Mandeville had also already pointed.

—∞—

Two 20th-century philosophers, Friedrich Hayek and Karl Popper, were among those who picked up on the by then much greater challenges posed by the rapid evolution of commercial society for minds evolved in a tribal setting.

We are, according to Hayek, bifurcated creatures. Our instincts and yearnings make us want to extend the rules of the face-to-face hunter-gatherer troop to the wider world. This would be (indeed has been) at best problematic, at worst disastrous. But neither can we apply the rules of the economic "extended order" to the family and community. "So we must learn to live in two sorts of world at once."

Hayek thus pointed to what he saw as the fundamental tension at the heart of modern society: "Man's instincts, which were fully developed long before Aristotle's time, were not made for the kinds of surroundings, and for the numbers, in which he now lives. They were adapted to life in the small roving bands or troops in which the human race and its immediate ancestors evolved during the few million years while the biological constitution of homo sapiens was being formed."

The "two-world tension," Hayek said, has been growing for a long time (although not long in biological terms). Trade took place over great distances at least 30,000 years ago (the latest research has stretched its origins back beyond 100,000 years ago). "By the beginning of the classical era," wrote Hayek, "life at the great centres of culture had become wholly dependent on a regular market process."

But ancient Greece held two warring systems: the traditional anti-commercial military state of Sparta, which looked back to the tribal world, and the more open commercial democratic state of Athens, where art and literature flourished, and which looked forward to a new, more open world. Hayek suggested that as far back as Plato and Aristotle there had been a "nostalgic longing for return to Spartan practice, and this longing persists to the present. It is a craving for a micro-order determined by the overview of omniscient authority."

Such a claim is controversial, not because the shadow of a simpler past does not indeed hang over our minds, but because Athens's combination of democracy and commerce had led to imperial ambitions that ended in oppression and destruction.

Given the brutal realities of the Peloponnesian War, which Athens lost to Sparta, one can understand why there was a backlash — a desire for a more secure order — that was rooted not merely in nostalgic cravings.

Hayek claimed that "an atavistic longing after the life of the noble savage is the main source of the collectivist tradition." But we might note that this "longing" was promoted primarily by aspirants to political power — by prospective noble chieftains rather than noble savages.

Man's struggle with modern society was also the theme of Karl Popper's great work, *The Open Society and Its Enemies*. Popper maintained that Western civilization had still not recovered from the shock of its birth: the transition from a "closed" tribal society "with its submission to magical forces, to the 'open society' which sets free the critical powers of man."

He wrote in the preface to the second edition of *The Open Society*, "I see now more clearly than ever before that even our greatest troubles spring from something that is as admirable and sound as it is dangerous — from our impatience to better the lot of our fellows." However, perhaps impatience to better the lot of our fellows is sometimes — if not usually — a cover for impatience to better our own lot. Indeed, an evolutionary perspective would allow no other conclusion.

Ayn Rand, who attempted to mount a moral defence of capitalism based on the problematic claim of the "virtue of selfishness," in fact highlighted the two-worlds problem, but did not pursue it because of her own blank-slate assumptions and rationalist biases. "It is morally obscene," she wrote, "to regard wealth as an anonymous, tribal product and to talk about 'redistributing' it. The view that wealth is the result of some undifferentiated, collective process, that we all did something and it's impossible to tell who did what, therefore some sort of equalitarian 'distribution' is necessary — might have been appropriate in a primordial jungle with a savage horde moving boulders by crude physical labor ... To hold that view in an industrial society — where individual achievements are a matter of public record — is so crass an evasion that even to give it the benefit of the doubt is an obscenity."

But might we perhaps be inclined to regard wealth as an "anonymous, tribal product" because our brains were formed during a long evolutionary period when wealth *was* mostly such a product?

—m—

To understand economics, says Steven Pinker, we have to "go to school." The problem even then is that "we depend on analogies that press an old mental faculty into service, or on jerry-built mental contraptions that wire together bits and pieces of other faculties. Understanding in these domains is likely to be uneven, shallow, and contaminated by primitive intuitions."

The evolutionary psychologist Paul Rubin confirms that "folk economics," which is another term for Henderson's do-it-yourself economics, has its origins in the very different environment in which our brains evolved. Folk economics, he writes, "evolved in our ancestors in circumstances where there was little in the way of specialization, division of labor, capital investment, or economic growth. It can explain the beliefs of naive individuals regarding matters such as international trade, labor economics, law and economics, and industrial organization."

Rubin suggests that the evolution of sedentary societies featuring a division of labour came too late "to have left a significant mark on our evolved preferences or intellects." In the ancestral environment, "each person would live and die in a world of constant technology and income. Thus, there was no incentive to evolve a mechanism for understanding or planning for growth. Indeed, to the extent that our ancestors lived on the

Malthusian margin, any changes in circumstances were more likely to be harmful than beneficial, so we would have had a tendency to be leery of change."

Steven Pinker stresses that education in many cases involves *unlearning* what our intuition tells us. This is particularly difficult because the subject matter of economics — personal exchange and wealth distribution — is intricately mixed up with the fundamentals of morality and politics.

Pinker acknowledges a raft of folk-economics or DIYE misconceptions: "People all over the world think that every object has an intrinsic fair price (as opposed to being worth whatever people are willing to pay for it at the time), that middlemen are parasites (despite the service they render in gathering goods from distant places and making them conveniently available to buyers), and that charging interest is immoral (despite the fact that money is more valuable to people at some times than others)."

My Cuban exile friend Ignacio's basic problem thus wasn't either Communist indoctrination or self-exculpation for his state-planning past, it was the structure of his mind. His belief in the power of central economic planning might have been boosted by growing up in Cuba, but his basic lack of appreciation of markets was innate. Ignacio shared it with most human beings (including many professional economists). But then he also shared the Smithian propensity to "better his condition," in this case by acquiring an air conditioner.

We are thus faced with the conundrum of people being natural traders but not natural economists. That's because, despite the deep-seated confusions of do-it-yourself economics, the roots of the modern market economy also and inevitably lie in universal evolved aspects of human nature, although certainly not "bestial" ones.

—⁂—

Just as humans have a language instinct and a moral instinct, they also — as Adam Smith pointed out — have a trading instinct. However, they have no intuitive appreciation of its wider systemic implications. That's because, in biological terms, the "system" has only just appeared.

Even a vague appreciation of the workings of extensive markets requires considerable intellectual effort, which most people are not prepared to make. The crucial point is that *they don't have to*, any more than they are required to have an understanding of their own circulatory or respiratory systems in order to stay alive. People in Western societies work; they get paid; they have access to a stunning array of goods and services. Although innovators, entrepreneurs and managers are essential drivers of the extended order, even they do not need to understand or appreciate it.

It is significant that Smith referred to trading as a "propensity" rather than an exercise in deliberate calculation. While trade may appear a rational activity, proto-humans must have started trading — with the result but not the *intention* of mutual benefit — before they became aware of what they were doing. Although Smith wrote that "nobody ever saw a dog make a fair and deliberate exchange of one bone for another with another dog," experiments have indicated that other primates may have crude trading instincts. However, trade with strangers is uniquely human. It is not greed that makes people effective traders, it is empathy, the ability to put themselves in the minds of others (although "mind reading" obviously facilitates trickery and fraud too).

In the earliest ages of human development, "truck, barter and exchange" would have been severely limited, as Smith (and Xenophon) suggested, by the size of the market. There weren't many trading possibilities for a small group of hunter-gatherers, who were likely more concerned with avoiding contact with other bands than with seeking it. Nevertheless, the origins of both the division of labour and trade — Smith's bases of economic advancement — already lay *within* the tribal band, attached to two fundamentals of hunter-gatherer life: sex and hunting.

The sexual roles of men and women — in particular the fact that women bear and nurture children over an extended period — seem to have co-evolved with the first great division of labour: between men as hunters and women as gatherers of fruit, nuts and berries. One form of early "trade" was also sex-related. It made adaptive sense for males to share with existing or prospective mates, who naturally evolved to find good providers attractive.

Sharing between hunters was also adaptive. Hunting was in any case usually a collective activity. It might have cost hunters little to give up some meat from a large kill, since it would rot anyway (before the development of preservation techniques); but ensuring a payback could be a matter of life and death. Humans seem to have developed a relationship of what has been called "equality matching" (I'll give you a haunch now if you return a haunch later). Equality matching is one of a set of four human social "relational models" identified by the anthropologist Alan Fiske. The others are communal sharing, authority ranking and market pricing.

Market pricing is, significantly, the most recently evolved, the least understood and the most easily morally condemned. Steven Pinker describes it as "the system of currency, prices, rents, salaries, benefits, interest, credit, and derivatives that powers a modern economy." Critically, he notes that it remains not merely "cognitively unnatural" but often morally taboo. As an example, Pinker points out that when it was first introduced, life insurance provoked moral outrage because it was seen as putting a monetary value on a human life, which we reflexively believe should be "priceless."

Pinker also acknowledges that "the momentum of social norms in the direction of Market Pricing gives many people the willies." But that reaction should occur only if you subscribe to such slippery-slope notions as capitalism meaning that "everything is for sale." In reality, moral taboos often prevent efficient market-oriented solutions to social policy problems such as health care and education.

—m—

Earlier I described my musings about what I would do if a friend needed a kidney. It seemed obvious that if I were to donate one of mine, my main compensation would be my friend's gratitude, although there might be reputational advantages too. I certainly wouldn't ask for payment.

The notion of selling — as opposed to donating — an organ appears to trigger some kind of ancient taboo, although there were no organ transplants in the ancestral environment. And when Adam Smith spoke of the universal urge to "better one's condition," he certainly never imagined that selling a kidney might be one possible route.

That issue was inadvertently thrown up by the announcement of the 2012 Nobel Prize in economics, which went to Lloyd Shapley and Alvin E. Roth for "the theory of stable allocations and the practice of market design." One of Roth's most thought-provoking applications of the theory had been to design a "market matching" system for kidney transplants. Since many donors are not biologically compatible with their desired recipient, Roth had set out to devise a system under which donors would swap donations with other donors who were a match with the person to whom they wished to donate. His system was undoubtedly a step forward in making donation systems more efficient. One intriguing related issue, however, was that kidney *sales* were banned in most developed countries. If asked why, most people might say, "Well, it's obvious." They might have a bit more trouble explaining *why* it should be obvious.

Given the state of medical science and the fact that most people can live healthy lives with only one kidney, a well-regulated market could save many lives, while helping out some of those in financial difficulty. However, the prospect of organ sales is almost invariably met with horror.

At the time of the Nobel announcement, the transplant policy issue was in the headlines in Canada because of an acute organ shortage in the province of Prince Edward Island. It had been suggested that a negative option might be introduced: unless people stipulated otherwise, their dead bodies would become spare parts for the government-managed health system. Although some found this notion objectionable, what was curious was that people appeared less exercised by the thought of the state expropriating their body than by allowing someone to freely choose to sell one of her own superfluous parts.

Just why this was so, and what it said about our moral psychology, was explored in *The Ethics of Transplants: Why Careless Thought Costs Lives*, by Janet Radcliffe Richards, a professor at Oxford. Her thesis was based not on the libertarian view that people should be allowed to do what they like with their own bodies, but on the fact that the "ethical" arguments of opponents of organ sales didn't make any sense according to the moral principles they claimed to espouse themselves.

Radcliffe Richards brought up the arresting point that poor Indian farmers reportedly commit suicide because of their debts. Surely they would prefer to sell a kidney. Would Western purchasers not be doing them a great favour? Seeking to stop "exploitation" by banning well-regulated organ sales, she noted, would be like trying to cure slum dwelling by bulldozing slums.

The ultimate question that she addressed was, Where do such immovable but problematic moral assumptions originate?

It is surely impossible to think about the removal of an organ under any circumstances without a reflexive wince. Put that together with trade, which has long been morally condemned (although Radcliffe Richards suggests that it is "morally neutral"), and you have a truly repulsive mixture. The issue is whether such moral revulsion may be inappropriate when set against the stated objectives of the morally revolted. Radcliffe Richards lacerated the failure to think about the practical consequences of unquestioned moral assumptions.

"It may be bad to live in a society where people really do need to sell their organs," she wrote, "but it seems still worse to live in one where they cannot do even that because the rich and healthy make themselves comfortable by prohibiting this conspicuously unpalatable manifestation of poverty and sickness, and by endless rationalizing to keep the contradictions in their moral systems out of sight. The price for such moral comfort is paid by the very people who are the supposed objects of moral concern, and it is too high. This is why serious ethics cannot be left to intuition."

She concluded that "moral seriousness" means not profound moral commitment but a willingness to examine whether profound moral commitment might in some cases be misguided. Radcliffe Richards raised particularly pertinent questions about moral condemnation of capitalism and why — as with the case of kidney sales — other policies that are claimed to be "moral" also tend to be counterproductive when they involve attempting to force market actors to cater to the allegedly disadvantaged. The classic examples are minimum wage legislation and rent controls, which inevitably wind up hurting the people they are designed to help.

Ironically, I believe, part of the failure to see the counterintuitive benefits of capitalism — and to acknowledge the unintended results of policies that seek to force the market in "moral" directions — arises from the fact that our minds were indeed conditioned by the circumstances of chopping up bodies, but not human ones.

—ɯ—

Throughout most of human history, and for all non-human social carnivores, the division of a collectively hunted carcass was a fundamental form of collective activity. This led to the evolution of hierarchies — authority ranking, in Fiske's terms — to prevent intra-pack or intra-tribal conflict.

Significantly, the division of a carcass was a zero-sum, political activity. One person could have a particular chunk only if somebody else did not. Today, of all our primitive anti-economic intuitions, that of the zero-sum mentality may be among the most pervasive, and the most potentially damaging to wealth and freedom.

In *The Rational Optimist,* Matt Ridley notes that "zero-sum thinking dominates the popular discourse, whether in debates about trade or complaints about service providers ... The notion of synergy, of both sides benefiting, just does not seem to come naturally to people. If sympathy is instinctive, synergy is not."

And neither are profits instinctively understood. Profits in a market economy overwhelmingly represent the value *added* by innovation and organization to the inputs of labour, raw materials and capital equipment. Or they arise from providing valuable services. They are the necessary spur to further innovation. However, the untutored mind is still inclined to see profits for one actor as representing a loss to one or more of the others involved; they are seen as something unfairly subtracted through the exercise of greed-motivated, exploitive "power" rather than added through the application of technical, entrepreneurial and managerial ingenuity.

Intriguingly, the zero-sum view of corporate activity has received academic support throughout business schools via "stakeholder theory," which is based on the belief that the interests of the corporate management and shareholders are achieved *at the expense of* workers, suppliers, customers, local communities and the environment more generally. It implies that the struggle for profits represents a Hobbesian war of all against all. Incidents such as the *Exxon Valdez* and BP Gulf of Mexico oil spills are seen not as accidents but as the inevitable result of relentless corner cutting at the public expense, examples of "externalizing" costs in order to increase returns to shareholders. That is, they are held up as examples of moral turpitude and greed.

In fact, the enormous cost of industrial accidents to the firms involved, along with the corresponding loss of valuable goodwill, suggests that the stakeholder take is upside down. In any sensibly managed company, the long-term interests of shareholders, customers, suppliers, employees and communities have to be carefully managed; but they are not ultimately conflicting, they are coexistent.

Zero-sum assumptions also seem to be at the root of persistent fears and warnings about "resource depletion." An inability to comprehend how we can produce ever more of something — and yet still have an *increasing* amount that is economically recoverable or the growing technical ability to find superior alternatives — is understandable given that our minds evolved in a world without technology (beyond crude implements), in which we might exhaust local resources.

Fear of resource depletion is also exacerbated by an inability to comprehend the sheer size of the earth's resource base. Hunter-gatherers lived in small local worlds, with no clue that they were inhabiting a vast planet. There was surely a significant degree of psychological projection in the interpretation of the first pictures of the earth from space: they were seen as confirming how small and finite the earth was, rather than how immense and full of limitless potential when combined with market innovation.

Depletion concerns tend to go with moral condemnation of "over-consumption" and accusations that current generations are robbing future generations (the claims at the heart of the "sustainable development" movement). Such thinking tends to be morally charged by the demonization of greed.

Some wonder why the depletionist mentality is not eradicated by the sight of the mounting cornucopia of capitalist production and resource creation. In fact, the greater the use of resources, the more convinced depletionists become that the day of reckoning has merely been postponed, and that it will be all the more terrible when it arrives. Their moralistic perspective is charged by an inability — or perhaps useful unwillingness — to see the economy as a process rather than a thing.

The economist Julian Simon made a famous bet with the professional doomster Paul Ehrlich, whose 1968 book *The Population Bomb* had predicted global famine before the end of the 20th century. Simon bet that a parcel of commodities — chosen by Ehrlich — would decline in price in the ensuing decade. Ehrlich lost the bet. He continues to preach doom and gloom.

Around 2005, depletionism hit the headlines again when a book called *Twilight in the Desert*, by Matt Simmons, a Texas investment banker, peddled a concept known as "peak oil." The seemingly obvious fact that petroleum reserves are finite and that production in any area will take the form of a bell curve, with a peak, was originally associated with the geoscientist King Hubbert. The theory was the subject of a 1998 article in *Scientific American*, by Colin Campbell, who predicted "the end of cheap oil." This claim had in fact been made pretty much since oil had first been discovered, but Campbell's article became a seminal text for peaksters because it was ultimately not about resource projection but about the "end of economics" and of civilization as we know it.

Simmons's specific claim was that Saudi Arabia's oil fields were in potentially catastrophic decline, and that the Saudis were keeping this information from the world. His assertions gained support as oil prices surged in the period up to mid-2008 to above $140 a barrel. However, this jump had much more to do with soaring demand from China, artificially cheap money promoted by the U.S. Federal Reserve and the fact that oil supplies tend to be "inelastic" in the short term. That is, it takes time to bring new production on stream, so unexpected increases in demand tend to lead to price spikes; similarly, unexpected declines in demand lead to price slumps, which is exactly what happened after the economic crisis hit in 2008.

The central flaw of peak oil theory has nothing to do with peaks or bell curves. It is Campbell's bizarre claim that peak production will lead to the "end of economics." Such claims can be made only by those who have never grasped the nature of economics in the first place.

In the real world of markets, projections of increased scarcity are reflected by higher prices, which promote conservation and make previously marginal supplies viable. Higher prices also boost the search for alternatives. In fact, within just a couple of years of Simmons's book, refinements in technologies such as horizontal drilling and hydraulic fracturing ("fracking") had made vast new petroleum supplies — in particular of shale gas — available all over the world, and had sent U.S. energy production rising once more.

The fact that Simmons, like many depletionists, was motivated by moralism was clear in his description of the market as a "500-pound wrecking ball." He also declared, "If you leave it to the invisible hand of Adam Smith, that could actually end up creating a gigantic noose that strangles us."

Typically, there was an unreflecting authoritarian centralist standing behind the moralist. Simmons, like Ignacio, wanted "more planning," and in particular draconian legislation to force behaviour that complied with his anti-oil, anti-market, anti-freedom agenda. The government should mandate how goods are moved. Workers should be forced to stop commuting and made to eat local food. Globalization should be halted.

Prehistoric assumptions may also help explain the pervasive — and fondly cultivated — notion of "exploitation" of workers, which arises from difficulty in comprehending the novel modern concept of voluntary "labour." For much of human existence, working for somebody else meant literally being a slave, likely captured in war and existing under compulsion of punishment or death. Critics of capitalism have always sought to link the relatively new phenomenon of the wage economy with this more ancient and oppressive form of relationship by calling workers "wage slaves."

There was indeed an overlap between the slave system and the emergent capitalist system, particularly in the use of slavery in the Caribbean and the United States to grow the sugar, tobacco and cotton that were an important part of the American and British economies during the Industrial Revolution. However, the two were ultimately incompatible. Any system that uses slavery contradicts the essence of ideal capitalism: freedom and voluntary relationships (Adam Smith was staunchly opposed to slavery). The moral climate that both promoted capitalism and was fed by it — with its emphasis on freedom and enlightenment — rendered slavery repugnant. As Don Boudreaux of George Mason University succinctly put it, "Capitalism exterminated slavery."

Whether the use of the term "wage slaves" represents a cognitive error, a rhetorical device or a combination of both, it feeds the notion that the solution is for working men to come together in potentially coercive coalitions, known as trade unions, to fight for better wages and conditions. But when it comes to the exercise of union power, the impact of forcing employers to raise wages above their market price is — paradoxically — to undermine jobs. To understand this requires a comprehension of economics, which is one reason why economics is not popular with trade unions (and why the term "trade union economist" is almost invariably a contradiction in terms).

During the Great Depression, the attempt to relieve hardship by legislating higher wages was one of the reasons why unemployment remained at such high levels for so long. And yet the same thinking persists today in minimum-wage legislation, whose inevitable economic impact is to price the neediest workers out of the market. Opposing minimum-wage legislation is uncomfortable because such opposition is ritually condemned as "hard-hearted." As Adam Smith acknowledged in *Moral Sentiments*, it is difficult to promote what you believe — or even know — to be right when everybody else is condemning you.

—◊—

Money is another relatively modern — and marvellously useful — invention whose nature and role we still have trouble grasping, even as we use it every day. Throughout its history, money has been not merely misunderstood but frequently demonized as the "root of all evil," a classic case of projecting a moral failing — greed — onto an inanimate object.

Originally, trade in goods was direct: it took the form of barter. Traders might swap so many arrowheads for a bearskin, but what if the guy with the bearskin didn't want arrowheads? Barter depended on a "double coincidence of wants." When barter would not work, another system of exchange developed quite naturally: "common currencies," commodities that people were prepared to take because they knew that others in their trading areas would accept them. These took many forms, from beaver pelts through strings of seashells to dried cod.

Such commodities varied greatly in quality. What would prove most useful and efficient was a scarce, easily portable substance of uniform quality that could be subdivided into smaller units and then, if necessary, put back together again. Precious metals, eventually in coin form, were the answer. Problems arose, however, when governments were predictably tempted by "debasement" — mixing base metals into their coinage or lowering the weight of coins. Eventually governments abandoned the gold standard altogether and turned to "fiat" money, which they manufactured and manipulated to pay bills, buy votes or "macromanage" the economy. The (latest) fruits of such money mischief fell after 2008.

The rapid evolution of paper money, credit and electronic money reflected the more general explosion in technology. Rapid, or even slow, technological advance simply wasn't a feature of the ancestral environment in which our brains were formed. The hand axe, for example, was a seminal technology but is estimated to have been "the latest thing" for about a million years. By about 40,000 years ago, changes in stone technology were coming relatively thick and fast, transpiring over only a few thousand years.

Paul Rubin suggests, "Given this low rate of technical change and innovation, there was no incentive to evolve a mental mechanism for understanding or rewarding innovation." Nevertheless, humans are amazingly adaptable and have always been quick to adopt new technologies, albeit while staring gift horses resolutely in the mouth.

Lack of appreciation of technological advance as an accelerating cumulative process means that people have difficulty taking in that *more* innovation — potentially an exponential amount — is coming down the pike, due to Julian Simon's "ultimate resource": human intelligence.

The economist Paul Romer writes, "Every generation has perceived the limits to growth that finite resources and undesirable side effects would pose if no new recipes or ideas were discovered. And every generation has underestimated the potential for finding new recipes and ideas. We consistently fail to grasp how many ideas remain to be discovered."

Mental shortcomings also seem to be behind ever-recurrent fears of "technological unemployment." New industrial technologies are almost invariable labour saving, but the experience of the past 200 years is that the labour so released is always absorbed by the work emanating from new technologies, products and services. The supply of employment-creating ideas seems endless.

Put economic growth and capitalist fortunes together with zero-sum "carcass" assumptions and it becomes easier to understand obsessions with the alleged "unfairness" of income and wealth "gaps." Such gaps were invoked as morally reprehensible not merely by the Communist propagandist Vladimir Shemiatenkov, but by the wife of the rector of the Canongate Kirk and the antiquarian print dealer on the Royal Mile in Edinburgh. More recently, they have been the focus of the "Occupy" movement, which came together toward the end of 2011 to protest not just income and wealth inequality but corporate power and the global financial system.

Within weeks of the first Occupy protest at Zuccotti Park in New York's financial district, there were hundreds of similar protests in other U.S. cities, and in more than 80 countries. Insofar as the movement was opposed to the bank bailouts in the wake of the 2008 crisis, it shared a cause with the right-wing Republican Tea Party movement.

The bank bailouts orchestrated by the administrations of George W. Bush and Barack Obama and by European politicians such as British prime minister Gordon Brown were in fact offences against capitalism, not "typical" of it. They were engineered as much out of desperation to preserve the illusion that governments could provide economic security as out of any desire to support Wall Street bankers (although governments certainly weren't short of former Wall Street bankers).

The Occupy movement claimed to represent 99 per cent of the population against an allegedly greedy capitalist 1 per cent. Anybody who suggested that blacks, women or gays could be judged on the basis of their group identity would have been roundly and rightly condemned as racists, sexists and homophobes. However, demonization on the basis of a statistical category — *relative* income or wealth — was not even questioned as a "moral" stance. Gaps are bad, period. Condemnation of disparities in wealth as inherently "unfair" and the association of relative wealth with repressive political power are reflexive human assumptions that, I believe, represent holdovers from the world in which our minds evolved.

In a comparatively free mass-market society, where people have varied abilities and levels of application, and where some talents — such as entrepreneurial acumen or outstanding entertainment and sporting ability — are highly prized, it is inevitable that there will be very large variations in income, and thus in wealth: that part of income that is saved and invested. Anti-gap morality appears to be based on the unquestioned zero-sum assumption that large accumulations of wealth have been gained "at the expense" of others by some form of political oppression. One classic metaphor for this politically useful misapprehension is the term "robber baron."

The term was popularized during the Great Depression as the title of a book by the journalist Matthew Josephson, who peddled the view, common since the end of the Civil War, that great industrial fortunes had been built on fraud and despoliation. In fact, business geniuses such as Andrew Carnegie, John D. Rockefeller and Cornelius Vanderbilt would have been among the greatest benefactors the world has ever seen even if they had never given a cent to charity. Thanks largely to Vanderbilt, freight charges in the United States fell by 90 per cent between 1870 and 1900. Carnegie brought steel prices down by 75 per cent in the same period, while John D. Rockefeller, even as he tried to control the chaotic oil market, cut the price of kerosene by 80 per cent.

The Robber Barons was published in 1934, when the climate was ripe for picking on capitalist scapegoats. President Franklin Delano Roosevelt had blamed the Depression on "economic royalists" (again conflating wealth with political power). Bashing the rich helped FDR to win by a landslide in 1936. His victory — and his continued assault on the rich — was followed by four more years of depression.

Castigation of capitalist wealth continues unabated, but here's another thought experiment. Nobody on earth has done more to widen the gap than Bill Gates, the founder of Microsoft. So would the world be a better place if Bill Gates — and all the other billionaire entrepreneurs — had never been born?

In fact, what the wealthy in a capitalist society are "guilty" of is not taking too much, but *creating* too much. Did Beethoven take more than his fair share of musical fame? Are bestselling authors accused of greed for taking "too much" of the book market? Did the Beatles grab an "unfair" share of pop music income in the 1960s (and since)? Did Monet, Manet and Renoir grab a disproportionate portion of the Impressionist "pie"? Such accusations are surely ridiculous. How can somebody take too much of something they have created themselves, albeit in the case of entrepreneurs and capitalists with the help of voluntary labour, and by standing on the shoulders of their myriad innovative predecessors?

The wealth of those in the Forbes 400 list of America's richest people is indeed stunning. The average net worth of those in the 2012 list was $4.2 billion, up $400 million *each* over the previous year. Bill Gates held on to the number one spot, with $66 billion, followed by Warren Buffett, with $46 billion.

The commentariat tended, tediously and predictably, to the view that this rise in average net worth "increased the chasm" between rich and poor, and expressed profound concern that the super-rich might "leave everybody else behind" (another example of Pinker's "eccentric" conceptual uses of language, equating wealth accumulation with abandoning fellow travellers).

However, the most remarkable and significant fact about the 400 was that 70 per cent had built their fortunes from scratch (the rest had inherited theirs from corporate builders). They couldn't have built those fortunes without creating many millions of jobs and vast amounts of wealth for their shareholders and communities, so how could their wealth be a source of concern?

If wealth gaps were to be bemoaned, and their reduction celebrated, then the member of the 400 who deserved the most praise in the 2012 list was presumably Facebook's founder, Mark Zuckerberg. The stock market flop of his company's 2012 initial public offering had left his net worth down $8 billion over the previous year. Did it appear sensible to suggest that what was needed for a more equitable society was more business failure and less creativity? (Zuckerberg returned to widening the gap in 2013, when his net worth leaped by $9.6 billion, to $19 billion.)

Income and wealth gaps are inevitably the object of envy, a moral sentiment that evolved to express disapproval of, and motivate action against, those thought to have more than their "fair share." From this perspective, envy of those who grow wealthy in relatively free capitalist societies through their success in serving others amounts to a cognitive "error." However, emotions are by definition not easily recalibrated. Moreover, envy will inevitably be cultivated by politicians as a justification for expropriation and redistribution on behalf of the inevitably greater numbers of have-nots, who, it should be noted, are never referred to as the "earn-nots."

In the vast majority of prehistory and history, relative wealth was indeed usually a reflection of political oppression and theft. But today, just as the Western rich are no longer "expropriators" (except when bailed out by governments, or when they get rich through government favours), so the (relatively) poor can arguably make no moral claim on a share of what they have not earned.

nine

The Invisible Metaphor

While we recognize the necessity of individual initiative
in industrial life, we hold that the doctrine of laissez-
faire is unsafe in politics and unsound in morals.
— From the founding platform of the American
Economics Association (1885)

In 2001, Adam Smith finally made it to the silver screen of the theatre named after him in Kirkcaldy. He was mentioned in that year's winner of the Best Picture Oscar, *A Beautiful Mind*. Smith's name emerged from the mouth of the actor Russell Crowe, who played the troubled mathematical genius and Nobel prizewinning economist John Forbes Nash Jr.

"Adam Smith," said Crowe, "was wrong."

The assessment emerged during a scene in a bar. It was concocted to explain the insight for which Nash won his Nobel. As a student, Nash was drinking with college buddies when a group of young women entered. One was a beautiful blond. The others were attractive, but not as attractive as the blond. Nash reasoned that if he and his friends all hit on the blond, then the other girls would be offended and most, if not all, of the guys would wind up with no girl at all.

"Adam Smith needs revision," declared Crowe-as-Nash. "Adam Smith said the best result comes from everyone in the group doing what's best for himself, right? Adam Smith was wrong."

Had the Sage of Kirkcaldy been reincarnated to witness this scene, he would likely have choked on his popcorn, spluttering that he couldn't remember ever writing about strategies for wooing wenches in taverns. Worse, the scene presented the conventional parody of Smith as someone who believed that self-interest — understood in the narrowest and most "selfish" of terms — was the route to the best of all possible worlds.

A Beautiful Mind was meant to be the true story of a brilliant man who sank into mental illness and not only recovered — helped by a long-suffering wife — but wound up with a Nobel in economics. Were Smith to examine Nash's insights, he might conclude that the discipline he had played a key role in formulating had undergone a precipitous decline in both scope and usefulness, and that Nash's Nobel was symptomatic of a drastic trivialization, fragmentation and perversion of political economy.

A broader examination of the history of economics might suggest that Smith's whole intellectual thrust had been corrupted and reversed. Conceived by him as a study that warned of political activism's limits and its dangers to the natural order of commerce, and to human welfare, economics had instead become a tool of activism.

Still, Smith had had a pretty good run for a hundred years or so, despite the moralistic thunderings of the likes of Robert Owen, Marx and Engels. Indeed, at the centenary dinner to mark the publication of *The Wealth of Nations* in 1876, held at the Political Economy Club in London and chaired by Prime Minister Robert Gladstone, William Newmarch, a prominent banker, economist and statistician, predicted that political economy would develop in a direction that would "reduce the functions of government ... within a smaller and smaller compass."

Few prognostications were ever more wrong.

Over the next hundred years, even as capitalists, entrepreneurs and managers continued to promote stunning innovations and amazingly efficient corporate organizations, along with creating unprecedented wealth, government began a period of spectacular growth, based simultaneously on the moralistic rejection of the alleged inequities, inefficiencies, instabilities and political dangers of laissez-faire and on the taxation and redistribution of its ever-flourishing benefits.

The violence done to Smith in *A Beautiful Mind* was just one in a long series of misinterpretations and attacks, which at least confirmed Smith's continued iconic status. To rationalist intellectuals, Smith's "natural order" has always seemed not merely implausible but downright objectionable, not to mention leaving them little room in which to exercise their own large brains and acute moral sentiments. A growing army of professional economists — cultivated and promoted by the political system — conspicuously did not share William Newmarch's free-market vision.

The founding platform of the American Economics Association declared, in 1885, "While we recognize the necessity of individual initiative in industrial life, we hold that the doctrine of laissez-faire is unsafe in politics and unsound *in morals*" (my italics). America might be the fountainhead of capitalism, but, as Yale president Arthur Hadley noted in 1896, American economists were "a large and influential body of men who are engaged in extending the function of government."

If there was one key metaphor that would be the lightning rod for opposition to free markets (if that's not mixing metaphors too much), it was that of the Invisible Hand.

—⚏—

For fans of capitalism, the Invisible Hand became synonymous with free individuals interacting commercially and having their actions informed and guided by the astonishing cybernetic feedback mechanism of the price system. Promoters of ever bigger government, by contrast, refuted the notion that even good results — let alone the best ones — could come from myriad disjointed individual decisions being guided by some mystical-sounding metaphor. People with capacious intellects and good intentions just *had* to be able to come up with something superior to a system based on "greed," and which produced inequality and cyclical slumps.

Many economists and economic historians have indeed praised the Invisible Hand as effusively as they have defined it expansively, but there is a problem here. Smith uses the phrase only once in *The Theory of Moral Sentiments* and once in *The Wealth of Nations*.

In *Moral Sentiments*, he suggests somewhat dismissively, "The rich ... are led by an Invisible Hand to make nearly the same distribution of the necessaries of life, which would have been made, had the earth been divided into equal portions among all its inhabitants." In other words, they "share the wealth" despite themselves. Hardly a ringing endorsement.

In *The Wealth of Nations*, Smith uses the term to refer to a merchant "naturally" supporting both the local and the wider domestic economy. "By preferring the support of domestic to that of foreign industry, he intends only his own security; and by directing that industry in such a manner as its produce may be of the greatest value, he intends only his own gain, and he is in this, as in many other cases, led by an Invisible Hand to promote an end which was no part of his intention."

This reference is problematic too, because it seems to suggest that Smith was promoting local investment over the foreign variety. In fact, Smith was referring to people's natural — and wise — tendency to stick to markets that they *know*. Also, the context of this passage was the artificial promotion of foreign trade by government, to which Smith was opposed.

Smith went on to write of the merchant, "By pursuing his own interests he frequently promotes that of society more effectually than when he really intends to promote it. I have never known much good done by those who affected to trade for the public good."

That last zinger was another insight for the ages.

What sort of guidance does the hand provide? Friedrich Hayek gave perhaps the clearest explanation of its ministrations in his seminal article "The Use of Knowledge in Society." Hayek pointed out that the issue in commerce wasn't one of planning versus non-planning, but of *who* should do the planning, and at what level. He noted that everybody plans according to their own perspectives and desires. The sort of knowledge people use in such planning is not analogous to scientific knowledge. It is "knowledge of the particular circumstances of time and place." It cannot be known by others, much less *in toto* by any individual or group. It cannot be captured by statistics or fed into government economic plans.

The key question is how to utilize all this dispersed knowledge. That is what the market does, by providing a vast arena for promoting, judging and rewarding efficiency and innovation. This fact, wrote Hayek, is a "marvel" but an unacknowledged and underappreciated one. Not only is the market not "designed," but those who participate in it "usually do not know why they are made to do what they do." This, suggested Hayek, is a good thing. He quoted the Cambridge philosopher Alfred North Whitehead, who had pointed out that "civilization advances by extending the number of important operations which we can perform without thinking about them."

However, there is a downside to this unconscious aspect of the natural order. If you don't have to think about it, you don't have to understand or appreciate it, and you become more vulnerable to taking "thoughtful" actions — or pursuing policies — that might damage or destroy it.

Smith had observed how people failed to appreciate the commercial complexity embodied in even the most apparently mundane products. To accommodate the simple needs of a labourer required an amount of cooperation that "exceeds all computation." Smith took as an example the workman's plain woollen coat, which, "as coarse and rough as it may appear, is the produce of the joint labour of a great multitude of workmen." He enumerated all the parts of the wool industry, all the merchants and carriers, all the elaborate machinery, from ships and mills to looms and furnaces, that would have been involved. Producing the rest of the workman's attire, and his tools, home, furniture and utensils, similarly required vast interconnected industries. "Without the assistance and co-operation of many thousands," wrote Smith, "the very meanest person in a civilized country could not be provided, even according to what we very falsely imagine, the easy and simple manner in which he is commonly accommodated."

Although Smith didn't use the term in connection with the coat, this is the "Invisible Hand" in all its productive but taken-for-granted glory. Indeed, Adam Gopnik, in the *New Yorker*, suggested that the woollen coat passage is the "crucial moment of vision" in *The Wealth of Nations*. If so, it is a vision that is still not widely grasped.

The cynical but insightful Mandeville had also cited apparently "simple" clothing as an example of how people took commercial ingenuity and cooperation for granted. "Man would be laugh'd at," he wrote, "that should discover Luxury in the plain Dress of a poor Creature that walks along in a thick Parish Gown and a course Shirt underneath it; and yet what a number of People, how many different Trades, and what a variety of Skill and Tools must be employ'd to have the most ordinary *Yorkshire* Cloth? What depth of Thought and Ingenuity, what Toil and Labour, and what length of Time must it have cost, before Man could learn from a Seed to raise and prepare so useful a Product as Linnen."

One of the best-known modern expositions of the Invisible Hand is Leonard Read's essay *I, Pencil*, in which a humble writing instrument outlines its own astonishing, and again unappreciated, genealogy. (Smith would have regarded a mass-produced pencil as a technological wonder. Read, who published his fascinating essay in 1958, would no doubt have been blown away by the internet or an iPhone.)

Read, who set up the Foundation for Economic Education — the first modern libertarian think tank in the United States — picked a pencil, when he could have chosen something much more complex, such as an automobile or airplane, to emphasize again how the most apparently simple objects are the result of a stunning amount of market-based cooperation. As Read's pencil noted, "Not a single person on the face of this earth knows how to make me."

Behind the unprepossessing combination of "some wood, lacquer, the printed labeling, graphite lead, a bit of metal, and an eraser" lay complex technology and organization that were nevertheless effortlessly facilitated by the market at myriad levels via the incentives of price and profit. The wood required "saws and trucks and rope and countless other gear." Each of those items in turn needed elaborate fabrication. The wood was shipped on railroads that represented a monument to innovation and organization. The pencil factory contained its own complex equipment to shape the wood and glue its separate sections round the pencil's graphite heart, which had been mined in Sri Lanka, processed with Mississippi clay and other chemicals, then extruded, baked and further treated. The pencil received six coats of yellow lacquer and was labelled with elaborately produced resins and carbon black. The brass ferrule had entire global zinc and copper industries behind it. The eraser tip was a "rubber-like product made by reacting rapeseed oil from the Dutch East Indies [Indonesia] with sulfur chloride, along with numerous vulcanizing and accelerating agents." The pumice came from Italy. Cadmium sulphide gave the eraser plug its reddish colour.

By Read's time, given the anti-capitalist political horrors of the 20th century, he could point out that failure to understand the power and benefits of free markets had been not merely counterproductive but disastrous. Comprehending the market process, which was infinitely superior to central planning, was not just the key to wealth, it was essential to freedom and prosperity. "The lesson I have to teach is this," concluded Read's pencil. "Have faith that free men and women will respond to the Invisible Hand."

In 1976, the Nobel laureate economist Milton Friedman wrote of *I, Pencil*, "I know of no other piece of literature that so succinctly, persuasively, and effectively illustrates the meaning of both Adam Smith's invisible hand — the possibility of cooperation without coercion — and Friedrich Hayek's emphasis on the importance of dispersed knowledge and the role of the price system in communicating information that 'will make the individuals do the desirable things without anyone having to tell them what to do.'"

More recently, Matt Ridley, in a 2012 lecture, "Adam Darwin," drew attention to the parallels between the Invisible Hand and Darwinian evolution. The common theme of Smith and Darwin, Ridley said, "is emergence: the idea that order and complexity can be bottom-up phenomena that need no designer. Both economies and ecosystems emerge."

Darwin — having read Smith — had applied the concept of the division of labour to the specialized species within the ecosystem of the Brazilian rainforest. But a Darwinian perspective held insights for economics and cultural evolution too, since, as Ridley noted, "ideas evolve by descent with modification, just as species do."

The natural market order produces amazing diversity and complexity without grand design, just as biological evolution has done. And although the advance of the natural market order is rooted — unlike the biological order — in the more or less conscious choices and innovations of humans, the process by which market success emerges is similar to the random mutation and selection of biological evolution. Just as in nature there have been vast numbers of maladaptations that have died out, so there are many commercial innovations that do not pass muster and fall by the market wayside.

Both nature and entrepreneurs are "tinkerers" within a system that passes judgment on the basis of the tinkerings' contribution toward survival and growth. Moreover, both systems are based — as Hayek and Read pointed out — on a literally incomprehensible amount of implicit information.

Technological evolution comes about, like biological evolution, by trial and error. Such advances are, suggested Ridley, incremental, inevitable and inexorable. The computer whiz Gordon Moore posited Moore's Law: the number of components on a silicon chip — that is, its computing power — doubles every 18 months. This kind of cumulative advance, noted Ridley, was in fact universal in commercial society. There is a law of accelerating returns that "appears to have marched imperturbably through the upheavals of the 20th century without breaking step."

In drawing analogies between biological and cultural evolution, Ridley suggested that the commercial equivalent of sex is exchange, which enables good ideas, like adaptively advantageous genes, to spread. This, Ridley stressed, is quite different from genetically based forms of cooperation such as symbiosis, food for sex or the social interactions of insects.

"Exchange," according to Ridley, "was the key invention that led to the explosion of technology and economic progress in our species: not language, or tools, or self awareness or big brains. We had all those for hundreds of thousands of years and remained rare and simple hunter-gatherers. It was when we invented exchange that the human revolution happened."

Societies that encourage internal exchange and open themselves to external exchange flourish. Closed societies stagnate. Smith's great insight was to understand the importance of specialization and exchange — of the division of labour and free trade. Since cultural innovation tends to increase with the volume of exchange, wrote Ridley, it is promoted by population density. The more people, the more ideas. On the other hand, isolated or shrinking populations can lose technology, as happened in Tasmania when it was cut off from the Australian continent.

It was time, suggested Ridley, to reclaim the word "collectivism" from the left and note how markets represent the greatest possible collective effort, although from the bottom up rather than from the top down. Surely, he pointed out, we should have grasped by now that top-down systems encourage selfishness rather than eliminating it.

Ridley also believed we hadn't seen anything yet. If the exchange of information and ideas, both in their pure form and embedded in products, was the essence of cultural evolution, then the internet, which enabled "ideas to have sex faster and more promiscuously than ever," promised unprecedented innovation, and thus prosperity.

Ridley stressed that the advances of capitalism had nothing to do with "social Darwinism," the notion that the biological imperative of "the survival of the fittest" should be adopted as social policy. In fact, quite the reverse. "Because bad ideas die in competition with good ones," Ridley noted, "people do not have to die. The more we allow our technologies and institutions to evolve, the more we can afford to keep the poor, the disabled and weak alive."

—ɯ—

Milton Friedman wrote his paean to Leonard Read's pencil in 1976, the 200th anniversary of *The Wealth of Nations*, but despite proliferating technological wonders, understanding of the Invisible Hand remained slim, particularly at the policy level; faith in it was even slimmer. Despite the Thatcher and Reagan revolutions, and the further stunning achievements in computers and telecommunications of subsequent decades, by the time Ridley delivered "Adam Darwin," the Invisible Hand was not merely still ungrasped, it continued to be ridiculed and vilified.

As commercial society and democracy expanded over the two centuries following Smith's death, the Invisible Hand acquired increasing importance and attracted increasing criticism. Smith's nemesis, Marx, in *The German Ideology*, made reference to "an English economist" who claimed that "the relation of supply and demand ... hovers over the earth like the fate of the ancients, and with Invisible Hand allots fortune and misfortune to men, sets up empires and wrecks empires, causes nations to rise and disappear."

This certainly gave a looming and threatening significance to the concept that Smith had never intended. Marx anticipated the more expansive meaning that the metaphor would come to have. It would increasingly be seen as the central insight of the Smithian system, which explains why it would become the object of everything from snide condescension to towering moral condemnation.

The concept of the Invisible Hand is not mystical, but it is counterintuitive, and requires intellectual effort to grasp. The point at which they "see" the Invisible Hand often represents the eureka moment for economists. Many never get it. One reason why many intellectuals and politicians consciously or unconsciously resist getting it is that it is potentially lethal to their interventionist pretensions. It suggests that deliberate tinkering "for the public good" is, as Smith suggested, likely to be counterproductive — analogous, perhaps, to a visible bull in a china shop.

Condemnation of the Invisible Hand inevitably comes heavily tinged with moralism. It is tainted, claim critics, whatever its results, because it guides people whose fundamental motivation is the sin of greed. (It is worth noting that Smith used the word "greed" only once in *The Wealth of Nations*, and he used it of governments and their greed for power.) This take ignores the *mutually beneficial* processes of the free market, which enable some people to become fabulously wealthy ("greedy") by providing goods and services that bring benefits to others (except to their commercial competitors, who are nevertheless spurred to their own further innovations).

That the business achievements of Bill Gates or the late Steve Jobs might be explained by massive greed is surely patently ludicrous. However, the greed taboo remains ever current. According to the now much-referenced *Wikipedia*, the Invisible Hand suggests that "greed will drive actors to beneficial behavior." Even after the collapse of Communism and despite the success of Reaganism and Thatcherism (or perhaps because of it), Lester Thurow, a Harvard-based popular economist, wrote in a 1992 book, *Head to Head*, "Too often, Adam Smith's 'Invisible Hand' became the hand of a pickpocket."

In *Twenty-First Century Capitalism,* the Marxist academic Robert Heilbroner shed crocodile tears for the alleged passing of the concept. "Nowadays," he wrote, "one does not much hear about the Invisible Hand, Adam Smith's marvellous metaphor for the market system. The system is all too visible in the form of corporate manoeuvres or garish advertising."

Joseph Stiglitz — who won an economics Nobel in 2001 for his work on "asymmetric information," the fact that buyers and sellers inevitably have different levels of knowledge — was another reflexive big government interventionist who treated the concept with disdain. He never tired of repeating that the hand "is invisible, at least in part, because it is not there." One wonders if Stiglitz ever considered where pencils — let alone iPhones — come from.

One of the most virulent attacks on the battered extremity came in a 2001 book, *Economic Sentiments*, by Emma Rothschild (the wife of another left-leaning Nobel prizewinning economist, Amartya Sen). Rothschild spun around the conceptual appendage like a malevolent spider, seeking to immobilize it with rhetorical stings and semantic silk. Like so many of her fretful left-liberal colleagues, she saw in Western countries not relatively happy people free to choose their own lives and enjoying an enormous range of commercial products and cultural and social possibilities, but individuals "imprisoned by their own discontent, or by their own cupidity, in a society of universal commerce."

In her desire to refute the ideologically offensive metaphor, Rothschild attempted to glove it with unalloyed evil. She claimed that it should be "understood in the setting of the 'bloody and Invisible Hand' of Macbeth's providence, or the 'Invisible Hand' which rebuffs and then hovers over the unfortunate hero of Voltaire's *Oedipe*." Her Invisible Hand was also a false god, allegedly the object of "reverence" by "fundamentalist" believers (none of whom she identified). She claimed that the concept is "extremely condescending about the intentions of individual agents." She said the Invisible Hand was also contrary to Smith's championship of enlightenment because its "subjects" were "blind."

But surely the concept is there to be grasped by anybody who is prepared to observe, study and think. It was rather Rothschild who — like Marx — was "blinded" by her moralistic assumptions. Nor are those operating within the realm of the hand, as Rothschild claimed, "puny and futile." They are not so much helplessly in the grip of a larger force as the *creators* of an extensive undesigned cybernetic system that provides them with signals and opportunities to fulfill their own objectives.

"Market power" is an object of obsessive concern for interventionists, so the hand is inevitably claimed to serve it rather than undermine it. Rothschild's Orwellian logic ran as follows: capitalist freedom leads to unequal wealth, which inevitably leads the economically powerful to attempt to buy political influence to rig the market. She was thus essentially peddling one of the party slogans from *Nineteen Eighty-Four*: "Freedom is Slavery." Indeed, Rothschild had Smith's metaphor do everything but jerk upward to shouts of *"Sieg heil."*

Academic hatred for the Invisible Hand can rarely have been more glaringly expressed than by the Oxford business school professor Colin Mayer in his 2013 book, *Firm Commitment: Why the Corporation Is Failing Us and How to Restore Trust in It*. This was Mayer's assessment of how the Invisible Hand works: "Just as rats rushing to leave a sinking ship re-establish its buoyancy, so in the individual pursuit of our own self interest we collectively confer benefits on those who lie on the other side of the market."

Mmm. I think somebody's psyche is showing.

In the book on which *A Beautiful Mind* is based, Sylvia Nasar further abused and misconstrued the Invisible Hand. She explained that the Nobel-winning "Nash equilibrium" claimed that in a "multi-player game, the game would be solved when every player independently chose his best response to the other players' best strategies." She admitted that "the Nash Equilibrium, once it is explained, sounds obvious, but by formulating the problem of economic competition in the way that he did, Nash showed that a decentralized decision-making process could, in fact, be coherent — giving economists an updated, far more sophisticated version of Adam Smith's great metaphor of the Invisible Hand."

Quite apart from the fact that Hayek's and Read's elaborations of the Invisible Hand were both highly coherent and sophisticated, Nash's insight was anything but broadly applicable. It applied only in limited situations where the participants had *perfect knowledge* of each other's intentions and strategies. How realistic or useful was that?

Game theory — of which the Nash equilibrium is an example — came to analytical prominence after the Second World War in a world where power struggles rather than cooperative relationships were seen to be the defining mode of social inter-action — that is, in a world dominated by politics rather than economics. Given, however, the tendency to misperceive and misrepresent markets as power struggles, game theory was claimed to be relevant to economics when in fact it usually wasn't.

Perhaps the best-known example of a Nash equilibrium is the "prisoner's dilemma," which Nasar rightly described as "the most famous game of strategy in all of social science." The pris-oner's dilemma is an example of how an individual pursuing what appears to be a "rational" course may produce subopti-mal results for both himself and his colleagues or, in this case, his co-conspirators. Foes of free markets eagerly embraced the game's implication that the pursuit of self-interest didn't neces-sarily produce the best results.

The dilemma as usually portrayed involves two criminals, arrested for a crime and incarcerated separately. If both stay silent, they receive a light sentence; if both confess, they receive a heavier sentence; but if one confesses (for both of them) and the other stays silent, the one who confesses gets off and his partner carries the can. The only logical "solution" to this game, whatever your partner does, is to confess, or, in the jargon of game theory, "defect." If he stays silent, you can get off by con-fessing; if he confesses and you stay silent, you receive the hefty punishment. The "best" cooperative solution would be if you both kept quiet, but you can't rely on that, so in seeking the least-worst solution, both players defect.

Nasar concluded, "Thus the Prisoner's Dilemma contra-dicts Adam Smith's metaphor of the Invisible Hand in eco-nomics. When each person in the game pursues his private interest, he does not necessarily promote the best interest of the collective."

This is utterly garbled. The prisoner's dilemma is not by any stretch of the imagination a model of economic behaviour. For a start, the game's participants are not engaged in voluntary commercial exchange; they are criminals. Cheating, lying and backstabbing are much more prominent as characteristics of *political* behaviour, and indeed the Nash equilibrium may be most useful for examining why governments engage in destructive policies such as imposing trade restrictions and subsidizing, or bailing out, companies or industries.

Worse, Nasar seemed ignorant of the fact that the prisoner's dilemma would be entirely stood on its head when a repeated series of "games" are played not by criminals seeking to minimize punishment, but by people seeking to maximize economic payoffs. Participants in classroom studies soon learn that cooperation is the best strategy.

Smith in fact acknowledged that there was more temptation for traders to cheat, that is "defect," in one-off deals. However, where there was "regular" — that is, repeated — commerce, he observed, participants were far more concerned with their reputation for fair dealing because it was in their own long-term interest. Reputation has commercial value. Not only did the Invisible Hand guide self-love toward serving others and promote stunning technological progress, it even encouraged virtuous behaviour.

Such a notion was repugnant to critics of markets, who considered them not merely agents of oppression and inequality but playgrounds of fraud, perpetually open to failure, and in need of minute regulation and fine tuning. They misrepresented and parodied those who supported the power and morality of markets not merely as supporters of "greedism," as the Nobel prizewinning economist Paul Krugman put it, but also as naive believers that humans were purely rational creatures, and markets "perfect." The insights of the new brain sciences were in fact recruited to suggest how irrational humans really were, and prone to error. Strangely, however, this new analysis — like older versions — seemed particularly one-sided, since it resolutely ignored the murky political and bureaucratic realities of those who were meant to do the fine tuning.

ten

The Rise and Fall and Rise
of John Maynard Keynes

*Here was one of the most famous and respected economists in the world
informing governments that the way to full employment was paved
with higher spending and lower taxes. What more attractive advice
could politicians wish for? Long regarded public
vices turned into public virtues.*
— Milton Friedman on John Maynard Keynes

I n a niche in the Keynes Room at King's College, Cambridge,
sat a large bust of the great eponymous economist, with a
cape draped over onc shoulder. He was proffering a small book.
His look was one of forbearance, an attitude essential for anybody trapped permanently in a university lecture room.

I was here attending a conference that happened to coincide
with the end of my 1993 trip between the tombs of Smith and
Marx. The conference's title — "Canada: The First Postmodern
Society?" — had been irresistible. It promised academic "folly
and presumption" on a large scale, and it did not disappoint.

First up to the podium was a gloomy Quebec academic who
spoke, with knitted brow, of the political fatigue and fragmentation caused by Canada's bilingualism and multiculturalism,
and of their impact on denying the possibility of a "grand narrative." Then came a professor who intoned at length on the

postmodern rejection of ontological assumptions, and posed the great postmodern question "Can identity exist?" She suggested that Canadian postmodernists "are less able to feel postcolonial optimism." Another academic declared that Canadians had "anxiety about an absent past."

A young woman from Quebec started promisingly, noting that postmodernism was a word "overused and underdefined," but then spoke of "a paranoid chase through multiple narratives," of "maternal symbolic economy" and of "social silence about women's bodies." She used "foreground" as a verb. They all did.

A man at the back of the room asked her a long, complex question about "underground subtexts challenging the linear." There was a postmodern silence. Eventually, the man answered himself, positing "an ethos of the unfathomable."

Later, Anthony (subsequently Lord) Giddens, a prominent left-wing British sociologist, stepped up to a podium to ritually dump on Thatchcrism, express regret that the Marxist model had not worked and call for a "new left synthesis." The crowd loved him.

The conference, while giving me another opportunity to revisit a place I loved, also presented a stark reminder of the stunning amount of gobbledygook spouted in academe. Some of the most dangerous was arguably put forward by the man whose bust sat in the niche, contributing mightily to the corruption of economics.

Keynes's theories, although many heirs of Adam Smith considered them fatally flawed, came to dominate public policy in the decades after the Second World War. The most obvious reason was their appeal to Smith's "men of system": those who reflexively believed that markets were immoral and unstable, and thus had to be regulated and "stimulated." They also appealed more generally to most people's unreflecting centralist assumptions that somebody should be "in charge." Unfortunately, since they flouted Smith's natural order, they were bound to come a cropper.

—⚲—

Already by the latter half of the 19th century, and throughout the 20th, the Invisible Hand — even as it continued as the organizing principle of market wonders that were seldom wondered at — would, from a theoretical perspective, wave frantically from the rising waters of interventionism. Smith was misrepresented, castigated and ultimately turned upside down. He had pointed out what was potentially beneficial about free markets and counterproductive about government intervention. Economics increasingly became about what governments should do to counter alleged market imperfections and inequities.

As the vote was extended and professional democratic politicians and bureaucrats sought to expand the scope of the state, they would increasingly look to economists to formulate and justify politically attractive intervention. Most governments weren't interested in hearing from people who told them that their initiatives were likely to be counterproductive, so the true heirs of Smith, who concentrated on the power of free markets and the dangers of intervention, were unlikely to achieve much influence, at least until the governments of Ronald Reagan and Margaret Thatcher came along.

Still, the Smithian perspective was never entirely extinguished in theory, even as it continued to flourish in fact. Toward the end of the 19th century it was championed by the great Cambridge economist Alfred Marshall (who gave his name to the piece of brutalist architecture where I carried out some of my own rather spotty studies as an undergraduate). Marshall, the greatest economist of his age, visited the factories of Manchester, just as Engels had done, and developed a fascination with poverty and how to improve social conditions, but he came to very different conclusions. He also travelled in, and was impressed by, the United States.

Marshall believed — as Smith had done — that America represented "the history of the future." He toured American factories and concluded that the division of labour had not led to the "mental mutilation" about which Smith had been concerned, much less to Engels's "social murder." He marvelled at Americans' geographical and social mobility, at the status of American women and at the country's sense of egalitarianism and absence of class consciousness. More generally, his first-hand experience of the ways of industry and business made him optimistic, in contrast to those like Marx who condemned the system based on economic ignorance and moral assumption, and without ever having been inside a factory

Marshall looked past the 19th-century morality plays framed by Malthus, Marx and John Stuart Mill — which concentrated on capitalist oppression of the overbreeding working classes — to point out that the cause of poverty was not oppression but, as Smith had implied, low productivity and underdeveloped "human capital." The answer to economic development was thus education and technology, which was spurred by competition. Marshall believed — like Smith — that the key to general wealth and welfare was enhancing "mental and moral capital." He noted the central role of business organization in innovation and bettering people's lives. He also refuted Marxist notions of immiseration, pointing out that the British working classes had in fact done well in the 19th century. His 1890 book, *Principles of Economics*, rejected socialism, embraced private property and competition, and was optimistic. But Marshall was leaning against the tenor of the times.

The most prominent, but increasingly lonely, champions of the Invisible Hand in the 20th century would be the heirs of the so-called Austrian School, notably Ludwig von Mises and Friedrich Hayek. Mises, who was Hayek's teacher, lived most of his life outside the academic mainstream, mainly because he saw the mainstream heading over a cliff and did not hesitate to say so.

Hayek's philosophy too was rooted in reflections on the insanities of nationalism, collectivism and government-printed hyperinflation, which he, like Mises, had experienced first-hand in Vienna after the First World War. Both men were incisive critics of government culpability in trade cycles and monetary mischief. One story tells of government advisors coming to ask Mises how to stop the inflation that was gripping Austria in the early 1920s. He told them to meet him later that day outside the building where banknotes were printed. When they arrived, he said, "Do you hear that noise?" It was the rumble of the presses. "Turn it off."

Mises and Hayek wound up fighting socialism on two fronts: in its extreme form as Communism, and in its more "moderate" forms such as fascism and social democracy, both of which permitted "fettered" enterprise under government regulation and control. On one front of their intellectual struggle, they refuted the theoretical possibility of full-scale central planning; on the other, they countered the promotion of mixed economies, which combined macroeconomic management with the extensive regulation and public ownership promoted by Herbert Hoover and Franklin Delano Roosevelt's New Deal, and by the socialist government in Britain after the Second World War.

In his book *Socialism*, published in 1922, Mises had explained how a socialist economy without the Invisible Hand of a market system to set prices was bound to be grossly inefficient. His critique was devastating but was largely ignored, because it was either counterintuitive or inconvenient. Hayek acknowledged the possibility, indeed the critical importance, of planning at the individual and corporate level but pointed out that grand, long-term economic plans at the national level were bound to come to grief. However, like Marshall before them, both Mises and Hayek were leaning against the intellectual conceits — and career self-interests — of the time.

Above all, the Great Depression would be interpreted by interventionists as a "failure of capitalism," which thus needed "saving from itself." In the conventional wisdom shaped by leftist academics and policy-makers, the culpability of government policies — in the form of monetary contraction, regulatory uncertainty and beggar-thy-neighbour trade restrictions — was downplayed or ignored. Instead, more government action was called for.

Adam Smith would stay out of favour for another 40 years, and even then his resurgence under the governments of Margaret Thatcher and Ronald Reagan would hardly be welcomed by the academic community. In the interim, one brand of economics was enthusiastically embraced by governments: that of the man immortalized by the statue in the niche at King's College.

—◊—

John Maynard Keynes was the son of a University of Cambridge lecturer. He achieved academic prominence first as a mathematician, then as an economist, at King's. He was an influential British Treasury official during the First World War, in which capacity he went to the Versailles peace conference. There, he pointed out that the huge reparation payments the Allies demanded of Germany were morally reprehensible, economically flawed and politically dangerous. He outlined his critique in a book, *The Economic Consequences of the Peace*, whose wisdom would eventually become abundantly clear.

Having achieved fame for castigating one set of dubious government policies, he then proved responsible for spawning another. His most influential work was *The General Theory of Employment, Interest and Money*, published, in 1936, in the depths of the Great Depression. In it, he refuted the Smithian notion of a self-correcting market economy. Full employment was not a natural state of affairs; thus corrective government action was essential.

The model of the self-correcting market depended on the free movement of prices, but Keynes noted that wages and other prices tended to be "sticky" on the downside, meaning that there is resistance to their falling due to factors such as trade union power. Thus he suggested that an economy could contract to, and be "trapped" at, a low level of activity, with high levels of unemployment. The market could "fail" at the most fundamental level (even though in fact the main problem was the tendency of unions — thanks to the coercive power granted them by politicians — to hold up market processes rather than the failure of the market processes themselves).

It would apparently never occur to market participants that prices and wages *had* to come down, at least until above-market levels had inflicted much misery. Keynes also suggested that a flight to cash could make a low-interest-rate policy ineffective in times of drastic downturns. Banks wouldn't want to lend. Consumers wouldn't want to borrow or spend. The only answer, he claimed, was for governments to step in to maintain "aggregate demand."

Keynes grew up in the great years of a British empire and firmly believed in noblesse oblige; he thought that politicians and bureaucrats could be counted on to do the "right thing" (despite the contrary evidence of Versailles). He approached policy as if it were being proffered to philosopher-kings. The economist James Buchanan called this attitude "the presuppositions of Harvey Road" (where stood Keynes's parental home in Cambridge). In a letter to Hayek, with whom he had a good relationship, Keynes wrote: "Dangerous acts can be done safely in a community which thinks and feels rightly, which would be the way to hell if they were executed by those who think and feel wrongly."

Among those who apparently thought and felt hardly at all were the "animal spirits," as Keynes called them, that drove business. The intellectual historian Jerry Z. Muller noted that Keynes had absorbed all the negative Dickensian stereotypes of 19th-century capitalism and suggested that his "deepest sentiments were closer to Marx and Engels." Keynes in fact rejected Marxism, but he shared Marx's moral condemnation of the "cash nexus" as capitalism's only alleged form of social cohesion. Indeed, Keynes even outdid Marx in moralistic rhetoric, never an easy task, throwing in a little environmental sensitivity for good measure.

"The same rule of self-destructive financial calculation governs every walk of life," he wrote. "We destroy the beauty of the countryside because the unappropriated splendours of nature have no economic value. We are capable of shutting off the sun and the stars because they do not pay a dividend."

Keynes's only use for capitalism appeared to be to provide the wherewithal to get rid of capitalism. "Avarice and usury and precaution must be our gods for a little longer still," he wrote. Muller also observed that Keynes had a "cultural antipathy to deferred gratification." Keynes described a "paradox of thrift": if everybody held on to their cash, the economy would decline; hence he recast the virtues of prudence and saving as potential vices.

Keynesian theory depended on highly debatable assumptions. The first was that government expenditure was a viable substitute for the private version in promoting economic growth. A devastating parody of this view was delivered by the economics journalist Henry Hazlitt. "So there you have it," wrote Hazlitt in his 1959 book, *The Failure of the "New Economics"*:

> The people who have earned money are too shortsighted, hysterical, rapacious, and idiotic to be trusted to invest it themselves. The money must be seized from them by politicians, who will invest it with almost perfect foresight and complete disinterestedness (as illustrated, for example,

by the economic planners of Soviet Russia). For people who are risking their own money will of course risk it foolishly and recklessly, whereas politicians and bureaucrats who are risking *other* people's money will do so only with the greatest care and after long and profound study. Naturally the businessmen who have earned money have shown that they have no foresight; but the politicians who haven't earned the money will exhibit almost perfect foresight. The businessmen who are seeking to make cheaper and better than their competitors the goods that consumers wish, and whose success depends upon the degree to which they satisfy consumers, will of course have no concern for "the general social advantage"; but the politicians who keep themselves in power by conciliating pressure groups will of course have *only* concern for "the general social advantage."

Keynesianism turned Say's Law (named for the great French economist Jean-Baptiste Say) — which essentially pointed out that you had to produce before you could consume — on its head. Keynes suggested that if you artificially stimulated consumption, you could bring about real production, and thus "prime the pump" of the economy. Hazlitt responded by citing a devastating satirical poem, "I Want to Be a Consumer," by Patrick Barrington, published in *Punch* in 1934. Here is part of it:

"And what do you mean to be?"
The kind old Bishop said
As he took the boy on his ample knee
And patted his curly head.
"We should all of us choose a calling
To help Society's plan;
Then what do you mean to be, my boy,
When you grow to be a man?"

"I want to be a Consumer,"
The bright-haired lad replied
As he gazed into the Bishop's face
In innocence open-eyed.
"I've never had aims of a selfish sort,
For that, as I know, is wrong.
I want to be a Consumer, Sir,
And help the world along."

"I want to be a Consumer
And work both night and day,
For that is the thing that's needed most,
I've heard Economists say,
I won't just be a Producer,
Like Bobby and James and John;
I want to be a Consumer, Sir,
And help the nation on."

Nothing could more succinctly have laid bare the notion that you could effectively "spend yourself rich."

Keynes's main attraction for economists and politicians was that he offered an economic model that put them in charge. He formulated a "macroeconomics" consisting of a set of statistical aggregates waiting to be manipulated by masterful policymakers. His fundamental model, Milton Friedman wrote, was of the economy as a hydraulic device, whose flows could be determined by pulling and pushing levers or twisting valves. Keynes also compared it to a motor car with a defective part, which thus needed economic "mechanics."

As Jerry Muller put it, "Keynes became the most influential economist in the Western world from the 1930s through the 1970s. That was in part because he offered a seemingly scientific rationale for what politicians wanted to do, in part because he provided economists with a self-image combining the authority of technique with high moral purpose, and in part because he created an arsenal of economic concepts that proved indispensable even to those who disagreed with his particular policy prescriptions."

Friedrich Hayek — although he greatly admired Keynes — was among those profoundly concerned about the implications of the state spending and control central to Keynesianism. In 1944, Hayek published *The Road to Serfdom*, which suggested that Keynesian interventions, plus even more intrusive measures such as nationalization of industries, would lead to disaster. Hayek's book proved wildly popular in the United States when a condensed version appeared in *Reader's Digest*. However, the occupying powers banned the book in Germany on the grounds that it would impair good relations with the Soviet Union.

The Austrians pointed out that government interventions, particularly of the monetary variety, were in fact not the solution to most economic disruptions but the cause of them. When governments attempted to stimulate activity by spending or holding interest rates artificially low, they in fact merely promoted "malinvestment," whose adverse consequences could not be avoided.

Government could certainly provide short-term jobs on public works, and there seemed to be an opening for Keynes in Smith's suggestion that government might provide what would be called "infrastructure," such as roads and bridges. But whatever government spent to "stimulate" demand would have to be paid for by borrowing and/or additional taxation down the road — thus sapping private consumption and investment — or by printing money and thus debasing the currency and undermining economic confidence.

Mixing up alleged "stimulus" with the more basic requirement that infrastructure serve economic development would inevitably lead to misspending on make-work programs directed at winning votes. Meanwhile the constant possibility of unpredictable debt-boosting governmental intervention would generate uncertainty, further damaging confidence and thus the climate for private investment. It was this resolute blindness to the political flaws of Keynesianism that suggested that its proponents were either naive or self-interested. Intriguingly, those who pointed to Keynesianism's flaws were not merely rejected; they were morally condemned and even persecuted for stating what they considered obvious.

—⁂—

When James Buchanan was awarded the Nobel Prize in economics in 1986, the media inevitably descended, seeking to encapsulate his work in a sound bite or a paragraph. When they thought they had grasped the insights for which Buchanan had won the prize, many reacted with shocked surprise. Was *that* all there was to it?

Stated simply, Buchanan's main contribution to political economy — via the theory of "public choice" — was to note that political actors behaved just like economic ones: they looked out for number one. Whatever good intentions they might profess, elected representatives and bureaucrats did not pursue the "public purpose" without regard for their own benefits. Their top priorities were to get, and stay, elected, and/or to expand their political/bureaucratic empires.

The media reaction to Buchanan's essential insight was "Every fool knows that!" But the intriguing point was that most academic economists apparently did not. Nor did they want to. Many lived in a world in which advice was given by philosopher-princes to philosopher-kings, and intentions were assumed to coincide with results. These assumptions were perhaps less naive than simply self-serving, although Buchanan understood where they were coming from. He had started there himself.

Buchanan acknowledged that his own intellectual development represented a journey from reflexive left to reasoned right, from sharing a pervasive belief that business was dangerous and needed to be controlled politically, to an appreciation of free markets and a realization of the profound flaws of economic intervention and macromanagement.

Buchanan had been brought up poor on a farm in Tennessee although his grandfather, an agrarian populist, had been governor of the state. The political pamphlets Buchanan read as a boy made the robber barons very real for him. He went to teachers' training college and then achieved a master's in economics, which left him, in his own words, "blissfully ignorant of the coordinating properties of decentralized market process" and open to "quasi-Marxist" arguments. After the war, during which he served in the U.S. Navy in the Pacific, he went to the University of Chicago.

"Those of us who entered graduate school in the immediate postwar years were all socialists, of one sort or another," he wrote in his autobiography, *Better Than Plowing*. That soon changed under the teaching of a Chicago economics professor, Frank Knight. Buchanan's appreciation of the power of the market developed into a growing skepticism about the political alternatives. Following a Fulbright Scholarship in Italy, his skepticism became full-blown conviction. This made him not just a renegade but an object of suspicion and condemnation.

To Buchanan's astonishment, the issue of whether interventionist methods would or could work within the democratic political institutions through which they inevitably had to be mediated was hardly examined. The most dangerous fallacy, Buchanan saw, lay in the profoundly influential thinking of Keynes. Buchanan's reward was to be vilified and ostracized for his apostasy.

Keynes assumed that governments would run budget surpluses during "good times" to compensate for the deficits required to "stimulate" the economy during downturns. Buchanan pointed out that this was naive. Keynes wasn't giving advice to Platonic guardians who would do what was best for society without personal consideration. Due to the "presuppositions of Harvey Road," Keynes's model politician was somebody like himself, independently wealthy and imbued with a public service ethic. The democratic reality, noted Buchanan, was quite different. In the rough and tumble of democracy, Keynesian policies would have to be executed by politicians who liked spending but didn't like taxing, because spending went with being re-elected, while taxing went with losing the government limo. They would almost inevitably put only half of Keynes's prescription into effect. The result would be ballooning public debt.

As early as 1954, Buchanan wrote a paper pointing out that Keynesian policy had been "developed in a political vacuum and that the precepts of his theory were unworkable in democratic settings." His colleagues told him not to publish such a document because "there are costs to being branded a heretic too early in one's career." Sure enough, Buchanan was ostracized for his views. He spent decades fighting an academic orthodoxy based on highlighting the inadequacies of free enterprise in order to justify macromanagement, regulation and fine tuning. His darkest period started with the Kennedy years, which he refused to romanticize as the second coming of Camelot, and continued through the rest of the "radical" 1960s, when he and his colleagues were accused of being "fascist." He eventually found academic asylum at Virginia Polytechnic Institute.

—⁂—

In the years after the Second World War, as Keynesianism was embraced by economic policy-makers, Adam Smith's teachings were considered embarrassingly old hat. Nothing more clearly indicated that than a conference in 1973 in Smith's birthplace, Kirkcaldy. There, a group of distinguished academics, politicians, businessmen and bureaucrats were invited by the local council to commemorate the 250th anniversary of Smith's birth.

Those attending included Arthur Burns, chairman of the U.S. Federal Reserve; Lord O'Brien of Lothbury, governor of the Bank of England; and the British Labour Party politician James Callaghan, who would become prime minister three years later. However, the star of the meeting was the celebrity economist John Kenneth Galbraith.

The local council had invited Galbraith over the protests of Smith's fans, but Galbraith was a big draw at the time. His bestselling books such as *The Affluent Society* and *The New Industrial State* catered to a fashionable distaste for "crass" materialism, and to a desire for bigger government to counter corporate "power" and compensate for capitalism's manifest shortcomings.

Despite the supposed "celebration," most of those present in 1973 — and in particular Galbraith — had come not to praise Smith but to bury him. The common policy view was that comprehensive government "management" of the economy — a notion that Smith had utterly rejected as the delusion of "men of system" — was now both viable and essential.

Smith was subtly put down by several participants as a "man for his times." Some, presumably to save the face of the long-dead fuddy-duddy, suggested that Smith would also have "moved with the times," and would now be a much greater fan of intrusive government. Lord O'Brien nevertheless acknowledged that Smith "would be amazed by the great growth in government expenditure, and, going with it, the great growth in government intervention in industry, which takes many forms, but which has occurred in all countries, including even the United States."

The validity of Keynesianism went unquestioned. Arthur Burns reported that although policy-makers hadn't *quite* perfected the system of macromanagement, experiments were "going forward." Jim Callaghan — whose British Labour Party, then in opposition, was contemplating a massive extension of government ownership of industry — allowed that he had developed considerable sympathies for the interventionism that Smith had refuted. However, the presentation that would surely have startled Smith the most came from Galbraith, who declared most forcefully that Smith had been overtaken by events. And about time too.

The heart of Galbraith's attack was that big government was needed not merely to macromanage the economy but to counter the dangerous power of big business. Perhaps Galbraith's most startling claim was that free trade was no longer important. National markets were large enough for any country. Here, as in so many things, Galbraith was merely following Keynes, who had claimed in the 1930s that the world might be more peaceful with less international trade and more economic "autarchy." (Ironically, Keynes wrote this just as Nazi Germany was putting such a program in place.)

When I first came upon the transcript of the 1973 conference in the Kirkcaldy library, 20 years after the event, it already read like a meeting of the Flat Earth Society. Delusions of state competence lay in ruins. The Communist economies (which Galbraith had elsewhere effusively praised) had collapsed. Government ownership of industry had everywhere proved to be a grossly inefficient financial sinkhole. Western governments — including, even especially, that of Canada — were only then beginning to struggle out from under the burden of two decades of feckless borrowing; their Keynesian pretensions to economic management had, as James Buchanan predicted, been subverted and overwhelmed by the more powerful urge to buy votes with borrowed money. In 1977, Buchanan co-wrote, with Richard Wagner, a devastating analysis of the Keynesian fallacy, *Democracy in Deficit: The Political Legacy of Lord Keynes*. "Keynesian economics," the book declared, "has turned the politicians loose; it has destroyed the effective constraint on politicians' ordinary appetites."

In fact, Keynesianism would be thoroughly discredited within just a few years of the Kirkcaldy conference. Jim Callaghan, shortly after he became British prime minister, admitted to a party conference, "We used to think that you could spend your way out of a recession, and increase employment by cutting taxes and boosting Government spending. I tell you in all candour that that option no longer exists, and that in so far as it ever did exist, it only worked ... by injecting a bigger dose of inflation into the economy, followed by a higher level of unemployment as the next step ... That is the history of the last 20 years."

John Kenneth Galbraith would, nevertheless, remain remarkably popular. That popularity sprang not from his analysis, which was comprehensively flawed, but from the fact that he catered to so many prejudices about the capitalist system, most of which were based on that popular stew of economic misunderstanding, moralistic rejection, historical skewing and political misrepresentation. Milton Friedman was among those who pointed out that Galbraith was not a scientist seeking explanations but a "missionary seeking converts." He was a moralist in economist's clothing.

Friedman pointed to another fatal flaw in postwar Keynesian theory. It was assumed that there was a stable relationship between inflation and unemployment, and that government could boost employment by juicing inflation. In his presidential address to the American Economics Association in 1967, Friedman had noted that such a trade-off would soon break down once inflationary expectations became embedded. The emergence of "stagflation" — accelerating inflation with no growth — appeared to prove him right.

The events of the 1970s — soaring oil prices during two OPEC crises, related currency turmoil following the abandonment of the dollar's link to gold and the collapse (at least for the time being) of the model of government as economic puppet master — were a turning point of sorts. They paved the way for the Thatcher and Reagan revolutions of the 1980s, with their emphasis on deregulation, privatization, personal responsibility and breaking the more perverse aspects of trade union power.

The bulk of mainstream professional economists tended to oppose such market-oriented moves. Nothing more clearly indicated their orientation than a letter to the *Times* of London in March 1981 by 364 British economists who condemned Prime Minister Thatcher's recent budget as having "no basis in economic theory" and threatening the country's "social and political stability."

During the budget debate, Thatcher had been asked if she could name even two economists who supported her policies. She came up with two names but later admitted she was relieved that she had not been asked for a third. Nevertheless, the 1981 budget marked the beginning of Britain's economic recovery from its long postwar decline. Clearly, mainstream economics had gone severely astray, confirming the persistent warnings of Cassandras such as Mises, Hayek, Friedman and Buchanan. However, Keynesianism had not been dispatched. It catered to too many useful misconceptions.

The lessons of economics are both counterintuitive and morally suspect, and thus subject to reflexive dismissal by every new generation. Hence, following the 2008 crisis, desperate politicians reflexively reached once again for those Keynesian knobs, valves and levers, and they still had plenty of support from Nobel prizewinning economists.

—␣␣—

The new, post-2008 Keynesian thrust came attached to the almost universal regurgitation of an old canard about "traditional" or "classical" or "neoclassical" economics, all of which had their roots in *The Wealth of Nations*: that those who promoted free markets were dunderheads who believed that people were perfectly "rational" and markets rationally "perfect."

In fact, Smith had never written anything about markets being perfect, or depending on human rationality. Indeed, he was a major analyst of human *irrationality*. Smith had pointed out that the business of the market was achieved by a rough "higgling and bargaining" and continued despite the "folly and impertinence" of government policy. The division of labour, he stressed, had come about as the "consequence of a certain propensity in human nature ... to truck, barter, and exchange one thing for another." It was a "propensity," not an exercise in unbridled rationality. Smith had also specifically refuted the notion that markets required perfection. "If a nation could not prosper without the enjoyment of perfect liberty and perfect justice, there is not in the world a nation which could ever have prospered."

He promoted free trade, but he never expected that it would be achieved. He wrote, "To expect, indeed, that the freedom of trade should ever be entirely restored in Great Britain, is as absurd as to expect that Oceana or Utopia should ever be established in it. Not only the prejudices of the publick, but what is much more unconquerable, the private interests of many individuals, irresistibly oppose it."

Beyond ignorance of these truly inconvenient historical facts, the Keynesian counterattack against alleged naive belief in human rationality and market perfection was rooted in a misreading — or perversion — of two modern economic theories: "rational expectations" and the "efficient markets hypothesis." These theories had nothing to do with Spock-like rationality or perfect markets (at least in the sense in which critics used the terms). Their relevant features were, respectively, that (a) people are rational enough not to be fooled — at least in the longer term — into thinking that printing money creates wealth, or that government expenditure is a substitute for the private variety (the essential conceits of Keynesianism); and that (b) markets reflect the state of current knowledge, which may prove misguided, and will inevitably be superseded, but which can't be second-guessed by governments.

All the old anti-capitalist caricatures and straw men — plus some new ones — were hauled out for ridicule. There were strident appeals for stronger regulation and more macromanagement, but remarkably few demands for analysis of why past regulation and macromanagement had failed. One claim was that the culprit for the crisis was deregulation, but while there had indeed been some deregulation, the real problem was the mountain of regulation that remained, which made the process of deregulation like a cross between a complex game of pick-up sticks and bomb disposal.

Keynesianism was dragged from the policy crypt and declared, by a very strange leap of logic, to have been "vindicated" by its mere application. This was analogous to a claim that the mere existence of the Flat Earth Society "vindicated" the theory of a flat earth. However, "stimulus" expenditures, when piled atop business bailouts and the unsustainable burdens of expansive welfare states, soon led into numerous national debt crises. Subprime mortgages were replaced in the headlines by much more dangerous subprime governments, particularly in Europe.

Keynesianism's return required a good deal of historical fudging and was accompanied by much moral posturing. Keynes's faithful biographer Robert Skidelsky looked through his rose-coloured rear-view mirror and declared that the Keynesian era had had a great deal to recommend it. "If we look at the historical record," he wrote, "the liberal regime of the 1950s and 1960s was more successful than the conservative regime that followed ... Economic growth was faster and much more stable in the Keynesian golden age than in the age of Friedman; its fruits were more equitably distributed; social cohesion and moral habits better maintained. These are serious benefits to weigh against some business sluggishness."

But "more successful" on whose assessment? Where might one view the tablets of this "historical record"? And how did one gauge "social cohesion" or "moral habits," except on the highly subjective "Fings ain't wot they used to be" scale?

Skidelsky fulminated like an Old Testament prophet against "the corruption of money." He denigrated the "offshoring" of jobs and bemoaned the "rape of nature." He suggested that the post-2008 situation was a "crisis of conservatism," a "moral crisis." He ritually bemoaned wage "gaps." He asserted his belief in "making markets well-behaved," as if they were unruly schoolboys. He claimed that "we" had to make globalization "efficient and acceptable." He resurrected the hoary question of whether economic growth makes people truly happy.

Skidelsky proudly admitted that Keynes was a moralist as well as an economist, clearly not grasping that moralistic economics might be a contradiction in terms (as established by Galbraith). Keynes "believed that material wellbeing is a necessary condition of the good life," wrote Skidelsky, "but that beyond a certain standard of comfort, its pursuit can produce corruption, both for the individual and for society." So, presumably, a guardian class of moralists had to decide — Morrie-like — on an acceptable dividing line between comfort and corruption.

Skidelsky claimed that Keynes "reunited economics with ethics by taking us back to the primary question: what is wealth for?" In fact, Keynes had separated economics from ethics by claiming that private income and wealth was just an aggregate collectivist carcass to be taxed, borrowed against and manipulated by policy wonks advising vote-hungry politicians. "The good life was one to be lived in harmony with nature and our fellows," wrote Skidelsky of Keynes's view, as if this represented some startlingly original insight rather than more Morrie-style Hallmark philosophy.

Certainly, when it came to that supposed Keynesian "golden age," the quarter century after the Second World War had indeed seen a surge of growth, but there was little evidence that this was due to wise macromanagement. Indeed, Keynesians had predicted a postwar slump due to the withdrawal of government spending. Meanwhile, social cohesion was far from evident in postwar Britain, particularly in the trenches of class warfare that Keynesianism encouraged by suggesting that governments, rather than countering union intransigence, should attempt to compensate for it by fiddling with inflation. Skidelsky's golden age was, after all, the world that also inspired Orwell's nightmare vision of *Nineteen Eighty-Four* and cultivated the ultra-radical unions that helped bring the British economy to its knees in the 1970s, a decade that Skidelsky seemed to want to shove down the Orwellian "memory hole."

Another Invisible Hand–biter who rejoiced in Keynes's alleged return from "the wilderness" was the Nobel laureate Joseph Stiglitz, the man who liked to claim that the Invisible Hand wasn't there. Stiglitz declared, "At one level, what is happening now [the resurgence of Keynesianism] is a triumph of reason and evidence over ideology and interests." The crisis, he claimed, established above all that free markets were not "self correcting."

But markets had never been free, and the fettered version had rarely been allowed to self-correct.

Among the works of premature Keynesian triumphalism was a book titled *Animal Spirits*, by George Akerlof and Robert Shiller. Akerlof was at the University of California, Berkeley, while Shiller taught at Yale. Akerlof had won a Nobel Prize in 2001; Shiller would share one in 2013. The authors claimed to be preaching Keynesian "inconvenient truth." Naysayers were dolts, shills or cases suitable for treatment. The book portrayed a world full of praise and silly enthusiasm for capitalism. The authors parodied "classical economics" as based on the belief — ho-hum — that people are perfectly rational and markets always stable. Yet again, they quoted nobody who held such a view, but claimed it went back to ... the Invisible Hand.

Akerlof and Shiller trotted out all the snide anti-capitalist canards: capitalism was exploitive; it might be based on consumer choice but it didn't produce what consumers *really* needed. Tediously but typically, they impugned John D. Rockefeller by pointing out that his father was a "snake oil salesman." They continued, "His son transformed his legacy into something more constructive, if highly controversial." But where might such "controversy" have arisen except in the robber baron rantings of anti-capitalists?

"Capitalism," they wrote, "fills the supermarkets with thousands of items that meet our fancy. But if our fancy is for snake oil, it will produce that too." There was truth in this, but no capitalist snake oil could match the policy snake oil of Keynesianism, which, suggested the authors, required wise governments to perform a "parental" role to those silly teenagers of the market. This role should be neither too strict nor too permissive: Goldilocks-onomics. Henry Hazlitt would have been rolling his eyes from the beyond.

Akerlof and Shiller in fact gave numerous examples of public policy screw-ups but refused to acknowledge that these might ever add up to a general case against interventionism. They admitted that the founding of the Federal Reserve in 1913 had been based on wild optimism about its potential for stopping business depressions, and that the Fed did not understand the boom of the 1920s and precipitated the slump of the 1930s. They conceded the role of the uncertainty created by FDR's policies. They pointed to the key role of government guarantees in creating the savings and loan debacle of the 1980s. They noted that the U.S. Securities and Exchange Commission had introduced dumb rules about "marking to market" that had allowed companies such as Enron to inflate their profits but had then subsequently weakened bank balance sheets during the 2008 crisis. They granted the role of Prohibition in creating disrespect for the law. They agreed that "the increasing complexity of our financial system makes it rare for economic institutions like deposit insurers or central banks to stay ahead of financial innovation." They bowed to the inadequacy of the

Basel rules on bank regulation. They cited the role of Andrew Cuomo, while he was secretary of the Department of Housing and Urban Development, in forcing the government-backed mortgage concerns Fannie Mae and Freddie Mac to aggressively increase lending to people who didn't qualify for mortgages. But none of this shook their faith in the perfectibility of policy. Indeed, like most policy wonks, they regarded the vast catalogue of government failure as a trove of knowledge from which to craft more and better regulation.

They claimed that "many government operations function well. And many private companies function poorly." The big difference — which they neglected to mention — was that private companies that function poorly go out of business (unless bailed out by governments), whereas poorly functioning government programs tend to stick around.

Akerloff and Shiller admitted that in the end they could not provide the "detailed" policy answers. Nevertheless they stressed "the urgency for setting up the committees and commissions to develop the reforms in financial institutions and the regulations that are so immediately needed." So there was the solution: more committees and commissions! There would always be a viable regulatory policy ... just over the hill.

Not all the new Keynesians were old Keynesians. One surprising convert to the cause was Richard Posner, a highly respected U.S. judge and expert in law and economics at the University of Chicago. Ironically, Posner had in the past been fingered as a leading proponent of hyper-rationalist market-oriented selfishness. Now, however, he appeared to have had a Damascene conversion, which he wrote about in *A Failure of Capitalism: The Crisis of '08 and the Descent into Depression*. He now parroted the mantra that the prevailing view in the economics profession was that individuals were "rational" and markets "perfect." And to prove his own new embrace of irrationality, he approvingly cited Keynes's most highly criticized — and indeed economically ridiculous — ideas, including support for destroying farm inventories, because that would stimulate production. Here was Mandeville's benevolent Great Fire of London redux.

Posner, like Keynes, dismissed businessmen as "animal spirits," subject to irrational exuberance one minute, "paralyzed" by fear into "hoarding" the next. This was where wise and competent government would step in to "arrest a downward economic spiral." "The government," wrote Posner, "must do everything it can to convince businessmen and consumers that it is resolute in working for economic recovery. An ambitious public-works program can be a confidence builder." In other words, government had to strive to fool all of the people at least some of the time.

Posner, although a legal expert, seemed strangely impervious to the impact of regulation in promoting the crisis. Jeffrey Friedman, a political scientist at the University of Texas, noted in a review of Posner's book that the "rational self interest" that Posner condemned was inevitably misguided by following the "tens of thousands of pages of the tax code" and the "millions of pages of the regulatory code."

Posner concluded that "we need a more active and intelligent government to keep our model of capitalism from running off the rails." But "active" we already had. "Intelligent" not so much. Governments' failure of intelligence lay not in the absence of IQ, but in that fatally conceited Keynesian conception, now embraced by Posner, of an economy as a machine with knobs and levers, and of the political class as philosopher-king/mechanics. It lay more fundamentally in an inability or unwillingness to acknowledge the power and sophistication of markets. In Posner's case, it amounted to the apparent abandonment of such knowledge in return for accepting the warm embrace of fashionable and "caring" statism.

Not long after Posner's "conversion," studies were already confirming that the main impact of post-2008 artificial stimulus had been to crowd out private investment in the short term and/or create a debt burden that would impoverish taxpayers and damage the economy in the long term. Five years later, economies had not recovered. Europe remained in a debt-fuelled crisis. And yet Keynesians had not lost the faith, precisely because morally based faiths are hard, if not impossible, to dislodge. Keynesian economists such as Paul Krugman claimed that the only problem with government stimulus was that there had not been enough of it. Just as the cure for misregulation was always more regulation, so the cure for debt-laden governments was more debt, or simply to print more money, which Fed chairman Ben Bernanke effectively did through so-called "quantitative easing."

The fact that attempts to pump more cash into economies had not promoted the general inflation at which the Keynesians aimed was claimed by some Keynesians as a vindication. Since they had stagnation but not inflation, they were right and the Austrians were wrong. Since bleeding the victim had not killed the victim, the scientific validity of bleeding had been established.

The inevitable "austerity" that followed from reining in government fiscal ineptitude was claimed to be heartless and unnecessary. Krugman called the Austrians "Austerians," suggesting that they were at heart economic sadists rather than simply real economists. The fact was that when economies recovered, recovery could come only from private ingenuity and investment. However, as Jean-Baptiste Say had pointed out, government propaganda could always confuse people about what caused or retarded economic growth.

Nobel prizewinner Robert Lucas suggested another reason why Keynesianism was back: "I guess everyone is a Keynesian in a foxhole." In other words, the revival of Keynesianism was primarily a reflection of sheer political desperation.

eleven

The Darwin Wars

The world has far too much morality ... The human moral sense
can excuse any atrocity in the minds of those who commit it.
— Steven Pinker, *The Better Angels of Our Nature*

For [Richard] Dawkins, the awful truth is that science is
unbiased, the universe is pitiless, and Mother
Nature is a discarnate Margaret Thatcher.
— Marek Kohn, *A Reason for Everything: Natural*
Selection and the English Imagination

When I came across evolutionary psychology, I was intrigued by its potential to help explain why people might
have problems with the concept of capitalism. I soon realized
that I was being gloriously naive. I found that it, like the social sciences more generally, seemed to be filled with those
who were emotionally inclined to bite the Invisible Hand and
smart enough to find copious rationalizations for doing so.
Indeed, at the very first conference on evolutionary psychology
that I attended, at Carleton University in Ottawa in 2004, one
of the organizers suggested during his opening remarks that
Communism and capitalism were similarly "artificial" systems,
and that capitalism had been "invented" by Adam Smith.

When I pressed him, he admitted that he hadn't actually read
any Adam Smith. When I pressed him further, he suggested that

if he did lack knowledge of capitalism, it was because he had never been particularly interested in money. Just like Morrie. He did admit, however, that he found a lot to admire in Chinese Communism.

At the same conference I discovered that, in the 1970s, the then relatively new field of evolutionary biology and psychology had been torn apart by — of all things — its allegedly "pro-capitalist" leanings. The first shots had been fired after the 1975 publication of the Harvard biologist Edward O. Wilson's book *Sociobiology: The New Synthesis*, which defined a discipline devoted to "the systematic study of the biological basis of all social behaviour."

Sociobiology was mostly *not* about humans. Wilson's specialty was ants. However, the book's final chapter, as Ullica Segerstrale (who was also at the Carleton conference) noted in her own book *Defenders of the Truth*, "suggested that human sex role divisions, aggressiveness, moral concerns, religious beliefs, and much more, could be connected to our evolutionary heritage, as it is represented today in our underlying genetic dispositions."

Far from being revolutionary, this seemed to me merely obvious. Moreover, as *Defenders of the Truth* made clear, Wilson's was hardly the first book to root human behaviour in a biological context and suggest certain powerful, indeed possibly ineradicable tendencies. There had been, among others, Konrad Lorenz's *On Aggression*, Desmond Morris's *The Naked Ape*, Robert Ardrey's *The Territorial Imperative* and Lionel Tiger's *Men in Groups*.

The root of opposition to a neo-Darwinian perspective appeared to lie in the belief that it somehow *promoted* red-in-tooth-and-claw, dog-eat-dog selfishness, whose demonized avatar was capitalism. In the parody of Darwinism that emerged in the wake of *The Origin of Species*, life — including human life — was seen as all eat-or-be-eaten selfishness. However, many animals, including humans, also take actions that appear to benefit others at their own expense. How could the evolution of such characteristics be explained? Wilson embraced the view that reciprocity and mutual help weren't the result of reason, cultural enlightenment or social contracts; they were written into our genes.

This theory had been promoted and elaborated in particular by the British biologist William Hamilton (about whom Segerstrale would write a biography, *Nature's Oracle*). Seemingly "altruistic" behaviour, Hamilton noted, can emerge once you accept that the crucial element in evolution is not the individual organism but its genes. Hence "self sacrifice" for the sake of relatives (who carry a degree of the same genetic material) could be adaptive, in that it increased the chances of the *genes'* survival within the related human vehicles that helped each other.

According to Hamilton's theory, we are programmed to be concerned for our relatives' survival, and to make sacrifices for them, because it serves the interests of our common genes. This behaviour was subsequently dubbed "kin selection." It purports to explain why, as a rule, blood is thicker than water. But it is also part of a multi-level process of "inclusive fitness," which embraces the evolution of altruism toward non-relatives. Of course, in the hunter-gatherer environment pretty much everybody in the tribe was related, so merely helping those nearby was adaptive, although it paid genetically to aid closer relatives more.

In the late 1960s and 1970s, Bob Trivers, a graduate student at Harvard when he first met Hamilton, pointed out that apparently altruistic acts to non-relatives would be adaptive if the payoff was greater than the costs. Indeed, this appears tautological. However, the phrase he used for this concept, "reciprocal altruism," is somewhat confusing. For most people, altruism is taken to involve self-sacrifice without any payback. Reciprocal altruism, by contrast, is very much about paybacks; it requires and adaptively cultivates an acute sense of who pays back and who does not.

The essential evolutionary "selfishness" of Hamilton's and Trivers's theories, which were embraced by Wilson and promoted by another British biologist, Richard Dawkins, in his book *The Selfish Gene*, proved anathema to the academic left.

Ironically, however, Wilson considered himself left-leaning, as did Dawkins. Bob Trivers, for his part, was a rabid anti-capitalist who hung out with the radical group the Black Panthers. Indeed, one commentator noted, "Actually, a review of the politics of leading sociobiologists would lend more credence to the contention that sociobiology is a Communist conspiracy."

Wilson's and Dawkins's main opponents were the Harvard scientists Stephen Jay Gould and Richard Lewontin, both of whom were Marxists. Thus the sociobiology conflict was essentially between the left and the farther left. The farther left was traditionally much more keen on nurture than nature. They tended to play down the role of innate, hereditary human tendencies and stressed the primacy of culture, a perspective that pervaded social science departments more generally. It was crucial to their ideological view that man's fundamental nature could be changed for the better by social engineering.

Franz Boas, the father of modern anthropology, had been keen to establish that all ethnic groups possessed similar basic mental abilities, and that differences were due to culture. This quite reasonable assumption was perverted to suggest not merely that *differences* between cultures had to be explained in cultural terms, but that *everything* about human behaviour had to be explained in terms of culture.

Aggression and acquisitiveness, it was claimed, along with gender roles, were merely cultural conditioning and could be eradicated by the right (that is, left) social arrangements. Wilson dubbed this culture-based approach to human nature the "Standard Social Science Model." (It was the conceptual bedrock of *Tuesdays with Morrie*.)

Shortly after the publication of Wilson's book, a group of Boston-area academics called the Sociobiology Study Group —

many of whom were also Marxists — wrote a letter to the *New York Review of Books* portraying Wilson as an ideologue whose science supported the "capitalist status quo." Wilson was associated by his opponents with "conservative hereditarians" and tarred with the brush of Panglossian naïveté and/or genocidal racism.

The study group acknowledged that there might well be genetic components to human nature, but denied that there were any universal tendencies toward "warfare, sexual exploitation of women and the use of money as a medium of exchange." This was a very revealing collection of tendencies, since it linked "primitive" aggression and sexual exploitation with one of the most sophisticated and beneficial of human inventions (although one ritually demonized by the left, and perpetually undermined by the machinations of governments).

The tone of such groups, observed Segerstrale, "was one of righteous moral indignation at dangerous 'biological determinist' theories and their creators." At the 1978 meeting of the American Association for the Advancement of Science, protesters mounted the stage and doused Wilson with water, chanting, "Racist Wilson, you can't hide, we charge you with genocide." Dawkins too was accused of being a genetic "determinist," particularly since he wrote of humans as "lumbering robots" and "survival machines."

The biology and neurobiology professor Steven Rose, another Marxist and Dawkins's nemesis in England, accused Dawkins of believing in a "philanderer gene" that *excused* male infidelity. Dawkins responded, "I am not advocating a morality based on evolution," but his opponents weren't listening. Moreover, if one wanted to fault Dawkins, it would be not for his determinism but for exactly the opposite. *The Selfish Gene* concludes, "We have the power to defy the selfish genes of our birth and, if necessary, the selfish memes of our indoctrination." Dawkins had postulated "memes" as evolved carriers of cultural evolution, "thought packages" that found homes in our minds. "We are built as gene machines and cultured as meme machines, but we have the power to turn against our creators. We, alone on earth, can rebel against the tyranny of the selfish replicators."

The key question was just how far this rebellion could or should go. Dawkins was a popularizer of neo-Darwinist theories but no fan of what he imagined they implied. When Dawkins referred to Darwinism, he often seemed to have social Darwinism in mind, or at least its parody as a doctrine that the weak should be left to fend for themselves. That doctrine's most grotesque offshoot was claimed to be Nazi eugenics, but the greatest fans of eugenics early in the 20th century were on the left. Aldous Huxley's *Brave New World* was a devastating satire of such conceits.

Significantly, capitalism and fascism were often conflated by the left. In fact, the two were contradictory. The conceptual heart of the Smithian natural order is private property, voluntary relationships and free trade, whereas fascism is based on self-sacrifice (to the state), although a degree of private business ownership is permitted. Nazism was a contraction of the words "national socialism," not "national capitalism." Nevertheless, the fact that some private businesses continued to operate under fascism (and even in some cases to partner with it, for example by using prison camp labour, as in the case of the German company I.G. Farben) was eagerly taken by the left to mean that capitalism and fascism were congenial cooperators.

Dawkins claimed that we are "entitled to throw out Darwinism" in our social and political life, "to say we don't want to live in a Darwinian world. We may wish to live, say, in a socialist world *which is very un-Darwinian*" (my italics). It didn't seem to occur to Dawkins that a "socialist world" might be considered very Darwinian indeed, if that meant a world charged with righteous collectivist tribal morality and blind to the positive effects — both material and moral — of the novel system of free-market capitalism.

Dawkins claimed that genes generated only tendencies that could be overridden. True, but some tendencies are more difficult to override than others. "We, that is our brains, are separate and independent enough from our genes to rebel against them ... We do so in a small way every time we use contraception. There is no reason why we should not rebel in a large way, too." However, it depended, again, on exactly which "large way" you were considering. Changing human nature isn't quite as simple as slipping on a condom. As Robert Wright pointed out, no man would be comforted by the information that his wife had used contraception when having sex with her tennis instructor. Could Dawkins treat the prospect of his wife having protected sex with another man with equanimity? The fact that he almost certainly couldn't indicates that "rational" redesign of our moral sentiments might not be as easy as he suggested.

Dawkins's opponent Stephen Jay Gould believed even more strongly that "our biological nature does not stand in the way of social reform." But, yet again, this entirely depended on how you interpreted our biological nature, and what type of social reform you had in mind.

Tellingly, Steven Rose attempted to link William Hamilton's theories with Thatcherism. Rose described them as "part of the tide which has rolled the Thatcherites and their concept of a fixed, nineteenth century competitive and xenophobic human nature into power." Rose's linking of competition and xenophobia said far more about his own ideology than it did about Thatcherism. Dawkins found this link with "parochial" British politics "annoying," although he too — like most leftist intellectuals (remember Simon Schama) — regarded Thatcherism as "Darwinian." Indeed, Dawkins had claimed that society was "continuously vulnerable to what I would see as degeneration to naked, raw Darwinism — a kind of Thatcherite society, which I see as closer to Darwinism."

That a demonic view of capitalism was at the heart of the issue was confirmed by the Sociobiology Study Group member

Stephan Chorover, who wrote of a capitalist society in which "human beings [are] regarded as so much raw material to be manufactured, manipulated, marketed, or (if powerful interests desire it) discounted, discarded, or destroyed."

Both Wilson and Dawkins were in any case more than eager to distance themselves from capitalism. To those who suggested that Darwinism had "right-wing, conservative" implications, Dawkins kept pointing out, with obvious frustration, the "fact-value distinction": that "is" does not mean "ought." Asked why accusations of right-wing bias persisted, he said: "Because the opponents of sociobiology are too stupid to understand that distinction between what one says about the way the world is, scientifically, and the way it ought to be politically."

He clearly thought it ought to be "leftwards inclined," which raised many questions about his own unexamined assumptions. "Is" might not imply "ought," but the deeper philosophical and moral issues are exactly how we know what "is" is, and where "ought" originates.

—⁂—

One aspect of this debate that fascinated me was the part that wasn't even debated or acknowledged: how rapidly evolving social arrangements — capitalism in particular — might render certain moral assumptions redundant or counterproductive, but how certain people or groups might hang on to those assumptions not just through inertia or because they were morally satisfying, but because they were adaptively useful.

Dawkins saw himself as part of a crusade against "viruses of the mind," that is, "irrational" belief systems such as religion, but he appeared subject himself to one of the most pervasive of such viruses: a reflexive academic demonization of the capitalist "extended order" and those thought to be its champions. Dawkins's mind had clearly been "occupied" by many left-wing mental viruses, such as a tendency to demonize the robber barons. As noted earlier, these "robbers" brought enormous good to society. Nevertheless, it has traditionally been regarded as the mark of intellectual sophistication and public concern on the left to ritually denigrate these great public benefactors.

"Rockefeller," Dawkins told an interviewer, "an immensely rich and powerful man, had imported a form of Social Darwinism into his political beliefs. He really felt that the weak should go to the wall, and the strongest should survive; it was right in business, it was right in capitalism that the economically strongest and most ruthless should prevail."

In fact, Rockefeller was a highly religious man and a renowned philanthropist, not to mention one of the greatest business geniuses of all time. His business competitors certainly found him "ruthless," but his achievements included inventing the modern business organization and bringing cheap kerosene to the masses. Moreover, the important thing about capitalists is what they contribute in their area of business specialization and in their personal philanthropy, not what they think about how the wider world works, which can often be intellectually muddled or dangerously wrong, as in the case of Robert Owen and Friedrich Engels. More tendentiously muddled, however, was Dawkins's reflexive equation of capitalist success with "ruthlessness" rather than prudence, organization and empathy with the consumer. As Matt Ridley pointed out, the great thing about emergent innovative markets was that by winnowing out bad ideas, they enabled more people to live and thrive. Such a view was simply inconceivable to those who demonized the market perspective.

In his book *A Reason for Everything: Natural Selection and the English Imagination*, Marek Kohn noted Dawkins's reluctance to delve into the nature of morality, especially his own. Kohn pointed out that Dawkins had spent a couple of years teaching at Berkeley in California during the Hippie Sixties and had thrown himself into the politics of the time and place. "He was swept some way towards the left," wrote Kohn, "and the tide did not bring him all the way back when it receded."

Dawkins reportedly didn't believe in the usefulness of field trips for zoology, so he didn't believe they were necessary before making pronouncements on social arrangements. According to Kohn, "His politics are conducted similarly to his science. They are based on principles, and just as universal Darwinism does not require visits to other planets, they do not require personal experience of the countries in question. The view from Oxford is sufficiently clear."

This ivory tower approach made Dawkins uniquely vulnerable not merely to the alluring memes of capitalist demonization but also to the related "fatal conceit" that society was there to be comprehensively remade by intellectuals such as himself. This approach tended to be accompanied by extraordinary moral conviction. The origin of such economics-challenged and historically problematic convictions demanded analysis, but it was hardly likely to get any from those who were consumed by them. Intellectuals were obviously less than open to the notion that their ideas for social reform might be based on irrational commitment, economic ignorance, the attractions of moral posturing, subconscious power lust or any combination of these weaknesses.

Kohn remarked on Dawkins's "absence of reflection ... about the basis of morality in a godless universe. Dawkins takes right and wrong as given, but has very little to say about the nature of the giver. Morality is a given in his own thinking, not because he has worked it out through reason, but because his mental atmosphere is electric with moral sentiments. When he perceives unfairness, he feels it intensely." The example Dawkins provided of an unfairness that gave him "an almost visceral pain" was George W. Bush's 2000 presidential election victory over Al Gore. Surely, in the great sweep of history, this hardly ranked with Stalin's gulags, Hitler's Holocaust or Mao's Great Leap Forward.

When Kohn asked Dawkins about work on establishing that our brains had powerful moral mechanisms built into them, he reported that Dawkins seemed reluctant to go there: "It is a project he would rather leave to others, while he concentrates on the human capacity to rise above human nature." "For Dawkins," concluded Kohn, "the awful truth is that science is unbiased, the universe is pitiless, and Mother Nature is a discarnate Margaret Thatcher."

In fact, Dawkins would eventually claim to have been converted to belief in the possibility of the scientific analysis of morality. He didn't have to stray too far intellectually for his Damascene moment. He found it in a 2010 book, *The Moral Landscape*, by one of his fellow left-liberal militant atheists, Sam Harris.

Harris's assault on religion was vicious to the point of being deranged. For him, faith was all about stoning, acid in the face and 9/11. "The boundary between mental illness and respectable religious belief can be difficult to discern," he wrote. And faith wasn't just mental illness, it was part of a plot. "Because there are no easy remedies for social inequality, many scientists and public intellectuals also believe that the great masses of humanity are best kept sedated by pious delusions." This was a regurgitation of Marx's view of religion as the "opiate of the masses." It never occurred to Harris that those who assumed that "social inequality" was something to be "remedied" might also need to examine their own moral foundations.

He did not seem to notice that the greatest problems around the world at the time his book was published were attached to the unsustainability of left-liberalism's moral ideal of welfare state redistributionism. As far as he was concerned, the problem was that left-liberals had just been too shy about adopting an aggressive moral agenda. "Moral relativism" had left the way open to wicked believers.

Certainly, understanding the clash between religion and secular commercial society — from the murderous resentments caused by what the scholar Bernard Lewis called the "failure" of Islamic society, through the struggles of the Catholic church with medieval bank interest, to evangelicals' objections to stem cell research — was crucial, but Harris made only the most tangential reference to the mass murder and poverty brought about by the modern secular religion of Communism. He demonstrated no such restraint in giving vent to his anti-business and anti-conservative bias. "We have all met people who behave quite differently in business than in their personal lives," he wrote. "While they would never lie to their friends, they might lie without a qualm to their clients or customers."

One couldn't help wondering if Harris had ever actually met a businessman.

"There is also," he continued, "the question of whether conservatism contains an extra measure of cognitive bias — or outright hypocrisy — as the moral convictions of social conservatives are so regularly belied by their louche behavior." Harris generously admitted that liberalism might be "occluded by certain biases," but the only one he could find was anti-white racism (which obviously couldn't be condemned too harshly).

He blithely suggested that "science should increasingly enable us to answer specific moral questions. For instance, would it be better to spend our next billion dollars eradicating racism or malaria." But his question led to much bigger ones: first, on what moral basis did Harris imagine that he and his fellow *bien pensants* were free to take (yet another) billion dollars of money earned by others; and second, why did grand top-down schemes fail in the past? (One significant reason why malaria was still so prevalent was the demonization and banning of DDT as the result of Rachel Carson's *Silent Spring*.)

"We must build our better selves into our laws, tax codes, and institutions," wrote Harris, boldly placing himself on the side of the (secular) angels. He appeared extraordinarily blind to the fact that what actually got built into laws, tax codes and institutions tended to be the self-interest of politicians, bureaucrats, government consultants and politically favoured businesses.

If Harris had wanted to address the gap between moral intention and perverse result, he might have looked at policies such as minimum wages and rent controls, but he didn't. Indeed, perhaps the biggest and most telling gap in Harris's perspective was that he seemed to have no comprehension of — or interest in — economics. The view from moral conviction, like the view from Dawkins's Oxford, was sufficiently clear.

Dawkins lavished praise on Harris's book. "I was one of those who had unthinkingly bought into the hectoring myth that science can say nothing about morals," he wrote. This was rather bizarre since he had himself been a prime promoter of such hectoring mythology. Nevertheless he claimed that *The Moral Landscape* had opened his eyes and promised to open those of other intellectuals. "Moral philosophers, too, will find their world exhilaratingly turned upside down, as they discover a need to learn some neuroscience."

Within a few months of the publication of Harris's book, Dawkins would be proved right, although not quite as exhilaratingly as he had imagined.

—m—

Early in 2011, the issue of academic bias in the study of human nature erupted once more. During a talk at the annual meeting of the Society for Personality and Social Psychology in San Antonio, Texas, Jonathan Haidt, a University of Virginia psychologist, asked how many of the thousand or so academics present considered themselves "conservatives."

Three hands went up.

Haidt pointed out that social psychologists obsess about representational skewing due to racism or sexism, and yet the virtual absence of conservatives among them was not even considered an issue. This, he suggested, was both remarkable and dangerous. Social psychologists were in danger of becoming a "tribal moral community" embracing "sacralized values" that might undermine objective research. Those sacralized values were overwhelmingly those of the liberal left, of which Haidt considered himself a member.

Haidt gave examples of how objectivity had been abandoned in the face of political correctness. Research into issues such as destructive aspects of black culture or possible genetic reasons for the absence of women in the highest reaches of math and science had become taboo. The economist and former U.S. Treasury secretary Larry Summers had been hounded from the presidency of Harvard for mouthing the latter heresy. "We psychologists should have been outraged by the outrage," said Haidt. "We should have defended his right to think freely."

Haidt's talk was respectfully received at the time, but when it was subsequently reported in the *New York Times*, it became a "dirty laundry" issue and provoked a backlash from angry fellow left-liberals, who suggested that if conservatives were "underrepresented" in academe, it was because they just weren't smart, curious, educated or open-minded enough.

The definition of "conservatism" shares some of the wildly fuzzy characteristics of the definition of "capitalism": everything but the kitchen sink can be tossed in. The members of the Soviet politburo in the 1980s were dubbed "conservatives," as are the current mullahs of radical Islam, so "conservative" is hardly synonymous with understanding or supporting capitalism. It depends entirely on what you are trying to conserve.

Adam Smith's truly conservative friend Edmund Burke, at the time of the French Revolution, had warned about the dangers of trying to remake society on "rational" principles. The Reign of Terror and the rise of Napoleon had amply confirmed his fears. Over the ensuing 200 years, conservatism broadly morphed as a political movement into an opponent of, and then merely a brake on, the long march of radicalism, which bred both Communism and modern democracy.

In his book *The Constitution of Liberty*, published in 1960, Hayek, one of the greatest proponents of liberty and capitalism, wrote a chapter titled "Why I Am Not a Conservative." He pointed out that Burkean opposition to rationalist conceits had transmogrified after the Second World War into something that Burke would not recognize: a willingness to go along with the advance of statism in the forms of economic "management," welfarism, protectionism and even state ownership.

It was this version of conservatism that came under attack by Prime Minister Margaret Thatcher, who, while nominally a conservative, was far more of a revolutionary against the statist status quo. She was, however, also a very firm believer in the "traditional" values of individual responsibility, family and community, and she was anything but xenophobic when it came to appreciating the material benefits and benign influence of global free trade.

Conservatism is thus a broad and complex term, like "the right," which is applied to a wide spectrum, from evangelicals who believe that the Bible is literally true to libertarians who embrace atheism and challenge tradition at every turn. Neither group tends to be overrepresented in the mainstream academic community.

Haidt's controversial claim in San Antonio was that his corner of social science might have been "broken" by left-liberal bias. "My research," he said, "like so much research in social psychology, demonstrates that we humans are experts at using reasoning to find evidence for whatever conclusions we want to reach. We are terrible at searching for contradictory evidence."

One of Haidt's declared objectives was to seek a truce in the culture wars raging in the United States by suggesting that the two sides were arguing past each other, since they adopted different weightings of moral dimensions. However, the difference between left and right is not merely a matter of a different moral weighting. It represents different interpretations of the most fundamental of moral issues, such as what constitutes "harm" and "fairness."

Haidt reopened sociobiology's can of worms and returned attention to what Darwinism and neo-Darwinism might have to tell us about our moral sentiments.

—w—

Adam Smith had postulated God as a "moral architect," but Smith's view that the moral sentiments might have been "designed" by the Creator to enable sociability didn't lead him to deny that the Creator's specifications were often far from perfect. Indeed, man might be the "moral animal," but the dark side of morality — which was displayed when "faction and fanaticism," that is, politics and religion, came into play — made him far more deadly than any other of God's creatures.

What light could Darwinism shed on these complex, conflicted sentiments? Darwin followed Hume and Smith in positing a moral sensibility that had co-evolved with social values and thus helped determine them. "Ultimately," he concluded in *The Descent of Man*, "our moral sense or conscience becomes a highly complex sentiment — originating in the social instincts, largely guided by the approbation of our fellow-men, ruled by reason, self-interest, and in later times by deep religious feelings, and confirmed by instruction and habit."

Morality was thus — as Hume and Smith had suggested — primarily a matter of *feelings*, a set of evolved emotional inclinations combined with a structured mental *capacity* to absorb values that have themselves evolved within the societies into which we are born and by which we are "socialized." Moral intuition is rooted in the logic of biological survival within a social setting.

That morality goes back deep into our evolutionary past is indicated by the fact that our closest relatives, the chimpanzees, display signs of what appears like moral behaviour. In *Good Natured: The Origins of Right and Wrong in Humans and Other Animals*, the primatologist Frans de Waal maintained that "evolution needs to be part of any satisfactory explanation of morality ... The fact that the human moral sense goes so far back in evolutionary history that other species show signs of it plants morality firmly near the center of our much-maligned nature. It is neither a recent innovation nor a thin layer that covers a beastly and selfish makeup ... It takes up space in our heads, it reaches out to fellow human beings, and it is as much a part of what we are as the tendencies that it holds in check."

De Waal also stressed that the tendency to moralize is pervasive. "The desire to dictate the behaviour of others is such a timeless and universal attribute of our species," he wrote, "that it must rank with the sex drive, maternal instinct, and the will to survive in terms of the likelihood of it being part of our biological heritage."

Darwin had confirmed that morality had a darker side, which lay in the importance for group solidarity of a willingness, even eagerness, to demonize outsiders and apostates, and to wage war. In *The Biology of Moral Systems*, Richard Alexander suggested that the ultimate roots of such morality lay in the adaptive value of living in larger and larger groups. Expanding group size was promoted by effectiveness in defence, not against wild animals but against other human groups. Alexander theorized that intergroup aggression led to an "arms race" of larger and larger social units, whose internal cohesion depended on adopting moral rules that enabled their members to restrain their selfish tendencies in order to live together, but to be united against and deadly toward opponents. Thus they were a key aspect of Hamilton's "inclusive fitness" in the broadest sense.

In the period of prehistory and through most of history, an emphasis on acting for the "common good" was essential to group survival in a world of intergroup predation. The flip side of internal cohesion was the tendency to demonize the "other." This helps explain the "us-and-them" orientation of human beings, and why we tend to apply different moral standards to the "in group" and the "out group." "Thou shalt not kill" was a commandment that applied only to members of your own "tribe." It certainly didn't apply to enemies. The ultimate expressions of tribal "morality" are genocide and, more recently, suicide bombing.

One of the great 20th-century students of morality and its fraught relationship with capitalism was Friedrich Hayek. Hayek was rare in bringing both a mastery of economics and an evolutionary perspective to the conundrum of why anti-capitalism — in the form of socialism — was both so attractive and so flawed as a social arrangement. For Hayek, as he laid out in his last book, *The Fatal Conceit: The Errors of Socialism*, the basic question was this: "How does our morality emerge, and what implications may its mode of coming into being have for our economic and political life?"

Hayek acknowledged the critical role of Adam Smith in analyzing the enormous cultural changes that elements of mankind were bringing about without any grand plan. "Adam Smith," wrote Hayek, "was the first to perceive that we have stumbled upon methods of ordering human economic cooperation that exceed the limits of our knowledge and perception." Those new methods inevitably clashed with more slowly changing moral values, which had often become embodied in religion, but which were present even among those who felt themselves free of religious "superstition."

One reason that moral sentiments are slow to change is that they are adaptively "designed" so that people believe them to represent transcendent values. For the moral sense to prove most effective, man cannot believe that it is a utilitarian trick played by evolution (even if he believes in evolution). Indeed, it is best, in evolutionary terms, for him not even to countenance such beliefs. To be most effective, the moral sense had to evolve so as *not to question* its own origins or validity, or the beliefs to which it adheres. Morality works best as a motivator if we believe that we are espousing "absolute" values or — in a scientific age — acting on the basis of undeniable objective "truths." Even moral relativists tend to be profoundly morally committed to their moral relativism.

One of the reasons why religion evolved was perhaps to cater to the adaptive sense that moral values are "carved in stone." Moses may have brought the Ten Commandments down from the mountain, but they had been evolving through myriad generations. Moreover, the tablets were far more than merely a trick to back up a set of socially useful behaviours with a little divine sanction. To see religion as merely a set of fairy tales, or an instrument of social sedation or control, is to miss how the concept of God fits with the evolved usefulness of moral certainty.

Religion has been under attack since the Enlightenment, and the horrors of religious extremism are still evident today. But religion — as the guardian and promoter of morality — served a crucial purpose in the evolution of civilization, and in fact still serves such a purpose in its more tolerant varieties. As Smith pointed out, "Religion, even in its crudest form, gave a sanction to the rules of morality long before the age of artificial reasoning and philosophy."

Hayek quotes Sir James Frazer, who, in *Psyche's Task*, pointed out that "superstition rendered a great service to humanity. It supplied multitudes with a motive, a wrong motive it is true, for right action; and surely it is better for the world that men should do right for wrong motives than that they would do wrong with the best intentions. What concerns society is conduct, not opinion: if only our actions are just and good, it matters not a straw to others whether our opinions are mistaken."

But what is "just and good"? And how might our views of these concepts differ between individuals and groups, and change over time? "God" reflects not only our adaptive sense of moral permanence but also morality's dark side. When the Israelite God dealt with the tribe's enemies, or sinners, He worked through smiting, drowning, and fire and brimstone.

Steven Pinker wryly describes the Ten Commandments as "the great moral code that outlaws engraved images and the coveting of livestock but gives a pass to slavery, rape, torture, mutilation, and genocide of neighbouring tribes." Today some fundamentalist Muslims regard it as the purest religious devotion to throw acid into the faces of little girls whose parents want them to be educated, or to shout "God is great" before incinerating or beheading other infidels.

Religion in Adam Smith's world was a great cause of civil strife and foreign war. The conundrum of how to persuade different denominations — in his time, Catholics and Protestants — to cohabit peacefully consumed political theorists and philosophers. The attacks of 9/11 and their aftermath brought the concept of religious war back into the limelight and made it easier to understand the concerns of Enlightenment philosophers.

What was intriguing was how many people in the West seemed inclined to believe that the most spectacular of all suicide bombing attacks might have some justification in the alleged inequities and depredations of capitalism. By contrast, Smith and many of his intellectual predecessors and contemporaries — such as Montesquieu and Voltaire — favoured the idea of commercial society because they believed that people tended to get along far better when they were trading and making money than when they were obsessing about salvation for themselves and damnation for their enemies.

As William Robertson, another figure of the Scottish Enlightenment, put it: "Commerce tends to wear off those prejudices which maintain distinction and animosity between nations. It softens and polishes the manners of men. It unites them, by one of the strongest of all ties, the desire of supplying their mutual wants. It disposes them to peace, by establishing in every state an order of citizens bound by their interest to be the guardians of public tranquility. As soon as the commercial spirit gains ... an ascendant in any society, we discover a new genius in its policy, its alliances, its wars, and its negotiations." A more succinct recent summary of this theory is offered by Robert Wright: "Among the many reasons I don't think we should bomb the Japanese is that they built my minivan."

Commercial society certainly doesn't preclude religious belief. Indeed, Max Weber argued that the "Protestant ethic," with its emphasis on saving and prudence, was essential to the rise of modern capitalism. Religion is necessary for many individuals, and as long as it doesn't cause them to fly airplanes into buildings, it can be a highly positive and cohesive force. Marxism demonstrated what can happen when you set up a secular alternative: tens of millions of corpses. And yet Marxist anti-capitalist "moral" perspectives persist to an astonishing degree in the academic community.

—w—

In his book *The Righteous Mind: Why Good People Are Divided by Politics and Religion*, Jonathan Haidt reiterated that his goal was to "drain some of the heat, anger, and divisiveness" out of the culture wars. He admitted that this was much more easily recommended than achieved. The problem, he suggested, is that our rational mind is like a small, somewhat conscious rider on a very large subconscious elephant. The rider doesn't guide the elephant, he acts as its press secretary, justifying what the elephant wants to do, and all the while imagining it was all his own idea. The elephant calls the shots, and the rider, while he imagines he is acting rationally, is "blinded" to alternatives and "bound" to those riding similar elephants, who find themselves travelling with the intellectual herd.

Haidt's take-home message for his fellow left-liberals — perhaps signifying his olive branch to the religious right — was from the Bible: take the log out of your own eye before concerning yourself with the specks of dust in the eyes of others. No advice could be more philosophically sound, and none harder to execute.

Haidt admitted that left-liberals had traditionally treated market-oriented conservatism as a mental disorder. He described his own growing doubts about such a characterization, which had come easily to him as the Yale-educated child of Jewish progressive parents.

He noted that left and right coalesced around differing visions of human nature. This "conflict of visions" goes back to at least the 17th century and is based on differing views of human perfectibility and the role of political power in bringing it about. The "constrained" or "tragic" vision — traditionally associated with the right — is of an inevitably flawed humanity that needs laws and institutions to keep it, and particularly its political elements, in check. It suggests that we should be perpetually on guard against the corrupting influence of power. It is reflected in the deliberate creation of counterbalance in the U.S. system's separation of political powers. The "unconstrained" vision — traditionally associated with the left — is of man as a perfectible creature whose nature can be changed for the better by wholesale institutional reform masterminded by intelligent and well-intended leaders.

While both sides believe in the importance of rules and institutions, the unconstrained view tends to imagine that all rules and institutions — and even human nature itself — can be remade by human intelligence, and that those who make these rules will not be corrupted by power. Such an orientation tends to not even countenance the possibility that the fundamental motivation of those who promote the unconstrained vision is power itself.

Haidt admitted that, as a moral psychologist, he had been led to change his views at least partly by the revelations of new sciences such as evolutionary psychology, which confirmed the insights of Hume and Smith. "When [Hume] died in 1776," wrote Haidt, "he and other sentimentalists had laid a superb foundation for 'moral science,' one that has, in my view, been largely vindicated by modern research ... [But] in the decades after Hume's death the rationalists claimed victory over religion and took the moral sciences off on a two-hundred-year tangent."

Haidt pointed to the irony that in a field in which it was essential to grasp the power of human emotion, two of the most influential moral philosophers after Hume and Smith — Jeremy Bentham and Immanuel Kant — were autistic. Bentham had suggested that the route to the good lay in utilitarian mathematics, using a "felicific calculus" to determine "the greatest good of the greatest number." Kant had said the key to morality lay in "deontological rights," which had to be accessed through the logic of the "categorical imperative" — by subjecting our actions to rigid analysis on the basis of whether they were universally applicable.

Significantly, both Bentham and Kant came before Darwin, whose theory of evolution was, Haidt suggested, the most powerful tool for analyzing the design of all living things — including humans — ever discovered. Haidt subscribed to the Darwinian view (as refined by the likes of Richard Alexander) that morality was an aspect of "group selection," and posited, "Early humans domesticated themselves when they began to select friends and partners based on their ability to live within the tribe's moral matrix." He emphasized the importance of religion for embodying moral systems. "Gods and religions ... are group-level adaptations for producing cohesiveness and trust."

Haidt compared our moral sense to our sense of taste, in that we have a number of different "receptors." He divided these broadly into concerns about harm, fairness, loyalty, authority, and sanctity, or purity. These receptors, he claimed, evolved in response to five original adaptive "triggers": caring for children;

the benefits of cooperation; the advantages of group solidarity; the need for hierarchy to avoid conflict; and avoiding contaminants. Haidt claimed that the main difference between left and right was that the left tended to be obsessed with harm and fairness, while the right had a more "balanced" level of concern across the five categories.

I certainly believe that Haidt was, and is, well-intended. The problem was that he still seemed to be carrying around much of the reflexive left-liberal baggage that (a) was blind to the Invisible Hand or claimed that its proponents were "fundamentalists"; and (b) tended to demonize "powerful" and allegedly feckless corporations as the justification for the "countervailing power" of big government, despite the fact that big government had historically been tyrannical, inept or both.

Haidt suggested in *The Righteous Mind* that "libertarians sometimes have a quasi-religious faith in free markets." However, while libertarians may indeed tend to have a bit too much faith in the power of reason to convert their opponents, their support for markets and their caution about trying to improve them are usually rooted not in mystical commitment but in conceptual appreciation and historical evidence. While Randian rationalism might itself be "blind," to write off proponents of free markets as "quasi-religious" or "fundamentalist" suggests that Haidt hadn't grasped the Invisible Hand. But, as noted, that hardly made him rare in his field.

A few years ago, on a visit to the website of the Human Behavior and Evolution Society, one of the main associations of evolutionary biologists, I found a page promoting peak oil theory and other neo-Malthusian anti-economic canards as indisputable sources of worry, to which HBES members should devote their attention. It had been posted by the website's editor. I contacted him and laid out why I thought fashionable analogies to reindeer population collapses and the fate of Easter Island were inappropriate. No civilization, I pointed out, had ever collapsed from being too capitalistic. In the end, the academic disengaged by saying that he hoped I was right, and that this was one debate he would be glad to lose.

Leda Cosmides and John Tooby are among the most brilliant of evolutionary psychologists, but in their 1994 article "Better Than Rational: Evolutionary Psychology and the Invisible Hand," they arguably confused a critical issue by claiming that natural selection was an "invisible-hand process." While this appeared superficially analogous to Matt Ridley's "Adam Darwin" claims that both biology and market processes were emergent, Cosmides and Tooby concluded that "economic theory can increasingly be grounded in the theoretically and empirically derived models of human decision-making machinery that are presently being constructed within evolutionary psychology." But you can't reduce an understanding of the emergent market to an analysis of human psychology. Understanding economics requires *transcending* reflexive psychological assumptions and concentrating — as Ludwig von Mises emphasized — not on the psychological roots of human action but on the action itself, which tends to be remarkably consistent, and on its systemic consequences, which tend to be not just beyond, but counter to, the intuitions of economic actors.

Of course, classical economics does imply certain things about human nature, and about its consistent reactions to commercial incentives and penalties. It says that taxation and welfare are both likely to reduce effort. It says that minimum wages will put poor people out of work. It says that rent controls will lead to less rental accommodation. None of these messages is amenable to a redistributionist mentality that assumes that "fairness" is based on the Robin Hood morality of taking from the rich and giving to the poor. Robin Hood — if he existed at all — lived in very different times.

What really required analysis by evolutionary psychologists — or so it increasingly appeared to me — was the "natural" misunderstanding and moral condemnation of markets. Cosmides and Tooby were on the right track in pointing out that analyzing mental structures would make it easier to understand why some ideas grab us more than others, but they didn't include failure to grasp the Invisible Hand as an example.

Other leading evolutionary psychologists not merely failed to understand the nature of markets, they continued to castigate capitalism on moral grounds. Richard Dawkins was one obvious example. Another, even more extreme, was Robert Trivers. In his 2011 book *The Folly of Fools: The Logic of Deceit and Self-Deception in Human Life*, Trivers indulged in a good deal of self analysis, but that didn't extend to the roots of his own rabid, '60s-style anti-capitalism. Indeed, he demonized "traditional economics" even as he made clear that he did not understand it.

In the book, which was dedicated to his friend Huey Newton, the Black Panther leader, Trivers equated capitalism with deception and condemned economics as lacking a "biological" basis. He wrote, "I have disagreed for thirty years with an alleged science called economics that has absolutely failed to ground itself in underlying knowledge, at a cost to all of us."

Trivers ranted about "the harmful effects of unrestrained economic egotism by those already at the top." He displayed a crude, demonize-the-rich, zero-sum mentality. "Are the wealthy unfairly increasing their share of resources at the expense of the rest of us (as has surely been happening) or are the wealthy living under an onerous system of taxation and regulation?" he asked. He examined "false historical narratives," but when it came to the most murderously delusional narrative of the 20th century, Communism, Trivers said only that the Soviets "provided a counterweight to rapacious capitalism."

Frans de Waal, whose writings on primates and morality I had greatly enjoyed and admired, nevertheless provided a telling example of the "unreflecting centralism" that was a key part of David Henderson's do-it-yourself economics in the introduction to his book *Good Natured*. He claimed that economists were getting used to the idea "that free market economies can be beaten at their own game by guided economies such as that of the Japanese." By the time his book was published, in 1996, the myth of Japan's statist success, with allegedly brilliant bureaucrats guiding private trade and investment, had already been exploded. Indeed, the Japanese economy would still be stagnant 17 years later.

In 2013, I got in touch with de Waal to ask him how he now regarded his previous assessment of Japan. He responded almost immediately, "As you know, I am no economist. I am less sure about top-down guided economies now, but since 2008 also less sure about deregulation. I think most economies fall somewhere in between, even in the U.S."

This reply was at least as fascinating as his 1996 statement, not least because it indicated that he regarded the fact that he was "no economist" as no reason not to continue to wade into economic policy issues. He was now "less sure" about top-down guided economies but also "less sure" about deregulation. It didn't seem to occur to him that his views on regulation — and deregulation — might be every bit as misguided as his earlier views on the reasons for Japan's economic performance. He was certainly right that all economies were "mixed," but this said nothing about which parts of the mix worked and which didn't, and why we might have trouble differentiating.

Then again, de Waal and Trivers were in many ways merely reflecting the conventional wisdom of leading popular economists. Trivers's main authority seemed to be the left-liberal Nobel prizewinner Paul Krugman, the man who had dubbed free-market enthusiasts supporters of "greedism."

Meanwhile a new branch of the dismal science had arrived on the scene that claimed to apply the insights of evolutionary psychology to market actors. It didn't appear any more enthusiastic about free markets than Keynesianism. Needless to say, its promoters were eagerly recruited as advisors by governments. It was called behavioural economics.

twelve

Homer Economicus

"D'oh!"

— Homer Simpson

B ehavioural economics became hot in the early years of the 21st century. It offered such non-astonishing insights as that human beings are not wealth-maximizing robots; that they procrastinate and lack self-control; that they behave with "irrational exuberance" one minute, then like Chicken Little the next; that they fail to pursue consistent long-term strategies; that they get obsessed by sunk costs (and are thus unwilling to abandon losing investments); and that, when they gamble, they get the odds all wrong.

This "new" field was rooted in the psychology of decision-making, particularly in financial markets. It was pioneered by the psychologists Daniel Kahneman and Amos Tversky. The insights they developed were called "prospect theory" and revolved around attitudes toward gains and losses, which often tended to depart from objective probabilities. Humans, they noted, are "loss averse": that is, they are inclined to value the loss of a unit of something more than the gain of a unit of the same thing. This is hardly surprising; indeed, it is implicit in the economic theory of marginal utility. Other things being equal, somebody who wants, and has, two loaves of bread is likely to place more value on a loaf being taken away than on a third loaf. Only an extraterrestrial — or an academic — might find that a novel idea.

In 2002, Kahneman won an economics Nobel Prize for his insights, which were laid out in a 2012 book, *Thinking, Fast and Slow*. We are, declared Kahneman, born to "jump to conclusions" on the basis of the most recent information, the "availability heuristic." We reconfigure the past through the "narrative fallacy," which manufactures nice tidy stories. We tell ourselves — via "hindsight bias" — that we knew what would happen all along. When it comes to guesses and decisions about issues or topics with which we are unfamiliar, we are influenced to an alarming degree by randomly generated numbers — the "anchoring effect." Similarly, subjects can be unconsciously primed to influence their thoughts and actions. For example, students involved in a study on the aged subsequently walked more slowly: the "Florida effect." Kahneman also identified an "affect heuristic," a rather grandiose name for the simple fact that likes and dislikes strongly influence our beliefs.

Kahneman made clear that his target was not human irrationality per se but what he called the "rational agent model," which he claimed had led economics astray. Kahneman's own "affect heuristic" made him particularly averse to the beliefs of Milton Friedman's Chicago School, which he claimed had a "hard edge." Not only were these free marketers naive, they lacked the milk of human kindness.

According to Kahneman, the rational agent model promoted the notion that people are "Econs," which was the behavioural economist Richard Thaler's shorthand for *Homo economicus*, that purely rational and selfish straw man that had long been a favourite for those seeking to rationalize government intervention. However, economics is based not on people being perfectly rational but on the systemic consequences of their actions, no matter what motivates them. It is the Invisible Hand that is "rational," dispensing bouquets and brickbats in accordance with how ingeniously, assiduously and efficiently participants pursue their own interests by serving the interests of others. Thus Kahneman flaunted intellectual superiority over non-existent foes when he declared that "life is more complex for behavioral economists than for true believers in human rationality." Like all those Keynesians who pooh-poohed the numbskulls who believed that people were rational and markets perfect, he didn't actually identify any "true believers."

Adam Smith, of course, had been all too aware that humans were irrational. Moreover, Kahneman's hoary claim that irrationality undermined free-market economics had been refuted by Ludwig von Mises more than 60 years earlier in his classic book *Human Action*: "The most popular objection raised against economics is that it neglects the irrationality of life and reality and tries to press into dry rational schemes and bloodless abstractions the infinite variety of phenomena. No censure could be more absurd. Like every branch of knowledge economics goes as far as it can be carried by rational methods. Then it stops by establishing the fact that it is faced with an ultimate given, i.e. the phenomenon which cannot — at least in the present state of knowledge — be further analyzed."

Milton Friedman, like Mises, observed that economics is not about individual psychology but about group behaviour. The economist Armen Alchian pointed out that not only do markets not need to be populated by rational maximizers, they don't even require individuals to be self-aware beyond pursuing their own interests. The market would still favour those who happened to come up with profitable ideas or allocate resources more efficiently. This perspective was reflected by Matt Ridley in his lecture "Adam Darwin," where he noted that both biology and markets worked on the basis of "tinkering" and "natural selection" by the relevant biological or market environment.

Kahneman posited that people have two mental systems: System 1, our "fast" intuition, which seeks stories to integrate into its world view, and System 2, the "slow," more logical and laborious process of deliberate reasoning. He said that System 1 is usually in charge. System 2 is lazy. Economic understanding requires System 2's logic and analysis, but that requires effort, which System 1 would rather not make.

Intriguingly, Kahneman did not address the fact that System 1 seems designed to reflexively — and hypocritically — reject the pursuit of self-interest (at least by others) as "selfishness" — the *Tuesdays with Morrie* effect. Nor did he suggest that it is easy and satisfying for System 1, with its desire for simple narratives, to fall for tales of an oppressive and greedy "1 per cent" of wealthy capitalists — the Occupy Wall Street effect — rather than coming to grips with the counterintuitive fact that it is only in the process of the 1 per cent becoming rich that much of the economic good for the 99 per cent is generated.

Reflecting his own biases, Kahneman appeared particularly keen to bring investment advisors and corporate leaders down to size, but while Kahneman was right that a chimp with a dartboard might indeed be able to beat a professional stock picker (one of the real insights of the much-maligned efficient markets hypothesis), his implication that you might be able to replace most chief executives with the janitor was implausible, to say the least. Certainly, there is much luck in corporate success, and corporate executives may benefit from a "halo effect." Also, many takeovers may be driven by managerial hubris, but if that happens, markets will provide comeuppance.

Kahneman noted the "planning fallacy" on the part of entrepreneurs who discounted the skills of other innovators, neglected their own ignorance and demonstrated an "illusion of control." But if mere business planning faced so many pitfalls, how nonsensical was the notion that governments could plan at a pan-economic or even global level? Corporate errors tended to be subject to swift market retribution. By contrast, not only could the consequences of policy errors drag on for years, but the same errors tended to be committed again and again out of a combination of political self-interest and economic incomprehension.

Behavioural economists, however, seemed resolutely uninterested in the psychological roots beneath the repetition of policy errors. Instead they claimed that personal quirks undermined "traditional economics" and thus justified more government intervention, which they called — with an Orwellian contradiction in terms — "libertarian paternalism."

Richard Thaler had accumulated a long list of allegedly "anomalous" behaviours. For example, some cab drivers set themselves a dollar target for a day's work, thus driving fewer hours when business was good, and more when business was bad. Thaler claimed this practice flouted "economic logic." Then there was the occasion when guests at Thaler's house couldn't stop eating from a bowl of cashews and thanked him for removing it, thus allegedly undermining the notion that freedom and choice are always good. A friend of Thaler admitted that he'd mow his own lawn to save $10 but wouldn't mow his neighbour's lawn for $10. Thaler also found out that people would cross town to save $10 on a clock-radio, but not $10 on a big-screen TV. Made no sense. Shouldn't a $10 saving be a $10 saving?

However, such trivial examples in no way refuted "economic logic" because there is no economic logic, outside of people acting according to their own needs and wants, which usually incorporate far more than financial calculation. For example, taxi drivers might drive longer on nice days simply because it's more pleasant. Whatever motivates them, it's their actions that count.

Other examples that the behavioural economists claimed to be "troubling" to conventional economic theory were similarly trivial. These included the "endowment effect," whereby people who acquired a mug in a laboratory game valued it more highly than those who didn't have the mug. So what? Did this undermine free trade or the logic of the division of labour? Did minimum wages and rent controls suddenly work after all? Were the theories that governments could borrow and spend economies back to health, or concoct effective industrial policies, thus validated?

Behavioural interventionists eagerly seized on the — again unstartling — facts that some people procrastinated in planning for their retirement, or failed to buy medical insurance, as prima facie evidence that the nanny state was needed, not so much to mastermind grand economic strategies as to produce beneficial little "nudges" to appropriate behaviour. Indeed, the bible of libertarian paternalism, published in 2008, was titled *Nudge*.

Co-authored by Thaler and another academic, the legal scholar Cass Sunstein, *Nudge* was subtitled *Improving Decisions about Health, Wealth, and Happiness.* Thaler and Sunstein claimed that since all choices are made within particular contexts, or "frames," policy-makers are obliged to become "choice architects," subtly rigging environments to stop people from making the "wrong" decisions. After all, didn't the private sector do much the same thing (although without such noble motives) by arranging products on supermarket shelves? According to *Nudge*, "Governments can get in on the act, too."

As evidence, the authors related — in an example whose bizarre triviality you could not make up — how Dutch airport authorities had reduced urinal spillage by 80 per cent by etching "target" flies into the porcelain. Given the right policy incentives, claimed Thaler and Sunstein, we could all learn to pee straight(er).

Kahneman's practical suggestions for "nudging" also looked a little trivial. For example, he wanted legislation to thwart the hidden persuaders by ensuring that products labelled "90 per cent fat free" had also to be labelled "10 per cent fat." The bigger problem was that once the idea of nudging took hold, there was no end to the initiatives that might be undertaken. Instead of labelling products "10 per cent fat," or forcing the display of voluminous small-print nutritional details in fast food restaurants (one of New York mayor Michael Bloomberg's favourite pieces of paternalism, along with his attempt to make large soda drinks illegal), why not address the obesity crisis by legislating full-length mirrors around all-you-can-eat buffets?

Knowledge of human nature is of course essential to making productive investment and good public policy, but the most astonishing aspect of behavioural economics as a policy tool was that it entirely missed the elephant in the room. This fact was beautifully exemplified by an article that Thaler wrote in the *New York Times* in 2009.

"This column is in praise of warning labels," Thaler began. "So let's begin with one: I am not your usual sort of economist." He then boldly knocked down the straw men of pure economic rationality. Such characters, according to Thaler, "are amazingly smart and are free of emotion, distraction or self-control problems. Think Mr. Spock from 'Star Trek.'"

Of course, like Kahneman, Thaler didn't name anybody who actually believed that such Spock-like characters existed, but his straw Vulcan was necessary to set up his own brilliant insight that "real people have trouble balancing their checkbooks, much less calculating how much they need to save for retirement; they sometimes binge on food, drink or high-definition televisions." Then came the insult piled atop the obvious: "They are more like Homer Simpson than Mr. Spock. Call them Homer economicus if you like, or just Humans." In other words, ordinary people were pretty much morons who needed superior intellects such as Thaler to tell them how to tie their economic shoelaces.

Thaler suggested that designing policies for Vulcans would be pretty easy: "The best policies give them as many choices as possible and simply assure that they have access to all the relevant information." So not only could you not trust markets to come up with multiple choices, you couldn't even trust Mr.

Spock to look after his own interests without a little government arm twisting, hand holding and calorie counting.

However, when it came to protecting the benighted Homers of the world, Thaler wanted lots of newly empowered bureaucrats standing around the open doors of empty stables. Take mortgages, for example, which had been at the heart of the subprime crisis. Thaler noted that mortgage documents were filled with awfully complicated details about things like interest rates and prepayment penalties. "How," asked the paternalistic professor, "can we help people make sense of all this?"

I have a suggestion: what about people actually reading the terms and conditions before they sign anything? What about government not encouraging — or forcing — lenders to make loans to people who can't understand mortgages, and who are naive enough to believe that government is looking after them?

Nah.

Thaler suggested that the state could "ban complex mortgages entirely," although he admitted this might choke off innovation. "A better approach," he wrote, "is to strive for maintaining diverse options by helping consumers make smart choices and avoid the most common pitfalls." So apparently the U.S. administration would sit the collective consumer down on its capacious knee, while lenders would be required to offer good old "plain vanilla" mortgages for the Homers of the world. To get anything more exotic, "borrowers might have to demonstrate that they understand the risks or have been aided by a certified mortgage planner." Certified like, say, the ratings agencies that had handed out AAA status to steaming packages of toxic mortgage crap?

But I still haven't got to that elephant. Thaler cited Homer Simpson as the typical klutz who needed government to save him from himself, but if Thaler wanted to call on the cartoon town of Springfield as the model community for justifying his Brave New World, shouldn't he look at local politics too? Who should be running the show but corrupt, incompetent, hypocritical, skirt-chasing, Ted Kennedy sound-alike Mayor Quimby.

D'oh.

Also, while Thaler recommended further fiddling with mortgage laws, he failed to note the astonishing array of existing paternalistic government institutions and programs that were designed to "assist" home buyers but that had in fact helped set up the 2008 disaster. Apart from the government-backed mortgage suppliers and packagers, Fannie Mae and Freddie Mac, there was the Department of Housing and Urban Development, the Federal Housing Finance Board, the Federal Housing Administration, the Federal Home Loan Bank and the Office of Federal Housing Enterprise Oversight. Then there were all those congressional acts, such as the Fair Housing Act (1968), the Equal Credit Opportunity Act (1974), the Community Reinvestment Act (1977), the Home Mortgage Disclosure Act (1975), the National Affordable Housing Act (1990), the Community Development and Regulatory Improvement Act (1994), the Home Ownership and Equity Protection Act (1994), the American Dream Down Payment Act (2003) — and many more.

Hadn't this whole regulatory morass been a classic example of "nudging"? American legislators had nudged lenders to issue subprime mortgages in order to nudge poor people to buy houses. Fannie Mae and Freddie Mac had aided the nudging through their support for packaging and guaranteeing bundles of mortgages. The Fed had artificially nudged interest rates lower in the aftermath of the internet bubble at the turn of the century, thus feeding the housing boom. And everybody had been nudged off a financial cliff.

Surely it wasn't the Homers who made the really dumb decisions, it was all the Quimbys in government and the nerdy Spocks in policy back rooms. Thaler in fact admitted that bureaucrats might make mistakes, but apparently their superior strength lay in being able to "hire experts and conduct research." But which experts? What research? "Fixing the problem is complicated," he concluded. "But a good first step is to make the mortgage lending process Homer-proof."

But how would you make it Quimby-, Spock- and Thaler-proof?

A comprehensive refutation of Thaler had in fact been eloquently delivered 250 years before by a French contemporary of Adam Smith, Anne-Robert-Jacques Turgot, who pointed to the folly of government intervention in the name of "consumer protection." Turgot commented that to expect government to prevent frauds "would be like wanting to provide cushions for all the children who might fall."

> To assume it to be possible to prevent successfully, by regulation, all possible malpractices ... is to sacrifice to a chimerical perfection the whole progress of industry; it is to restrict the imagination of artificers to all narrow limits of the familiar; it is to forbid them all new experiments ...
>
> It means forgetting that the execution of these regulations is always entrusted to men who may have all the more interest in fraud or in conniving at fraud since the fraud which they might commit would be covered in some way by the seal of public authority and by the confidence which this seal inspires in consumers ...
>
> Thus, with obvious injustice, commerce, and consequently the nation, are charged with a heavy burden to save a few idle people the trouble of instructing themselves or of making inquiries to avoid being cheated. To suppose all consumers to be dupes, and all merchants to be cheats, has the effect of authorizing them to be so, and of degrading all the working members of the community.

Note that the nanny state has in fact gone exactly in the direction of Turgot's parody, with comprehensive regulations about the dangers of playground equipment and children's helmets.

Meanwhile the massive Ponzi schemer Bernie Madoff made sure to align himself with the public authority of the New York Stock Exchange. Finally, as Turgot predicted, corporate and consumer legislation tends to treat business as guilty until proven innocent, while electors, consumers and investors are lulled into the false belief that governments can provide them with "security."

There is no doubt that irrationality stalks human behaviour, but the pretensions of behavioural economics to root it out and correct for it seemed to be astonishingly one-sided. Needless to say, behavioural economics was eagerly embraced by governments covering the full political spectrum: that is, from the gung-ho interventionist to the merely cynical, poll-guided interventionist.

President Obama, during his first term, appointed Cass Sunstein to head the White House Office of Information and Regulatory Affairs. The British coalition government led by Conservative prime minister David Cameron hired Richard Thaler as a consultant and set up a Behavioural Insight Team, nicknamed the "nudge unit," to persuade people, as the *Guardian* put it, "to behave in a more socially integrated way."

—៣—

Daniel Kahneman did, however, point to one key human failing that helped explain the inability to grasp economics (even as he seemed to have problems grasping it himself). He called it the tendency for humans to believe that "What You See Is All There Is," or WYSIATI. He noted that "the human mind does not deal well with non events," another key factor in economic incomprehension. People have a problem appreciating the economic consequences of bad policy because those consequences often consist of things that *do not happen* — investments not made because of political uncertainty, jobs not created because of the policy-promoted misallocation of resources.

Indeed, this point had been made forcefully by Frédéric Bastiat in his essay *Ce qu'on voit et ce qu'on ne voit pas* (What is seen and what is not seen), and the theme was expanded upon by Henry Hazlitt in his 1946 book, *Economics in One Lesson*. As Hazlitt wrote: "The art of economics consists in looking not merely at the immediate but at the longer effects of any act or policy; it consists in tracing the consequences of that policy not merely for one group but for all groups."

Toward the end of his book, Kahneman touched on another leftist meme: that, as the Beatles put it, money "can't buy me love." The related academic claim is that aggregate measures such as gross national product are not merely crude but misleading. Kahneman suggested that one day an "index of human suffering" would be included in national income statistics.

Would that include the mental anguish caused by those peddling pretentious flapdoodle such as "gross national happiness"?

—ɯ—

The idea that people's desire to better their condition might suck them into a materialist nightmare of competitive "envy and emulation," as Mandeville put it, and thus destroy their finer instincts has long been a staple of anti-capitalism. A corollary of this view is that economic statistics don't measure happiness, and thus need to be replaced.

The man most associated with the notion of the political promotion of happiness was that autistic moral philosopher Jeremy Bentham. Bentham, who lived from 1748 to 1832, was the father of social utilitarianism, the idea that it was the business of policy to secure the "greatest happiness of the greatest number." This pretension required measurement, and Bentham came up with a "felicific calculus" to measure pleasure in units he called "utils."

Bentham was not only one of the originators of "cost-benefit analysis," he was influential in providing other rationalizations for the expansive, redistributive state, including the notion that a unit of money is of more benefit to a poor man than to a rich man. Hence government can increase social welfare simply by taking from the Biblical rich man, Dives, and giving to the poor man, Lazarus. Robin Hood was a social utilitarian.

In the good old days, gross national product, or GNP (the total money-measured production of the citizens of a country, whether at home or abroad), provided a rough measure of overall national output. Such statistics were always dangerous, not primarily because they provided an inappropriate measure but because they were the raw material of government planning and macromanagement.

As state planning stumbled, reflexive anti-capitalists turned — while persisting in supporting state planning — to attacking markets not merely through human irrationality but by assailing GNP. Look, they would say, manufacturing bombs and tanks contributes to GNP. So does repairing wrecked cars. Thus capitalism rejoices in war and car crashes. (In fact, it was Keynesianism that promoted the barmy idea that deliberate destruction was a useful promoter of economic activity.)

The pursuit of happiness is hardly a novel concept. Just read the U.S. Declaration of Independence. Nevertheless, the hoary truism that wealth and happiness are not synonymous became embodied in the concept of "gross national happiness," or GNH, a metric reportedly conjured up by the "Dragon King" of the extremely poor Himalayan country of Bhutan. GNH would incorporate all that was important, rather than merely that which could be recorded in money terms.

Westerners have always concocted mythical Shangri-Las or peoples, sometimes just for fictional fun, but often as a means of criticizing their own societies. That was the origin of the "noble savage." Ayn Rand's heroes, by contrast, headed off from an ungrateful anti-capitalist world at the end of *Atlas Shrugged* for a capitalist mountain Nirvana — Galt's Gulch. The left's supposedly non-fictional equivalent emerged as Bhutan, where erecting GNH was the brainchild of the country's fourth king, Jigme Singye Wangchuck, who had had to interrupt his education at British boarding schools in 1972 to take over from his father.

The notion that anybody considers economic growth the "ultimate good" was, of course, nonsensical. Nobody in her right mind imagined that national aggregates of economic output equated directly with happiness. Nevertheless, economic growth based on higher productivity — that is, more output of goods and services, more access to them, plus more free time — was what most people, given a free choice, seemed to want, including the Bhutanese, who sought to escape the drudgery of subsistence farming. However, according to green socialists and champions of "environmental justice," it was more happy-making (at least for themselves) to preserve blanket coverage of old-growth forest than to improve the material well-being of the 60 per cent of Bhutan's population who lived in poverty.

Meanwhile, if economic growth wasn't generally a "good thing," why would the UN-based "development community" have been trying to promote it — with astonishingly little success — for over 50 years? Could it be that their very failures had prompted the embrace of GNH?

Anybody who was truly concerned with happiness as the main objective of life almost certainly wouldn't be trying to do anything as stupid as measure and aggregate it. The notion that happiness might be summed at the national level bespoke exactly the type of wonkish calculation that GNH purported to transcend. If you really thought that GNP was such a dumb idea, why would you bother putting the words "gross national" in front of anything? In fact, the UN already had a Human Development Index, which went heavy on education or indoctrination and longevity and light on income, thus enabling socialist paradises such as Cuba to shine in the rankings.

GNH's murky metrics even made their way into the midst of the 2008 global crisis as the result of an initiative by French president Nicolas Sarkozy. Sarkozy had established the International Commission on the Measurement of Economic Performance and Social Progress, headed by two leading leftist Nobel prizewinning economists, the ubiquitous Joseph Stiglitz and Amartya Sen. The task of Stiglitz and Sen had been to confront "dissatisfaction" not just with the state of statistical information but with alleged "overreliance on free market principles."

"If the market was the solution to all problems and was never wrong," asked Sarkozy during a speech to present his pet economists' findings, "then why are we in such a situation?" But whoever claimed that the market was "the solution to all problems"? Markets reflected the consequences of commercial activity and policy. It was humans that screwed up, especially pretentious policy-makers. Markets merely handed out the prizes and penalties.

According to Sarkozy, one way of avoiding future crises would be to incorporate measures of such joys and aggravations as vacations, recycling, household chores and traffic congestion. He did not mention the contribution to well-being of physical attributes and sex, but presumably they would have to be included.

During a visit to a manufacturing plant in Normandy the week before his GNH speech, aides to the vertically challenged president had sought out the factory's 20 shortest workers as the backdrop for a photo op. So should dissatisfaction about height "gaps" be factored into GNH? Obviously, the more expansive the definition of GNH, the more farcically immeasurable.

Stiglitz laid out his thoughts on the inadequacy of traditional statistics in a newspaper article. "Are statistics giving us the right signals about what to do?" he pondered. But his question begged more fundamental ones, such as: Who was this "us" and what did it plan to "do" with these "signals"? Stiglitz noted that "what we measure affects what we do," but what he really meant was "what governments measure determines what governments do." Measurement is crucial to judging policy success, but it also tends to be the mother of activism, on the basis of the delusional conviction that if you can measure it, you can improve it.

Stiglitz believed there were opportunities to "improve metrics." He claimed that policy wonks were now in a better position to assess well-being and gather the relevant data, employing such insights as that losing a job meant more than just loss of income. But who, except a newly arrived Martian or an ivory tower academic, would not know that? And how would you measure this additional "loss"? Meanwhile somebody had also apparently just clued Stiglitz in to the obvious fact that "social connectedness" was important.

"It should have been obvious that one couldn't reduce everything to a single number [GNP]," concluded Stiglitz. But it had only ever been wonks such as himself who had imagined that such an exercise was desirable, or possible, in the first place. And now they were trying to make the "single number" even more expansively ridiculous.

Jeremy Bentham didn't have only GNP to answer for. He was also at the root of another interventionist conceit, that of the comprehensive oversight, and regulation, of the economy: the "not a sparrow shall fall" delusion.

—⁊⁊—

Bentham believed that what was needed to make sure nobody messed up was to keep comprehensive watch — literally. He proposed a vast system of "panopticons," or "inspection houses," whereby institutions such as factories, schools, hospitals and prisons would be subject to central surveillance. It would all be done with mirrors, part of the purpose of which was that those under surveillance would not know if they were being watched. (Orwell elaborated this nightmare in the ubiquitous "telescreens" of *Nineteen Eighty-Four*.)

In the wake of the 2008 crisis, the concept or conceit of regulatory "macroprudence" began to catch on. It was based on a vision of the tribunes of regulatory governance not merely overseeing individual institutions, sectors and markets, but taking a grand panoptic view that looked above and beyond all the grubby self-interest to the big global picture, and thus furnished an early-warning system for the market. The threat was Kafka; the reality, more Keystone Kops. It represented just more of the same system that had conspicuously failed in — and had arguably greatly exacerbated — the crisis. Now, however, the regulatory system would be improved by having even more coordinating committees, with new national overseers swapping reports with bigger and more expansive regional and international oversight groups.

The Keynesian prefix "macro" had become the herald of policy pretension. That pretension started with human irrationality and alleged market failure, and leaped straight to the conclusion that what was needed to deal with "systemic" problems was stratospheric oversight, masterminded by the best and the brightest (overlooking the fact that the best and the brightest also happened to be human). Such a boatload of knowledge had in fact already existed when the collateralized debt obligations and the credit default swaps hit the fan. It was called the Financial Stability Forum, or FSF, and had been created as part of a new global "financial architecture" some 10 years previously.

As noted earlier, economic metaphors often tell us more about the flawed thought processes of those coining them than about the situations they are meant to illuminate. The notion of "financial architecture" was inevitably appealing to policy Frank Lloyd Wrights, but it was based on an inappropriate image of economic "structure" and how markets worked. The key point about markets is that they are organic institutions that essentially build themselves.

The Financial Stability Forum proved practically useless in stabilizing anything ahead of the 2008 crisis. Unembarrassed by its failure, however, the G20, at its April 2009 meeting, blandly reshuffled the regulatory deck and created a "new" Financial Stability *Board*, FSB. According to a study for the C.D. Howe Institute by Nick Le Pan, a former superintendent of financial institutions in Canada, the FSB would have a "more interventionist mandate, more follow-up, better staff support, better links to the IMF, early warning exercises, and improved reporting to G-20 finance ministers and central bank governors." That is, more and bigger bureaucracies organizing more and bigger meetings to keep an eye on all the things they missed before, while some new crisis inevitably crept up on the blind side.

Even if it were possible to coordinate this roiling mass of old and new agencies, and even if they were populated by the smartest bureaucrats the world had ever seen, they still likely wouldn't spot the — inevitable — next crisis, or be able to grasp why the existing one persisted. As Alan Greenspan wrote in the spring of 2008, "We will never be able to anticipate all discontinuities in financial markets. Discontinuities are, of necessity, a surprise." And never more surprising than to regulators, macroprudential or otherwise, whose main motivation, conscious or not, is to expand their empires and whose main impact is to create a false — and thus dangerous — sense of security.

Regulators claimed that globalization threatened massive instability because now financial "contagion" could spread literally everywhere on earth. But it is not the spread of capitalism — which thrives on diversity — that threatens contagion but the spread of common forms of regulation.

The peculiarities of the regulatory mentality at last received a psychological once-over by the University of Kiev's Slavisa Tasic in a paper titled "Are Regulators Rational?" "Rarely," wrote Tasic, "have behavioural arguments been used to question the knowledge and rationality of policymakers and regulators." He suggested that if regulators appeared congenitally incapable of grasping that regulation created more problems than it solved, that was because they *were* congenitally incapable.

Tasic noted that the limitations of regulation had already been laid out by Hayek, who had pointed out that the essence of the market was dispersed knowledge to which regulators, by definition, did not have access. This created "an insurmountable epistemic limitation." It wouldn't matter how expert policymakers were in cognitive psychology; they still couldn't solve the dispersed knowledge problem. Regulators were also subject to "illusions of competence."

Tasic observed that despite regulatory failures, "the rise of the regulatory state still largely meets public approval." That appears to be a natural consequence of "unreflecting centralism." If you assume that an economy can best be planned from the centre, you also imagine that it can be more easily regulated. Enthusiastic regulators were, declared Tasic, of necessity ignorant and deluded. They suffered from the "meta-cognitive" problem of being not merely ignorant but unaware of their own ignorance.

The psychologist Abraham Maslow formulated a personal "hierarchy of needs" that stretched from breathing and eating at one end to such aspirations as saving Africa at the other. He was also credited with the profound, if comic, insight that if the only tool you have is a hammer, then everything looks like a nail. Regulators are perhaps more like people whose only tool is a shovel. When they find themselves in a hole, they are inclined to keep digging.

As Tasic wrote, "Adverse unintended consequences are pervasive across regulatory areas, and yet when they are recognized, the typical policy answers are new attempts to fix the omissions of the previous regulation." It is rarely if ever countenanced that regulation itself might be the problem.

Regulators reflexively imagine that the failures of any system hatched by numerous committees and commissions is merely to have more and bigger such committees and commissions; they believe that the more they fail, the more they have to learn from. The regulatory mentality constantly believes that the answer to failures of oversight is to create a new overarching bureaucracy.

Those macromaniacs who cannot see the trees for the wood suggest that the picture might be clearer from outer space. They are firmly convinced that they have a broader perspective than those benighted souls who warn against fiddling with markets until you understand them. All the regulators really lack, they claim, is sufficient power. Which brings us to that elephant in the room, or, perhaps more appropriately, the chimpanzee in the psyche.

thirteen

The Chimpanzee in the Room: Darwinian Politics

The source of all these evils was a thirst of power, from
rapacious and ambitious passions ... Such things ever will
be, so long as human nature continues the same.
— Thucydides, *The History of the Peloponnesian War*

Free markets lead to thinking, that eternal enemy of politicians.
— P.J. O'Rourke, *On the Wealth of Nations*

"There you go with that 'we' again."
— Jack Lemmon to Tony Curtis in *Some Like It Hot*

Adam Smith had intended to write a third book, on the principles of government, but never completed it. He had the related papers destroyed before his death. Smith was perhaps diverted by taking the post of commissioner of customs in Edinburgh. However, P.J. O'Rourke, in his book *On the Wealth of Nations*, suggests that it may not have been just a matter of being preoccupied or succumbing to what Smith described as the "indolence of old age."

"Smith was a moral philosopher," writes O'Rourke. "It may be that at some point he realized politics isn't a good place for philosophy and is no place for morals." This assessment, while tongue-in-cheek, contains a good deal of truth.

At the Kirkcaldy gathering in 1973 to celebrate the 250th anniversary of Smith's birth, at least one academic was present who had expressed some degree of skepticism about the symposium's pervasive assumption of wise and selfless public administration. Ironically, that voice belonged to Andrew Skinner, the man I would meet 30 years later in Glasgow and who would suggest that Smith might not have been concerned *enough* about the positive potential of policy.

"Smith," Skinner had declared in Kirkcaldy, "suggested that *homo politicus* may be subject to the same self-interested motives as *homo economicus* ... It is probably true to say that this problem has received significantly less attention than its due."

Skinner's observation appears blindingly obvious to everybody except — strangely — politicians, policy wonks and mainstream social scientists. But pointing out that it was senseless to propose policies without taking political self-interest into account tended to be a career-limiting move. Vituperation had been poured on Hayek for *The Road to Serfdom*. James Buchanan's skepticism about the application of Keynesianism in a democratic setting (whatever Keynesianism's more fundamental economic flaws) had led to personal vilification. Interventionists, it seemed, were far from amenable to criticism of their plans for a "better world." Like Marx, they tended to dismiss opponents as "self-interested," while taking for granted their own pristine and selfless objectivity. Good intentions were assumed to lead directly to good results.

The pursuit of self-interest in the market is in fact quite different from the pursuit of self-interest in the political arena. While the former may be subject to perpetual hypocritical condemnation, it can only produce gains by catering to others. Political self-interest appears often to be driven by subconscious urges that resolutely seek to cloak their true objectives, even — indeed especially — from themselves. Political "elephants" are devious animals. Similarly, academics who serve the interests of politicians appear to be extraordinarily one-sided in their concerns about human imperfection, like those with a form of brain damage that enables them to see only one side of a clock face.

Keynes, that leading light of 20th-century economic interventionism, acknowledged the potential dangers of power but declared that as long as those who wielded it had noble orientations, then everything would be fine. Milton Friedman noted wryly that while Keynes claimed to agree with Hayek's message in *The Road to Serfdom*, he seemed to have singularly failed to grasp the chapter headed "Why the Worst Get on Top."

Adam Smith had realized that the Leviathan of government was essential to restrain violence, administer justice and provide defence against external enemies, but he also realized that it was perpetually dangerous. Indeed, *The Wealth of Nations* was aimed at disrobing the destructiveness of intrusive mercantilism.

Smith was highly cynical about politicians and their pretensions and described how "faction" — that is, political partisanship — led men to lose all sense of balance or fairness. He specifically rejected "men of system," who treated economic actors as so many chess pieces, and castigated the "folly and presumption" of state planners. He noted the short-term orientation of politics, referring to "the skill of that insidious and crafty animal, vulgarly called a statesman or politician, whose councils are directed by the momentary fluctuations of affairs." He also wrote, "There is no art which one government sooner learns of another, than that of draining money from the pockets of the people."

Sure enough, the wealth of commercial society would inevitably invite a political struggle for its "spoils," along with the relentless search by politicians for rationalizations for ever greater levels of taxing, spending and regulation.

Smith had realized that it was unwise to sell his prescriptions as revolutionary. Rather, he stressed their benefits for the state. If the state wanted to increase its revenues, it should step back from trying to guide the economy. The vast wealth unleashed by the efflorescence of capitalism, combined with ongoing confusions about the system, meant that the state would wind up both interfering more and reaping more.

Smith had suggested that people had a trading instinct and a moral instinct, insights confirmed by modern studies in evolutionary psychology. But what about a political instinct? Insofar as politics is ultimately about the use and restraint of competitive violence in pursuit of resources, it has deep roots in evolutionary history, both human and animal.

—m—

I had mixed memories of Lady Mitchell Hall, an auditorium set amid the modern architectural curiosities of the University of Cambridge's Sidgwick site. I used to suffer through eye-glazing economics lectures there as an undergraduate. Now I was back, with infinitely more enthusiasm, on a spring evening in 2005, to hear a talk by the Harvard biologist Richard Wrangham titled "Why Apes and Humans Kill." I wanted to know more about what insights animal ethology (the study of creatures in the wild) might offer about the origins of politics.

Wrangham started by describing the opposing views of human nature and violence put forward by the philosophers Jean-Jacques Rousseau and Thomas Hobbes. Rousseau thought humans were naturally peaceable; Hobbes thought violence was fundamental. Wrangham's conclusion was that humans tended to be "Rousseau at home and Hobbes abroad."

Wrangham pointed out that chimpanzees had once been assumed to be peaceable. Research had proven otherwise. At the borders of their territory, chimps in groups frequently ambushed and killed isolated members of neighbouring tribes. He showed a disturbing video of such a killing. Males were more likely to kill or be killed than females, and the killings were opportunistic. They depended on outnumbering and immobilizing the victim by grabbing his arms and legs as he was bitten and beaten to death. Aggression was obviously evolutionarily adaptive, concluded Wrangham. Killing neighbouring males meant the opportunity to expand range, capture females, gather more resources and thus have more offspring.

Wrangham did not pursue this theme, but the reproductive rationale for violence continued down human history, perhaps most spectacularly in the case of Genghis Khan, the 13th-century Mongol conqueror whose empire at the time of his death extended from the Caspian Sea to the Pacific Ocean. "The greatest joy a man can know," Genghis is reported to have said, "is to conquer his enemies and drive them before him. To ride their horses and take away their possessions. To see the faces of those who were dear to them bedewed with tears, and to clasp their wives and daughters in his arms."

As Stephen Pinker writes in *The Better Angels of Our Nature*, "Modern genetics has shown this was no idle boast. Today 8 percent of the men who live within the former territory of the Mongol Empire share a Y chromosome that dates to around the time of Genghis, most likely because they descended from him and his sons and the vast number of women they clasped in their arms."

Wrangham meanwhile noted that although humans were adaptively violent, they were so to a much lesser degree than chimpanzees. The level of violence in hunter-gatherer tribes was between 150 and 1,000 times *lower* than in chimpanzee society. The level of violent deaths in modern industrial societies was much lower than among pastoralists and farmers. He attributed this disparity to the specialization of armies, and to the fact that the bulk of the population did not become involved in warfare. He conspicuously did not attribute it to the essentially non-violent nature of commercial society.

Wrangham pointed out that lethal warfare on the modern scale was quite alien to the evolutionary period. It was likely to be exacerbated by the fact that "leaders" didn't get hurt. Also, said Wrangham, we tend to have "positive illusions" about our own relative power (this observation came with a cute slide of a kitten looking in a mirror and seeing a lion). We are also inclined, he said, to ignore "intelligence" that doesn't fit our preconceptions.

This remark led to a ripple of knowing nods and murmurs through the Cambridge audience, who seemed to take it as a cryptic reference to the then-recent American occupation of Iraq. In fact, Wrangham made no reference to Iraq, but he did use another controversial example.

He suggested that the 1961 Bay of Pigs invasion — in which U.S.-trained Cuban exiles launched an attack on Cuba, where Fidel Castro had seized power two years before — was a prime example of delusional tendencies. He noted that President John F. Kennedy had subsequently said that he couldn't believe how stupid he had been to back the invasion. Wrangham went on to claim that there was no evidence to support assertions that there were 30,000 people on the island ready to join the rebels.

I found this example intriguing because I happened to know something about the subject. I wrote a book, *Family Spirits*, about the Bacardis, a family of Cuban exiles who still controlled one of the world's most popular liquor brands, and the project had involved a good deal of research on Cuban history, interviewing many Cuban exiles and a trip to Cuba.

I knew that Kennedy had in fact betrayed the Cuban exiles and their American CIA colleagues at the Bay of Pigs by withdrawing crucial air cover during the attack. I also knew that Fidel Castro had used the attack as an excuse to kill or imprison thousands, which meant that Wrangham's denial of extensive opposition to Castro on the island was, to say the least, moot.

I also did not see how the Bay of Pigs could be equated to any glib overestimation of American power. The problem was not power, of which the United States had an abundance, but unwillingness to use it against a dictator who enjoyed considerable popularity among the American chattering classes. Another factor was wariness of Soviet intervention, which Kennedy's irresolution at the Bay of Pigs in fact subsequently encouraged, leading to the Cuban Missile Crisis.

Wrangham offered no observations on similarities between chimpanzee politics and Cuban Communism. But Cuba had, since the "triumph of the revolution" in 1959, been very much like a chimpanzee society. Its citizens had been oppressed by an alpha male who had both charisma and a coercive coalition of followers to stamp out dissent. (He also had many lovers, although not on the Genghis scale.) Fidel Castro was a classic example of "Hobbes at home." Unlike an alpha chimpanzee, however, he could talk. And talk. Also, his ruling group had a monopoly of lethal weapons, which meant they could control a much larger number of people with a relatively small group of — intriguingly hairy — "dominants" (Castro's revolutionaries were known as *los barbudos*, "the bearded ones").

This repressive, essentially primitive regime — with its banning of private property and free speech, and its grossly inefficient top-down system of economic control — had for decades been supported and lauded by leftist Western intellectuals, who stressed Fidel Castro's good intentions. Indeed, I had little doubt that most of this Cambridge audience had distinctly more negative feelings about George W. Bush or Margaret Thatcher than about Fidel Castro.

—⁂—

One of the reasons I had been eager to meet Ignacio, the former Cuban central planner, and his wife, Iliana, was that I had then recently started work on the Bacardi book. When I told them I was planning to visit Cuba, Iliana asked me to take presents to her family in Havana, including U.S. dollars, which it was illegal for Cubans to possess. The money was for Iliana's sister and brother-in-law, who were attempting to build a house.

Cuba had long fascinated me. The conventional wisdom, which I had heard parroted time and again, was that Cubans might not enjoy as much political freedom as in the West, but "just look" at all the good things Fidel Castro had done for them. Look at the "free" health care and education. And if the regime did have problems, they were mainly due to the U.S. trade embargo. Maybe Castro had never held elections, said the apologists, but he was "popular." Meanwhile the situation in Cuba was declared to be undoubtedly better than it had been "before," under the regime of the dictator Fulgencio Batista. Then, Cuba had been run by the Mafia (heck, hadn't you seen *The Godfather: Part II*?), and Batista's misrule had enjoyed the support of the United States, which had suppressed Cuban political independence throughout the 20th century.

Western Fidelistas had expressed delight over the Bay of Pigs. The subsequent missile crisis — when the Americans confronted the Soviets over installing nuclear missiles on the island, and the Soviets backed down in return for a U.S. non-invasion pledge — was treated as evidence that the West had to get along with Communism. And what was so wrong with Communism anyway? How free were we, *really*?

—m—

After arriving in Havana and spending a couple of days retrieving lost luggage, I took a Turismo taxi to an address in the suburbs. There, Iliana's father met me at the curb and guided me into an alleyway and up some dingy stairs into a tiny apartment. The fridge was in the living room, along with a ghetto-blaster and a small television. Cockroaches scampered here and there. I delivered the gifts Iliana had given me: towels, shirts, shoes and socks, tights, razor blades, toothbrushes, blouses, stereo headphones and batteries.

Iliana's father shared the apartment with his wife, two of his other daughters, one of their husbands and two children. One of the daughters, who was divorced, taught at the university and was eager to practise her English. She declared that she wouldn't like to live in the United States because she would be afraid of being murdered.

The father clearly wanted to say something, but I left without hearing what it was, at least for the moment. At the end of the evening, the other daughter and her husband, to whom I had given the dollars, drove me back to my hotel in the sidecar of their motorcycle. They were effusively grateful for the money. It was difficult to get anything done in Cuba without American dollars, they said. The peso was virtually worthless.

A day or two later, following a Kafkaesque experience organizing travel arrangements, I took a plane to Santiago de Cuba, which had been the Bacardis' home city and business base. The Cuban government had given me a "program," which included the services of a guide. At one of my stops, I met a young museum curator who, I sensed, did not like my Communist minder. Later, I returned to chat with him.

His name was Jorge. He started out peddling the party line but soon realized that I wasn't responding like a typical Western fellow-traveller, so he began to tell me what he really thought. Jorge said that nobody had a private life in Cuba because of the so-called Committees for the Defence of the Revolution. These were government-appointed street-level busybodies who literally came to look in your window for evidence of crimes such as "unexplained wealth."

People were desperate to escape the island's poverty and repression. Jorge mentioned friends who had set out in shark-infested waters to swim miles to the American base at Guantánamo (before it became an internment camp for suspected terrorists in the wake of 9/11).

We discussed the West's perception of Cuba. Jorge mentioned a TV interview with Fidel by Maria Shriver, which had been shown in Cuba. Jorge commented, "Fidel got away with giving her the 'You don't have a free press either' bullshit."

Jorge offered to take me sightseeing. We drove in my rental Lada into the little town of El Caney, where a weekly barrel of beer — a *pipa* — had just been delivered. It was a strange scene: men of all colours, shapes and sizes drinking out of improvised containers on a street lined with Fords and Buicks from the 1950s. A drunken gaucho clattered down the street on a little pony. Through a window, a television sported an episode of *The Benny Hill Show*. Friends of Jorge's opened the local music hut and organized an impromptu concert. A good time was had by all.

I saw Jorge several more times in Santiago. He helped me find the man who had been the head of the Bacardi factory's labour union. The octogenarian unionist, who was almost blind, said that the island sorely missed the capitalist Bacardis.

When I returned to Havana, I took Iliana's family to my hotel for a mediocre buffet meal. Afterwards, her father guided me conspiratorially to one side. "Here," he said, "we live at the will of one man. If he says that day is night, then everybody says it is night. Everything is his gift. If we get meat once in 15 days, we must be grateful. If we do not, we must not complain.

"We live," the old man concluded, "in a big prison."

—〰—

Richard Wrangham had studied the interaction of chimpanzees in the wild, and it wasn't pretty. Frans de Waal's fascinating book *Chimpanzee Politics* dealt, by contrast, with the subtle manoeuvrings within a captive colony of chimpanzees at the Burgers Zoo at Arnhem in Holland. De Waal wrote, "The social organization of chimpanzees is almost too human to be true ...

Entire passages of Machiavelli seem to be directly applicable to chimpanzee behaviour."

De Waal's study indicated an astonishing complexity of "political" coalition building by males, whose ever-tenuous position depended on far more than merely physical strength. Conflict resolution was an essential part of chimp society and involved elaborate rituals of recognition, grooming and mediation. Alpha males, meanwhile, often ruled by intervening in fights on behalf of weaker parties, and by displaying "generosity." They were essentially running for office. Power, noted de Waal, was very much related to sex.

The political world of our hunter-gatherer ancestors was necessarily much more complex than that of chimpanzees, particularly once language had evolved, but it was ultimately based in the same Darwinian imperatives. Men hunted in groups because it was more efficient. They found ways to divide kills without excessive intergroup violence, leading to the evolution of hierarchies. But hierarchies were always subject to disruption by aspiring male power seekers, just as in de Waal's chimp colony. Men competed for and abducted women from neighbouring tribes. Indeed, according to Napoleon Chagnon, whose studies of the Yanomamo tribe of South America made him the most famous — and controversial — anthropologist of his era, competition for women was at the very heart of war, which, far from being unnatural, was the constant condition of primitive tribes.

Hobbes was right.

Chagnon was controversial precisely because he upset the cultural anthropologists' fondly held Rousseauian notions about the noble savage (similar to those of the peaceful chimp). He also refuted their claim that all war was about resources. He observed that even when they lived above subsistence, the Yanomamo still constantly raided rival villages. Moreover, they were not "egalitarians." Kinship ties determined status and dominance. Worst of all, his meticulous research established that being a killer was adaptive. Killers got more offspring (as Genghis Khan's widespread genetic heritage confirms).

For his pains, Chagnon was accused of everything from data faking to genocide. Anthropologists who felt they had a moral duty to protect primitive people (although you couldn't call them "primitive" because all cultures were "equally valid") rejected Chagnon's conclusions because of how they thought they *might* be interpreted.

The Yanomamo offered a look back to man's "lowly origins," but civilization elsewhere had moved on, albeit amid continuing violence and predation. The key issue of politics, as noted by the American political scientist Harold Lasswell, was "who gets what, when, and how." That applied as much to Chagnon's "fierce people" as it does to today's parliaments and congresses.

The fundamental, crude question on which politics is based is "Where's mine?" More threatening, since there is violence in numbers, is the explicit or implicit question "Where's ours?" Most subtle — and Machiavellian — of all is the claim that you are speaking not for yourself, but for others: "Where's theirs?"

"Speaking up on behalf of others" is thus at once both the most noble-sounding and the most potentially devious posture of human politics, in particular modern democracy. It has been at the heart of the redistributionist ethic since Marx: "From each according to his abilities, to each according to his needs." Which is to say, the vanguard of the proletariat would "speak up" for the needy, and thus justify taking from those with the abilities.

The importance of coalitions, with their threat of violence in numbers, goes deep into animal history. Chimpanzees don't need to sit down to plan an attack on any unfortunate male who wanders into their territory. Lethal mobbing is in their genes. Any human (almost invariably a man) who has been in a confrontational situation such as a bar fight subconsciously weighs the odds attached to "fight or flight" without needing a course in game theory.

Literally "speaking up" for others required the evolution of language, which brought with it plotting, persuasion and reputational manipulation via gossip. Language also meant that there could be debate about political alternatives. Hence rhetoric, the use of language to win an argument, would have been gradually born over myriad generations before flowering in ancient Greece. The great historian Thucydides warned about the dangerous power of political rhetoric, whose manufacture was the business of "sophists." It could be used to motivate mobs and justify regimes via state religions and self-serving "ideologies," as Karl Marx would point out.

Ironically, Marx concocted one of the most pernicious ideologies of all, but he couldn't have done so without appealing to a whole suite of hunter-gatherer moral assumptions that were triggered by misreading — or misrepresenting — as *political* or *coercive* the employment relationships and wealth accumulation essential to capitalism and inevitable under it.

Political power comes from coercion or authority. Jonathan Haidt contended that authority is an aspect of morality, but it is also a system through which moral rules are imparted to others. Authority appears obviously preferable to coercion, but it contains its own dangers.

—m—

Deference to authority evolved as a biological or cultural adaptation that not merely reduced violence but enabled the spread of social norms and useful knowledge without everybody having to work things out for themselves. The tendency to believe and follow authority is what makes us educable and the spread of civilization possible, but it also makes us vulnerable to miseducation or political exploitation.

In the 1960s, the social scientist Stanley Milgram undertook a famous study of the dangers of reflexive obedience to authority. His experiment was partly inspired by the trial of Adolf Eichmann, a Nazi Holocaust facilitator who famously claimed that he was merely "following orders." (Eichmann was the inspiration for Hannah Arendt's phrase "the banality of evil.")

In the Milgram experiment, unwitting volunteers were told that they were to play "teachers," and their apparent co-volunteers were the "learners." When the learners failed to give correct responses, the teachers were instructed by a stern white-coated "experimenter" to administer increasing electric shocks. Despite their mounting unease, more than two-thirds of the teachers delivered shocks to the maximum level, despite the complaints, screams and even apparent passing out of learners (who were in fact acting).

"I observed," wrote Milgram, "a mature and initially poised businessman enter the laboratory smiling and confident. Within 20 minutes he was reduced to a twitching, stuttering wreck, who was rapidly approaching nervous collapse ... And yet he continued to respond to every word of the experimenter, and obeyed to the end."

As the library of knowledge has expanded exponentially, and society has grown more complex, we have to rely more and more on various "authorities" for our perspectives on the wider world. As individuals, we can experience and read and think only so much. How do we choose? In the ancestral environment, the status that went with authority would have been attached to particular characteristics or skills, such as bravery, strength or animal tracking. We evolved to give credence to people with status, no matter how acquired. This can have bizarre, even comic results.

One example of confusing the status of achievement in one field with knowledge of matters in quite another was the notion that astronauts might be able to help us with theological issues, as if going to the moon had really put them closer to God. Another surely strange notion is that rock stars and actors might have useful things to say about environmental science or economic development. (Of course they might, but certainly not as a result of winning Grammys or Oscars.)

Humans are not merely prone to defer to authority, and to be "groupish" in their thinking; some are also strongly inclined to seek authority, which originates in the enhanced mating potential attached to higher status. However, aspiring to power is a dangerous business, as de Waal's chimps — not to mention Shakespeare's plays — make clear. Coalition building is essential for any successful aspirant to power, be it in a chimpanzee tribe or a run for the White House. That's where the "speaking up for others" algorithm comes in useful. It also helps if you believe it yourself, which seems to be one of the reasons why self-deception evolved. The adaptive benefits of deception are obvious; self-deception is more intriguing.

Self-deception — which was so devastatingly exposed by Bernard Mandeville in *The Fable of the Bees* and also highlighted as a major human flaw by Adam Smith — seems to have come about as the result of a subtle evolutionary "arms race." The evolutionary biologist Robert Trivers wrote, "If ... deceit is fundamental to animal communication, then there must be strong selection to spot deception and this ought, in turn, to select for a degree of self-deception, rendering some facts and motives unconscious so as not to betray — by the subtle signs of self-knowledge — the deception being practiced. Thus the conventional view that natural selection favours nervous systems which produce ever more accurate images of the world must be a very naive view of mental evolution."

As with our natural *non*-reflectiveness, this is surely a shocking revelation. Our brains evolved not just to fool others, but to fool ourselves ... the better to fool others. And we don't want to know about it. To few people would that characteristic be more valuable than politicians.

David Livingstone Smith notes that according to the theory of Machiavellian intelligence, "double-dealing and suspicion might have been the driving forces behind the explosion of brainpower that emerged in monkeys and apes." Such intelligence has been both greatly elaborated and, he claimed, suppressed to the level of the subconscious. "A portion of the brain developed special expertise in dishonesty, cleverly weaving useful illusions out of biased perceptions, tendentious memories, and fallacious logic."

This fits neatly with Haidt's notion of a subconscious "elephant" who might thus be seen as the devious, power-hungry ventriloquist for a rider who neither realizes that he's a dummy nor wants to know. Machiavellian elephants are useful because they also "read" other elephants and guide the politically inclined toward expressing sentiments and policies that appeal to their "constituency." The fact that those sentiments and policies do not conform to economic reality — and they can't possibly, since economic reality is both counterintuitive and unappealing — is not their primary concern. Indeed, there should be a "natural" subconscious tendency to cater to others' delusions if those delusions serve our interests.

Frans de Waal too supported the view that the human pursuit of power is both self-concealed and subconscious. He quoted the social psychologist Mauk Mulder, who conducted experiments that demonstrated that there is a taboo surrounding the word "power." Men prefer to speak of "carrying responsibility," "being in a position of authority" or "helping others by taking decisions out of their hands."

De Waal notes, "Machiavelli was the first person to refuse to repudiate or cover up power motives. This violation of the existing collective lie was not kindly received. It was regarded as an insult to humanity."

More precisely, it was a crucial insight into the nature of politics and politicians.

—ᴍ—

Politicians (and their Machiavellian elephants) quite naturally encourage powerful primitive collectivist assumptions that aid their cause, such as promoting the existence of an all-embracing "we." We (that is, the genuine "all of us") are suckers for "we" (that is, politicians claiming to "speak on our behalf") because the "we" we have in mind is the much smaller, more manageable and more collectivist "we" that comprised the tribal groups of no more than about 150 people in which our minds evolved.

Once a society reaches a relatively low threshold of size and complexity, comprehensive direct consultation becomes effectively impossible. The practical problem of consultation has been addressed by "representative democracy." But politicians are not "us."

When Marx revealed his coercive redistributionist formula, he was invoking a powerful collectivist tribal principle. He was also being far too unsubtle in admitting that Marxism involved the expropriation of some for the promised benefit of others. Then again, Marx wasn't trying to win an election, even though his formulation was designed to appeal to the majority of have-nots. Modern democratic politicians are far more subtle. Those with the abilities and the needs are now simply subsumed under the great "we" of a society that is allegedly defined by how well "we" look after "our" disadvantaged.

This aspiration does in fact reflect on our natural community spirit, but it is also a convenient cover for power-seeking elephants, whose riders may be firmly convinced of their own unwavering commitment to the "disadvantaged." The problem arises when the tribal redistributionist ethic, which was ultimately based on hierarchy or the threat of force, comes up against a historically novel market system in which goods are not "collective" and force tends to produce unintended results.

Steven Pinker points to the dangers of "we" as "the pronoun in the machine." He writes, "If the 'we' is truly unfettered by biology, then once 'we' see the light we can carry out the vision of radical change that we deem correct. But if the 'we' is an imperfect product of evolution — limited in knowledge and wisdom, tempted by status and power, and blinded by self-deception and delusions of moral superiority — then 'we' had better think twice before constructing all that history."

Matt Ridley, in his "Adam Darwin" thesis, pointed to the similarity of biological and free-market evolution. Both are "natural" and "emergent." The former has no Grand Designer and the latter doesn't need — indeed, by its nature can't afford — one. "Success" is ultimately dependent on the ecosystem of commercial choice. As Adam Smith said, in such a system the consumer rules, or at least should.

Ridley noted that technological advance tends to be "incremental, inevitable and inexorable," ever onwards and upwards. But what about politics? Political systems are rivalrous in a Darwinian sense, and the relatively free, fettered capitalist West appears to have outlasted its Communist alternative, which lingers only in the gulag states of Cuba and North Korea. But Western democracy — like all forms of democracy — contains its own dangers. It is an error to imagine that because democracies are capitalistic, democratic systems are friends of capitalism.

The "vile maxim" of Smith's feudal "masters of mankind" had been "All for ourselves, and nothing for other people." The new political masters of democracy profess undying concern for "the people." Certainly, this is an improvement, even if it involves hypocrisy, but it comes with its own problems.

Skepticism about the dangers of democracy goes back a long way. Plato was concerned that it would inevitably lead to tyranny as the masses were manipulated by a political class. Alexis de Tocqueville too wrote of the potential "tyranny of the majority." Joseph Schumpeter pointed out that democracy was merely a means of deciding things, and that such decisions might well be unjust or perverse. For example, majority support for burning witches or persecuting Jews didn't make these activities "right."

The journalist H.L. Mencken wrote that "democracy is a pathetic belief in the collective wisdom of individual ignorance." Ayn Rand suggested that democracy is "a social system in which one's work, one's property, one's mind, and one's life are at the mercy of any gang that may muster the vote of a majority at any moment for any purpose."

Churchill pointed out that, whatever its faults, democracy seemed better than the alternatives. Then again, he was a democratic politician, and one who had numerous ideological incarnations before he found his role as the leader of Britain during the Second World War.

The great thing about modern democracy is that it allows the electorate to periodically throw the rascals out, even if that means throwing a new bunch of rascals in. But electorates are perennially prone to folk economics — that is, bad and dangerous policies, which politicians are more than happy to promote if it will get them elected.

Significantly, Churchill was tossed out of office after that war by a socialist party that promoted policies of Marxist-inspired redistribution and state control that would prove little short of disastrous. Those policies remain as attractive as they are flawed. Attractive because they appear to embody the spirit of communal sharing and selfless public service, while catering to the bias that economies are best "planned" from the top, by "leaders." Flawed because unreflecting centralism fails to grasp the workings and benefits of dispersed markets, which are all too easily parodied as the reign of unfettered greed, while welfare states tend to grow out of control, issuing promises that increasingly have to be met by incurring debt, and are thus unsustainable.

Forceful redistributors invariably rationalize their activities partly by invoking the "greed of the rich," who need to be made to pay their "fair share," and partly by invoking the "positive rights" of those who are "disadvantaged." Positive rights sound good, but they are both morally and practically problematic.

"Negative rights" relate to individual freedoms. They are primarily about the right to be left alone to pursue one's own objectives in free association with others. They are at the heart of the political revolutions that made the Industrial Revolution possible. Positive rights, by contrast, are rooted in a collectivist or redistributionist ethic that declares, for example, that all individuals deserve an "adequate" standard of living, regardless of personal effort.

The seminal statement of positive rights is often identified as the "Four Freedoms" speech made by President Franklin Delano Roosevelt in his State of the Union address in 1941: freedoms of speech and religion, and freedom from want and fear. Freedom from want was different from the others, and problematic. If it meant some form of social insurance against temporary unemployment, then it appeared quite reasonable, although all government-run programs tend eventually to run out of control. If it meant the "right" to a job, then it further opened the door to problematic government policies of job creation, which in fact tended to undermine the economy unless they were designed to remove barriers from private investment. If it meant the right to income without a job, it was even more problematic, because somebody else had to be persuaded, or forced, to supply the wherewithal.

Those forced to do the paying were thereby not merely less free but possibly less inclined to make as much effort, particularly if higher earnings went not merely with higher levels of taxation but with greater levels of moral condemnation. (So it was with FDR's demonization of the rich in the 1930s, Obama's similar demonization throughout his term of office and the Occupy movement's condemnation of the "1 per cent.") At the same time there was the perpetual danger of welfare breeding dependence, which tends to destroy self-esteem and social relationships, as happened under the Great Society programs of President Lyndon Johnson.

This gets to the heart of the problem with the "trade-off" argument, which was used as a justification for regimes such as those of Fidel Castro. The "trade-off" is not simply between less freedom and more equality, because less freedom also means less wealth creation that would benefit all. In return, the regime may provide only the forced equality of poverty, as Communist Cuba all too clearly indicates.

Trade-offs that move from freedom to redistributive equality move into a repressive cul de sac. Milton Friedman noted that those willing to trade freedom for equality are likely to end up with neither.

This brings us to a fundamental difference between left and right in how they define "fairness." Left-liberals interpret it as promoting equality by forced redistribution — the securing of "positive rights." The right tends to emphasize "proportionality": since market incomes tend to reflect talent, effort and social usefulness, they should not be considered merely the source for some collective social pot, with higher incomes not just "fair game" for redistribution but the source of opprobrium. The right also stresses inevitable problems of dependency.

Jonathan Haidt acknowledges that left-liberals are "often willing to trade away fairness (as proportionality) when it conflicts with compassion or with their desire to fight oppression." The problem Haidt does not acknowledge is that left-liberals are not "trading away" anything of their own. They are indulging their "compassion" with other people's money, which inevitably implies its own form of oppression. That they require a justification for taking it helps explain the relentless invocation of "the gap" as something that must be closed in the name of social justice. It also explains the constant tendency to demonize some of the most useful people in society: it's a rationalization for taking their money.

Steven Pinker, too, suggests that "the major political philosophies can be defined by how they deal with the trade-off [between equality and freedom]. The Social Darwinist right places no value on equality; the totalitarian left places no value on freedom. The Rawlsian left sacrifices some freedom for equality; the libertarian right sacrifices some equality for freedom."

However, the use of the word "sacrifice" is in no way consistent as we move along the alleged trade-off scale (which begins with a "social Darwinist right" that exists only, if at all, in remote, heavily armed mountain huts). By this calculus there is no difference between somebody who takes your money, and somebody who does not take your money. After all, both are making "sacrifices." The first is sacrificing *you*; the second is sacrificing the interests of the potential recipients of your money. These are hardly moral equivalents.

The philosopher John Rawls (he of the "Rawlsian left") proposed that redistributionist arrangements should be formulated behind a "veil of ignorance," as if made by ethereal individuals who have no idea of their own talents or ambitions. In other words, they don't know if they are destined to be haves or have-nots. What this effectively means is that such "contracts" are decided by people such as Rawls, claiming to speak *on behalf of* the necessarily voiceless unborn: a sophistic twist on the oldest political trick in the book.

—m—

The Darwin Wars of the 1970s — which, I noted, were between the left and the farther left — seemed to frighten many evolutionary psychologists away from the political implications of their field of research. Paul Rubin nevertheless suggested in his book *Darwinian Politics* that cognitive errors were at the root of many left-wing policies. One element that I believe he failed to notice was the importance of that subconscious urge to power.

Rubin declared it "surprising" and "puzzling" that intellectuals supported more government, but surely many intellectuals derive their status and power from the policy advice that expansive government demands. It is more than what Hayek called the "fatal conceit" or Haidt dubbed the "rationalist delusion." It might be a conceit, but it is far from delusionary insofar as it serves political and bureaucratic self-interest, which tends to be psychologically suppressed.

Steven Pinker leaned toward evolutionary psychology's "right-wing" policy implications, but he was obviously aware that he was operating in an academic and political minefield. In the preface to his book *The Blank Slate*, Pinker suggested, "Nor does acknowledging human nature have the political implications so many fear." But then that depended, surely, on what they feared.

The fears to which Pinker referred likely related to the social Darwinism demonized by Richard Dawkins: the claim that capitalists believed that the weak should "go to the wall." But perhaps the elephants of power-seeking moralists were rightly fearful about what evolutionary psychology might have to tell them about their eager embrace of erroneous economic assumptions. One obvious elephant response would be to throw up a moralistic smokescreen, or perhaps a dust cloud.

—⟋⟍—

The 2007 Human Behavior and Evolution Society conference — at the beautiful campus of William and Mary in Williamsburg, Virginia — had a session specifically devoted to politics, but its presenters appeared eager to avoid controversy. This was most obvious in the final presentation, by a young academic from the London School of Economics. He concluded that an evolutionary perspective offered no particular comfort to either the right or the left. From the floor, I suggested that evolutionary insights should surely help us explain why "leftist" policies that produced perverse results — such as minimum wages and rent controls — kept being brought back. He appeared not to have a clue what I was talking about.

To suggest the inconclusiveness of the issue, the young academic had flashed the covers of two books on the screen behind the podium: *A Darwinian Left*, by the philosopher Peter Singer, and *Darwinian Conservatism*, by the political science professor Larry Arnhart. I subsequently read both books and found them anything but inconclusive.

In *A Darwinian Left*, Singer admitted that evolutionary psychology was as devastating to the left-wing cause as history had been, but he refused to give up the good fight, attempting — in Richard Dawkins style — to rise above the fray in a hot-air balloon of moral self-inflation.

"It is time for the left," he wrote, "to take seriously the fact that we are evolved animals." He also acknowledged that there are indeed biological reasons for a preponderance of male CEOs and politicians, and that social engineering has its limits. He conceded that "those seeking to reshape society must understand the tendencies inherent in human beings, and modify their abstract ideals in order to suit them." But it didn't seem to occur to him that the aspiration to "reshape society" might itself require some critical analysis.

Singer acknowledged that Marx's view of a malleable human nature reflecting "the ensemble of the social relations" had been utterly wrong, and that his "vanguard of the proletariat" had been a recipe for repression and mass murder. Yet Singer clung to the notion that evolutionary theory could tell us nothing about moral values. Thus we were — to paraphrase and parody Milton Friedman — "free to choose socialism," albeit a "new" version. One major problem was what this new socialism might look like.

Just as the British socialist sociologist Anthony Giddens had called in 1993 for a "new left synthesis," Peter Singer claimed that the left needed "a new paradigm." This seemed analogous to suggesting that theories of a flat earth or a geocentric universe might be saved via a "new paradigm" that left their fundamental assumptions intact. Singer gave ground on many points but refused to surrender the bedrock of his belief: a demonic parody of heartless capitalism.

"If we shrug our shoulders at the avoidable suffering of the weak and the poor, of those who are getting exploited and ripped off, or who simply do not have enough to sustain life at a decent level," he wrote, "we are not of the left. If we say that that is just the way the world is, and always will be, and there is nothing we can do about it, we are not part of the left. The left wants to do something about this situation."

The implication — typically — was that the non-left had no such compassionate concern. Singer meanwhile clung to the fundamental misinterpretation of economic relations as a power struggle rather than a cooperative exercise. He tediously conflated the competition of the market with that of "the jungle," demonized free trade and peddled images of noble trade unions under siege.

Singer didn't seem to have noticed that billions of people were being lifted from poverty around the world not by "compassionate" aid or forced redistribution but by increasingly free commercial cooperation. Moreover, he wrote as if the elaborate civil societies and generous welfare systems of advanced capitalist countries — the institutional embodiments of social concern — simply did not exist.

He continued to conventionally bemoan the allegedly rising "gap" between rich and poor. He couldn't bring himself to abandon Marx's condemnation of the naked "cash nexus." He claimed that "modern market economies are premised on the idea that we are all dominated by acquisitive and competitive desires." But who had ever stated this ridiculous straw man "premise" except anti-market ideologues?

Typically, he portrayed the market as a zero-sum game and dredged up an indicted Wall Street criminal, Ivan Boesky, and the fictional character Sherman McCoy, hapless anti-hero of Tom Wolfe's satire *The Bonfire of the Vanities*, as its typical denizens. He persisted in seeing a "competitive society" as the black to the white of his "cooperative society." He also delivered the hackneyed claim that money can't buy you happiness, and that, as a result, "public policy ... can ... appeal to the widespread need to feel wanted, or useful, or to belong to a community — all things more likely to come from cooperating with others than from competing with them."

But here he was not only misrepresenting market competition, he was failing to grasp the fundamental insights of neo-Darwinism — not to mention Enlightenment philosophers going back to Adam Smith and beyond. People are *by nature* cooperative and generous, and nowhere as cooperative and generous as under systems of "gentle commerce." (Significantly, Singer, in a common Freudian slip, misidentified Smith's Invisible Hand as a more sinister-sounding "hidden hand.") Public policy, far from promoting community, had been a proven destroyer of traditional values and communities as it intruded into or took over more and more aspects of social life.

Singer inevitably returned to the same old tried-and-failed socialist solutions: more redistribution, more central planning, all based on the parody of markets as the root of all evil. "When the free operation of competitive market forces makes it hazardous to walk the streets at night, governments do well to interfere with those market forces to promote employment." He seemed blind to the possibility that the "root cause" of much street violence was not the market but welfare ghettoization, or simple failure of the fundamental Smithian governmental responsibility of policing.

Singer's "new" left would somehow promote "genuine" altruism. As his slim, allegedly anti-Darwinian ray of hope, he cited blood banks, but contribution to blood banks is entirely explicable in terms of our evolved tendencies to feel sympathy and seek satisfying esteem within our communities. (After 9/11, I had immediately gone to give blood in Toronto. I couldn't get near the donation centre because of a massive lineup.) Thus Singer, despite claiming to have grasped the negative implications of neo-Darwinism for socialism, seemed, like the Bourbons, to have "learned nothing and forgotten nothing."

Larry Arnhart's *Darwinian Conservatism*, by contrast, pointed out that the "tragic" or "realist" view — that man is imperfect in both knowledge and virtue, and thus needs a political system in which power is constrained and balanced rather than being unleashed to "reshape" society — was abundantly borne out by the insights of Darwinism.

"A Darwinian science of human nature shows," he wrote, "how these conditions for ordered liberty conform to the natural desires of the human species as shaped by evolutionary history." The problem, which Arnhart didn't address, is that not everybody prizes liberty, at least liberty for others. He was thus perhaps too kind to the professed noble goals of socialism when he wrote that "socialists are driven by a utopian vision of a society without private property where all people share resources selflessly for the communal interest of all." But was that a genuine "vision," or a superficial Machiavellian rationalization eagerly embraced by potential vanguards of the elephant herd who got to make the rules, expropriate and dole out the "communal" property, and "manage" the economy?

Given the urge to rationalize power, it was inevitable that politicians would — as we have seen — tend to favour those brands of economics that rejected the Invisible Hand, emphasized "market failure" (and market "heartlessness") and promoted government intervention. They would also be blind both to their own motivations and to the adverse consequences of their policies. After all, they'd been built that way. We all are.

In *Thinking, Fast and Slow*, Daniel Kahneman's most arresting — even depressing — conclusion was that teaching psychology is mostly a waste of time, because people will ignore evidence that conflicts with their beliefs. This is just another way of agreeing with David Hume's insight that reason is a slave to passion; with Jonathan Haidt's conclusion that the "elephant" is in charge; and with David Livingstone Smith's insight that our minds are designed to reject the conclusions of studies of our minds. The irony was that Kahneman didn't seem to consider how his insight might apply to his own views about "traditional economics." (Of course, I have to be on guard for my own potential pro-market psychological biases too.)

One of Kahneman's more bizarre suggestions was that politicians should protect the public not merely from real threats but from *irrational* fears as well. In fact, there are few sources, or stokers, of irrational fear more dangerous than government.

—⁂—

The opening of Moscow McDonald's in 1990 had coincided with both the crumbling of the Soviet Union and the bicentennial of the death of Adam Smith. To celebrate the bicentennial, there had been an exhibition and conference in Edinburgh. Its attendees included a gaggle of Nobel laureates in economics. Other laureates sent academic papers to be read for them. These men were theoretically Smith's heirs, but they had all grown up in an era when Smith's free-market theories had been regarded as crude and unsophisticated. Indeed, some had been unembarrassed fans of the Soviets' "noble experiment" or admitted they had entered economics to prove that socialism worked.

The program for the Edinburgh exhibition, titled *Morals, Motives and Markets*, asserted, "Modern economic analysis constructs models of human behaviour and uses computers and statistical data to map this process at work and predict changes in it." One exhibit featured a computer with a program in which players could put themselves in the position of the British Chancellor of the Exchequer. By fiddling with government expenditures, tax rates and the money supply, they could attempt to bring down unemployment, stop inflation and balance the budget.

Nobody, it seemed, thought to square such pretensions with the quote from *The Wealth of Nations* featured in the exhibition's doorway: "It is the highest impertinence and presumption, in kings and ministers, to pretend to watch over the economy of private people." And wouldn't any Chancellor be a member of that breed to which Smith referred cynically as "that insidious crafty animal, vulgarly called a statesman or politician"?

The exhibit and the conference spoke volumes about economics' drift into both abstruse mathematical model-building and down-and-dirty economic manipulation for political purposes, the very antitheses of Smith's thrust. Many economists had retired to the ivory tower to pore over an ever-growing flood of statistics, which they attacked with matrix algebra and analytical geometry. Those models were eagerly sought by politicians eager for guidance on intervention.

The oldest laureate represented at Edinburgh was Jan Tinbergen, a Dutchman who had won the first Nobel Prize in economics in 1969. His academic paper suggested that the "birth of econometrics [data-based mathematical economics] meant the transformation of economics into a mature science." Such a view was far from universal. Indeed, some believed it represented dangerous delusion.

Statistics were the raw material of economic modelling, the servant of the twin conceits of government forecasting and planning, which Smith, Marshall, Mises, Hayek and Friedman had refuted and which were at that very moment coming so spectacularly unstuck in the Soviet Union.

Economic models were only ever Rube Goldberg–type conceptual contraptions, bound to be inaccurate for the simple reason that they could never either mirror the complexity of reality or forecast the essentially unknowable developments on which economic growth ultimately depended. What couldn't be measured was inevitably left out. The American Theodore Schultz, one of the laureates more in touch with reality, suggested that economics had abandoned Smith's notion of the critical importance of "human capital" — that is, what was inside people's heads — presumably because it couldn't fit it into any equation.

Nevertheless, even though their interventionist ideas had received an enormous setback in the previous decade, many of the laureates were keen to assert that the important thing was that their moral sentiments were in the right place. Jan Tinbergen was not embarrassed to admit that he had entered economics "to find a scientific base for a socialist order."

Significantly, socialism — the notion that governments could guide economies both more efficiently and more morally than the Invisible Hand — wasn't the conclusion of Tinbergen's studies any more than it had been for Marx. It was his starting point, his unshakable *moral* conviction. He saved his political praise not for Margaret Thatcher or Ronald Reagan, leaders who had together sought to hold back the advance of the megastate, but for Mikhail Gorbachev, the man who had cluelessly presided over the inevitable collapse of Soviet Communism.

Paul Samuelson was perhaps the most prominent representative in Edinburgh of the many followers of the macromanagerial pretensions of John Maynard Keynes, even though Keynesianism had collapsed in a heap in the previous 20 years (and would be back to collapse again in the wake of the 2008 crisis). Samuelson was famous for introducing complex mathematics into the profession. His predictions had included that the United States would suffer a postwar depression (it had boomed) and that the Soviet Union would likely surpass the United States in economic performance (it was collapsing). He had described capitalism as being like a car without a steering wheel, a telling analogy since it betrayed the aspirations of himself and those like him to "steer" the economy. Like many of his brethren, Samuelson saw market failure everywhere. Depressingly, he was the author of America's best-selling economics textbook.

Samuelson's presentation had a few kind words for Smith, but was otherwise almost a parody of the discipline's increasing obscurity. "Thus," he wrote in his conference paper, "in 1933, Bertil Ohlin revolutionized Ricardian trade theory by explicit use of Smith-Walras-Cassel cost-price equations; and he did so for the explicit purpose of formulating a Heckscher-Ohlin model of non-labour factor endowments that negates the Ricardian comparative advantage cost constancies."

Got that?

The laureate Wassily Leontief's paper, by contrast, decried economics' increasing use of mathematics and modelling. "Mathematical formulation," he declared, "permits theoretical model-builders to secure the internal logical consistency of their constructs but leaves the question of their factual relevance entirely open."

Nevertheless, if their interventionist pretensions were under attack, several of the laureates were not prepared to go down without a fight. The French laureate Maurice Allais declared, "I don't agree with the statement, as many people are saying, that the meaning of what we are seeing in Eastern Europe is the definite victory of the market economic system. That is not right, because if I look, for example, in my own country, so many people are agreeable to what they call humane socialism."

This raised that pregnant issue of why what was "agreeable" to so many people — not merely reflexively, or in theory, but in terms of bureaucratic and political career prospects — might not work in practice. The fruits of Allais's "humane socialism" could be seen in Europe 20 years later.

Other laureates too were clearly miffed at the reported death of the centrally planned economic dream. James Tobin declared that the collapse of Communism represented rather a victory for the "mixed economy" — in which government and business "worked together" — rather than Reaganism or Thatcherism. "We don't have any right to be complacent about our own organization of economic and social affairs," he claimed, "to think that wholesale deregulation and trusting everything to market forces, whatever that means, will solve our problems. There is some irony that the victory of Adam Smith over Lenin comes just at the time that capitalist economies face very serious problems that markets are not probably able to solve well."

So there. Meanwhile the idea that the government half of the "mix" might still be the problem remained on the "invisible" side of the analytical clock.

Allais declared, "In my opinion, what we need just now in Europe is some moderate protection against the outside world, particularly in agriculture but also in the textile industry and in ship building."

Was that whirring sound the patron saint of free trade revolving in his nearby grave? Smith had been against government economic intervention except under certain strictly limited circumstances. Instead, as this conference made clear, economists had become the handmaidens of intervention. This process had become ever more self-reinforcing. When it came to advising governments, non-believers in planning and macroeconomic management and skeptics about the pitfalls of the perpetual expansion of the "welfare state" mostly needed not apply.

It wasn't so much that you couldn't teach old economists new tricks as that economists perpetually sought to find new ways of justifying their unshakable, morally based interventionist pretensions. The proud socialist Jan Tinbergen fretted about overpopulation, pollution and the distribution of income, "which," he bemoaned, "is terribly unequal." Amazingly, at least for a Nobel prizewinning economist, Tinbergen spoke about the prospect of "running out of resources." However, he saw a ray of hope in the ability of grand transnational organizations such as the United Nations Environment Programme (UNEP) to deal with environmental problems at the global level.

The reference was profoundly significant, because instead of rolling over and dying in the wake of its manifest failures, socialism was morphing in a new, environmental direction, under the aegis of "sustainability." The UN, and in particular organizations such as UNEP, would be central to the push, at the heart of which was, as ever, anti-capitalism. The grand new cause was the theory of projected catastrophic man-made global warming.

fourteen
Moral Climate

*In reading the history of nations we find that whole communities
suddenly fix their minds upon one object, and go mad in its pursuit;
that millions of people become simultaneously impressed with
one delusion, and run after it, till their attention
is caught by some new folly.*
— Charles Mackay, *Memoirs of Extraordinary
Popular Delusions and the Madness of Crowds*

*Violent zeal for truth hath an hundred to one odds
to be either petulancy, ambition, or pride.*
— Jonathan Swift, *Apophthegms and Maxims*

In 2009, I attended a conference in New York City organized by the Heartland Institute, a Chicago-based libertarian think tank. Its theme was skepticism about the theory of catastrophic man-made global warming. At the end of one of the sessions — on the unfolding disaster of European "green" energy policies — a young man spoke up from the back of the room, declaring that he had never witnessed "such hypocrisy." How, he asked, could the panellists sleep at night?

One of the puzzled presenters asked the young man with which parts of their presentations he disagreed.

"Oh," said the young man. "I didn't come here to listen to the presentations."

Philip Tetlock, a psychologist at the University of Pennsylvania, coined the term "psychology of taboo" to describe the tendency to regard some perspectives as so morally wrong as to be both beneath contempt and beyond examination. Tetlock had asked his students their opinions on a number of contentious issues, including buying and selling human organs, auctioning adoption licences and buying one's way out of jury duty. They tended to be offended at even being asked to consider such proposals.

Significantly, buying organs, adoptees or a way out of jury duty involves the intrusion of commerce into "moral" issues: care, family and civic duty. Whereas commercial values are all about haggling, moral values tend to be seen as absolute and non-negotiable. Evolution has "designed" us to regard them that way to make them more effective as motivators. The dark side of non-negotiability is that it involves demonization of those who hold alternative views. They are, by definition, "immoral" and likely wickedly motivated.

How can these hypocrites sleep at night?

The psychology of taboo has blanketed arguably the dominant scientific and political issue of the last decade of the 20th century and the first decade of the 21st — which, to be clear, is not "global warming" or "climate change" but the *theory* of catastrophic projected man-made climate change *due to* global warming. (Global warming and climate change are thus not strictly interchangeable terms, although they tend to be used as such.)

Few dispute that there was a slight overall warming in the 20th century, of around 0.8 degrees Celsius. No sensible person denies that the climate changes. The issues are the causes of temperature movements, the case for projected catastrophe and the viability and implications of draconian policies proposed to prevent it.

In a rational world, dealing with any threat from man-made global warming should be a matter of cost-benefit analysis. One problem is that such a calculation is enormously complex and depends on the science being known and the economics clear. However, cost-benefit analysis — which is in any case perpetually open to being rigged — and moral issues make for uneasy bedfellows. Indeed, merely to suggest such a "weighing" of economic costs and benefits is to invite that psychology of taboo.

How, in any case, say the believers, could "normal" pedantic scientific standards of testability and falsifiability be applied, when "proof" could mean global calamity? Those who dared to question science or policy were prepared to play Russian roulette with the planet. And when it came to fairness, the rich nations had taken more than their "fair share" of the atmosphere's "services," and thus should step back and leave more for the poor, for whom somebody had to "speak up." To take requisite action would require unprecedented power, although now it would take the form of vast schemes of global bureaucratic cooperation rather than a direct global dictatorship. Not global government, just "global governance."

When it comes to harm and fairness — the two moral "receptors" Jonathan Haidt described as the biggest concerns of left-liberals — climate change is like Red Bull, not merely because of the alleged existential threat to humanity, but because the main culprit is the old enemy: capitalist big business, in particular the fossil fuel industry. Skeptics were thus to be discounted or ignored on moral grounds. Even if they weren't financially — or even wickedly — motivated, they were clearly biased by their irrational "fundamentalist" commitment to perfect markets.

—w—

Jon Haidt hadn't let conservatives off the hook in his controversial 2011 speech in San Antonio. While acknowledging that left-liberal assumptions might have blinded social scientists on some issues, such as race, he suggested that "climate change denialism" was an example of conservative moral bias, of another "community ... protecting their sacralized free markets."

Although Haidt was to be congratulated for recognizing left-liberal biases, his objectivity seemed to have limits. His term "climate change denialism" implied refusal to see unarguable "truth" and amounted to demonization. The term "denialism" implied mental disorder, when what was really under debate was a theory about the distant future. Haidt had also inevitably fallen prey to that moral dimension that he claimed was much more important for the right than the left: "authority," in this case the authority of "settled" science.

Haidt was certainly correct in implying that the theory of catastrophic man-made global warming was about much more than the prospect of worse weather. It represented an attack — indeed an unprecedented attack — on capitalism and the free markets on which it depended. It claimed that the Invisible Hand had dropped the ball when it came to the most vital game of all: human survival. Haidt claimed that fans of the Invisible Hand were more concerned with their metaphor than with scientific objectivity.

Economists have always recognized that industrial activity may generate pollution that inflicts costs on third parties. Such externalities have to be dealt with through the market — by a deal between polluters and pollutees — or controlled by regulation or mitigated by innovation. However, in the notion that industrial emissions would lead to mighty floods, unprecedented droughts, violent storms and international conflict we see the mother of all externalities.

There is no such thing as a climate "crisis." No extreme weather event has been linked, or can be linked, to human causes. Global warming is, according to the preponderance of analyses, meant to be beneficial up to at least 2050. Yet the proposed solution to this allegedly massive *prospective* problem was to curb industrial emissions of carbon dioxide and other greenhouse gases via gargantuan international agreements. Developed countries had to tax or otherwise restrict fossil-fuel-based industrial activity. They also had to promote energy alternatives such as windmills, solar panels and biofuels and subsidize "clean" development in the Third World as part of a new foreign aid thrust.

One obvious problem was that these "new" development policies were variants of the same old top-down industrial strategies and redistributionist foreign aid schemes that had been outright failures in the past. The more fundamental issue, however, was the solidity of the science.

—⚏—

Thomas S. Kuhn, in his classic book *The Structure of Scientific Revolutions*, pointed out that science is a much messier process than generally recognized. Scientists adopt and commit to theoretical "paradigms," which then become fundamentally unquestionable. "Professionalization" of any paradigm leads to "an immense restriction of the scientist's vision and to a considerable resistance to paradigm change." This stance, said Kuhn, is hardened even further if moral values are involved.

Science had clashed with morality and religion before Darwin presented the ultimate challenge to man's self-esteem. Just a few centuries before Darwin there had been consensus among the Western cognoscenti that the world had been created in seven days, was flat and stood at the centre of the universe. Giordano Bruno, the 16th-century Italian philosopher, had been burned at the stake for daring to suggest that the earth moves.

The origins of the universe may be beyond the bounds of human comprehension, but scientists now believe that the earth's evolution took place over billions of years and can be best understood by sciences such as astrophysics, chemistry and biology. The advance of science, along with its popular dissemination, has meant that few people now believe that the earth is flat or the universe geocentric, although many still believe in divine Creation.

Belief in a flat earth is not essentially moral. It is, rather, intuitive "folk" physics. How could you stand on the bottom of a giant ball? You'd fall off. But the notion that the earth was the centre of the universe was very much mixed up with man's assessment of his own God-given, and God-like, significance.

Weather has often been seen as an instrument of divine retribution. Poseidon and Zeus wielded storms and thunderbolts. Many Biblical tales have a powerful environmental element: the rain of fire and brimstone that fell on Sodom and Gomorrah; the plagues of Egypt; Noah's Ark. Indeed, the story of the Flood bears remarkable similarity to current climate concerns. Bad behaviour (in the form of greed, crass materialism and attendant greenhouse gas emissions) will lead to a mighty inundation (caused by the melting of the polar ice caps), which requires a Custodian to preserve all the earth's animals (guarding biodiversity with policy "arks"). We seem here to be as much in the realm of Joseph Campbell's mythology as we are dealing with physics or chemistry.

Belief in extreme weather is particularly prone to the feature of human psychology known as "confirmation bias." There is always extreme weather happening somewhere, indeed at many places, all over the earth, so if you are worried about climate catastrophe, you will find lots of examples to feed your anxiety. Believing is seeing. You will also be inclined to dismiss any contrary view. Ears have walls.

It was inevitable, for example, that Superstorm Sandy in 2012 would be linked to man-made global warming, which also proved a convenient scapegoat for politicians eager to avoid blame for having failed to take measures protecting the citizenry against an entirely predictable event (as with Hurricane Katrina in 2005). But there is nothing unusual about these "extreme weather events," which have not been increasing, despite the claims of Munich Re, the German insurance giant. Insurance companies are naturally concerned about catastrophic events, but they can also use such projections to justify rate hikes. Greater weather loss figures are relentlessly cited by alarmists, but these have nothing to do with more bad weather. They are due to ever more valuable property being damaged in extreme-weather-prone areas. Manhattan has seen bigger storms. Sandy was caused by a confluence of events — primarily hurricane winds and a high tide. There is no way it could be linked scientifically to human activity.

However, that's where confirmation bias comes in. If you are inclined to believe in man-made global warming, you will see the hand of man in every weather event, and you will easily be persuaded that things are getting "worse." And confirmation bias isn't just for lay people. To paraphrase the Doobie Brothers again: what a scientist believes, he sees, even if those beliefs do not happen to coincide with reality. Indeed, Thomas Kuhn suggested that a scientist, as the captive of a paradigm, is "like the typical character of Orwell's 1984, the victim of a history rewritten by the powers that be."

But is it not far-fetched to suggest that the entire science community might have been corrupted by ideology, or so easily manipulated, even if they were in the grip of a Kuhnian paradigm? In fact, another critical factor that contributed both to accepting the potentially catastrophic "problem" and to believing that it could be rationally "solved" was that scientists tend toward reflexive anti-capitalism, "unreflecting centralism" and economics-challenged Malthusianism. Albert Einstein was one of the greatest scientists of all time, but he wrote of the "economic anarchy of capitalist society" and strongly advocated a "planned economy."

Being brighter than average, but embracing folk-economic assumptions, scientists are more susceptible to the belief that what the world needs is more deliberate organization "from above" by people such as themselves — what Hayek called the "fatal conceit" of rationalist constructivism. Rupert Darwall also suggested in his book *The Age of Global Warming* that scientists tend to have a "cultural aversion to learning from the past. For them, history is not so much a closed book as irrelevant to the problems of the future."

Haidt had acknowledged the leftist bias of the social science community, but that bias is found, perhaps surprisingly, in the natural sciences as well. A 2005 study by the academics Stanley Rothman, S. Robert Lichter and Neil Nevitte found that "three out of four biologists and computer scientists now place themselves to the left of centre, as do about two thirds of mathematicians, chemists, and physicists." Indeed, among physicists, the study found that self-described Democrats outnumbered Republicans in American universities by more than ten to one.

One of the first great policy wonks, Francis Bacon (1561-1626), had projected a New Atlantis — a society that would be run by scientists on the basis of "facts." The libertarian economist Murray Rothbard castigated Bacon as "the prophet of primitive and naive empiricism, the guru of fact grubbing." Rothbard wrote, "No scientific truths are ever discovered by inchoate fact-digging. The scientist must first have framed hypotheses; in short, the scientist, before gathering and collating the facts, must have a pretty good idea of what to look for, and why." "Capitalism did it" is a particularly appealing catch-all hypothesis for many alleged social evils, from gaps in wealth (where capitalism is indeed "guilty") to poverty (where it is certainly not). The notion that the industrial emissions of a feckless and greedy system might be threatening the planet nicely fitted the demonic profile.

Baconian thinking had been behind the founding of the British Royal Society. In *Gulliver's Travels*, Swift had parodied the early Royal Society's pretensions in his floating island of Laputa, which was inhabited by distracted boffins who were not merely impractical but tyrannical. In the modern era, nobody foresaw the dangers of technocracy better than U.S. president Dwight Eisenhower. Most people are aware of Ike's warning in 1961 about the "military-industrial complex." Less often quoted is his observation that "in holding scientific research and discovery in respect, as we should, we must also be alert to the equal and opposite danger that public policy could itself become the captive of a scientific-technological elite." Karl Popper too noted the dangers to an open society of science being controlled by a "small group of specialists." In fact, catastrophic climate theory would cultivate a relatively large group of specialists because climate touched everything. Never had a scientific theory been both so morally charged and so full of political — and career — potential.

—⚏—

The *annus mirabilis* for putting global warming on the political map was 1988. It was the year of a major climate conference in Toronto; of the creation of the UN's Intergovernmental Panel on Climate Change (IPCC); of a significant speech on the issue by Margaret Thatcher — an unlikely early supporter of a cause that promoted global economic controls; and, most significantly, of dramatic testimony before the U.S. Congress by James Hansen, a climate scientist with the space agency NASA. "The greenhouse effect has been detected," Hansen told the Senate Energy and Natural Resources Committee, "and it is changing our climate now." Hansen was a protegé of Al Gore, then a presidential aspirant. If, as Steven Pinker subsequently suggested, the threat of climate change became "the occasion for a moralistic revival meeting," Al Gore would be its Elmer Gantry.

As it happened, 1988 produced a particularly hot summer in most of North America. (It was the summer my Cuban friend Ignacio was looking for his air conditioner and claiming there should be more "planning.") But the timing of Hansen's heated testimony was not accidental. Timothy Wirth, a powerful Democratic politician, admitted in a 2007 PBS interview, "We called the Weather Bureau and found out what historically was the hottest day of the summer . . . So we scheduled the hearing that day, and bingo, it was the hottest day on record in

Washington or close to it." Wirth also admitted that associates had gone into the hearing room the night before and opened all the windows to make the room as hot as possible, to thwart the air conditioning.

Thatcher's support for the theory — she declared before the Royal Society that humanity might have "unwittingly begun a massive experiment with the system of the planet itself" — suggested that the hypothesis could hardly be written off as a left-wing plot. Although her speech received (unlike Hansen's testimony) almost no coverage, Thatcher's own status and authority were critical in putting global warming on the international agenda and setting Britain on the path to becoming — at considerable cost — a "champion" of draconian policy. (The Iron Lady would subsequently modify her views.)

The subsequent, oft-repeated claim that climate science was "settled" — which was itself essentially unscientific — was rooted in the alleged authority of the IPCC. We all have to rely on authority for most of what we believe, but, as the Milgram experiments confirm, authority can be used to lead us astray. The IPCC was politicized from the start. It had been created to press a particular — and particularly useful — scientific viewpoint. As a 2010 report by the InterAcademy Council, a representative body of national science academies, acknowledged, the IPCC stood at the intersection of science and politics. That is a problematic location for those aspiring to objectivity, but a fruitful one for those aspiring to power.

IPCC assessment reports (there had been four up to 2007, with a fifth due in 2013-14) were voluminous exercises involving scores of "peer-reviewed" studies, which people took to mean "rigorously vetted by acknowledged experts." The sheer number of those experts (most often cited as 2,500) constituted, according to catastrophists, an unassailable "consensus." In fact, most of those studies were not about climate at all, but about the consequences *if* global warming accelerated. The IPCC's climate studies contained numerous caveats, but few people read them.

Instead, the media and public were guided to "Summaries for Policymakers," which tended to be slanted toward the generation of scary headlines. Lord Andrew Turnbull, the former head of the British civil service, and a skeptic, commented that they should have been called "Summaries *by* Policymakers."

The reports were in fact not offering predictions, although most people imagined they were. They were creating "scenarios" of the if-then variety. Richard S. Lindzen, professor of meteorology at MIT and a prominent skeptic, pointed out that these were "scary scenarios for which there is no evidence."

In fact, other scientists had already admitted alarmist bias. Stephen Schneider, a notable Stanford professor who in the 1970s had been an ardent proponent of a theory of catastrophic global cooling, suggested in 1989 that scientists had to offer up "scary scenarios" to get attention. "On the one hand," he observed, "as scientists we are ethically bound to the scientific method, in effect promising to tell the truth, the whole truth, and nothing but — which means that we must include all the doubts, the caveats, the ifs, ands, and buts. On the other hand, we are not just scientists but human beings as well. And like most people we'd like to see the world a better place, which in this context translates into our working to reduce the risk of potentially disastrous climatic change. To do that we need to get some broad based support, to capture the public's imagination. That, of course, means getting loads of media coverage. So we have to offer up scary scenarios, make simplified, dramatic statements, and make little mention of any doubts we might have. This 'double ethical bind' we frequently find ourselves in cannot be solved by any formula. Each of us has to decide what the right balance is between being effective and being honest. I hope that means being both."

Some within the IPCC had in fact pointed to a more fundamental politicization, beyond what was apparent in the "Summaries for Policymakers." After the second report, Frederick Seitz, a leading physicist and former president of the U.S. National Academy of Sciences, said that he had never witnessed a "more disturbing corruption of the peer-review process." There was a two-stage problem: corruption of peer review when it came to the underlying climate studies, and cherry picking when it came to the summaries drawn from them.

—m—

Climate has changed since the earth first cooled and solidified. The spot where I now sit was once (in fact, numerous times) buried under hundreds of metres of ice. Nobody disputes the so-called greenhouse effect, which is essential to life on earth as we know it. Heat from the sun is reflected from the earth's surface in the form of infrared rays, and a portion of these rays is trapped in the atmosphere by various greenhouse gases, GHGs, of which water vapour is in fact the most significant. Carbon dioxide, however, is the GHG that gets all the attention.

The average global temperature (although itself a fraught concept) has risen by something less than 1 degree Celsius in the past century, at the same time as concentrations of carbon dioxide have increased, because of industrial emissions. Carbon dioxide levels rose from 290 parts per million before the Industrial Revolution to around 400 ppm by 2013. However, one of the first caveats of logic is that correlation does not mean causation. Certainly, according to atmospheric physics, increases in carbon dioxide levels should, other things being equal, lead to small increases in temperatures, but other things are never equal in the massively complex system of the earth's climate. Moreover, catastrophic projections depend on computer models that assume powerful positive feedbacks, thus multiplying the temperature effect of the increased carbon dioxide.

The term "greenhouse effect" is misleading, since garden or commercial greenhouses trap heat by the physical barriers of their glass roofs and walls, thus preventing air circulation from dispersing it. In the atmosphere, by contrast, air turbulence is one of the factors that make predicting the weather so difficult. To complicate matters further, greenhouse growers often *do* pump carbon dioxide into their facilities, but this is not what makes them hot. Carbon dioxide promotes plant growth. More of it goes with a greener earth.

By the beginning of 2013, contrary to official forecasts, there had been no global warming for some 16 years. All computer models had predicted higher levels of warming over the previous 40 years than had actually occurred. This suggested that "the science" needed at least to be revisited. However, pointing out such facts resulted not in acknowledgement of the need for sober reassessment but in anger, as did all questioning of the official scientific paradigm.

Skeptics were demonized as deranged "deniers" or, worse, as "shills" for the giant fossil-fuel-producing corporations, which were allegedly waging a vast campaign of disinformation. One man ranked as finger-pointer in chief.

—⚏—

Al Gore has claimed that his moral perspective on the environment arose from a personal epiphany. In the introduction to his 1992 book, *Earth in the Balance: Ecology and the Human Spirit,* Gore wrote that, in 1989, he had seen his son almost killed in a car accident, not long after he had lost a presidential campaign and turned 40. "This life change," he explained, "has caused me to be increasingly impatient with the status quo, with conventional wisdom, with the lazy assumption that we can always muddle through." Thenceforth Gore had wholeheartedly embraced hellwards-in-handbasket environmentalism. In fact, he had already brought James Hansen to Congress on a predictably hot day.

"What a striking contrast between the awesome power and efficiency our economic system displayed in its philosophical rout of Marxism-Leninism," wrote Gore, "and the abject failure of the very same system to even take note of the poisoning of our water, the fouling of our air, the destruction of tens of thousands of living species every year."

Gore was wrong on all counts. Marxism-Leninism had arguably never been routed "philosophically," only in fact. Marxist assumptions about the evils of capitalism were still widespread. Moreover, far from failing to take note of the environment, the United States had been invaded by something approaching environmental hysteria in the previous two decades.

Frances Cairncross, then the environment editor of the *Economist*, pointed out in her book *Costing the Earth*, which was published around the same time as Gore's, that environmental regulations were costing the United States over $100 billion a year. One of the pieces of legislation she cited for outstandingly expensive ineffectiveness was the so-called Superfund law to clean up hazardous chemical dump sites. Passage of that controversial law had been championed by Gore.

Earth in the Balance was a bible of alarmism that seemed to indicate far more about Gore's own needy psyche than it did about the state of the world. Moral epiphanies of the kind that had inspired Gore's book didn't necessarily make people think very clearly. Injured egos often search for grand causes. Radical environmentalism appeared a particularly attractive refuge for the troubled soul. Subsequent events would make Gore's soul even more troubled.

After he lost to George W. Bush in the disputed 2000 presidential election, Gore went into messianic overdrive, taking jeremiads about the "climate crisis" on the lecture circuit, where he found a willing congregation. That crusade was portrayed in the Oscar-winning 2006 documentary *An Inconvenient Truth*.

The movie was a propaganda masterpiece. It showed the stolid former veep presenting his paradoxically slick message — complete with sophisticated visuals and clever props — to rapt audiences. The presentation was interwoven with his personal story and shots of his global travels in pursuit of his environmental white whale. As with Captain Ahab, however, travel seemed to narrow Gore's mind. Whether he was at the North Pole, at the South Pole or in the Amazon, he appeared to see only one conclusion: Apocalypse Soon.

Unless, that is, we started listening to him.

Gore, typically, treated all skeptics as apostates, who either had been corrupted by naked self-interest or were suitable cases for psychiatric treatment. "Fifteen per cent of the people believe the moon landing was staged on some movie lot and a somewhat smaller number still believe the earth is flat," he claimed. "They all get together on a Saturday night and party with the global warming deniers."

But much of what Gore claimed to be the "truth" wasn't inconvenient: it was plain wrong. His eye-catching presentations — especially mounting a hydraulic hoist to indicate carbon dioxide levels literally heading through the roof — were brilliantly effective but utterly misleading.

As the psychologist Daniel Kahneman pointed out, humans are not very good with numbers. How do we put that carbon dioxide rise in parts per million — from 290 to 400 — into perspective? What would it look like on a graspable scale, and in a reasonable perspective?

Let's say the contents of the atmosphere are displayed on a chart a kilometre high, which would be roughly three times the height of the Empire State Building. The amount of carbon dioxide in the atmosphere in the early 21st century would equate to about the height of a low coffee table, and the increase since before the Industrial Revolution to the height of a coffee mug. This is not to say that such a minuscule change in the composition of the atmosphere might not have significant effects; it's just that — as Gore's shtick with the hydraulic hoist indicated — "evidence" was being presented in the most alarming way.

Gore's film was filled with assertions that were dubious or simply untrue, including the claimed clear causal link between carbon dioxide levels and temperatures. Even Bert Bolin, the first head of the IPCC, noted that Gore's suggestion that carbon dioxide levels determined ice ages was entirely wrong.

Contrary to Gore's assertions, Hurricane Katrina — which had devastated New Orleans and which Gore featured prominently — could in no way be attributed to man-made global warming. Antarctica was not melting. Polar bear populations were in fact flourishing. Greenland's ice cap was in no danger of slipping into the sea. Gore's "facts" regarding the links between global warming and disease — particularly malaria — were refuted by health specialists. His claim that the rate of extinction was currently 1,000 times historical levels was based, again, on computer models supported by no physical evidence whatsoever. A British high court, in response to a parent's objection to the film being shown in government schools, found Gore's movie to be "misleading" in nine respects when compared with the scientific conclusions of the IPCC.

Gore's most egregious claim was that there was no credible scientific disagreement with his point of view. Any skepticism, he claimed, was a product of a manipulated "corporate" media. In fact, Gore's film was greeted with an almost complete *lack* of skepticism in the mainstream media, which overwhelmingly bought into claims that those who denied the conventional alarmist wisdom were shills or cranks.

Gore claimed that the moral aspects of climate change placed it "beyond politics." But moral issues are the deepest motivators of — and justifications for — political activism. As Paul Slovic of the Oregon Research Institute, a leading psychologist of risk, points out, "Defining risk is ... an exercise in power."

What Gore really seemed to be claiming was that we should move past "quibbling" about objective truth and get straight to draconian action, which just happened to coincide with his own brand of politics: more regulation and bigger government; more redistribution both within and between states; and more government support for "alternative" energy (in which Gore was a major investor).

An Inconvenient Truth wasn't the only factually challenged, morally charged, climate-related blockbuster of 2006. That year also saw the publication of a report for the British government by Sir Nicholas Stern, the chief economist at the Treasury and former chief economist of the World Bank. The Stern Review had been commissioned by the Chancellor of the Exchequer at the time, Gordon Brown, to address a scathing critique of U.K. climate policy by a committee of the House of Lords. Significantly, it was released the same week that Brown announced a new environmental advisor: Al Gore.

The review — whose main text ran to 550 pages — was accompanied by a government press release that cut straight to its arresting conclusion: that the costs of unabated climate change would be the equivalent of at least 5 per cent of global GDP each year, and as much as 20 per cent "or more." The price of avoiding the worst impacts could be "limited to around 1% of Global GDP each year."

Spend 1 per cent of global GDP to save between 5 and 20 per cent of global GDP? It seemed like a no-brainer, especially since you would be addressing what Sir Nicholas (later, for his services to the Labour government, ennobled to Lord) Stern described as "the greatest market failure the world has ever seen." But such a claim was invalid for the simple reason that the world hadn't "seen" it. Few reporters thought to ask where this alleged ecological and economic holocaust was actually taking place.

The Stern Review was a thoroughly political document. The most flagrant way in which it cooked the economic books was by using an artificially low "discount rate" to exaggerate the present costs of alleged future catastrophe. Individuals discount the future by deciding, say, that a bird in the hand is worth two in a year's time, but Stern rejected actual rates of discount — which are most commonly reflected in market interest rates — as being too high, and "myopic." His review suggested that "a high rate of discounting the future" — that is, the actual rate used by real people — "will favour avoiding the costs of reducing emissions now." The review conspicuously failed to point out that an artificially low rate, by contrast, would favour current intervention by exaggerating the present value of future costs, and thus would be politically attractive to interventionists.

Stern's supposed ethical trump card was that the market had no way of accounting for the fate of people a hundred years hence. Future generations, claimed Stern, "lacked representation." To discount the future was to cheapen the lives of the unborn. One obvious response might be to note that capitalism had done a commendable job of looking after its future generations in the previous two hundred years, especially when set against centrally planned alternatives of the type Stern was proposing.

Bizarrely, Stern suggested that the unborn of the distant future should have equal "weight" with present generations. "Are there any persuasive ethical arguments," he asked, "for discrimination by birth date?" Such thinking certainly put abortion out of the question, but it also suggested that those who had not even been *conceived* might rank with those living now. It was a proposition out of Jonathan Swift, or perhaps George Orwell.

The Stern Review was as widely criticized by professional economists as it was lauded in the media, which meant that the criticisms tended not to get too much coverage. Critics pointed out that apart from his cooked discount rate, Stern ignored adaptation. He assumed people would sit around while water lapped at their ankles. He also invariably cited worst-case scenarios.

Richard Tol, one of the world's leading environmental economists and himself an IPCC contributor, described Stern's prophecies as "preposterous" and concluded that Stern himself was "alarmist and incompetent." However, Stern's conclusions served political interests, whose aspirations were unprecedented anywhere outside the old Soviet Union.

In 2007, the IPCC and Al Gore shared the Nobel Peace Prize for promoting an issue that had set the nations of the world at each other's throats.

—m—

The Kyoto Accord — which emerged from negotiations subsequent to the mammoth 1992 UN Conference on Environment and Development in Rio de Janeiro — projected a vast scheme of coordinated international action to restrain emissions. Under the subsequent Kyoto Protocol, which was signed by more than 150 countries, just 40 industrialized nations — accounting for not much more than a quarter of man-made global emissions, and excluding the United States and Australia — promised to cut greenhouse gas emissions to below 1990 levels by 2008-12.

Some of those who signed on — Canada in particular — did so without a clue about how they would achieve these objectives, although there was one potentially very expensive way out. The development agenda was to be served by poor countries selling "credits" for non-emissions to rich countries, thus effectively monetizing non-activity.

By the time Kyoto was ratified and came into effect in early 2005, it was obvious that signatories were going to miss their targets. Canada's emissions were around 30 per cent above its Kyoto commitments. The most glaring flaw in the policy — if, that is, it was really intended to cut down on greenhouse gas emissions rather than simply halt growth, install more government control and promote global redistribution — had become even more obvious. Developing countries, in particular China and India, which were destined to become the greatest emitters of GHGs, faced no restrictions and fiercely resisted adopting them. But perhaps the most dramatic fact about Kyoto — which had led to political Sturm und Drang at every level — was that even if its commitments had been met, the projected impact on average global temperatures would have amounted to a decrease of 0.1 degree Celsius by 2050.

The Kyoto process and the search for an inevitably more draconian agreement to replace it were already falling apart toward the end of 2009, when, just before another vast climate meeting in Copenhagen, a cache of emails to and from one of the IPCC's principal nodes of climate data, the Climatic Research Unit (CRU) of the University of East Anglia, was — depending where you stood on the climate issue — "hacked," "stolen" or "liberated." What they revealed appeared to confirm Thomas Kuhn's insights about the jealous guarding of paradigms and Jon Haidt's point that even scientists tended to form "tribal moral communities" that can be both "blinded" and "bound" by their assumptions.

—m—

The long-term temperature record is an important issue for climate theory. Temperature readings are taken from a limited number of weather stations, some of which are located near heat sources (although "official" science claims to adjust for this). Satellite data are more reliable but go back only a relatively short period. When it comes to more distant past temperatures, and the amounts of carbon dioxide in the atmosphere, scientists have to rely on "proxies": that is, on inferences drawn from sources such as tree rings and ice cores.

The Hockey Stick — a long-term temperature graph that appeared to show that the previous millennium had consisted of 900 years of moderate temperatures followed by an upward swoosh in the 20th century to coincide with rising man-made carbon dioxide emissions — was built upon a reconstruction of pre-thermometer temperatures derived from tree rings. It had been carried out by a team led by an ambitious and aggressive young University of Massachusetts paleoclimatologist named Michael Mann. His co-authors were Ray Bradley and Malcolm Hughes.

The Hockey Stick was eagerly embraced by the IPCC. As Lawrence Solomon pointed out in his book *The Deniers*, "More than any other single piece of evidence, [the Hockey Stick] made global warming a serious popular and political issue."

The graph was the star exhibit of the IPCC's Third Assessment Report in 2001. The year 1998 was declared to have been the warmest of the past millennium. Mann was soon appointed a scientific advisor to the U.S. government. He moved to the University of Pennsylvania and became the recipient of hefty research grants. In 2002, *Scientific American* named him one of "50 leading visionaries in science."

The Climategate emails suggested that something beyond mere reconstruction was afoot. Mann featured prominently in the exchanges, but their central figure was the head of the CRU, Phil Jones. The emails showed that Jones and his colleagues had engaged in doctoring data, attempting to influence peer review, hiding or destroying information to avoid freedom-of-information requests and deliberately plotting to exclude skeptics both from receiving relevant information and from participating in the IPCC process. They also revealed the frustration of IPCC scientists that the global warming trend seemed to have stopped. Jones subsequently admitted, "My colleagues and I accept that some of the published emails do not read well."

Many of the emails referred to attempts to frustrate or block inquiry into the Hockey Stick by two Canadians, Steve McIntyre and Ross McKitrick. McIntyre, a retired mining engineer who happened to be a mathematical genius with Terminator-like persistence, had become particularly suspicious of the science behind the Hockey Stick. The graph was just "too neat." It reminded him of the sort of charts produced by mining promoters. He was joined in his investigations by McKitrick, an economics professor at the University of Guelph.

When McIntyre had contacted Mann asking for details of his reconstruction, Mann at first refused, then revealed his data only slowly and grudgingly. Phil Jones, in the same vein, had sent an amazing response to an Australian researcher asking why he, Jones, should provide the Australian with data "when your aim is to try and find something wrong with it." But of course that is exactly why data and methods should be made freely available: to see if there is something wrong with them.

One of the most incriminating emails was from Phil Jones, referring to a "trick ... to hide the decline" in proxy data. For the period after 1960, a tree ring study by Keith Briffa, another paleoclimatologist belonging to what McIntyre called the "Hockey Team," had indicated declining temperatures. The problem was that actual thermometer readings were rising. The "trick" wasn't some ingenious algorithm, as suggested by its perpetrators; it involved substituting actual readings for the proxies without drawing attention to the fact.

Nor was the "adjustment" a mere technical detail. Tree rings are of necessity problematic because other factors beside temperature influence growth. Also, they inevitably reflect conditions only in particular areas. Briffa's proxies' failure to coincide with recorded reality after 1960 created obvious credibility problems for the Hockey Stick. Its 900-year straight "handle" had — conveniently — eliminated both the Medieval Warm Period, when the Vikings were farming in Greenland, and the Little Ice Age, when fairs were regularly held on a frozen Thames. If temperatures were as warm or warmer a thousand years ago, then the claim that 20th-century warming was unprecedented was weakened.

McIntyre and McKitrick's relentless digging revealed that Mann's conclusions rested on dodgy statistical manipulation of a small amount of data from a few unreliable proxy trees in very specific locations. The deeper they dug, the more they found shoddy work and cherry picking of data. And they were not the only ones questioning the work of the CRU. The British climate blogger Andrew Montford wrote two diligently researched books, *The Hockey Stick Illusion: Climategate and the Corruption of Science* and *Hiding the Decline: A History of the Climategate Affair*, in which Mann and his colleagues emerged as an unresponsive clique, who, like any dedicated "tribal moral community," were inclined to demonize their opponents.

Mann wrote to Marcel Crok, a Dutch investigative science journalist, "I hope you are not fooled by any of the 'myths' about the hockey stick that are perpetrated by contrarians, right-wing think tanks, and fossil fuel industry disinformation." Mann claimed that McIntyre and McKitrick "had suspiciously close ties with the fossil fuel/energy industry." This was untrue; they had no ties at all to that industry.

Mann also declared that giving McIntyre the computer code for his research would amount to "giving in to ... intimidation tactics." But McIntyre published his entire correspondence with Mann, and there was nary a trace of "intimidation."

As a result of political interest in the Hockey Stick affair, two inquiries were launched by the U.S. Congress. One was brief and superficial. The other, headed by Edward Wegman, a prominent statistician, found McIntyre and McKitrick's critique "valid and compelling." Wegman concluded that Mann's claims for 1998 as the hottest year in a millennium "cannot be supported by his analysis."

The behind-the-scenes shenanigans to thwart McIntyre and McKitrick revealed by the Climategate emails confirmed that peer review had — at least in some cases — become a corrupted process whose purpose was to support the catastrophist hypothesis rather than test it. It had become a professional Kuhnian paradigm, rendered all the more unquestionable because of its moral element.

While "breaking" the Hockey Stick didn't conclusively demolish the theory of catastrophic man-made global warming, it did indicate major problems both in the science and with the IPCC process, since nobody had spotted the Mann data's deficiencies (in fact, as an IPCC lead author, Mann had reviewed his own work). It also confirmed that the IPCC might put useful propaganda before good science.

—m—

As fascinating as the Climategate emails themselves was the reaction they provoked. Governments that had committed to the climate catastrophe paradigm tended to leap into white-wash-cum-demonization mode. The White House spokesman Robert Gibbs claimed, "I think that this notion that there is some debate ... on the science is kind of silly." The UK's secretary of state for climate change, Ed Miliband, branded Nigel Lawson, a respected former British Chancellor of the Exchequer and climate skeptic who had called for an inquiry into the emails, a "climate saboteur." (Lawson would found the Global Warming Policy Foundation, an influential think tank that concentrated on the policy flaws attached to climate alarmism rather than defects in the science.) Prime Minister Gordon Brown thundered about "behind-the-times, anti-science, flat-Earth climate sceptics."

There was a widespread effort to downplay the emails. They were said to prove nothing; to be the notes of only a small group of researchers out of the thousands who allegedly had built "the consensus"; to have been taken "out of context"; to be merely an attempt to discredit the IPCC, or to sabotage the imminent Copenhagen meeting. Nevertheless, three UK inquiries into Climategate were set in motion, one by the House of Commons Science and Technology Committee and two by the University of East Anglia (UEA), which was thus essentially examining itself.

According to a subsequent review of these reviews by Andrew Montford, all were hurried, had unclear terms of reference and contained panel members who were clearly biased in favour of climate catastrophism. The parliamentary hearing lasted only half a day, since an election was in the offing. Its chairman referred to skeptics as "deniers." Inquiries treated the objects of the inquiry, Phil Jones and his team, with kid gloves, while skeptics and critics were mostly ignored. None of the inquiries asked McIntyre and McKitrick to appear. The small number of CRU studies examined by one of the UEA inquiries, chaired by Lord Oxburgh, a committed environmentalist, were selected by the CRU itself. The other UEA inquiry, chaired by Sir Muir Russell, included, according to Montford, "several vocal supporters of the manmade global warming hypothesis." Penn State carried out a similar inquiry about Michael Mann but concluded essentially that he must be a good scientist; otherwise he wouldn't be receiving so much in research grants.

True believers waited for Al Gore to lead them through the Valley of Climategate. Gore eventually appeared on CNN, claiming that the emails were more than 10 years old (in fact, they included messages sent almost up to the date of their release in 2009) and amounted to a mere discussion of "arcane points." What this was really about, he said, was "people who don't want to do anything about the climate crisis taking things out of context and misrepresenting them." Gore never elaborated on what the correct "context" was, nor exactly what had been "misrepresented."

—w—

The 2009 Copenhagen talks on a successor to Kyoto fell apart amid mutual recrimination, but worse was to come for the credibility of the global warming industry. Early in 2010, the IPCC's claims of rigorous peer-reviewed science began to unravel further when it was revealed that the authors of the most recent (2007) report had included alarmist claims that they knew were inaccurate in order to push the political agenda. The most astonishing was the claim that there was a 90 per cent probability that all the glaciers in the Himalayas would disappear by 2035. There had been no significant questioning of this claim until late in 2009, when the government of India had published a discussion paper that pointed out that there was in fact no sign of any "abnormal" retreat in the Himalayan glaciers.

IPCC head Rajendra Pachauri had rejected the Indian paper as "voodoo science." However, Pachauri's bluster soon deflated when the source of the IPCC's Himalayan claims was revealed. The 2035 figure had come from a World Wide Fund for Nature (WWF) pamphlet, which had in turn taken the data from a story that had appeared in the British magazine *New Scientist*. That story, written in 1999, had quoted a prediction by an Indian climate scientist, Syed Hasnain, that all the glaciers in the central and eastern Himalayas could soon disappear. The claim had no research basis. However, it flew from the *New Scientist* via the WWF straight into the 2007 IPCC report, by which time it wasn't just the central and eastern glaciers of the Himalayas that were projected to disappear, but all of them.

Georg Kaser, an Austrian glaciologist and IPCC contributor, revealed that he had notified his IPCC colleagues of the "huge" Himalayan mistake in 2006. "This number is not just a little bit wrong," he said, "it is as wrong as can be wrong ... It is so wrong that it is not even worth discussing." However, Kaser had blown no public whistles. Moreover, he went on to reject "IPCC bashing" even though he admitted that the process had, in this case, "entirely failed."

The lead author of the relevant IPCC chapter, Murari Lal, rejected the notion that the IPCC had screwed up. "The IPCC authors did exactly what was expected from them," he said.

Never were truer words spoken. The IPCC's central task — no matter how dedicated and rigorous individual "experts" were — had always been not to examine science objectively but to make the case for man-made global warming — and, by extension, for global economic control — by any means available. Lal subsequently admitted that he had known the data were faulty but had included the information because "we thought that if we can highlight it, it will impact policy-makers and politicians and encourage them to take some concrete action." But why would anybody take "concrete action" to address an exaggerated, or even falsified, threat unless it was the political action itself that was the main object of the exercise?

—⚏—

In the wake of Glaciergate, the UN, in March 2010, announced an "independent" inquiry into the IPCC by the InterAcademy Council (IAC). Astonishingly, Secretary General Ban Ki-moon exonerated the IPCC in advance. "Let me be clear," he said, "the threat posed by climate change is real ... Nothing that has been alleged or revealed in the media recently alters the fundamental scientific consensus on climate change."

The IAC report appeared in September 2010. It suggested that the IPCC needed an overhaul and criticized its head, Rajendra Pachauri, for "straying" into advocacy. It acknowledged that there was indeed a "debate" over climate science and recommended that the IPCC look at alternative climate models.

The report was buried without trace.

It turned out that the Himalayan glacier claim was far from the only alarmist assertion from a non-peer-reviewed source in the IPCC reports. Late in 2011, a Canadian journalist and blogger, Donna Laframboise, published a book with the arresting title *The Delinquent Teenager Who Was Mistaken for the World's Top Climate Expert*. It delivered a devastating portrayal of the IPCC as a thoroughly politicized organization, issuing reports whose authors were not the world's leading scientists but frequently wet-behind-the ears graduates or ardent activists. They were often selected on the basis of gender and national "diversity" rather than expertise. She also pointed out that the IPCC had been thoroughly infiltrated by environmental non-governmental organizations, in particular the WWF. The IPCC's much-vaunted "peer review," she concluded, amounted to a "circular, incestuous process. Scientists make decisions as journal editors about what qualifies as peer-reviewed literature. They then cite the same papers they themselves played midwife to while serving as IPCC authors." She noted that there was always time — even after official deadlines — to insert fresh alarmism: "26 references to the Stern Review were added to 12 different IPCC chapters after the work of the expert reviewers had already been completed."

Laframboise established that Pachauri's claim that IPCC science was all "peer reviewed" was bunk. Along with a team of volunteer researchers, she discovered that more than 5,000 references in the 2007 IPCC report were from "grey literature" such as WWF leaflets. Another of her coups was to gain access to at least some of the responses to a questionnaire the InterAcademy Council had sent to IPCC authors as part of its inquiry. Far from "consensus," those responses indicated widespread concern, confusion and distrust.

Laframboise concluded, "The IPCC ignores the consensus among hurricane experts that there is no discernible link to global warming. It ignores the consensus among those who study natural disasters that there is no relationship between human greenhouse gas emissions and the rising cost of these disasters. It ignores the consensus among bona fide malaria experts that global warming has not caused malaria to spread. In each case the IPCC substitutes its own version of reality. In each case that version of reality makes global warming appear more frightening than genuine experts believe the available evidence indicates."

She also recorded the moralistic vitriol that her skeptical inquiries had unleashed. "It is peculiar, indeed," she wrote, "that people who see things differently try to link my climate views to racists, Holocaust deniers, child murderers, mental illness, and the tobacco industry ... Whatever happened to tolerance and mutual respect?"

The simple answer seemed to be that when ardent moralism rears its self-righteous head, in the form of the psychology of taboo, tolerance and mutual respect disappear, along with any inclination even to listen to what your demonized opponents are saying. As Adam Smith said, when "faction and fanaticism" — that is, politics and religion — come through the door, the Impartial Spectator tends to be shoved out the window.

It was in fact common for skeptics to be linked with repugnant but entirely unrelated beliefs. Nigel Marsh, chairman of Leo Burnett, the giant advertising agency that advised the WWF, declared, "I'm an optimist about climate change. The human race eventually abolished slavery and gave women the vote. We eventually work it out." The implication was clear: if you "denied" catastrophic anthropogenic global warming, then you were the kind of person who would support slavery and keeping women barefoot and pregnant in the kitchen.

—⁂—

Far from undermining climate catastrophism, the embarrassments of Climategate, Glaciergate and critiques of the IPCC such as those of McIntyre and McKitrick, Montford, Laframboise and even the InterAcademy Council were largely discounted or ignored. Hockey Team captain Michael Mann declared that the team had been entirely exonerated.

Indeed, the critiques appeared to harden the stance of leading scientists and scientific institutions. One arresting example was the British Royal Society, the venerable institution that had once been the haunt of Newton and Darwin. One of the Royal Society's presidents, Bob May, told a journalist, "I am the President of the Royal Society, and I am telling you the debate on climate change is over."

At the time of the IPCC's Third Assessment Report, the one that had prominently featured the Hockey Stick, the Royal Society took the lead in organizing 17 national science academies to sign an editorial statement, which appeared in the magazine *Science*. "It is now evident that human activities are already contributing adversely to global climate change," it declared. The letter backed the IPCC as "the world's most reliable source" on climate science and claimed that there was much that could be done to "reduce the emissions of greenhouse gases without excessive cost." Such a claim was quite outside the expertise of any pure science academy, and it reflected scientific naïveté about economic policy.

In 2005, the Royal Society organized another document designed to pressure members of the G8 ahead of their meeting at Gleneagles in Scotland. It also issued a pamphlet rebutting skeptics, and — disgracefully — pressured the media not to publish dissenting views.

Toward the end of his term of office as president of the Royal Society, May (now Lord May) characterized those who questioned the official science of climate thus: "On one hand, you have the entire scientific community and on the other you have a handful of people, half of them crackpots." He pointed to the existence of a climate change "denial lobby," allegedly funded by the "hydrocarbon industry."

May's successor Sir Martin Rees came out strongly in support of the Stern Review. He also presided over a campaign against the oil company ExxonMobil. In 2010, Rees was replaced by Sir Paul Nurse, a Nobel prizewinning geneticist, who claimed that Climategate was "the greatest scientific scandal that never happened." Nurse subsequently linked skeptics with those who rejected evolution and believed that the weather might be changed by prayer.

Perhaps the most egregious example of the Royal Society's support for treating skepticism as the result of ignorance or psychiatric disorder came with the grant, in 2013, of a Wolfson Research Merit Award — designed to attract and keep academic talent in Britain — to Stephan Lewandowsky, an Australian cognitive scientist who had recently moved to the University of Bristol. The award was for a project titled "The (Mis)information Revolution: Information Seeking and Knowledge Transmission."

Lewandowsky's other work already provided a window into the lurid fantasies of those who were so committed to the paradigm of climate catastrophism that they had abandoned all trace of objectivity or balance. In May 2013, the journal *Psychological Science* carried a paper by Lewandowsky and his co-authors Klaus Oberauer and Gilles Gignac with the title "NASA Faked the Moon Landing — Therefore, (Climate) Science Is a Hoax: An Anatomy of the Motivated Rejection of Science."

The paper was based on a "survey" that invited agreement or otherwise with statements such as: "In July 1947, the U.S. military recovered the wreckage of an alien spacecraft from Roswell, NM, and covered up the fact." "The claim that the climate is changing due to emissions from fossil fuels is a hoax perpetrated by corrupt scientists who want to spend more taxpayer money on climate research." And "U.S. agencies intentionally created the AIDS epidemic and administered it to Black and gay men in the 1970s." But the survey had been posted almost entirely on non-skeptical websites, thus inviting fraudulent responses by those pretending to be skeptics and "exposing" themselves as paranoid nutbars.

Steve McIntyre, the man who had broken the Hockey Stick, called Lewandowsky's study "a landmark of junk science — fake results from faked responses."

The paper typically misrepresented the mainstream skeptical position. Its most revealing claim (revealing about its authors, that is) was that "endorsement of free-market economics predicted rejection of climate science." But this assertion conflated skepticism about the effectiveness of policy (the main stance of organizations such as the Global Warming Policy Foundation) with the untrue claim that skeptics "rejected" science, when what they actually did was to question a theory.

It got worse. Lewandowsky suggested that endorsement of free markets went with rejection of the link between HIV and AIDS and denial that smoking caused lung cancer. This was allegedly due again to "rejection" of any form of science that implied regulation.

The study meanwhile demonstrated the one-sided view of ideology that was a trademark of the left. It admitted that climate science was "politicized," but apparently only for those on the right. Perhaps the most effective instant rebuttal of the thesis contained in the paper's title — that climate skeptics tended to believe that the moon landing was faked — was that two famous skeptics, Harrison Schmidt and Buzz Aldrin, had in fact been to the moon.

Lewandowsky had previously spoken out against free speech if it meant — according to his definition — "spinning." This would of course mean the end of all political discourse, but it indicated the peculiar psychology of those who felt themselves to be guardians of "the truth" and dismissed skeptics as believing that "gravity is a left-wing conspiracy."

This was apparently the Royal Society's idea of good science.

Ironically, Lewandowsky, while accusing skeptics of being conspiracists, believed in a vast right-wing media conspiracy that had allegedly corrupted coverage and confused the public, who would otherwise be "clamouring for more concerted mitigation efforts." In fact, the situation was almost entirely the reverse. The media tended to be far more alarmist than the public.

The muffling of the scandals surrounding the Hockey Stick and Climategate, plus the fierce denigration of "deniers" and fossil fuel industry "shills," pointed not merely to the problem of Kuhnian paradigms but to the issue of how this particular paradigm fit so neatly with anti-capitalist assumptions, which were in turn rooted in varying degrees of economic ignorance, anti-market moralism and the urge for political power.

The Hockey Stick graph had been used as a promotional tool for a political agenda, building a rationale for unprecedented global economic control. While national governments had largely fallen into line with the catastrophist hypothesis, universally expressing concern and policy commitment, this was very much a transnational agenda centred in the UN.

Michael Mann wrote in one of the Climategate emails about letting "our supporters in higher places" deal with McIntyre and McKitrick. But who were these "supporters in higher places"? Keith Briffa wrote, "I know there is pressure to present a nice tidy story as regards 'apparent unprecedented warming in a thousand years or more in the proxy data' but in reality the situation is not quite so simple." Where was that "pressure" coming from for this "nice tidy story"?

Ultimately, Jones, Mann and his colleagues were merely foot soldiers in a bigger ideological battle to use the environment as a rationale for assuming global economic control. In other words, the really intriguing question was who was pulling the political strings of the IPCC, or, more fundamentally, what was the source of the ideological thrust that characterized the IPCC in the first place.

Andrew Montford wrote, in his first Climategate book, of one of the early climate meetings, "One can almost detect the germ of an idea forming in the minds of the scientists and bureaucrats ... Here, potentially, was a source of funding and influence without end. Where might it lead?" But people's psychological "elephants" like to keep such thoughts to themselves. The elephants' "riders," the promoters of catastrophism, tended to articulate nothing but concern for the planet and a burning desire to speak up for the vulnerable.

Montford's second book on the Climategate affair came to much starker conclusions. "As we look back over the ten years of this story, the impression we get is of a wave of dishonesty, a public sector that will spin and lie, and lie again. If one lie fails then another lie is issued and if that fails they simply lie again. And all this happens without fear of the consequences. Everyone involved ... appears quite certain that their mendacity will go unpunished no matter what."

However, just as it seems improbable that scientists might have consciously admitted to themselves that they saw climate as a rich source of funding and influence, so too it seems unlikely that many of those involved saw themselves as liars. They were concerned with *moral truth*, with saving the world and poor people, and with fighting a greedy and feckless corporate-backed foe, who was all the more vicious and devious because you couldn't actually identify the great secret web of his activities.

The Hockey Team and their cohorts ridiculed the notion that they were involved in some sort of global plot. What was intriguing was that there were few examples of anybody actually *accusing* them of such shenanigans. Their elephants were perhaps engaged in a little pre-emptive defence. Matters of mutual self-interest do not need to be articulated any more than chimpanzees need to speak in order to ambush a member of a neighbouring tribe. Among humans, the lust for power almost invariably cloaks itself in high moral purpose. What higher moral purpose could there be than adopting the role of "global saviour"?

fifteen

Global Salvationism

*The urge to save humanity is almost always
a false-front for the urge to rule.*
— H.L. Mencken, quoted in *The Cynic's Lexicon*

Twenty years after coining the concept of do-it-yourself economics, the former OECD chief economist David Henderson became convinced that there were dangerous new ideas abroad, although they continued to have a lot to do with economic misunderstanding. He was particularly concerned about what he called "global salvationism," which had captured much of the corporate community. He laid out his concerns in a book, *The Role of Business in the Modern World*.

Global salvationism, he wrote, was a quasi-religious belief based on two articles of faith: environmental alarmism, and the assertion that Third World poverty was due to the West taking more than its "fair share" of global resources. Both problems were declared to require top-down political solutions of the type that had failed abysmally in the past, only this time those solutions would incorporate the participation of big business. Giant corporations, in this view, should accept more "social responsibility" for what were, ultimately, political objectives.

Henderson pointed out that the focus of the putative global master plan was the bland-sounding notion of "sustainable development," which was based on the view that without extensive new globally coordinated government controls, the world was doomed because of global warming, species extinction, resource depletion and any number of other apocalyptic scenarios. He went on to identify the key elements of and institutions promoting what he called "new millennium collectivism." He described the UN's 1992 Rio conference as a seminally dangerous event but noted that the salvationist movement went back to the early 1970s, and in particular to another UN environmental conference, at Stockholm in 1972 (of which Rio marked the 20th anniversary). He identified the founding of the United Nations Environment Programme (UNEP), which had emerged from the Stockholm conference, as a "landmark."

The 1992 Rio conference had been important for two reasons, wrote Henderson: its success in promoting climate change as a threat to mankind, and the fact that radical non-governmental organizations (NGOs) had been allowed into the proceedings, thus permitting an activist minority to hijack the conference agenda or, perhaps more accurately, to support the agenda of those who had let them in.

When it came to infecting the corporate sector with salvationist ideas, Henderson pointed to the importance of organizations such as the World Economic Forum (WEF), which held an annual conference at Davos in Switzerland, and the World Business Council for Sustainable Development (WBCSD). What I found surprising was that Henderson — a charming man whom I tracked down and interviewed in London — was unaware that one man had been critical to all the seminal meetings and organizations he identified: the 1972 and 1992 UN conferences and the formation of UNEP, the WEF and the WBCSD. I knew this man because I had been tracking his career for many years. He was the missing prince in Henderson's salvationist Hamlet. More than that, he was virtually a one-man psychological compendium of the links between professed high moral purpose, flawed critiques of capitalism and rationalization of the urge to power. His name was Maurice Strong.

When Kofi Annan, then the new secretary general of the United Nations, turned up at the White House in January 1997 for his first official visit, the press corps hardly noticed the pudgy, bland-looking little man with the clipped moustache who had also climbed out of the limo. Somebody once said that you wouldn't pick Maurice Strong out of a crowd of two. Here was the proof.

Annan had brought Strong along because Strong was considered close to President Bill Clinton's vice-president, Al Gore, who had also seized upon the environment as a major political issue. Annan and Strong were also due to visit the Republican-led Congress, which was demanding UN reform as the price of paying more than $1 billion in back dues. Strong was in charge of that reform program. The *Economist* wrote that Annan had appointed Strong, "a Canadian businessman, to co-ordinate the reform program, paying him just $1 a year, to underline the push for economy."

That Strong should be described as a "Canadian businessman" seemed woefully inadequate. Strong had always been a conundrum. He had spent his life straddling the public and private sectors, but his "success" in the public sector differed stunningly from a never-ending series of pratfalls in his personal business affairs. His fans regarded him as a saint, but most of his critics maintained that he was just in it for the money, using government connections for private gain. I had come to believe that it was a good deal more complex than that. Strong was the very model of UN Man, denizen of a world that mixed the noblest and most expansive of intentions with the most disappointing — and often perverse — of results.

When I met Strong's second wife, Hanne Marstrand, in Vancouver in the early 1980s, she said that people had told her that Maurice was "either a genius or a fraud." She said she still wasn't sure. Strong had been present when she made this remark. He had smiled, perhaps taking delight in keeping people guessing. Then again, perhaps he wasn't quite sure himself.

To his admirers, Strong approached the status of global saviour (the term had been used of him long before Henderson had coined "global salvationism"). Robert McNamara, the archetypal numbers-based policy wonk who had been head of the Ford Motor Company, U.S. secretary of defence and head of the World Bank, had told me that "Maurice is activated by a deep interest in human welfare." But Strong's vision of human welfare was controversial, to say the least. He was a committed socialist and radical environmentalist, and his career had been riddled with controversy over conflicts of interest.

Strong's curriculum vitae read like a parody of overachievement: more than 40 honorary degrees (although he had never gone to university); pages and pages of past and present chairmanships, directorships and associations that — tellingly — did not differentiate between the public and private sector; a list of awards that looked more like a catalogue of *all* the awards available on earth: the Jawaharlal Nehru Award for International Understanding, the Brazilian National Grand Order of the Southern Cross, the Swedish Royal Order of the Polar Star, the Blue Planet Prize, the International Saint Francis Prize for the Environment, the Charles A. Lindbergh Award and on and on. These awards, which had also been won by the likes of Mother Teresa, Yasser Arafat and Archbishop Desmond Tutu, placed Strong squarely in the top ranks of the secular sainthood, those whom John Kenneth Galbraith had once embraced as "we, the socially concerned."

Strong was often viewed as a career pinball, careening this way and that with no larger purpose than to do well for himself. Others saw something far more sinister. An article in the *National Review* once described him as the "indispensable man" at the centre of a "creeping UN power grab." Certainly, his professed good intentions, his vast network of contacts and his extraordinary skills in navigating the bureaucratic thickets of the international community had led to his being dubbed the ultimate "Rolodex socialist."

Strong's lionization within the UN system also had a good deal to do with his unparalleled ability to generate a seemingly endless stream of do-good initiatives, which required ponderous and expensive studies, elaborate conferences, the creation of new institutions and the promotion of (agenda-appropriate) sections of civil society. All this came attached to myriad person-years of well-paid employment for bureaucrats, consultants, NGOs and retired politicians.

I had interviewed Strong a number of times over the years and found that he seemed to speak in tongues when it came to explaining his belief system. He talked in rationalizations. "People accuse me — and I'm guilty — of moving a lot," he told me, "but although I do change instruments, I don't change causes. Basically I am a socialist in the ideological sense that I believe the principal purpose of economic activity is to meet the social goals of society. I am a capitalist because I believe that the capitalist system is the best way of doing it."

However, behind Strong's sunny demeanour, extraordinary networking skills and vapid ideology lay an apocalyptic world view based on acute environmental alarmism and demonization of the capitalist system, even as he wheeled and dealed within it. Strong put his grim perspective on unashamed display in his 2000 autobiography, *Where on Earth Are We Going?* The book's first chapter was titled "Report to the Shareholders, Earth Inc.," and dated 1 January 2031. This "corporate" format was highly revealing. Who might pen such a document other than somebody who imagined himself the prospective CEO of the planet?

In Strong's dismal imagined future, "the human tragedy is on a scale hitherto unimagined." There have been unprecedented extremes of weather. The North American prairies are experiencing their 10th year of drought. "Water vendors with armed guards roam the streets of Los Angeles." Hundreds of thousands of people have just died in Washington from a heat wave. There are plagues of insects and rodents. Malaria has turned New Orleans into a "shrinking fortress held only with poisonous amounts of lethal pesticides."

Not all is bleak. There is a good guy running Germany, a "benevolent dictator" seeking "to ensure that all Germans work together for the common good and share equitably in both the sacrifices and the benefits achieved." There are other "scattered islands of sanity and order" to be found. One such is in Crestone, Colorado: "A community created as a spiritual retreat in recent materialistic times has proven a haven for the virtues of sustainability, harmony and 'ethical husbandry.'" Strong was too modest to note that he had founded the community in question, whose background wasn't quite as Utopian as advertised.

There would be, according to Strong, other bright spots. "Everywhere, indigenous people are rediscovering their traditional way of life." And order was being restored by "volunteer security corps." People had turned away from science and toward religion, and this was a good thing.

The brightest prospect — according to Strong — lay in forecasts that two-thirds of the world's already diminished population might be wiped out, "a glimmer of hope for the future of our species and its potential for regeneration." Surely anybody who regards two-thirds of the human race being wiped out as a "glimmer of hope" betrays a very ambivalent attitude toward humanity.

Strong himself asked whether this chapter was "just sour fantasy, the dismal fiction of a doomsayer? Many readers will [see it as] the ravings of an activist with a hidden agenda." But just when it seemed that he might be on to himself, he declared that his scenario was all "entirely plausible." According to Strong, to seek proof of his assertions or pursue rational analysis of his vision would be irresponsible. All he needed was the power to act. Now. Before it was too late.

Strong had led an amazing life. Born to modest circumstances in the little town of Oak Lake, Manitoba, he had run away from home as soon as he could, pursuing a series of picaresque adventures as cabin boy, fur trapper, prospector and teenage financial whiz kid.

He was, he claimed, haunted by the spectre of an economic system that had, during the Great Depression, "broken down." For leftists, the Great Depression has always been one of the treasured memes of capitalist failure and a key rationale for government intervention, but Strong perhaps cleaved to this rationale more than most because he had suffered it. As a boy he ate dandelion and pigweed. He saw his father wrap his feet in rags before going out into the bush to cut wood. He witnessed his educated mother losing her mind.

Strong explained that he was profoundly influenced by a newspaper story about the formation of the United Nations that had — literally — blown across his path one day. Henceforth, he had fixated on a career in international affairs. Already demonstrating a remarkable ability to network with important people, he headed down to work as a minor functionary in the fledgling UN organization but soon returned to Canada to apply for work in government. Rejected because of his lack of qualifications, he decided that he would use business success as a back door into public service.

Strong became an oil and gas analyst, worked for a company called Dome Petroleum in Calgary, then went into the petroleum business for himself. Before you could say "Horatio Alger," he was running a large, politically connected company called Power Corp., a Montreal-based conglomerate with interests in energy, finance, industry and real estate. He used Power as a springboard to Ottawa, where he created the Canadian International Development Agency (CIDA) to pursue his Robin Hood vision of doing good in the Third World.

Thenceforth Strong proceeded to cut a swath through the international community, criss-crossing the globe in a constant whirl of initiatives, agendas and grand schemes for solving the problems of poverty. For the most part, they failed, but Strong became a star because bureaucracy thrives not on solving problems but on elaborately addressing them via meetings, conferences, initiatives, studies and programs, which Strong conceived at a dizzying rate.

Then he discovered the potential of the environment.

"I knew," he wrote, "there was a role for me to play here ... I also began to sense one of the great underlying truths of environmental politics: the environment is supranational. It transcends the nation state. At the very least it has to be dealt with multilaterally."

The modern environmental movement is often traced to Rachel Carson's book *Silent Spring* (1962), a bible of chemophobic catastrophism that was followed by other doom-laden bestsellers such as Paul Ehrlich's *The Population Bomb*, the Club of Rome's *The Limits to Growth* and E.F. Schumacher's *Small Is Beautiful*.

At the first Earth Day in 1970, Paul Ehrlich described global prospects thus: "In ten years all important animal life in the sea will be extinct. Large areas of coastline will have to be evacuated because of the stench of dead fish." The biologist and future presidential candidate Barry Commoner declared, "Civilization will end within 15 or 30 years unless immediate action is taken against problems facing mankind. We are in an environmental crisis which threatens the survival of this nation, and of the world as a suitable place of human habitation."

Such was the zeitgeist at the 1972 UN Conference on the Human Environment in Stockholm, which Strong was asked to organize and chair. There, Strong achieved his first apotheosis as captain of Spaceship Earth. In a BBC interview at the time, Strong suggested that the prospect of doomsday had to be taken seriously, given humanity's unprecedented impact on the environment.

The natural world was being destroyed, he said, so there was a need for "control." Strong asked whether man would be "wise enough" to subject himself to the required discipline. "We must adopt a much more cooperative attitude," he said. A much more cooperative attitude, presumably, toward being controlled.

The authoritarian neo-Malthusianism that lurked beneath the catastrophic projections was on abundant display in *The Limits to Growth*. The study on which the book was based had been commissioned by the Club of Rome, yet another group of self-appointed global guardians who had assigned themselves to examine what they called the world "problematique." According to the book's blurb, its authors' "inescapable conclusions are beyond anyone's grimmest fears."

They had studied the future "with the aid of a giant computer" and it was a place of resource exhaustion, ecological "overshoot" and civilizational collapse. The authors admitted that their model might not be perfect, but asserted that *their conclusions wouldn't change*. They thus confirmed that theirs wasn't a scientific hypothesis to be tested; it was an unshakable — albeit economics-challenged — moral conviction.

The junk modelling of *The Limits to Growth* was based on the primitive zero-sum assumption that what was needed for the present poor and future generations to thrive was for the rich to abandon materialist lifestyles. There was only so much to go round, and it was disappearing fast. According to *Limits*, what was needed was a "totally new form of human society" and the imposition of a "sustainable ... global equilibrium" that inevitably involved the sacrifice of "certain human freedoms" for "other freedoms such as relief from pollution and crowding and the threat of collapse of the world system." Population and investment had to be rigidly controlled. In short, this was a pseudo-science-based call for global eco-dictatorship, a monstrous extension of Plato's vision of an "arrested state" presided over by incorruptible guardians.

Strong demonstrated his extraordinary diplomatic skills before Stockholm in 1972, where developing nations stated their concerns that the West's growing environmental obsessions might lead to attempts to retard their own growth. He persuaded poor countries to attend, and he recruited the British intellectual Barbara Ward to stitch development and the environment together, which she did in the concept of "sustainable development." (Ward had also coined the phrase "Spaceship Earth" in a speech she wrote for Adlai Stevenson.)

Ward played a role in many ways similar to that of Beatrice Webb for a previous generation of British politicians. She provided political leaders who were perpetually desperate for ideas with rationales for action. Originally an editorial writer for the *Economist,* Ward had been sent by the British government to Washington during the war to win support for the war effort. There she developed a group of American admirers. She struck up a lifelong friendship with J.K. Galbraith, who secured her a post in Harvard's economics department. She was appointed Albert Schweitzer Professor at Columbia University and was the first woman to give the Harvard commencement address. She received substantial backing from the Carnegie Foundation. In the 1945 U.K. election, she campaigned for Labour. She contributed to Lyndon Johnson's 1964 Great Society speech. Ward was friends with the first generation of African leaders — Kwame Nkrumah of Ghana, Julius Nyerere of Tanzania, Jomo Kenyatta of Kenya, Kenneth Kaunda of Zambia — all of whom were disastrous for their countries. Indian prime minister Indira Gandhi was an admirer. Ward was on Pope Paul VI's Commission for Justice and Peace. Strong declared that working with her was a "dream come true."

Ward was a firm believer in world government and a harsh critic of capitalism, which she cast as 300 years of "reckless expansion." She rejected the market and called for a global Marshall Plan to distribute 1 per cent of rich nations' GDP to poor nations. Strong commissioned Ward and René Dubos to write a book whose title said it all: *Only One Earth.*

Another of Strong's diplomatic master strokes was to persuade Indira Gandhi to give the conference's keynote speech. She blamed the profit motive for wrecking the environment and keeping people poor. After Stockholm, Strong helped mastermind the creation of the United Nations Environment Programme, of which he became the first head. Like the socialist economist Jan Tinbergen, he sensed that the future of socialism lay in the environment.

As Rupert Darwall notes in *The Age of Global Warming,* the first environmental wave was arrested by the Yom Kippur War and the OPEC crises of the 1970s. Rising oil prices and economic disruption were seized upon by Malthusians as proof that they were right, but the crisis was the result of the kinds of lousy dirigiste policies that they espoused, not imminent resource exhaustion.

Strong's psychological elephant had acute sensitivity to the shifting possibilities of political power and naturally gravitated toward intrusive energy policies. As a man with considerable experience both in the oil industry and in Ottawa, he was appointed in 1976 by the government of Pierre Trudeau to be the first chairman and president of the Canadian state oil company, Petro-Canada. Strong quickly moved on, but the entity he helped create would become a bloated carnival of waste. (I wrote a book about it: *Self-Serve: How Petro-Canada Pumped Canadians Dry.*)

Strong's second global coming was in 1992, at the huge UN Conference on Environment and Development that he organized in Rio. He had certainly not been idle in the intervening years. Apart from being the first president of Petrocan, he also headed the huge provincial-government-controlled electricity utility Ontario Hydro, and he undertook a raft of roles within the UN, including African famine relief. He also became involved in myriad messy private business schemes.

The Stockholm agenda was kept going at Rio through the continued promotion of sustainable development. It had received a boost with the 1987 report of the UN's Brundtland Commission.

Gro Harlem Brundtland was another lifelong socialist. She had been enrolled by her father in the children's section of the Norwegian Labour Movement at the age of seven. She went on to become Norway's prime minister on three separate occasions. The mandate for the self-appointed commission of "eminent persons" that would bear her name, which had set itself up in 1983, was to prepare "a global agenda for change" in the face of the alleged "interlocking crises" of failing economic development and deteriorating environment.

Behind the commission's bland definition of sustainable development as "development that meets the needs of the present without compromising the ability of future generations to meet their own needs" lay the implicit accusation that free markets and the broader "extended order of human cooperation" were *un*sustainable and that what was needed to fix them was greater political oversight and control. At root, sustainable development was yet another assault on the Invisible Hand, "unreflecting centralism" gone global, only now business would be permitted as a manacled partner via the "social responsibility" of the corporate sector.

Sustainability had profound conceptual and practical problems quite beyond its implicit denial of any "natural order" that might both create wealth and protect the environment. How could anybody possibly know the "needs of the present," let alone the needs of the future? Indeed, how could anybody gauge the "needs" of even a single individual, or compare those of any two? Moreover, although there was no way of measuring needs, we could be sure that not all present needs were being met, so why should those of the future? In fact, the sustainable developers believed that assessing needs wasn't a problem; they would tell humanity what its needs should be.

The giveaway that primitive zero-sum thinking was at the root of all this lay in the assumption that the needs of the future might be better taken care of if the needs of the present were restricted. In fact, capitalist wealth had never been "taken" from the future; it had always been the foundation for continuous betterment.

Sustainable development — despite the evidence of history and James Buchanan's doctrine of "public choice" — assumed that the political agents who would "sustainably" control the new world order would be omniscient, wise and personally disinterested. They were merely concerned with "speaking up for" the planet and the future. The enormous personal power they demanded was merely a function of the size of the problems they faced. Would you have them do nothing?

The basis for sustainable development was the same old fundamental misunderstanding — or misrepresentation — of the role and function of markets in signalling scarcity, rewarding innovation, encouraging the efficient use of resources and promoting the search for new technologies. It also ignored the future-pointing genetic imperative of our concern for our children; or rather it exploited it, by promoting the hoary myth that markets functioned on the basis of short-sighted selfishness and thus of "robbing the future," the meme peddled by the Stern Review.

Sustainable development rendered zero-sum "carcass economics" gargantuan — and seized the intellectual imagination — because the carcass was now presented as the "whole earth." The seminal image of the new holistic, moralistic but still essentially economics-challenged world view was the photo of the earth as a "Blue Marble," taken from an Apollo spacecraft.

Wasn't it obvious from this picture that we had "only one earth," with finite resources and limited "carrying capacity"? How could a growing world population that demanded a better and richer life not drive itself into crisis? After all, there was "only so much to go around." Apart from prospective resource exhaustion, there was the obvious threat (or at least assumption) of worsening pollution.

In fact, the image of "one earth" offered no new insight; it was merely used to confirm economic misconceptions, bolster moral outrage and justify draconian action. Indeed, the interpretation of the picture of earth from space was an indicator of how far technology had outstripped our primitive assumptions, but how those primitive assumptions continued to frame all novel developments.

The word "sustainable" was an Orwellian term designed not to clarify thinking but to block it. After all, who could support unsustainability? Friedrich Hayek had once identified "social" as the ultimate "weasel word" that sucked the life from nouns to which it was attached, often reversing their meaning. Hence "social democracy" was a cover for a non-democratic agenda, "social justice" a code for forced redistribution and "social market economy" a term for an economy with crippled markets. Similarly, sustainable development essentially meant stopping — or severely constraining — development, at least in the advanced countries, while pursuing socialist-style, top-down programs in poor nations.

The apocalyptic vision that Strong eagerly embraced was predicated on the conventional view that free markets were obsessed by the short term, and that people were giddy grasshoppers. In his autobiography, he moralistically — and Morrie-like — bemoaned "a culture of materialism and self-gratification" and trotted out numerous sophistic rationalizations and non sequiturs. Some people had once argued for slavery and child labour, and against traffic lights; hence anybody who doubted man-made climate change and the need for draconian global regulation was a reactionary, marked by prejudice and wicked self-interest (not to mention being a fan of slavery and enemy of road safety). We already had lots of rules, he wrote, so why not more — lots more — as "preconditions for freedom." But it was, again, a very strange form of freedom if "gratifying" ourselves was to be censured or banned.

Inevitably, and conventionally, Strong bemoaned "the gap" between rich and poor. During one of our interviews, I had asked him that leading question about whether the world would be better if Bill Gates had never been born. Strong became visibly agitated. I was challenging what was meant to be an unquestionable moral precept, one to which the psychology of taboo applied. He was "morally dumbfounded." He had no answer. Nobody was meant to ask the question.

Being philosophically incoherent in no way precluded being a strategic and tactical mastermind. Strong had been extraordinarily successful at promoting his grim world view, partly because its fretful contours were reflexively shared by so many others, but also because he was a genius at promoting and manipulating not only the UN system but also the vast and growing interlinked web of private charities, capitalist foundations and environmental NGOs that, ironically, were the fruit of capitalism. He had helped build his activist NGO constituency partly by using public money, and had made sure that activists had access to both cash and the corridors of power.

Strong's principal tactic was to create or co-opt public agencies and private foundations that could be used to finance his agenda by shovelling money to activists. He used influence over both public and private funds to help support and grow a radical constituency of NGOs that claimed to represent civil society. It was very clear which type of NGO Strong favoured, since he had asserted that "business ... tends to look on NGOs as ideological opponents." (In fact, big business would wind up funnelling money to these harsh critics to buy them off.)

The British journalist John Lloyd, in a lengthy pamphlet titled "The Protest Ethic," credited Strong with unleashing the NGOs. "In the 1990s," wrote Lloyd, "the development movement began to grow exponentially. The UN began a series of major conferences on global issues; at the first of these, on the environment in 1992, the event's general secretary, the Canadian Maurice Strong, allowed all interested NGOs to participate." Lloyd quoted Robert Savio, chairman of the Rome-based news agency Interpress: "At a conference where the majority of the delegates were diplomats operating according to the instructions of their governments, and frequently without any emotional involvement in their actions, the arrival of a sea of people with passions and deeply held commitments upset the traditional mechanism of diplomatic consensus."

In fact, Strong had been pursuing this strategy since before Stockholm in 1972. It appeared that he was trying to do nothing less than seize the reins of global power by passing off the radical groups that promoted his agenda — groups that in fact represented a tiny activist minority — as the voice of "global democracy."

Strong's approach seemed somewhat analogous to Lenin's manipulation of the "soviets," the organizations that gave their name to the Soviet Union. The soviets were committees of workers that first appeared in 1905. Although their call was for reform, not revolution, Lenin saw that they might be infiltrated and used to subvert parliamentary democracy. By April 1917, his Bolsheviks were calling for "the rapid transfer of all state power into the hands of the soviets." In September of that year, Lenin declared, "All power to the soviets." He then staged a coup but, as the historian Paul Johnson points out, he "astutely made the greatest possible use of the spurious legitimacy conferred upon his regime by the Soviets." If Maurice Strong and his ilk had a slogan, it seemed to be "All power to the NGOs."

Of course, there was no hope of Strong literally seizing power, except in his wildest fantasies, which, perhaps surprisingly, he seemed quite willing to share. Strong's autobiography proved revealing about his apocalyptic visions and scarcely concealed hatred for capitalist society, but another insight into the Machiavellian recesses of his psyche had appeared in an interview he gave in 1989. In it, he had described the "plot" of a novel he claimed to be contemplating. The setting was the annual meeting of the World Economic Forum at Davos.

According to Strong's plot, rich countries would be presented with an ultimatum to stop destroying the environment, by a "group of world leaders." When they refused, "this group of world leaders form a secret society to bring about an economic collapse. It's February. They're all at Davos ... They have positioned themselves in the world's commodity and stock markets. They've engineered, using their access to stock exchanges and computers and gold supplies, a panic. Then they prevent the world's stock markets from closing. They jam the gears. They hire mercenaries who hold the rest of the world leaders at Davos as hostages."

Perhaps Strong was just playing to his own stereotype, having a little mischievous fun with his reputation as an aspiring global ruler. Then again, maybe his psychic elephant had just gone on a rampage. Either way, his "plot" should certainly have stirred interest in what was really going on in the Swiss mountains.

Strong had been instrumental in inserting his radical NGO constituency into the Davos proceedings. "There can be no doubt," declared the WEF website, "that NGOs are now influential actors in every major policy debate on the global agenda." But how had they become so influential? Because the forum's navigators had helped make them so. By 2012, a basic WEF membership cost $55,000, with another $27,000 to attend Davos. Hundreds of corporate "partners" paid the WEF hundreds of thousands of dollars each annually to be part of the show. NGO representatives were let in for free.

The NGOs were a clever device for suggesting that Strong's agenda had somehow bubbled up from the "grass roots," when in fact it was Strong who was providing both the seeds and the fertilizer. Indeed, one of Strong's persistent tactics was to claim that he was merely answering some public "call to action" when it was he himself who had set up the call in the first place.

Anybody who wanted to understand what Strong's version of NGO World would look like just had to read *Agenda 21*, the meddlesome wish list that his acolytes put together at Rio. The 800-page doorstop suggested interference at every level of human activity, right down to the recommendation that "national programmes are needed to encourage men to share household tasks equally with women."

Another telling Rio document was Strong's so-called Earth Charter, between whose politically correct lines — again — lay dreams of global control. According to the charter's typically doomsterish preamble, "The dominant patterns of production and consumption are causing environmental devastation, the depletion of resources, and a massive extinction of species ... Fundamental changes are needed in our values." A left-wing magazine described the charter approvingly as a "shared positive vision ... for anti-capitalism."

Despite all his talk of consensus and democracy, meanwhile, time and again Strong declared that behaviour would have to be modified and transgressors punished. "The single greatest weakness of the existing international legal regime," he said in an interview published in 2002, "is the almost total lack of capacity for enforcement." Strong wanted the UN to be able to raise its own funds through taxation of the "global commons," or through a "Tobin tax" on international capital transactions. The next step would be a full-time international police force or army under UN control. A force for good.

—m—

Strong turned the 1992 Rio conference into a must-attend global policy shindig. Never had so many world leaders attended one event. The conference led five years later to the Kyoto Protocol, the treaty that would allegedly address both climate change and development. Countries had tried — and failed — to promote aid by top-down methods for decades. Now this goal was to be yoked to controlling the weather.

Strong's mammoth twin pretensions were not the end of the story. His modest proposal at Rio had been for a "system" to manage not just world poverty and global climate, not just particular organizations and issues but, as suggested in *Agenda 21*, everything. "We must devise," he declared, "a new approach to co-operative management of *the entire system of issues*" (my italics).

One could imagine this fantasy originating in academe, hatched by unworldly boffins, but how could a man of Maurice Strong's vast political and bureaucratic experience hold it, unless he was advocating a system that was much less "cooperative" than he would have people imagine? Strong's pretensions of "global governance" amounted to Hayek's fatal conceit on stratospheric stilts.

"We are all gods now," declared Strong, "gods in charge of our own destiny, and gods can't be capricious." But divine aspiration seemed to clash alarmingly with Strong's own real-world experience. He wrote in his autobiography of "swinging the ever-cumbersome apparatus of government into action." He noted that "government officials know how to resist and often bury the initiatives of their political masters." Of the UN, he wrote, "Petty politics and small-mindedness constantly interfere with the UN's work." The vast institution's personnel policies, he admitted, "always favour politics ... over competence."

Yet this bunch of corrupt, incompetent foot-draggers were somehow to manage "the entire system of issues." Talk about regulatory "illusions of competence." Meanwhile, shouldn't Strong's own distinctly spotty business record have taught him the limits of what could reasonably be managed? Time and again he admitted to "neglecting" his business affairs. Observers were presumably to interpret this as a mark of Strong's selflessness rather than his lack of managerial competence, and yet a man who admitted to having problems managing relatively small enterprises wanted to set up a system to manage everything.

Strong's business affairs were a perpetual mess, not least because they were frequently steeped in politics. His attempts to be a kind of one-man mixed economy constantly came crashing down. Those who had worked with him in his early days in Calgary recalled that he was full of ideas, but that "you always had to clean up after him." Over the years he had dabbled in greenmail and troubled franchise operations. There had been controversy when it was discovered that a European merchant bank with which he had been involved had taken a fee from his old employer, Petro-Canada, for advising on a takeover. In the early 1980s he had emerged as the central figure in a Canadian government plot to seize control of a state-sponsored company called the Canada Development Corporation, whose shares had been sold to the public with a guarantee that there would be no political interference.

Perhaps the weirdest, but most telling, example of the complex relationship between Strong's private affairs and his global saviour persona occurred at that "spiritual retreat" in Crestone, Colorado, that he had mentioned in his autobiography. Strong, through a typically convoluted chain of dealings, had wound up with a ranch called the Baca. He had given some of the land to religious sects, who had built everything from underground Zen Buddhist monasteries to exotic prayer towers. Strong's wife, Hanne, dubbed the area the "Valley of the Refuge of World Truths." The *Rocky Mountain News* called it, perhaps more accurately, a "Disneyland of the Spirit."

However, the Baca was more than just a spiritual refuge. It sat atop a huge and valuable aquifer. Strong formed a company to pump the water but ran into strong local opposition. "I thought that it might be a very good example of sustainable development," Strong told me, "but what I did not understand was the political dynamics of the valley. [Also] my partners ganged up on me because I was setting aside land for ecological and spiritual groups."

So Strong admitted to not grasping the political dynamics of one remote and sparsely populated valley, and failing to understand his business partners, but he could simultaneously claim that he had a handle on supervising the whole world. Meanwhile one could surely have a Freudian field day with somebody who had acquired a huge subterranean resource, from which he hoped to reap large profits, and had then, literally, covered it with multi-religious philanthropy.

Strong would also run into problems in Costa Rica, where, after Rio, he had set up his personal NGO, the Earth Council, as a "watchdog" to keep up the pressure for *Agenda 21* and for action on climate change. The council was also designed to seed further new NGOs to spread the gospel of sustainable development and push the Earth Charter (which had been rejected at Rio). Strong had already become embroiled in conflict-of-interest allegations in Costa Rica over a tourist development, for which he had been harshly criticized by local native groups. Now the Costa Rican government claimed that the Earth Council had illegally sold land that the government had granted it for a headquarters. The council responded by fleeing the country and setting up in Toronto.

While the Costa Rican fandango had been unfolding, a much larger scandal was brewing. As usual, the story was complex.

Around the time Strong was visiting the White House in 1997, controversy had erupted over his involvement in a recycling company called Molten Metal Technology, whose price had soared following praise from Al Gore in an Earth Day speech. Subsequently, when the government cut grants on which the company relied, its shares slumped. Civil suits accused Strong and others of insider trading. Strong said he had been forced to sell his Molten Metal shares not because he knew that the hazardous waste was about to hit the fan, but because he had "neglected" his affairs while running the Rio summit. He needed the Molten Metal cash to fund other ventures. In particular, he needed the money for a petroleum exploration company called Cordex Petroleum.

—⁂—

A shadowy South Korean businessman takes a cardboard box full of dollar bills from a representative of the Iraqi dictator Saddam Hussein. He deposits the cash in a Jordanian bank. Subsequently, he writes a million-dollar cheque on the account to a highly placed UN official, which he delivers personally in New York. The scenario reads like something out of John le Carré, but the details are real. The highly placed UN official who received the cheque was Maurice Strong.

The transaction was uncovered by a commission set up in 2004 to investigate the corruption surrounding the UN-administered oil-for-food program, from which Saddam Hussein reportedly siphoned billions. The investigation, led by the former Federal Reserve chairman Paul Volcker, implicated a raft of UN officials and their relatives, including the son of Secretary General Kofi Annan, previous secretary general Boutros Boutros-Ghali and Benon Savan, who had administered the program. The commission's report also found that Strong had been on the receiving end of that tainted million, although he claimed he had no idea of its source.

The man from whom Strong took the cheque was Tongsun Park, a Korean lobbyist who had previously enjoyed 15 minutes of infamy in the 1970s as a conduit for bribes to U.S. congressional officials, an affair dubbed "Koreagate." Strong said that he had taken Park's "investment" because he needed to buy out one of the investors in Cordex, to whom he had given a "put," that is, an option to sell the shares back to Strong.

Strong admitted that the option's exercise had placed him in "financial difficulty," so he had called Park, with whom he had a business and personal relationship. (The two men had tried to sell nuclear reactors to South Korea on behalf of Atomic Energy of Canada. Park had also provided offices for Strong in New York.) Park was now also doing business with Saddam's regime and persuaded the Iraqis that investing in Strong's company would buy influence. Strong asserted that he knew nothing of such promises.

Strong subsequently claimed that the Volcker report exonerated him. In fact, the report concluded that Strong was "in a position to know or suspect the source of Mr. Park's funds." It also confirmed that Strong had received a personal "benefit," and that he had "provided inconsistent accounts of his receipt of the money from Mr. Park." Cordex subsequently foundered. Strong moved to Beijing.

Given this convoluted trail of corporate controversy, one key question was why Strong, if his priority was saving the world, was involved in business at all. The answer seemed to be that he not merely hankered — quite normally — after financial independence but, more important, liked to leave the impression that he was an ultra-wealthy do-gooder, a latter-day Carnegie, Rockefeller or Ford. In this — that is, in leaving an impression — he was largely successful. He had been described even by one of his harshest critics as a "billionaire eco-warrior," but in fact Strong had never been enormously wealthy, although he had always been enormously ambitious. (One of those interviewed by the Volcker inquiry was Al Gore. Gore reported that when he had asked Strong who might be a worthy successor to Boutros Boutros-Ghali as UN secretary general, Gore had been "surprised when Mr. Strong replied that he himself would be interested in the position.")

Strong did indeed have extraordinary money power, but it was never *his* money. It came from his influence over the expenditures of the UN, national governments and major capitalist foundations, which, ironically but typically, had been increasingly captured by those with anti-capitalist sentiments. When the media magnate Ted Turner set up his own foundation to support UN activities, Strong was at the front of the line for a board appointment.

Strong had long before worked out that the secret to being taxpayer-funded and yet effectively beyond political control was to access the substantial but often loosely supervised funds made available for foreign aid, the environment and other "good causes." Indeed, Strong set up institutions to access these funds and funnel them to his environmental NGO constituency. Such entities included UNEP, CIDA and the Canadian-based International Institute for Sustainable Development, all of which in turn funded activist NGOs and "the agenda" either directly or indirectly.

Strong's involvement in the oil-for-food scandal confirmed for some the long-held suspicion that he was "just in it for the money," but far more significant was the radical disconnect between this affair — yet another in a long line of untidy private business entanglements — and Strong's widely supported plans to set up structures to rule the world. While the oil-for-food affair had cost him his influential position at the heart of the UN, the political movement he had helped promote continued to grow. By far the most significant rationale for Strong's schemes of grand central control was the alleged threat of catastrophic man-made global warming, which was closely linked to the grand narrative of anti-capitalism.

One major way in which global salvationism differed from traditional anti-capitalism was that instead of merely acknowledging corporate greed and environmental fecklessness, it declared that corporate power now had to be harnessed for the "common good." As well as supporting sustainable development, big business had to embrace "corporate social responsibility," CSR, although it certainly shouldn't expect the drumbeat of condemnation to soften.

What exactly was CSR? We might start with the ever-perceptive Adam Smith's advice that "we must in all cases attend to the nature of the thing, without paying any regard to the word." From a semantic perspective, a dead giveaway should be that CSR contained Hayek's weasel word "social," in this case compounded by appeals to "responsibility." Thus CSR — like sustainable development — was cast as a proposition with which it was impossible to argue. To question its murky metrics or suggest hidden agendas was to risk being decried as "anti-social" or "irresponsible," or accused of wanting to outlaw philanthropy and trash the environment; to reveal yourself as a blinkered fundamentalist ideologue who believed in the "magic" of markets and subscribed to the view that employees, suppliers and local communities should be treated with contempt.

—ɷ—

In his best-known work, *Capitalism, Socialism and Democracy*, published in 1942, Joseph Schumpeter projected that capitalism would falter for three reasons. First, the entrepreneur's work — which was in any case "unheroic" — was being "routinized" by specialized departments within large corporations, where, for example, research and product development were funded on an ongoing basis. Second, the critical sense of proprietorship would be weakened as shareholding became dispersed and professional management became the norm. Finally, capitalism not merely tolerated but funded a "scribbling set" of intellectuals and academics who sought to undermine it. These latter were the "judges" who had "the sentence of death in their pockets."

Schumpeter was too pessimistic about the ongoing role of the entrepreneur. However, the problems of professional management and the weakening of the sense of proprietorship were very much wrapped up with that third issue: the success of the scribbling set in peddling subversive ideas.

The embrace of global salvationism by the corporate sector would have come as no surprise to Schumpeter. "Perhaps the most striking feature of the picture," he wrote, "is the extent to which the bourgeoisie, besides educating its own enemies, allows itself in turn to be educated by them. It absorbs the slogans of current radicalism and seems quite willing to undergo a process of conversion to a creed hostile to its very existence ... This is verified by the very characteristic manner in which particular capitalist interests and the bourgeoisie as a whole behave when facing direct attack. They talk and plead — or hire people to do it for them; they snatch at every chance of compromise; they are ever ready to give in; they never put up a fight under the flag of their own ideals and interests ... The only explanation for the meekness we observe is that the bourgeois order no longer makes any sense to the bourgeoisie itself and that, when all is said and nothing is done, it does not really care."

Milton Friedman too noted business's suicidal tendencies. In an article in the *New York Times* in 1970, Friedman declared that social responsibility doctrines were "pure and unadulterated socialism." He pointed out that an executive was an employee of the owners of the corporation, to whom he had direct responsibility "to conduct the business in accordance with their desires, which generally will be to make as much money as possible while conforming to the basic rules of the society, both those embodied in law and those embodied in ethical customs."

Friedman did not suggest that the executive was a profit-maximizing automaton with no other interests. "Of course, the corporate executive is a person in his own right," he wrote. "As a person, he may have many other responsibilities that he recognizes or assumes voluntarily — to his family, his conscience, his feelings of charity, his church, his clubs, his city, his country." However, if he started indulging these "responsibilities" in his role as the executive of a public company, he was doing so with his shareholders' money. He was effectively adopting the role of government: taxing some in order to give to others. Adopting the redistributionist role of the tribal alpha male might be highly satisfying for many executives, but Friedman noted that such businessmen were "unwitting puppets of the intellectual forces that have been undermining the basis of a free society these past decades."

Echoing Schumpeter, Friedman commented on how confused businessmen tended to be in the political or ideological arena. "They are capable of being extremely far-sighted and clear-headed in matters that are internal to their business. They are incredibly short-sighted and muddle-headed in matters that are outside their businesses but affect the possible survival of business in general."

Friedman conceded that community activities or charitable contributions might well make sense as ways of generating valuable goodwill, but that these actions were not then "social responsibility." They were part of the proper profit-making function of the corporation.

"It would be inconsistent of me," concluded Friedman, "to call on corporate executives to refrain from this hypocritical window-dressing because it harms the foundation of a free society. That would be to call on them to exercise a 'social responsibility.' If our institutions, and the attitudes of the public make it in their self-interest to cloak their actions in this way, I cannot summon much indignation to denounce them."

Nevertheless, Friedman said that the embrace of CSR by businessmen helped to "strengthen the already prevalent view that the pursuit of profits is wicked and immoral and must be curbed and controlled by external forces. Once this view is adopted, the external forces that curb the market will not be the social consciences, however highly developed, of the pontificating executives; it will be the iron fist of Government bureaucrats."

In fact, the "external forces" that evolved to control corporate activity turned out to be not just bureaucrats but those radical NGOs — Maurice Strong's children — that would go beyond mere "scribbling" to outright coercion through do-not-buy and misinformation campaigns aimed at corporate customers. These NGOs took advantage of what might be dubbed "Friedman's loophole," his suggestion that executives had to conform not just to laws but to "ethical customs."

The problem is that ethical attitudes toward modern institutions such as business corporations tend to be informed by primitive assumptions, which can be politically exploited. As Mandeville pointed out, and Morrie confirmed, popular ethical attitudes tend in any case to drip with fashionable anti-materialist hypocrisy. Also, as Schumpeter noted, corporations tend to respond to attack not by standing up for free enterprise principles or the capitalist system, but by apologizing, and even hiring their enemies as "consultants."

The embrace of CSR and global salvationism required the perpetuation of a convenient misreading of the nature of corporate "power." One key assumption at the heart of corporate condemnation was that control of economic resources was synonymous with oppressive political power. The corporation was like a greedy person who got rich by exploiting others and despoiling the environment. According to "stakeholder theory" — the academic embodiment of zero-sum carcass economics — management was declared to be concerned exclusively with shareholders, *to the exclusion, and at the cost,* of all others with whom they dealt.

This take was based not merely on primitive confusion but on failing to grasp — or actually rejecting — how important reputation is to corporate success, which in turn is ultimately rooted not in the exercise of power but in serving consumers. It also ignored the vast web of laws and regulations that are themselves based on the notion that markets and property rights offer no — or at least insufficient — protection to workers, communities or the environment.

—∞—

Earlier I described the leftist academic Emma Rothschild's use of Orwellian logic to suggest that the Invisible Hand leads to oppression. Since capitalist freedom results — because of different levels of talent and application — in unequal wealth and the emergence of large corporate entities, this corporate wealth will inevitably seek to pervert politics and rig the market. Freedom is slavery!

In 2011, Rothschild and her husband, the left-liberal Nobel laureate Amartya Sen, jointly delivered the Adam Smith Lecture in Kirkcaldy (a choice that would surely have surprised Smith). Rothschild's most bizarre claim was that Smith, since he was skeptical of states, might therefore be in favour of world government. But she also misrepresented him on the key issue of the relationship between money and power.

Rothschild noted that in his 1784 revision of *The Wealth of Nations*, Smith had claimed — "rather boldly" — that "wealth, as Mr. Hobbes says, is power." She was clearly trying to leave the impression that Smith agreed with Hobbes. In fact, Smith was quoting Hobbes because he wanted to point out that wealth was *not* synonymous with power. Smith went on, "But the person who either acquires, or succeeds to a great fortune, does not necessarily acquire or succeed to any political power, either civil or military. His fortune may, perhaps, afford him the means of acquiring both, but the mere possession of that fortune does not necessarily convey to him either. The power which that possession immediately and directly conveys to him, is the power of purchasing."

Smith acknowledged that wealth *could* be used to pursue political power, and certainly in his day entities such as the East India Company exercised enormous political power because of privileges granted by the state. But Smith's fundamental message in *The Wealth of Nations* was that commercial activity could and *should* be separated as far as possible from the influence of the state, not merely because commerce was far more productive and innovative in a free market, but because state interventions tended to be counterproductive, while a powerful state — far from restraining business — was the main means by which businessmen could corrupt markets. Without political influence, business fortune had to depend entirely on success in serving consumers.

Marx, who was obsessed by power and how to justify it for himself, regarded it as obvious that the bourgeoisie would seek to subvert the state in its own interests. Corporations would also engage in a death struggle with each other in pursuit of monopoly. Marxists believed that capitalists would engage in a feeding frenzy of concentration until, according to Marx's anointed heir, Karl Kautsky, there would only be one giant corporation left.

These reflexive fears and confusions re-emerged with every generation and grew with the size of business enterprises. Despite the jobs created, and the enormous benefits brought to consumers by Rockefeller, Vanderbilt and Carnegie, the "progressive" movement and its muckraking media allies concentrated on the "ruthlessness" with which these great businessmen dealt with their business competitors, and focused on their elaborate corporate structures, their relationships with eminently corruptible politicians and their allegedly culpable "secrecy."

The corporate sector inevitably came under concerted attack again during the Depression, when it provided a useful scapegoat and convenient political bogeyman. One of the key tracts of the time was Adolf Berle and Gardiner Means's *The Modern Corporation and Private Property* (which was still on the reading list when I studied economics at Cambridge). Berle and Means's concluding paragraph read: "The rise of the modern corporation has brought a concentration of economic power which can compete on equal terms with the modern state ... Where its own interests are concerned, it even attempts to dominate the state. The future may see the economic organism, now typified by the corporation, not only on an equal plane with the state, but possibly even superseding it as the dominant form of social organization."

This was utterly confused, and arguably not innocently so. States had coercive power. Corporations had purchasing power. The two were quite different, although the state relentlessly sought to coerce or co-opt the corporate sector's wealth-generating ability to its own ends. FDR's New Dealers declared that more political power was necessary to take on these "malefactors of great wealth."

Before the 1936 election, Roosevelt declared, "I should like to have it said of my first administration that in it the forces of selfishness and of lust for power met their match. I should like to have it said of my second administration that in it these forces met their master." Bashing business helped him to a landslide.

The war led to a necessary rapprochement between businesses and governments. This indeed led to sometimes disgraceful "cooperation" — for example, in the case of the company I.G. Farben and the Nazis. Wartime cooperation led to a potential peacetime threat on the Allied side too, as President Eisenhower stated in warning of the "military-industrial complex." However, when George Orwell wrote *Nineteen Eighty-Four*, he saw the main political danger not in capitalism but in anti-capitalism, whose propaganda was served by his fictional "children's history textbook." Similarly, Hayek's *Road to Serfdom* emphasized how the greater powers sought by the state would inevitably lead to oppression.

In the postwar years John Kenneth Galbraith castigated the alleged awesome power of "technocratic" corporations. At that 1973 conference in Kirkcaldy to mark the 250th anniversary of Adam Smith's birth, Galbraith claimed that it was the very success of the corporation that had made Smith's notions of minimal government untenable.

In Galbraith's world, corporations were ever more powerful entities ruled by ever more short-sighted executives who engaged in the production of ever more trivial or dangerous products, such as intercontinental ballistic missiles, plastic grass and genital deodorants. For Galbraith's corporate managers, the brass ring was the key to the executive washroom.

Galbraith's presentation in Kirkcaldy asserted that Smith's contention that consumers and competition were the main constraints on business behaviour was simply not true any more. The "sharp and obvious distinction" between 1776 and 1973, according to Galbraith, was that the business corporation was now so large that it threatened to subvert the state. Indeed, in many cases it already had.

"The modern great corporation," declared Galbraith, "controls prices and costs, organizes suppliers, persuades consumers, guides the Pentagon, shapes public opinion, buys Presidents and is otherwise a dominant influence in the state. It also, alas, in its modern and comprehensively powerful form figures not at all in the accepted economic theory. That still holds the business firm to be solely subordinate to the market, solely subject to the authority of the state and ultimately the passive servant of the sovereign citizen." According to Galbraith, traditional market economics was invalid because "there is no I.T.T. in the system."

Galbraith's reference is profoundly ironic. ITT started life as International Telephone and Telegraph, and was built into a conglomerate by a man named Harold Geneen. ITT was once almost universally pilloried by the scribbling set for having the temerity to seek to protect its overseas investments from Communist expropriation, but its allegedly awesome power proved to be illusory. Geneen ultimately admitted that conglomeration wasn't necessarily such a great idea. Within a few years of the Kirkcaldy conference the company was brought to heel not by governments but by the markets that Galbraith claimed had no more power. Who now remembers ITT or Harold Geneen? Such inconvenient historical facts were easy to forget, indeed almost impossible to remember because they didn't fit "the narrative," and there were always examples of corporate malfeasance, corporate welfare or industrial accidents to feed confirmation bias.

Misunderstanding of the market as a power struggle inevitably led people to assume that "big" would always drive out "small." The moral psychologist Jonathan Haidt, despite his admirable commitment to try to understand those who failed to hold left-liberal beliefs, still bristled with memes that went straight back to *The Communist Manifesto*. In *The Righteous Mind*, he wrote that "during the twentieth century, small businesses got pushed to the margins or to extinction as corporations dominated the most lucrative markets." He offered no source for this claim or evidence of it.

Insofar as big business ever did "drive out" small, it was because "big" offered something that consumers preferred. It was, for example, not supermarkets or big-box stores that put butchers (such as Keith's in Kirkcaldy), bakeries or mom-and-pop stores out of business; it was the voluntary migration of the stores' customers. Meanwhile, even the largest corporations were in fact under constant threat from nimble innovators. Specialist butchers, bakeries and craft breweries were able to make a comeback as they appealed to consumers' desire for novelty and variety.

One of the most significant features of business in the final decade of the 20th century and the first decades of the 21st was how start-ups in computer and internet-related businesses such as Microsoft, Apple, Google and Facebook grew to become, in a single generation, some of the largest corporations in the world. If the older behemoths such as IBM had vast political power, wouldn't they have used it suffocate these upstarts in their cradle? (In fact, companies did often seek to use the legal system to hobble competitors.)

Depressingly, however, the new billionaires soon learned to mouth anti-corporate platitudes and point to their own exceptionalism. When the internet search engine company Google's founders, Sergey Brin and Larry Page, preached in their corporate philosophy that "you can make money without doing evil," they merely strengthened the notion that money making and evil had been traditional business partners, like Scrooge and Marley.

Mark Zuckerberg, founder of Facebook, stressed that making money was just a means to an end (as if it wasn't so for everybody): "We don't build services to make money; we make money to build better services." Facebook was "built to accomplish a social mission — to make the world more open and connected." Zuckerberg said he just wanted his social missionaries to press the "like" button so they could "discover the best products and improve the quality and efficiency of their lives." Sounded great, except that Zuckerberg also felt compelled to talk, like a good global salvationist, about addressing "the large worldwide problems we face in job creation, education and health care."

And yet perpetual breast beating and assertions of good intention didn't appear to shift perceptions of dangerous power. Indeed, Haidt suggested that when it came to business power, James Cameron's movie *Avatar*, which featured a genocidal corporation laying waste to an idyllic planet, represented a "quite believable" projection. Earth, he wrote, could be "run by corporations that have turned national governments into their lackeys." Haidt concluded, "The only force left on Earth that can stand up to the largest corporations are national governments, some of which still maintain the power to tax, regulate, and divide corporations into smaller pieces when they get too powerful."

But it was only through truly "powerful" — that is, coercive — governments that corporations could ever become burdensome or dangerous. Banks and auto companies did not bail themselves out; their rescuers were governments. However, since big government was a "sacralized value" for left-liberals, they tended to be blind to the inconvenient fact that the bigger and more powerful the government, the more corrupt, incompetent and dangerous it was likely to be, and the more inclined to try to co-opt the corporate sector by offering successful companies subsidies and unsuccessful giants bailouts. Like Keynes, left-liberals persisted in the belief that — despite the voluminous evidence of history — everything would be fine as long as the "right people," i.e., themselves, were in charge.

"When conservatives say," declared Haidt, "that markets offer better solutions than do regulations, let them step forward and explain their plan to eliminate the dangerous and unfair externalities generated by many markets." But here — apart from ignoring the myriad laws, rules and regulations that already exist, often with perverse results — he seemed to be taking the slippery-slope rhetorical position that those concerned about the *dangers* of political power and potentially perverse regulation wanted *no* government, and *no* regulation. He also appeared blind to the adverse consequences for any corporation discovered — or even perceived — to be trying to shove externalities onto the public. In fact, the main problem for corporations in the early 21st century was having externalities greatly exaggerated, or entirely falsified. Still, some "enlightened" businessmen were more than prepared to bear, publicize or even greatly exaggerate the charges of environmental rape and pillage that were now central to the anti-capitalist critique.

sixteen

The Greenest Businessman in America

*The whole notion of economics has to change, and measure success
in different terms from the ones that have been drilled into our
heads from the time we were babies, since Adam Smith.*
— Ray Anderson, founder of Interface

All censure of a man's self is oblique praise.
— Samuel Johnson

Ray Anderson was a businessman and a sinner. That combination was hardly likely to shock anybody. However, Ray Anderson's self-confessed sin put mere greed, exploitation or malfeasance in the shade. It was that, as a capitalist and an industrialist, he was a plunderer of the earth's resources and a polluter of its environment, not to mention a thief from future generations. He was the very epitome of unsustainable development.

As the founder and chairman of Interface, one of the largest carpet companies in the world, the Georgia-based businessman (who died in 2011) appeared to be a powerful witness for his own prosecution, not to mention that of capitalism more generally. The notion that business is fundamentally crooked has long been a staple of anti-capitalist critiques, but the idea that corporations were literally destroying the earth was a relatively new addition to the charge sheet.

Following an "epiphany" in the early 1990s, Anderson had begun sharing his massive *mea culpa* with appreciative congregations of the environmentally concerned all over the world — a kind of John the Baptist warm-up act for Al Gore's *Inconvenient Truth* crusade. In 2004 Anderson began to reach a wider audience through his starring role in an award-winning Canadian documentary called *The Corporation*. Anderson was the only representative of the business community to survive the film relatively unscathed, but then the film didn't have to condemn him: he did that himself.

The Corporation promoted the core sacralized anti-capitalist belief that large businesses are powerful, destructive and fundamentally evil. If they were individuals, it claimed, they would be psychopaths. (This accusation represented what Friedrich Hayek called "naive anthropomorphism," the notion that a corporation was analogous to a human being and thus should display moral attributes such as caring and sharing, particularly since it was so "rich.")

The film used interviews with corporate executives, marketers and even free-market icons such as Milton Friedman to assert that corporations, "the dominant institution of our times," were essentially manipulative "externalizing" machines that shoved their costs onto society. *Stakeholder Theory: The Movie*. The benefits of corporations received no screen time at all.

The corporate system was said to be analogous to — here we go again — slavery. Corporations were claimed to have always been handmaidens and cheerers-on of fascist and dictatorial governments, promoters of birth defects and cancer epidemics that sought to privatize rainfall and gag free speech. *The Corporation* was replete with images of sharks and Frankenstein monsters, with scenes of smokestacks and smog.

Celebrity left-wingers old and new were trotted out to make the case against corporate capitalism, from the American linguistic philosopher Noam Chomsky to the Canadian shopping philosopher Naomi Klein. Prominent too was the American radical anti-capitalist filmmaker Michael Moore.

The most surprising — and perhaps even most eloquent — condemnation of capitalism came from Ray Anderson, with his arresting admissions of sin and plunder. "We are leaving a legacy of poison and diminishment," he said, staring resolutely into the camera. "We are robbing the future." This amounted, he said, to "intergenerational tyranny." And then, calmly and with a some-how incongruous smile, he concluded, "It's the wrong thing to do."

Later in the movie, Anderson explained how he had come to the cause. After 21 years as an entrepreneur, he had been called upon to speak to his employees about what the company was doing for the environment. Desperate for inspiration, he was given a book, *The Ecology of Commerce*, by Paul Hawken. Anderson had been horrified by Hawken's catalogue of destruction and extinction, and particularly haunted by the phrase "the death of birth," which had been coined by the biologist E.O. Wilson.

Anderson described Wilson's characterization as a "spear in the chest." His subsequent address to employees had reportedly left everybody in tears and led to a "change of paradigm" for his company. Anderson claimed that he had realized that he had been taking "the way of the plunderer." He believed the day would come, he said, "when people like me will wind up in jail." "The Industrial Revolution," he concluded, "is not working."

Just before Anderson's final appearance in the movie, Michael Moore came onscreen to say that he was genuinely puzzled by why corporations would support his work, which, after all, slammed corporations. He opined that it must be because they ultimately stood for nothing, and would — as Lenin had suggested — manufacture the rope for their own hanging as long as they could make a buck out of it.

As an observation about business's ideological short-sightedness, Moore's assessment seemed depressingly accurate. Anderson then came back to note, effectively, that his own rope would be recycled. He talked about climbing "Mount

Sustainability" while, paradoxically, leaving "zero footprint." For once in the movie, a positive graphic appeared about a corporation, noting that Interface had become one-third more "sustainable" since 1995.

The film ended with a call for us to do something, anything, to get the world back into "democratic" hands. Such a world — whose outlines were somewhat vague — would apparently be driven by endless town hall meetings.

—⁂—

Anti-business businessmen are a much less rare phenomenon than most people might imagine, but how could anyone have taken Anderson's self-flagellation seriously? If you think you are sinning, there is surely only one moral solution: to stop. Ray Anderson's answer, however, seemed to be to go on a regimen of industrial "sin lite." Yet his performance in *The Corporation* attracted hardly a trace of skepticism, at least publicly.

The film as a whole also received overwhelmingly positive reviews. The *Economist* described it as "a surprisingly rational and coherent attack on capitalism's most important institution." Ray Anderson was singled out by more than one review — including that in the *Wall Street Journal* — as the film's "star" or corporate "hero." *BusinessWeek* described him, apparently without irony, as "the movie's mahatma." *Newsday* declared that Anderson's commentary was "a breath of fresh air, given the litany of societal crimes elsewhere committed by slaves of the bottom line."

No details of this litany were provided, or perhaps felt necessary. No such slaves were identified.

Toronto's *Globe and Mail* painted him as a "hopeful" example of "business leaders who have faced the ugly facts." Again, the "ugly facts" seemed to be regarded as too obvious to require elaboration.

Almost everybody appeared inclined to take Ray Anderson at his own word, but it was hard not to notice that, for a sinner, he appeared mightily self-satisfied. Still, he surely deserved to be taken more seriously than some of his fellow critics of capitalism. After all, he wasn't just a wild-eyed left-wing theorist; he was an entrepreneur, the founder and largest shareholder of a significant public company, where, he claimed, his theories were being implemented.

Was he sincere? Was he right? (Of course, these are two very distinct questions.) Was capitalism destroying the earth? Had Ray Anderson really discovered a new and more benign approach to business that might be imitated by other companies? Or was he a hypocrite, wrapping himself in a cloak of green as a marketing tool? Then again, might he be — to use another of Lenin's insightful assessments — a "useful idiot," blithely peddling dangerous ideas whose implications he simply didn't understand? Where, exactly, was this guy coming from?

—ɯɯ—

Ray Anderson was born in the little Georgia town of West Point, just off Highway 85, an hour's drive southwest of Atlanta. Sitting astride the Chattahoochee River, West Point is a mix of struggling industrial enterprise, old southern money and bedroom community. The main street is low-rise and low-rent, but just up the hill are some beautiful old houses. Under a blue sky on a crisp spring day, resplendent with porches sporting American flags and front yards bedecked with blossoming magnolias, they are pure Norman Rockwell.

Atop a hill on the west side of town is a reconstructed earthwork known as Fort Tyler, which had the distinction of being the last fort to fall in the Civil War. Unfortunately, Robert E. Lee had surrendered at Appomattox a week before. Those who died defending Fort Tyler perished for a lost cause.

On my visit, in 2004, I discovered as I read the detailed plaques that led up to the fort that, from an economic point of view, West Point has an even more intriguing history. Before the Civil War, the town had briefly boomed as the embodiment of a satirical proposal put forth by the economic satirist Frédéric Bastiat: a "negative railroad."

Bastiat, who died in 1850, was a stout defender of free markets and a skeptic about economic policy, especially that hatched by self-interested businessmen. Perhaps his most famous satire of naked commercial self-interest masquerading as good public policy was the "Petition of the Candlemakers," which demanded that window blinds be shut because of unfair competition from a "foreign source": the sun. (Ironically, given governments' tendency to embody satire in policy, the sun has now, via subsidies for solar power, truly become the source of "unfair competition.")

Bastiat's proposal for a negative railroad was based on a real petition from certain burghers of Bordeaux. When they heard that a railway was to come through the city, they suggested that there might be a gap in the line at the town, which would enable them to thrive commercially by transporting goods between the two termini.

Why stop there? Bastiat had asked. Why not have gaps at other major cities? Indeed, if gaps were such great promoters of economic activity, why not have one huge gap, a "negative railroad."

"Gap" status actually befell West Point in the years before the Civil War, although apparently for technical reasons. A railroad line had reached West Point from Montgomery, Alabama, in 1851. Another line was built to the town from Atlanta in 1854. The gauge of one line was four inches wider than the other's. This meant that, just as under the proposal of the business interests of Bordeaux, goods had to be unloaded and carried from one line to another. While this represented something of a boon to West Point, it meant a much greater burden to shippers and travellers. It also meant that when Union troops were sweeping through the South in 1865, West Point was a natural target because supplies were piled up there, awaiting transfer at the bottleneck.

The defence of the town, in particular the manning of the earthworks on the hill, was left to Brigadier General Robert C. Tyler, an enigmatic figure who had risen through the ranks during the war and was recuperating at one of the town's hospitals from the loss of a leg. The flag that flew above the fort had been stitched by the ladies of the town and presented to Tyler earlier. He declared that were the flag to be brought down, his body would be found at the bottom of the flagpole. By the end of the action, which took place on Easter Sunday, April 16, 1865, he had been as good as his word.

—ɯ—

Ray Anderson, the third son of an assistant postmaster, had always been ambitious and competitive. His career, like that of General Tyler, would intersect both with the embodiment of economic fallacy and with commitment to a coercive political cause — although, like the general, he didn't see it that way.

Anderson won a football scholarship to Georgia Tech, then went to work in the carpet business. As he rose through the management ranks at a company called Milliken, one of his jobs was to start up a carpet tile operation, a concept that had been developed in England. Anderson saw that carpet tiles had a big future — a future that would get much bigger with the need to have easy access to the underfloor wiring so necessary to the early stages of the computer and telecommunications revolutions. Anderson left Milliken to develop carpet tiles in partnership with a British company, Carpets International. Over the coming two decades, Carpets International would be one of the dozens of acquisitions Anderson would make on the way to building Interface into one of the largest flooring companies in the world.

A couple of miles east of Fort Tyler sits the Ray C. Anderson plant, or "RCA," as it is known. The afternoon shift was just pouring into the packed car park as I arrived. I was given a lightning tour, then sped up Highway 85 to the company's main plant at LaGrange for another tour. I asked the manager at LaGrange about Anderson. I said I understood that he hadn't had much to do with actually running the place for most of the past 10 years.

"No," acknowledged the manager, "he's off saving the world. And that," he added quickly, "is a good thing."

—⁂—

A couple of weeks after my trip to West Point, I caught up with Ray Anderson in Vancouver. He was there to give a couple of speeches, appear at a special private screening of *The Corporation* and take part in a panel discussion at a major environmental conference. Vancouver was looking spectacular. The rhododendrons were blooming, the sun shining and the snow-capped mountains glistening in the distance, somewhat incongruous circumstances perhaps for a conference whose theme was that the environment was going to hell.

I met Anderson at the Sheraton Wall Hotel. Across Burrard Street, at St. Andrew's-Wesley Church, the following Sunday's sermon was advertised: "Believing Your Own Press."

Anderson emerged from a conference room and shook my hand firmly. Seventy years old, of medium height and athletic build, he came across as a charismatic good ol' boy who was clearly on a mission. I asked him about his "epiphany," and he proceeded into a sermon that he had given hundreds, if not thousands, of times.

"I was 60 years old, 10 years ago, and this occasion arose when I had to make a speech to a task force about our environmental vision," he said. He said he hadn't thought about the issue but by chance was given a copy of *The Ecology of Commerce*, by Paul Hawken.

"Hawken's book landed on my desk and reading that book was the source of the epiphany ... The central theory of Paul Hawken's book is that the biosphere is in long-term systemic decline. The biggest culprit is the industrial system, and the only way out of this mess is for corporations that are doing the damage to lead the way out. I took that message very personally."

I asked him if he didn't underplay the huge amount of human wealth and welfare generated by the capitalist system.

"But it's all at the expense of the earth," he said. "What kind of wealth is that, generated at the expense of the earth?"

I asked him if the earth had a value independent of human values.

"If all that wealth destroys the earth, what will be left for the next generation?" he shot back, dodging the question. "Can you see any other way [but destruction]? You look at the earth. It's finite, 8,000 miles in diameter, and if we continuously chew up nature to produce stuff that ends up in landfills, in time we convert earth to waste and what do you have left in terms of a livable planet? What's the wealth worth then? What economy can survive without air? What economy can survive without water, and energy and materials and pollination and seed dispersal and flood control and climate regulation?"

Concluding that these were rhetorical questions, and not an invitation to debate, I asked him if he considered himself a capitalist.

"Absolutely," he said. "I'm also an industrialist and an entrepreneur and as competitive as anybody you're likely to know. Hawken would say that the only problem with capitalism is that nobody's tried it. We think of capitalism and we focus only on financial capital. We ignore human capital and natural capital."

Who, I asked, was this "we"?

"The members of this industrial system," he said.

"But you're a member of the industrial system and you don't think that way," I noted.

"I'm called a radical industrialist," replied Anderson. "I'm still a plunderer," he said, "but only two-thirds as much as I was."

"So plundering is just using resources?" I asked.

"It's stealing our grandchildren's future," he responded. "The plunderers will someday be put in jail for stealing our grandchildren's future. Any businessman is a plunderer if he is in the business of raping nature, as I am. This plundering has been going on for 292 years." According to Anderson, the invention of the Newcomen steam engine to pump water from English mines was where it all started.

I decided that it was time to insert a bit of likely unwelcome skepticism. "For 292 years of plundering," I suggested tentatively, "when I look around I don't see a plundered world."

"That's because you're not looking in the right place," said Anderson. "If you had flown over British Columbia or Washington State and seen the clear-cutting ... It's a matter of destroying habitat for countless species. Who are we to be so presumptuous to think that we have life and death power over other species?"

I moved on to *The Corporation* and its disturbing propaganda techniques.

"I disclaim all responsibility," laughed Anderson. "I just interviewed those guys three years ago, and I was as surprised as anybody to see the way I showed up in that film."

Despite my at times skeptical questions, Anderson's genial, charming persona really slipped only once during our interview. In *The Corporation*, Anderson had suggested that "not a single scientific paper in the past 25 years has indicated anything but that the biosphere is in decline."

With that assertion in mind, I asked him, "Have you read Bjørn Lomborg's *The Skeptical Environmentalist?*"

"Enough to know that it's bullshit," he snapped. "And I've heard enough scientific commentary to know that it's bullshit."

I pressed on, noting that Lomborg's central assertion (as I described in an earlier chapter) was that the world was *not* going to hell in a handbasket.

"And he's dead wrong. I haven't read the book myself but I've read the opinion of people I respect who say it is not scientifically based, it's not good science, and he's wrong. Hawken told me that. And Peter Raven, probably America's leading authority on biodiversity. And I've gone to other members of my advisory team, and they've said that it's absolute crap. As I understand it, there was no peer review. There is no independent third-party validation of the things he says."

Lomborg's book had investigated alarmist claims about resources and the environment and found that they were either without substance or grossly exaggerated. His conclusions generated a furor among environmentalists. They did not, for the most part, address his facts or arguments, but hurled personal smears and peripheral pseudo-academic claims, including the one picked up by Ray Anderson: that Lomborg's work had not been "peer reviewed." In fact, all his data came from peer-reviewed sources. Thus Lomborg's book became subject to the "psychology of taboo." Even to read it would have given it spurious validity; it should never have been published. Indeed, Anderson's expert Peter Raven — director of the Missouri Botanical Garden and president of the American Association for the Advancement of Science — had joined others in writing a letter to Cambridge University Press suggesting exactly that.

Raven had also declared that Lomborg "distorts statistics and statements to meet his own political end." Raven described environmental skeptics as "false prophets and charlatans." He claimed that the basis of the "sustainable society" lay in FDR's "Four Freedoms" speech (the one that erected the problematic claim to "positive" material rights). Although Bjørn Lomborg was apparently not permitted to bring politics into scientific affairs (which in fact he hadn't), Raven clearly did not regard this stricture as applying to himself.

Scientific American printed an 11-page rebuttal of *The Skeptical Environmentalist* filled with sneering dismissal. Lomborg was said to have a "rose-coloured point of view." He had offended against "the literature." He was accused of "discounting the value of biodiversity," and asserting that "the only value of forests is harvestable trees." Reviewers in the journal *Nature* compared the book to "a bad term paper."

The most intriguing assault on Lomborg came via something called the Danish Committees on Scientific Dishonesty (DCSD), a branch of the Danish Ministry of Science, Technology and Innovation. The DCSD relied mainly on the criticisms that had appeared in *Scientific American*, and virtually ignored Lomborg's rebuttals. Astonishingly, its "working party" criticized *Lomborg* for "personal attacks" and for "belittling researchers." The DCSD suggested that it was "out of keeping with good scientific practice" to "bypass specialist scientific fora." Most revealing, it claimed that Lomborg's work would never have achieved prominence but for its "positive" coverage in the United States and in the *Economist*. It continued, "The USA is the society with the highest energy consumption in the world, and there are powerful interests in the USA bound up with increasing energy consumption and with the belief in free market forces."

So there it was. Bjorn Lomborg's sin was out in the open: he was seen as being on the side of those who believed in "free-market forces."

The DCSD stopped short of accusing Lomborg of "gross negligence" but said that his work was "deemed to fall within the concept of scientific dishonesty." The judgment was immediately and enthusiastically taken up by the environmental establishment. However, when Lomborg complained, the Ministry of Science, Technology and Innovation launched its own inquiry. A year later it produced a scathing rebuttal of the DCSD, finding that its decision on Lomborg was "emotional," not backed up by documentation and "completely void of argumentation" for its claims of dishonesty and lack of good scientific practice.

Lomborg was exonerated, and yet the mud had obviously stuck, as the assessment of Ray Anderson and others who relied on the "authorities" of the environmental movement made clear. This begged a much larger question: why would Ray Anderson and so many others — including prominent scientists — be so violently opposed to the notion that the world *wasn't* going to hell in a handbasket?

—⁓—

Paul Hawken had a simple message: "Business is destroying the world." How? Through "the greed of the rich and powerful." "Quite simply," wrote Hawken, "our business practices are destroying life on earth. Given current corporate practices, not one wildlife reserve, wilderness, or indigenous culture will survive the global market economy. We know that every natural system on the planet is disintegrating."

At the centre of *The Ecology of Commerce* were the core sacralized claims of modern anti-capitalism: that corporations were entities that thrived by dumping their problems onto others; and that they were enormously and dangerously powerful, with a power that rivalled and excelled that of nation-states.

The book seemed to reflect a troubled psyche more than a troubled world. Hawken's earth was a dystopian place of teeming masses breeding exponentially, of fetuses with impaired immune systems, of mothers with chemical-laced breast milk, of human bodies too toxic to be put in landfills, of creatures poisoned by the industrial system, of ancient forests wiped out, of species eliminated wholesale, of mountains of waste, of potential climate apocalypse.

Hawken's image of commerce was a demonic parody that nobody could, or would, possibly defend. "The conservative view of free-market capitalism asserts that nothing should be allowed to hinder commerce," he wrote, without citing anybody who actually held such a view. He went on to claim that "defenders of the status quo sometimes cite the Book of Genesis," but he didn't identify these blinkered Bible thumpers.

Unspecified "business ideologues" allegedly regarded species extinction as a "so what" issue. However, wrote Hawken, "we can't turn our backs on the web of life that sustains us, and live in a biological vacuum engineered by technology." We weren't told who was recommending this biological vacuum.

It wasn't just business as usual that Hawken didn't like; it seemed to be people more generally. He depicted humans as weeds and parasites, compared them to thoughtless life forms such as algae or reindeer and castigated them as merely "one species" that was taking more than its "fair share."

According to Hawken, "Corporations are creating ... an environment of deadening commercial strip centers leading in and out of our towns and cities, garbage trains loaded with trash and toxins, and Bhopals where 200,000 people are sick or dead or dying. It is a world where fewer and fewer people benefit from the grosser and more swollen acts of commerce, a world in which the small things, the seemingly inconsequential forms of life, are extirpated with disdain, but to our ultimate peril."

Consumers were portrayed as morons easily manipulated into buying dreck. "Products have become increasingly shoddy and ill-formed," claimed Hawken. "The over-packaged chotchkes, the gummy bears and injection-molded refrigerator magnets, the 'Green Forest' ecological paper towels, the nacho-flavored, shrink-wrapped, ready-to-eat popcorn, the perfumes made of aromatic hydrocarbons refracted from Texas crude ..." (Note that Hawken condemned refrigerator magnets while ignoring the technological wonder of the refrigerator.)

In Hawken's world, trade, in particular international trade, was bad. Small, local and labour-intensive were good. "A restorative economy," wrote Hawken, "is not going to lead to a life of dulling comfort and convenience ... We should be prepared to bid farewell to energy- and resource-consumptive luxuries such as Chilean strawberries and nectarines flown in daily during New York winters."

Indeed, Hawken welcomed the prospect of greater scarcity and declared, "The purpose of all these suggestions is to end industrialism as we know it." He admitted that "people will not cut back on their possessions and wants on their own." So clearly the cuts had to be made for them. The rest was simply a matter of "imagination ... We have to be able to imagine a life where having less is truly more satisfying, more interesting, and of course, more secure."

Intriguingly, in line with the theme of co-opting business as well as condemning it, the companies that we had just been told were greed-driven exploiters were somehow to become the leaders of this sustainable Brave New World, where waste was to be not merely cut down but eliminated. Energy was to come from hydrogen and sunshine, which would meet our needs "as long as those needs do not continue to involve a runaway, frenetic world of cars, planes, commuting, and travel." Competition was to be banned.

All this implied a level of economic and social control that Hawken never explicitly acknowledged. He wrote vaguely of a "consensus-building, collaborative approach." Except that the consensus had already been reached. People had the freedom only to agree. Anybody who disagreed was "in denial."

Hawken projected Utopian visions of creating the world anew. "Imagine what a team of designers could come up with if they were to start from scratch, locating and specifying industries and factories that had potentially synergistic and symbiotic relationships." But wasn't that exactly what Soviet-style central planning — which had always and everywhere proved disastrous both to freedom and wealth — was all about? Hawken's ignorance of — or blindness to — economics, politics and history was stunning.

The culprits of present and future disasters were clearly identified. "We have spent too much time and money," wrote Hawken, "making the world safe for upper-middle-class white men." Men, presumably, such as Ray Anderson, which made it all the more curious that Anderson would so enthusiastically embrace Hawken's hate-filled thesis.

—◊—

Amid Hawken's catalogue of environmental horror, it was assertions about species extinction, the "death of birth," that Anderson declared were, above all, a "spear in the chest." Part of Anderson's angry rebuttal of Bjørn Lomborg to me in Vancouver had been his claim that the earth was losing "60,000 species a year."

"What species?" I asked.

"What does it matter what they are?" he replied. "They are part of the web of life. We have no idea how their demise might affect us."

Anderson had been stunned to learn that, according to Hawken, "we are losing 27,000 species a year," even though the figure seemed to be fairly flexible. Indeed, on the same page as that 27,000 figure, Hawken had declared that we were losing between 20,000 and 100,000 species a year, with the danger of losing 20 per cent of all species on the planet in the next 20 to 40 years.

Since these alarming figures were so central to Ray Anderson's "epiphany" and his ongoing concerns, not to mention staples in the literature of the environmental movement, it's worth having a closer look at them, and in particular at what Lomborg had to say about the issue in *The Skeptical Environmentalist*.

Where did the notion that tens of thousands of species were being eliminated annually come from? According to Lomborg, the seminal source was a 1979 book called *The*

Sinking Ark, by the British academic Norman Myers. How was the figure arrived at? Myers had noted that the current accepted rate of extinction at the time he wrote was *one* species a year, but then he quoted a source from a 1974 conference that "hazarded a guess" that the rate might now have reached 100 species a year, if we counted not just animals and birds but all life forms *including those not yet discovered.* Myers then went on to "suppose" that one million species might be lost in the final quarter of the 20th century. That would equal 40,000 a year. And that was his argument. From one a year, to a hundred, to 40,000, in three easy steps, with figures plucked from thin air.

If species loss had a root cause, it was said to be loss of habitat. A rule-of-thumb correlation between species and habitat had been formulated by E.O. Wilson in the 1960s. If 90 per cent of habitat was lost, he estimated, then half the species would disappear. Subsequently, an American biologist, Thomas Lovejoy, had built a model for the WWF to bolster Myers's figures. He assumed that most species lived in the rainforest and estimated that if you cut down half the forest, you would lose one-third of the species.

How did all these speculations and models fit with the real world? Lomborg pointed out that the forest of the eastern United States had been reduced to fragments totalling just 1 to 2 per cent of its previous area. This had resulted in the recorded extinction of one forest bird. The Puerto Rican rainforest had been cut by 99 per cent, but just seven of 60 bird species had become extinct. Although 86 per cent of the Amazon rainforest remained intact, almost 90 per cent of the Atlantic rainforest had been cleared in the 19th century. Lomborg pointed out that the Brazilian Society of Zoology could not find a single known species that had been rendered extinct.

The World Conservation Union (IUCN) is the organization that keeps the official "Red List" of endangered species. It acknowledged that there were severe problems with apocalyptic estimates, yet intriguingly, when the controversy blew up over Lomborg, it was clear on whose side the IUCN stood. Its director general, Achim Steiner (who later headed the UNEP), wrote to the *Economist*, which had strongly supported Lomborg: "Mr. Lomborg is right in cautioning against apocalyptic scenarios. But it is wrong to suggest that species extinction, climate change and pollution are imaginary environmental problems."

Lomborg had never suggested any such thing. He had merely pointed out that it would be sensible to gauge just how serious such problems were before taking costly action to counter them. Steiner's claim was typical of the repeated use by environmentalists of slippery-slope rhetoric. If you questioned any tenet of the alarmist green litany, you were instantly accused of claiming that there were "no environmental problems."

Significantly, Steiner also acknowledged that the actual rate of recorded global extinction over the previous 500 years had been *two a year*, while some 5,400 species of plants and animals were considered *at risk* (out of some 1.6 million known species). This was a very, very long way from 40,000 or 60,000 or 100,000 species becoming extinct annually.

In the *Scientific American* critique, one of those entrusted with refuting Lomborg was Thomas Lovejoy, whom Lomborg had comprehensively criticized in *The Skeptical Environmentalist*. Lovejoy had claimed that "Bjorn Lomborg discounts the value of diversity," but he had presented no evidence of such a claim. Lomborg had merely defended Norman Myers — the 40,000-a-year man — as a person who "deserves credit for being the first to point out that the number was large and at a time when it was difficult to do so accurately."

With their "scientific" claims under attack, alarmists simply cranked up the hyperbole. Norman Myers continued to talk of "the opening stages of a human caused biotic holocaust." The leading doomster Paul Ehrlich, author of the wildly inaccurate book *The Population Bomb*, claimed in another tome, *Betrayal of Science and Reason*, "But biologists don't need to know how many species there are, how they are related to one another, or how many disappear annually to recognize that Earth's biota is entering a gigantic spasm of extinction."

This was science?

—※—

I asked Ray Anderson if there had been any personal loss or tragedy that primed him for the epiphany he experienced after reading Hawken's book. He had avoided the question, but when I read the book that Anderson wrote a couple of years into his conversion, *Mid-Course Correction*, there it was, right in the prologue. Anderson had effectively been forced to kick himself upstairs following problems at Interface during the recession of 1991-93 and the introduction of a new management team, led by a charismatic manager named Charles Eitel.

Anderson had had some problems letting go of the reins of power. To ease the transition, Eitel had brought in a psychologist, one J. Zink, who was a specialist in marriage counselling and family therapy. Those specialties were appropriate because Anderson frequently referred to Interface as his "child," and few people give up custody of their children easily.

Part of the therapeutic process of transition was a series of "conversations" between the managers and the psychologist, which were turned into yet another book, called *Face It: A Spiritual Journey of Leadership*. The book contains some fascinating insights into the obvious problems that any corporate founder has in handing over under such circumstances: the struggle with acknowledgement of inevitable mortality, jealousy of the new "saviour" and, above all, what to do next.

In Anderson's own words, "The new management team took hold of operations quickly and effectively, and my job became one of turning loose, getting out of the way, staying out of the way, and being head cheerleader. That's a big change after 21 years of 'nose to the grindstone,' autocratic, hands-on management. I began seriously to question my role, what it should be, and indeed if I had one.

"Then ... I discovered an urgent calling and an unexpectedly rewarding new role for myself."

Like Al Gore and Maurice Strong, Ray Anderson decided that he had to save the world. He had already been convinced that global salvation would require economics — or at least economics as he understood it — to be tossed out the window.

"The whole notion of economics has to change," he was quoted as saying in *Face It*, "and measure success in different terms from the ones that have been drilled into our heads from the time we were babies, since Adam Smith."

Ray Anderson had clearly never read Adam Smith, but no comment typified more clearly the Scottish sage's role as lightning rod for moralistic anti-capitalist sentiment, which had now gone thoroughly green.

—※—

As a first step toward installing his "different" measure of success, Anderson had rapidly hired a group of environmentally concerned consultants and advisors who confirmed that the world needed saving and that Anderson could be in the vanguard of saving it. He dubbed them the "Eco Dream Team."

The Eco Dream Team blended a weird and wonderful mix of genius, Sixties convictions, mystic environmentalism, opportunism and flim-flam, offering huge and expansive visions. In the event, its members proved much better at borrowing ideas than at coming up with viable new ones. Hawken, of course, was a leading member. Other key players included the alternative-energy maven Amory Lovins and his wife, L. Hunter Lovins, and a Los Angeles-based environmental design expert named John Picard.

Amory Lovins had first achieved fame/notoriety in the early 1970s as the guru of small-scale, renewable solutions to the alleged "energy crisis," which he predicted would lead to persistent shortages (but didn't). He peddled the so-called "soft path," which featured a proliferation of backyard windmills and biogas digesters. Lovins had predicted that by the year 2000, the United States would be producing 35 per cent of its commercial energy "softly." He was out by a factor of perhaps 100.

Undeterred, Lovins continued to claim that the world could, within a generation, increase its energy efficiency by a factor of 10. Key to — and typical of — the practicality of this claim was a concept called the Hypercar, a vehicle of mythical characteristics in every sense. Lovins told *Fortune* magazine in 2000, "It will be roughly four to eight times as efficient as a car of comparable size. You can make it a 110-mile-to-the gallon large SUV or a 200-mile-per-gallon family sedan. In either case it will perform like a Jaguar." Elsewhere he declared that the wonder vehicle would combine "Lexus comfort and refinement, Mercedes stiffness, Volvo safety, BMW acceleration [and] Taurus price." Oh, and this hydrogen-fuel-cell-powered vehicle would be a *source* of energy too. Instead of plugging your car into your house, you would plug your house — or workplace — into your car. As for emissions, there would be only pure water, which led Lovins to suggest — possibly tongue-in-cheek, but then again possibly not — that the Hypercar might be equipped with an on-board espresso machine.

With admirable chutzpah, Lovins suggested that the billions of dollars that the auto companies were spending on alternative vehicles was somehow all due to his inspiration and innovative ideas, a gigantic investment in his vision. In fact, the automakers were investing primarily because of the threat of California legislation mandating that manufacturers' fleets contain a proportion of zero-emission vehicles, and because of increasing political pressures the world over to abandon the internal combustion engine in the face of climate hysteria.

In technical terms, Lovins in fact had very few, if any, original ideas. His Hypercar was built conceptually on assuming that hydrogen fuel cells would become economic, on ignoring the massive expense of hydrogen fuelling infrastructure, on using all the lightest (and most expensive) materials and on the blithe assumption that "scale" would bring costs down.

John Picard was another eco-visionary who wasn't going to be left behind in the wild idea department. Like Anderson, he had experienced a tear-jerking epiphany — in his case while watching an MTV public service announcement about decimation of the rainforest. Picard lived in Marina del Rey in a recycled-metal house with state-of-the-art computer and internet technology. He had specialized in energy-efficient renovations for Hollywood's super-rich, had helped "green" Sony Studios and had retrofitted the cars of celebrities such as Ed Begley Jr. and Priscilla Presley to run on natural gas (which by 2013, with a surge in cheap natural gas production, wasn't looking like such a bad idea). Picard's future world had "intelligent carpet" that uploaded the newspaper through your shoes into your spectacles.

Picard had in fact already played a seminal part in Ray Anderson's epiphany. As a consultant to Southern California Gas Co.'s Environmental Resource Center, whose carpet contract Interface had been chasing, Picard had told the company's regional sales manager that Interface just didn't "get it." The sales manager had, allegedly by chance, been given *The Ecology of Commerce* and passed it up the line to Anderson.

One of Picard's stipulations for Interface getting the contract had been that the carpet should be leased, which meant that the supplier took responsibility for both upkeep and recycling. Hence had been born the first "Evergreen Lease," which Anderson was soon persuaded was the wave of the future.

Under the Dream Team's guidance, Anderson committed to cut out all use of petroleum and replace it with solar energy, and to install "closed-loop" production systems leading to zero waste, harmless emissions and resource-efficient transportation. All this was very easy to say, but much more difficult, if not impossible, to do.

This grand vision, as peddled by the Lovinses and Paul Hawken, was called "natural capitalism." It was based on pricing somehow mandated to reflect those allegedly "real" values, in particular the value of "ecosystem services." Beyond that, it was largely pie in the sky. The productivity of natural resources was to stretch "5, 10, even 100 times further than they do today." There were to be "solutions-based business models," "whole-system design" and "lean manufacturing." However, when it came to practical ideas, the examples that the three used came almost entirely from what companies were already doing — that is, from capitalism's ongoing process of resource saving and technological innovation.

In a book that the three Dreamers wrote in 1999, they talked up Interface as "leading the way to this next frontier of industrial ecology." They touted a new wonder floor covering called Solenium that used 40 per cent less material and lasted four times longer than ordinary carpet, "an 86% reduction in materials intensity." The problem was that within a couple of years, because of technical problems and lack of consumer interest, Interface had discontinued the product.

They also claimed that there was high demand for carpets from Interface's "recently opened solar-powered carpet factory." Only Interface didn't have a solar-powered carpet factory. Interface's California plant had an array of photovoltaic cells that provided around 2 per cent of the plant's electricity and a fraction of 1 per cent of its overall power usage. This minimal amount of expensive solar energy was "dedicated" to the manufacture of the *tufting* in a certain type of carpet, the remainder of which was manufactured with conventional non-renewable energy.

Although Interface certainly cut waste and emissions and improved its efficiency, the practical contributions of the Eco

Dream Team appeared to have been marginal. The only one cited was "biomimicry," the idea of a carpet designed like a "forest floor." This hardly sounded like a "new industrial revolution." The three Dreamers talked up Interface's "shift to service-leasing business," through John Picard's concept of the Evergreen Lease, but the leasing scheme never caught on either.

Perhaps the most telling "contribution" made by the Eco Dream Team was their input to Interface's 25th-anniversary celebration at the Wailea resort on Hawaii. The first reaction of Paul Hawken when he heard about the location — which had been selected by Charlie Eitel — had been outrage. He claimed that tourism was "destroying the islands and the native culture." Eventually, however, the Dream Team decided they would turn up, but only if they could set about changing the resort's "culture." They would submit it to an "eco-audit" and demonstrate how you could live in five-star modesty. They would turn off the air conditioning, shut down the fountains, cut down the number of bath towels, suspend pesticide use and compost restaurant wastes. They even suggested that guests take their garbage home with them. The conference itself, meanwhile, was organized as a massive guiltfest about the state of the earth.

The event received an award for being the "corporate meeting of the year," but success didn't come cheap. The Eco Dream Team's "conservationist" intervention at Wailea wound up more than doubling its cost, to $8 million.

Charlie Eitel didn't survive too long after he had turned Interface around. In mid-1999, he "resigned to pursue other interests." He told the *Atlanta Journal-Constitution*, "I have had a great six years at Interface, and I will miss all of my friends there. But it is time to do something else — including spending time with my family." According to insiders, Eitel was fired by Anderson for his reluctance to go off the environmental deep end and his unwillingness to impose the costs of Anderson's crusade on shareholders, and yet there seemed to be little or no overt shareholder discontent about Ray Anderson's management.

The largest institutional shareholder of Interface at the time I interviewed Anderson was a Chicago-based investment manager. I spoke to the analyst who followed Interface. She appeared unconcerned that the share price was pretty much where it had been 10 years before, when Ray Anderson had had his epiphany. I asked her what she thought about Ray Anderson's confessions of sin and plunder. She sounded a little uneasy. "Is throwing your garbage out of the car window a sin?" she asked, somewhat obscurely. She admitted that for some people Ray Anderson might seem a little extreme, but she said that his crusade was all about everything gradually getting a little bit better. I begged to differ, noting that his stance was about massive and fundamental change, and about denigration of capitalism as a whole. She waffled, and spoke of the importance of "sustainability." I asked her to define the term. She couldn't.

—⁂—

So how far did Interface manage to climb up "Mount Sustainability" after Ray Anderson's epiphany? It claimed cumulative savings of hundreds of millions of dollars, but one key question was how much of those savings were the result of the natural trend to economize resources and recycle wastes, leaving aside any eco-epiphanies.

The employment of cost-effective, resource-saving technologies is good business, not some grafted-on moral imperative. The law is there to prevent corporations from externalizing their costs at the expense of others. Some companies may wish to go beyond the law for marketing or even "moral" reasons, but then we get into problematic territory, since such measures — unless they attract sufficient customers — will carry a cost in lost market share, employment and profitability. Ultimately they may threaten the survival of the company itself.

The irony was that Anderson's "moral" stance led not merely up "Mount Sustainability" but down the road to criticism and inevitable failure, at least from a radical ecological perspective. Ray Anderson had fallen under the sway of those who claimed that *all* resource extraction was unsustainable. Thus being 25 per cent of the way to sustainability merely served to emphasize that you were 75 per cent *un*sustainable. Moreover, the easiest savings had already been made, from what Anderson called "low-hanging fruit." Then what?

Most glaringly, the great commitment to ditch petroleum and embrace alternatives, mainly solar, stalled. The proportion of energy Interface derived from renewable sources had reached just over a third of total energy use by 2007, but was still around the same level five years later. The surge in petroleum prices up to 2008 provided a fillip to renewables, but it provided an incentive to everybody, not just to sinners and plunderers. By 2013, the heavily government-subsidized solar industry was in trouble worldwide.

The most pointed accusation against Ray Anderson was surely that he was a hypocrite, not in wanting to economize on resources — all sensible businessmen want to do that — but in his moralistic hyperbole. When Ray Anderson said he was a sinner and a plunderer, what he was really saying was that *other* industrialists were sinners and plunderers. As Adam Smith's sparring partner Samuel Johnson observed, "All censure of a man's self is oblique praise." Anderson was really saying that he, possibly alone in his time, had seen the light, like Robert Owen 200 years before. In fact, although Ray Anderson saw himself as a maverick, his views and attitudes were entirely reflective of an unreflective corporate zeitgeist.

Ray Anderson didn't appear to realize that he had allied himself with people who ultimately aimed at the destruction of the capitalist system. Mark Achbar, one of the producers of *The Corporation*, said that although he was "impressed" by Anderson, "we cannot rely on the CEOs of the world all having epiphanies while simultaneously reading Paul Hawken's *The Ecology of Commerce* ... One way or another, corporations must be forced into sustainability, or else we are collectively doomed."

Sustainability was obviously attractive to those who liked to apply force.

After visiting Interface's Georgia facilities, as I drove back up Highway 85 under a beautiful blue sky, I was listening to a piece on the satellite radio by the Norwegian composer Edvard Grieg. Grieg had apparently written it to reflect his concern about "materialism." It was this same base materialism, I reflected, that meant that I could now enjoy his music, beamed from space, while driving in comfort toward Atlanta's glistening towers.

What is fascinating is not just that people fail to appreciate such stunning advances, but that they see them as a source of guilt. More than one Interface employee told me that, because of Ray Anderson, he felt bad about driving his car; but of course they had to feel that way. If they followed the logic of their chairman, by driving they were destroying the earth and robbing the future. How could such a belief not be a spear in the chest?

Ray Anderson died of cancer on August 8, 2011, at the age of 77. An obituary in the *Economist* noted that he died "loaded with honours and awards as the greenest businessman in America."

That Anderson was widely applauded and subject to scarcely any critical analysis indicated that he was firmly in the mainstream of global salvationism. Indeed, far from differentiating him from his fellow big businessmen, his professed views were all too depressingly conventional.

seventeen

Bill Gates and the Pitfalls of Philanthrocapitalism

*I have never known much good done by those who affected
to trade for the public good. It is an affectation, indeed,
not very common among merchants, and very few words
need be employed in dissuading them from it.*
— Adam Smith, *The Wealth of Nations*

I n January 2008, Bill Gates gave his final keynote speech at
the razzle-dazzle Consumer Electronics Show in Las Vegas.
He was due to step down from his executive role at Microsoft in
July, although he would stay on as chairman.

His presentation was preceded by a mockumentary about
his "last day at work." It featured, among others, Barack Obama
(then a presidential aspirant), Steven Spielberg, George Clooney,
Jon Stewart, Hillary Clinton, Al Gore and Bono.

The theme of the mini-movie, which portrayed Gates as a
nerdy, absent-minded klutz, was the faked discomfort, incredu-
lity or outright annoyance of these moguls, stars and politicians
at Gates's entreaties that they might help him transition to a
new career as a rap artist, movie star, co-anchor, running mate,
colour commentator or rock guitarist.

Matthew McConaughey, who had been voted the Sexiest
Man Alive by *People* magazine in 2005, appeared as Bill's personal

trainer, helping him to do one rep with a bar carrying no weights. "Am I ready to take my shirt off?" asks Gates. "Not yet," says McConaughey.

The video was funny, but it raised pertinent questions about Bill Gates's next incarnation. Far from looking for a job as a talking head or sex symbol, Gates was convinced that he had far more important things to do. Specifically, he planned to devote himself to the Bill & Melinda Gates Foundation, the philanthropic organization to which he had already committed the bulk — more than US$30 billion — of his fortune. The foundation had been promised a similar-sized stash by Bill's close friend and bridge partner Warren Buffett, "the world's greatest investor."

If Bill Gates had never had a philanthropic bone in his body, he would still rank as one of the greatest benefactors of mankind. He developed products that greatly increased people's ability to communicate, be productive, grow wealthier, help others and enjoy themselves. He created tens of thousands of jobs directly, and millions indirectly. Stock in Microsoft made millionaires of literally hundreds of his employees, who were pillars of their communities. It also bolstered the savings and retirement accounts of many, many more. But all that clearly wasn't sufficient for Gates, who had had enough of doing a good that was arguably "no part of his intention," in Adam Smith's phrase. Now he wanted to do intentional, conscious, conspicuous good; to prove that he had never been in it just for the money.

The point of the Las Vegas mockumentary was that Gates was obviously ill equipped for many jobs. However, he felt himself suited to a gargantuan task that had eluded so many: improving the lot of people in poor nations other than by investing in ("exploiting") them and thus helping them help themselves onto the escalator of capitalism. The Gates Foundation's aspirations were mammoth. It sought to address, if not cure, some of the Third World's most intractable ills, including AIDS, malaria and tuberculosis. It also wanted to start an African green revolution.

In many ways, Gates appeared the true successor of Andrew Carnegie, the Scotsman who rose from the humblest of beginnings to become, in his own time, a steel tycoon and the richest man in his world. Carnegie had said, "The man who dies rich, dies disgraced." He had decided to devote the bulk of his time in later life to broader social issues. Apart from the many libraries he endowed, one of his main concerns was the promotion of world peace. Significantly, he made his mark at the beginning of a century that saw ruinous wars.

Carnegie's several foundations were significant in another way. As noted, one of the ironies of capitalist foundations was that they were easy targets for capture by anti-capitalists such as Maurice Strong. The Carnegie Endowment for International Peace provided the most spectacular example when it chose Alger Hiss, a man subsequently discovered to have been a Communist spy, as its head in the 1940s. More recently, foundations attached to the great names of capitalism — from Rockefeller and Ford to Hewlett and Packard — provided funding to radical environmental causes such as closing down development of the Canadian oil sands because of the oil sands' alleged threat to the climate.

Like Ray Anderson and other businessmen going back to Robert Owen and beyond, Bill Gates had a sense of personal exceptionalism that led him — albeit with the best of intentions — to denigrate the very system that had made him so rich, and that had cultivated his benevolence. It also led him to cleave to the belief that big problems required big, top-down solutions that necessitated the corporate sector to partner with governments and often ideologically driven NGOs, and to "lever" taxpayers' dollars. He had fallen hook, line and sinker for the cause of global salvationism.

Gates and Buffett also put conspicuous pressure on their fellow billionaires to make a "Giving Pledge," under which signatories would atone for their creation of wealth and jobs by committing to give away the bulk of their fortunes. Far from making their fellow super-rich look good, the duo's conspicuous initiative merely bolstered the impression that they needed to have their arms twisted to donate.

—ɯ—

Bill Gates became pumped with moral purpose. This made him — typically — intolerant of those who saw things differently. The year before his performance in Las Vegas, during a panel discussion on poverty at Davos, Gates had had an intriguing clash with William Easterly, a development expert from New York University. In 2006, Easterly had written a devastating analysis of the failures of foreign aid, *The White Man's Burden: Why the West's Efforts to Aid the Rest Have Done So Much Ill and So Little Good*. Easterly calculated that some $2.3 *trillion* had been spent on aid over the previous 50 years, with precious few results in stimulation of economic growth or lifting people out of poverty.

Gates had already declared that he "hated" Easterly's book. At Davos, according to a report in the *Wall Street Journal*, Gates, "his voice rising, snapped back that there are measures of success other than economic growth — such as rising literacy rates or lives saved through smallpox vaccines. 'I don't promise that when a kid lives it will cause a GNP increase,' he quipped. 'I think life has value.'"

Gates thus invoked one of the primary moral imperatives — "saving lives" — as the justification for his actions. He also — allying himself with the gross national happiness crowd — implied that there was too much emphasis on economic growth. However, while no sensible person would suggest that "GNP is everything" (although growth is broadly synonymous with better lives), Gates's orientation raised a thorny issue: what happens when you "save lives" *without* boosting GNP?

Friedrich Hayek had addressed the issues of population control and development aid with discomforting clarity: "Morally, we have as little right to prevent the growth of population in other parts of the world as we have a duty to assist it. On the other hand, a moral conflict may indeed arise if materially advanced countries continue to assist and indeed even subsidize the growth of populations in regions, such as perhaps the Sahel zone in Central Africa, where there appears to exist little prospect that its present population, let alone an increased one, will in the foreseeable future be able to maintain itself by its own efforts."

This analysis suggested that the consequence — the ineluctable Malthusian logic (where Malthus would, for a change, be right) — of Gates's pursuit of his moral imperative would be increased population, along with increased poverty or dependence. The misery would inevitably swell to a larger crisis involving more human suffering unless the real problems of underdevelopment — primarily the absence of the rule of law — were addressed.

No amount of aid could ever compensate for a dictator such as Robert Mugabe, whose tyrannical regime brought death, disease and starvation to Zimbabwe on a horrendous scale. Indeed, it was more likely to keep him in power and make the situation worse. Mugabe highlighted that one obvious reason for the failure of aid was political corruption. "Aid," wrote Easterly, "shifts money from being spent by the best governments in the world to being spent by the worst. What are the chances that these billions are going to reach poor people?" Peter Bauer, the great British aid economist, had pointed out that foreign aid tended to flow from "poor people in rich countries to rich people in poor countries."

Aid appeared to be another example of the general principle asserted by the Oxford philosopher Janet Radcliffe Richards: that moral seriousness consisted not in ardent commitment but in thinking through our moral assumptions — and policies

— to check whether they would actually achieve the purposes we intended (unless of course our primary purpose was to look good). The heart of the conundrum of ineffective foreign aid involves the application of some of the most admirable of moral sentiments to situations that are quite different from the circumstances in which those sentiments evolved, and in which they were adaptive and effective: that is, the face-to-face tribal environment of reciprocal altruism.

The real "gap" problem in foreign aid lay not in wealth differentials but in both the literal and the metaphorical distance between donors and intended recipients; literally in terms of geography, and metaphorically in terms of human capital and institutions. The greater the distance between donor cup and recipient lip, the greater the likelihood of the donations' disappearance into the pockets of scam artists, institution builders, consultants, corrupt administrators and politicians. Easterly wrote that in their eagerness to perpetuate the government-to-government top-down aid model, the aid community's big planners were inevitably forced to play down the role of bad governments. The UN's necessary fantasy was that there were "well-governed low-income countries," but there was no such animal.

There was a great deal of flawed ideology at the giving end too. The modern UN-centric foreign aid paradigm was built by people such as Maurice Strong on a socialist model of top-down economic planning. It was a classic example of David Henderson's unreflecting centralism, boosted by moral condemnation of market processes. It was rationalized by the idea that greedy, exploitative capitalism (which was equated with slavery and colonialism) had been the root cause of underdevelopment.

Aid's moral foundation was thus a combination of guilt promotion and an unquestioning (and unquestionable) belief that the solution to poverty lay in Robin Hood redistribution from the "greedy" rich to the "dispossessed" poor. Its central economic conceit was that development could — and had to — be promoted and nurtured from above rather than through Smith's bottom-up "natural order," whereby the desire to better one's condition, once mediated through the division of labour and free trade under the rule of law, leads to broader social cooperation and improvement.

The top-down aid vision's latest and greatest incarnation was the UN's Millennium Development Goals, or MDGs, the massive do-good package unloaded in 2000 by UN Secretary General Kofi Annan, under the guidance of "men of system" such as Maurice Strong and Jeffrey Sachs, the Rand-phobic director of the UN Millennium Project. Easterly fingered Sachs as the great new intellectual proponent of unworkable top-down aid. He pointed out that not only did Sachs propose 449 separate interventions to achieve 54 MDGs in a 451-page report with 3,300 pages of technical annexes, he had recommended that Kofi Annan should run the plan *personally*.

Subsequently, Annan had seemed only too happy to acknowledge that the MDGs were failing, but his conviction was unwavering because failure was never seen as a reason for questioning redistributionist goals or methods, just as regulatory failure never undermined the urge to regulate. These were "moral imperatives" and thus not to be doubted. Rather, failure was interpreted as indicating the need for more bureaucratic fine tuning. And more money. That was one of the reasons why Bill Gates was such a welcome convert to the cause.

What was unusual about Gates was that, unlike Ray Anderson, who accepted the parody of Adam Smith as the avatar of short-sighted selfishness, Gates pointed to Smith's moral sentiments as the answer to global poverty. He even claimed to have a solution to the real Adam Smith problem: the uneasy fit between the slowly evolving, and often conflicted, moral sentiments and the novel world of *The Wealth of Nations*. All you had to do, according to Gates, was stitch Smith's two books together.

—⚬⚬⚬—

A few weeks after his gentle roasting in the Las Vegas mockumentary, Bill Gates was at Davos again, citing, of all things, *The Theory of Moral Sentiments*. Indeed, he quoted its opening sentence: "How selfish soever man may be supposed, there are evidently some principles in his nature, which interest him in the fortune of others, and render their happiness necessary to him, though he derives nothing from it except the pleasure of seeing it."

Gates was attempting to recruit Smith to what he called a "creative capitalism" that would somehow merge *Moral Sentiments* with *The Wealth of Nations*. According to Gates, creative capitalism "takes this interest in the fortunes of others and ties it to our interest in our own fortunes in ways that help advance both. This hybrid engine of self-interest and concern for others can serve a much wider circle of people than can be reached by self-interest or caring alone."

But Gates was in fact merely regurgitating the confusions of those who asked whether man was motivated *either* by self-interest *or* by sympathy. As Smith and other philosophers understood, and as modern studies of the "modular mind" confirm, man is motivated by both, in varying degrees, at different times, depending on the circumstances.

One key difference in Smith's time was that 18th-century merchants were usually operating on their own behalf, or on behalf of partners with whom they had close personal associations. Modern corporations, by contrast, were owned by large numbers of anonymous shareholders and managed by professionals. Shareholder interests could be more easily compromised by executives who wished to appear "enlightened," or who regarded it as merely pragmatic to buy off rather than oppose those who would damage their reputations, and thus their stock price. This process was accelerated as large institutions such as pension funds began to hold significant blocks of stock. These institutions too fell under the control of professional managers who could be pressured to pressure their corporate counterparts.

Bill Gates needed little persuading that corporate executives should join the salvationist crusade. Capitalism, according to Gates, was failing the Third World because corporations were not giving enough emphasis to products and services for the poor. Salvationist corporations should be out there doing economic missionary work, the reward for which would be not profit but "recognition." Failure to march behind the salvationist band, by contrast, would presumably mean moral condemnation.

Gates even suggested that companies devote their "top people" to poverty issues, but the principal job of public companies' top people was to create wealth and look after the interests of the shareholders who employed them. Corporations were wealth-generating machines, and the wealth they generated facilitated enormous philanthropy, but, as Milton Friedman declared, charity should come from the owners of the wealth, not its managers.

Managers wanted — and employees often demanded — to be seen as "good corporate citizens," which meant involvement in local charities and other good causes, but turning them into global social agencies would divert them from their main task, and perhaps undermine it completely. Certainly, companies that operated in poor countries often built schools and medical facilities for local communities as well as providing jobs, but this was in no way a departure from capitalist principle (except for those who preached that capitalism was all about greed and selfishness) — merely an indication of how the pursuit of profit led naturally to a broader good.

Gates had been captured by the notion that such good had to be forced. He came up with some horrifying ways for governments to "encourage" corporations to become involved in the developing world. These included making drug approval for pharmaceutical companies conditional on developing drugs for "diseases of the poor." However, such a scheme effectively threatened to penalize drug companies that refused to get into the "neglected disease" business. It also would have created a bureaucratic nightmare of discretionary review.

And it wasn't just companies who should join his crusade. It was taxpayers too. One might have thought that trying to find outlets for the Gates Foundation's billions would be a full-time job even for a genius of Gates's stature, but apparently he now saw part of his task as not only "spurring other companies into action," with government wearing the spurs, but also "leveraging" his contributions by recruiting unwitting taxpayers.

—⁓—

Adam Smith specifically pre-refuted Gates's idea of corporate social responsibility when he wrote, in *The Wealth of Nations*, "I have never known much good done by those who affected to trade for the public good." Now, however, businesses were tripping over themselves to claim that they were trading "for the public good." However, what poor countries lacked was not corporate do-gooders but the Smithian essentials of "peace, easy taxes, and a tolerable administration of justice."

Smith seems to have been more fundamentally opposed to the notion that easing hardship or promoting development in other countries was any of our business — a position shockingly out of kilter with conventional modern sentiment. Those who believe that Smith might have been automatically appalled at the modern income "gap" or at the materialist self-indulgence of capitalism — or that he was a proto-Galbraith — would be profoundly discomforted if they were actually to read him.

In *Moral Sentiments*, Smith rebuked "whining and melancholy moralists, who are perpetually reproaching us with our happiness, while so many of our brethren are in misery, who regard as impious the natural joy of prosperity, which does not think of the many wretches that are at every instant labouring under all sorts of calamities, in the languor of poverty, in the agony of disease, in the horrors of death, under the insults and oppression of their enemies." He described this as "artificial commiseration."

Smith also wrote, "All men, even those at the greatest distance, are no doubt entitled to our good wishes, and our good wishes we naturally give them. But if, notwithstanding, they should be unfortunate, to give ourselves any anxiety upon that account, seems to be no part of our duty." Hardly anybody in polite Western society today would dare to admit that they had no anxiety about the distant poor. Indeed, the Gates Foundation made the bizarre claim that "every life has equal value." But did Bill and Melinda really regard the lives of their own children as of no more value than that of any child anywhere?

Smith castigated such bogus "stoic" doctrines of "universal love and brotherhood": the idea that we should weep as much for the death of a stranger as we do for a father or a brother. The climate issue had taken stoic posturing to a whole new level. The Stern Review had suggested not only that all lives should be considered equal, but that distant future generations should be given equal weight with those of people living today.

Or am I being too hard on Lord Stern? Had there been a genuine alteration in what Smith called the "original constitution of our frame"? Were we genuinely more concerned for those at a distance, or those allegedly threatened in the future? Or was that merely what social and political pressures demanded? Was the circle of human concern genuinely widening, or did we rather perhaps swim in a rising tide of Mandevillean hypocrisy and "artificial commiseration," boosted by those for whom promoting commiseration had become a self-inflating and profitable profession?

In fact, human nature hadn't changed too much since the time of Adam Smith. What certainly had changed was (a) the amount of wealth available to be given away, elicited by moral blackmail or forcibly expropriated, which in turn fed a professional class of redistributors and aid specialists; (b) the impact of technology on our moral sentiments; and (c) the involvement of celebrity.

Wealth enabled charity, which is based on Smithian sympathy and the genetic imperative to burnish our reputations. Where technology came into play — another of the enormous differences since Smith's day, and perhaps the most important when it came to stimulating sympathy — was that we could now see the distant poor. We were — as Smith emphasized — sympathetic creatures, and we were particularly sympathetic to the sight of abject poverty. In those countless millennia before television, the only poverty we ever saw was the poverty of our own tribe or community. This deprivation, through evolved sympathetic "pain," spurred us to action; we deployed adaptive instincts that promoted mutual aid and group solidarity.

We thus evolved to find images of suffering disturbing. We felt the reflexive urge to share with those we saw deprived (unless they had been demonized or dehumanized as enemies or outsiders). Scenes of disaster — such as those of the 2004 Asian tsunami, or the 2010 Haitian earthquake, or Superstorm Sandy in 2012, or Typhoon Haiyan in 2013 — elicited enormous charitable contributions, which could only be considered a reflection of the very best in human nature.

Smith suggested that even if we did develop genuine concerns for the distant poor, it wouldn't do us much good; but now money could be transferred instantly across the world. Contributions to Oxfam or World Vision at least assuaged guilt and probably gave most contributors a biochemical "good feeling." It would be churlish to suggest that no good was ever done by international charity. However, the act of digging a well or donating a goat did not address the much larger problems of corrupt government, demonization of foreign investment or condemnation of the "exploitation" of workers (who are often desperate to be exploited).

The final factor in promoting the modern foreign aid bandwagon was celebrity. According to *Time* magazine, Bill and

Melinda Gates rendered global health care "cool." Bono made poor-country debt relief "sexy."

Bono became the outstanding example of aid-promoting celebrity. People would undoubtedly have thought it strange if William Easterly or Milton Friedman had suddenly started delivering edicts on rock music, but few seemed to find it strange that a pop musician should start dictating aid policy. But then Bono appealed to the simplistic notion that improving people's lives was primarily about handing over money or forgiving debt. Perhaps the most amazing aspect of the Bono hagiography was that fans — including such unlikely star-huggers as the crusty retired U.S. senator Jesse Helms — suggested that Bono had "absolutely nothing to gain personally as a result of his work," as if being idolized as a champion of the poor carried no status or corresponding personal satisfaction.

If debt relief was a much thornier issue than portrayed, the question of intervening in health care to "save lives" was, as Hayek suggested, even more problematic. Health care was such a contentious political issue because it brought the best in evolved humanity — sympathy and the urge to protect and care for others — up against the failure to appreciate either the workings of markets or the implications of technological advance. The intense taboo against even a well-regulated market in kidneys illustrated the difficulties. What made medicine even more of a hot-button issue was the opportunities for moralistic and political posturing "on behalf of" the poor and diseased, and against market "greed" and corporate "power."

—∞—

In 2006, I attended a conference in Toronto titled "Access to Medicines as a Human Right." It took place at the University of Toronto's Munk Centre, a small institution funded by the Canadian entrepreneur Peter Munk, who had founded the world's largest gold company, Barrick Resources. Yet again, it seemed, a great capitalist was facilitating a festival of anti-capitalism.

Given the conference title, it was perhaps not surprising that the private health sector came in for a hammering, along with "post-Cold War neo-liberal triumphalism." Corporations were variously described as "predators," "profit-maximizing robots" and "zombies." They were declared guilty of criminality for not making drugs available to the poor. One participant even invoked the Nuremberg trials of Nazi mass murderers as an appropriate model for non-compliant corporations.

The conference's keynote speaker was Thomas Pogge, a German philosopher and director of the Global Justice Program at Yale. Along with Peter Singer, the philosopher who was seeking a "new paradigm" for the left, Pogge was a leading proponent of "positive" medical rights. (Bill Gates's notions about incentivizing drug companies to address Third World problems had originated with Pogge and Singer.)

Some conference attendees recommended "dangling carrots" in front of pharmaceutical corporations to achieve policy objectives, but most seemed to think that what was needed was more "stick." Carrot programs tended to be attached to vast bureaucratic schemes. Pogge promoted one such in which drug companies would be rewarded according to their "impact on global health." Singer had written, "In an ideal world, the amount of money we spend on medical research to prevent or cure a disease would be proportional to its seriousness and the number of people who suffer from it." However, this would be an "ideal world" only for those who put little or no store on individual freedom or its impact on human ingenuity and the genuine greater good. Typically, in Singer's ideal world collective security would be enhanced by depriving individuals of freedom. People in developed countries had to be deprived of the right to spend their own income or wealth to save or better their own lives, or the lives of their children, so that professional redistributors might feel the warm glow of conspicuously trying to save "poor lives."

Singer regarded it as reprehensible that 90 per cent of medical research went toward conditions that were responsible for only 10 per cent of the deaths. "Millions of people die every year from diseases for which no new drugs are in the pipeline," he wrote, "while drug companies pour billions into developing cures for erectile dysfunction and baldness." In Singer's ideal world, research into such frivolous medical conditions would presumably be outlawed. He seemed to be subject to the primitive zero-sum delusion that research into erectile dysfunction and baldness somehow crowded out research into diseases of the poor rather than making such research more likely.

Even greater self-inflating satisfactions would come from applying "sticks" to promote requisite corporate behaviour; conference attendees were mostly cynical about the potential of *voluntary* CSR. These sticks would force companies to dispense — or facilitate the provision of — "needed" drugs for a "reasonable" price. Thus had emerged "compulsory licensing" to generic manufacturers of big pharma's patented drugs for diseases such as HIV/AIDS. Pharmaceutical companies that resisted such pressures were inevitably pilloried for "selfishly" trying to protect their property rights. How, demanded activists, could anybody talk about property rights when lives were at stake?

The issue was inevitably soaked in cant. When there was a dispute between the repressive government of Thailand and Abbott Laboratories, based in Chicago, a Thai government official wrote, "Compulsory licensing is used to protect public health and save lives. Such matters should not be politicized." But expropriation — for however worthy a cause — is the most fundamental of political issues, since it has potentially disastrous long-term consequences for both economic development and medical research.

Many rationalizations were put forward at the Munk Centre conference to justify expropriation. One professor suggested that drug companies should be considered similar to physicians, who *must* treat emergencies and put themselves in harm's way for the sake of their patients. Apart from suggesting that the Hippocratic Oath made you a slave, this proposal reflected the usual problem of naive anthropomorphization, suggesting that companies were like rich, selfish, psychopathic individuals. Companies are in fact nothing like doctors. They are created and run primarily to manufacture profitable products for the benefit of their customers, shareholders and society more broadly. Initiatives such as compulsory licensing make pharmaceuticals less attractive investments and thus retard drug development.

This was the kind of ineluctable market logic that redistributors in general, and compulsory licensers in particular, seemed incapable of grasping. They saw pharmaceuticals through a zero-sum perspective: drugs were things to be expropriated for the poor here and now, rather than the result of a process that would be disrupted by curtailing property rights, which would hurt everybody in the long term.

Presented with the way the world actually worked, they said, well, it just *shouldn't* work that way. The government patent system had been set up "for the public good," they pointed out, and was thus malleable. True, but while rules might be infinitely malleable, private actors are not. To strong-arm pharmaceutical companies served only to undermine drug development. Indeed, compulsory licensing amounted to applying Third World standards to First World companies, with potentially Third World results.

The rush to "save lives" was having perverse impacts beyond the market for drugs. The African HIV/AIDS epidemic had brought in a tsunami of public and private funds, but a vast array of initiatives and programs were, as usual, creating havoc. According to a devastating 2007 critique in the magazine *Foreign Affairs*, "The Challenge of Global Health," by Laurie Garrett, senior fellow for global health at the Council on Foreign Relations, much of the cash was "leaking away without result."

Garrett's article reflected many of Easterly's themes. For example, most global health schemes were of the top-down, grand-planning variety, demanding Soviet-style metrics. Aid was often tied to short-term numerical targets — numbers of people on drugs, children in orphanages, condoms distributed — that might ignore or aggravate larger systemic problems and drain local health-care resources. Inefficient bureaucracy soaked up a huge chunk of funds, although nowhere near as much as simple corruption. Meanwhile, aid got "stovepiped" down narrow channels to specific diseases that happened to be in the First World headlines, ignoring less trendy but more deadly conditions. As Garrett wrote, "There is no dysentery lobby or celebrity attention given to coughing babies."

Another Africa-wide problem created by the AIDS/aid tsunami was the medical brain drain, either to donor agencies or to developed countries. In poor countries, aid agencies and NGOs were sucking up not just health workers but economists, accountants and translators. On a larger scale, Garrett pointed out that dramatic increases in external health-care funding could lead to the destabilization of a poor country's economy, undermining the resources available for development. All the best local talent wound up working for the "aid industry." The surge of funds also threatened to produce local inflation and thus, ironically, further hardship for the poorest of the poor.

Garrett observed that the shibboleths of socialized medicine ruled the aid world, in particular the taboo against profit; but she stressed that profit orientation was in fact essential if truly "sustainable" systems were to evolve. She concluded that the current system amounted to putting poor nations on the permanent, and increasing, dole: a US$20-billion annual charity program whose demands grew constantly without solving the problems addressed, indeed possibly aggravating them.

Garrett inevitably came under attack from the mavens of the aid industry, such as Jeffrey Sachs, who wrote, "Those of us on the front lines of this fight" — i.e., sitting in a big, expensive townhouse at the Earth Institute in Manhattan — "do not recognize her black-and-white contrasts."

However, more and more critics were coming forward to refute Earth Institute thinking. One was a Zambian woman named Dambisa Moyo, whose credentials included a PhD from Oxford and stints at Goldman Sachs and the World Bank. On the heels of Easterly and Garrett, Moyo launched a further incisive attack on the aid paradigm in her 2009 book, *Dead Aid*. She explained that aid didn't merely feed corruption; it meant that African governments didn't have to listen to their own people because they didn't rely on them for taxes. The taxpayers upon whom the African kleptocrats relied were those of developed countries, for whom aid effectiveness was a matter of only passing interest. The aid industry also painted the African picture as bleakly as possible in order to keep the donations coming, but these images put off investors, who were Africa's only real hope.

Moyo's book resulted in yet another sophistic attack from Sachs's Earth Institute. Brett House, the institute's senior macroeconomist, suggested that Moyo's claim that "no country on Earth has ever achieved long-term growth and reduced poverty in a meaningful way by relying on aid" was refuted by the fact that every emerging market had received aid. This of course confused receiving aid with the aid being effective. The spectacular development successes of China and India had certainly not come about because of foreign aid. Moreover, they had come as a result of the *abandonment* of top-down state planning. House wrote, "World Bank data show that the proportion of people living on less than $2 a day in Africa has gone down slightly since 1981." He did not concede — perhaps because he could not conceive — that development had occurred *despite* aid rather than because of it.

A 2011 report from the Brookings Institution — *Poverty in Numbers: The Changing State of Global Poverty from 2005 to 2015* — pointed out that the world was in fact living through one of the most dramatic, indeed unparalleled periods of poverty reduction in global history, but that it had little or nothing to do with debt relief or aid flows. It had to do with investment and economic growth. According to the report's authors, Laurence Chandy and Geoffrey Gertz, nearly half a billion people escaped the poverty threshold of US$1.25 a day between 2005 and 2010. They expected another 300 million to follow them in the ensuing four years.

Ironically, this meant that the main Millennium Development Goal — of halving global poverty between 1990 and 2015 — had already been achieved, although it had little or nothing to do with the UN's grand plans. The Brookings report noted that developing economies had grown by 50 per cent in real terms in the previous six years, despite the 2008 financial crisis. This growth was not restricted to China and India but extended to previously benighted economies such as those of Bangladesh, Tanzania, Ethiopia, Vietnam, Uganda, Mozambique and Uzbekistan.

Africa was still the epicentre of poverty, but improvement was lagging only relative to other faster-growing areas. Poverty in sub-Saharan Africa had in fact dropped below 50 per cent for the first time in 2008, and was projected to fall below 40 per cent by 2015.

—m—

Aid activists seemed perpetually blind to past failures and easily able to persuade themselves that poverty reduction was a result of aid rather than capitalism. What kept them motivated was moral self-inflation, blindness to — and condemnation of — the Invisible Hand, and the constant search for new "threats" to the poor. The greatest new threat was climate change. Indeed, the alleged impact on the poor was one of the reasons why questioning the official science was considered morally reprehensible. To be a "denier" was virtually to promote poverty. Rich nations had put all that "extra" carbon dioxide into the atmosphere, so they had to cut back on fossil-fuel-fed growth and let the Third World have its development "share": classic carcass economics bolstered by the threat of environmental apocalypse.

Catastrophic global warming not only provided a new justification for aid, it also promised carrots and sticks to corporations to transfer industrial activities to developed countries. Rich countries, or corporations, could ship cash in return for emissions credits, politically manufactured pieces of paper gifted bureaucratically to poor countries. Or they might obtain credits by funding "clean development." However, while they might buy credits and provide alternative energy, there remained staunch opposition to their "exploiting" resources, and people, in developing countries. That stance was scathingly exposed in a 2006 documentary, *Mine Your Own Business*.

The film did not receive either the publicity or the accolades won by Al Gore's *An Inconvenient Truth*, or by the films of Michael Moore, but it certainly raised inconvenient questions about the dark side of environmentalism. *Mine Your Own Business* was the brainchild of the Irish filmmakers Phelim McAleer and Ann McElhinney. It had been conceived when McAleer — while a reporter for the *Financial Times* of London — was covering opposition to a mine proposed by a Toronto-based company, Gabriel Resources, at Rosia Montana in Romania. The fight had been spearheaded by a Swiss journalist turned environmentalist named Stephanie Roth. Roth — consciously or unconsciously reflecting the imagery of Marx and Engels — had claimed that Gabriel and other mining companies were "modern-day vampires" (Rosia Montana is in Transylvania). In 2005 she had been awarded the Goldman Environmental Prize, the "Green Nobel."

McAleer was disturbed by the campaign's misrepresentations and set out to expose what he thought grassroots activism was really about: well-funded multinational environmental groups descending on impoverished villages and depriving them of jobs and a future. He saw that many, if not most, NGO claims were greatly exaggerated or entirely false. Rosia Montana was not an idyllic community whose "traditional lifestyle" needed preservation. It was a desolate and polluted village whose streams literally ran red-brown with toxic chemicals. The vast majority of its dwindling population were desperate for the good jobs that Gabriel offered. The local unemployment rate was around 70 per cent. Moreover, Gabriel's project would reclaim much of the area polluted by feckless state-owned mining operations. Gabriel CEO Alan Hill declared, "This is a mine to clean up a mess." McAleer approached Gabriel about funding a film, to which the company agreed. This of course left him open to inevitable accusations of bias, as opposed to the allegedly "pure" motives of the much better-funded NGOs. McAleer and McElhinney wound up on a picaresque adventure that took them not only to Romania but to other proposed mine sites in Madagascar and Chile.

The film was stunning because it combatted prejudice, fantasy and outright lies with images that refuted thousands of weasel words. Images spun from afar about Rosia Montana's happy-family small holdings were contrasted with the reality of desolate landscapes and decrepit hovels with no running water and crumbling outhouses.

The most devastating and lasting image of professional environmentalism came in the form of an interview with Mark Fenn, the World Wide Fund for Nature's man on the spot in the fight against a Rio Tinto mine in Madagascar. Fenn was at least on site, but then that was mainly because he was building a luxury home there to go with his $35,000 catamaran.

In a stroke of genius, the filmmakers had decided to take along on their travels a young Romanian miner named George. He was present to hear Fenn declare that the Madagascar mine would ruin the local town's "quaintness," and that poor people were happier, smiled more and had less stress in their lives. "I live in poverty," George told Fenn, who plowed on to suggest that if the locals acquired money, they would just spend it on fripperies such as beer, stereos and jeans. Fenn claimed that the locals didn't value housing, nutrition and education. George apparently felt like punching him, but managed to restrain himself.

At Pascua Lama in Chile, the site of a mine proposed by Toronto-based Barrick, McAleer again found a community desperate for jobs but being manipulated by multinational activists. An English environmentalist was shown claiming, from the depths of London's darkest Islington, that mining would damage "sacred mountains." The film showed that local opposition to the mine came mainly from big landowners, who were concerned about losing their workers to higher-paid jobs.

The development economist Deepak Lal was left to deliver *Mine Your Own Business*'s bottom line: much of corporate-bashing, CSR-spewing, anti-development environmentalism was effectively an attack on the world's poor.

—⚏—

The problem with Bill Gates's "philanthrocapitalism" — a term coined by the *Economist* — and Giving Pledge was that they fed the impression that capitalism does not promote benevolence or charity without arm-twisting. His attempts to pressure corporations into joining his global salvationist crusade again fed the notion that there was a moral vacuum at the heart of commerce. By doing so he allied himself with anti-development forces that threatened the poor.

Gates's crusade in no way appeased the Occupy movement and its demonization of the rich. In fact, Warren Buffett effectively joined with the Occupiers in affirming that the rich didn't pay enough taxes, a claim that became one of President Obama's main themes in the 2012 election campaign.

Just ahead of that election, a new rich-bashing tome appeared titled *Plutocrats: The Rise of the New Global Super-Rich and the*

Fall of Everyone Else (note the bad case of zero-sum mentality embedded in the title). Written by Chrystia Freeland, then the digital editor at the media giant Thomson Reuters, it was the modern equivalent of Matthew Josephson's *Robber Barons*.

Freeland made a good deal of the fact that certain disgruntled billionaires had — unwisely, as they subsequently admitted — compared the Obama administration to that of Hitler. Intriguingly, however, the term "plutocracy" had been eagerly embraced by both the Third Reich and the Soviet Union to denigrate U.S. capitalism.

The rich were a Marxist "class," according to Freeland. This led her to be puzzled that "they" might be unhappy with President Obama. After all, hadn't he bailed out Wall Street? In fact, "the rich" who weren't involved in Wall Street — the overwhelming majority — had every reason to be unhappy with the bailouts, since they were the ones who would have to pay disproportionately for them.

Freeland's primitive, popular prejudices were repeatedly betrayed by her metaphors, as in her evocation of the "winner-take-all economy." She condemned "oligarchs ... who see themselves as deserving victors in a cutthroat international competition." She suggested that recent developments meant that "our intuitive beliefs about how capitalism works haven't caught up with reality."

But the real problem is that "we" have no "intuitive" understanding of capitalism, because the system has emerged so recently in human evolution. Our "intuitive beliefs" are inclined to reject the system, even as we enjoy its benefits. We can, it seems, have our cake and condemn it too.

eighteen

Conclusion: Still Spinning
After All These Years

*The uniform, constant, and uninterrupted effort of every man to better
his condition, the principle from which public and national, as well as
private opulence is originally derived, is frequently powerful enough
to maintain the natural progress of things toward improvement,
in spite both of the extravagance of government and of the greatest
errors of administration. Like the unknown principle of animal life,
it frequently restores health and vigour to the constitution, in spite,
not only of the disease, but of the absurd prescriptions of the doctor.*
— Adam Smith, *The Wealth of Nations*

The year after *The Wealth of Nations* was published, Smith
accepted a position as commissioner of customs in
Edinburgh. Some have regarded this decision as hypocritical,
or at least ironic, but it was neither. Smith believed in a minimal
state, but he recognized that any state needed revenues to conduct its legitimate business. These revenues had to be collected
as efficiently as possible. Moreover, in becoming a customs official Smith was following in the footsteps of the father he never
knew.

Smith moved with his mother and a cousin, Jane Douglas,
to Panmure House, on the Royal Mile just above the Canongate,
which was then Edinburgh's fashionable residential quarter.
"The Scottish nobility," wrote one of Smith's biographers, John

Rae, "had their town-houses in its gloomy courts, and great dowagers and famous generals still toiled up its cheerless stairs."

Smith approached his new position with typical resolution, but not without a sense of humour. "About a week after I was made a Commissioner of the Customs," he wrote to a friend, "upon looking over the list of prohibited goods ... I found, to my great astonishment, that I had scarce a stock, a cravat, a pair of ruffles, or a pocket handkerchief which was not prohibited to be worn or used in Great Britain. I wished to set an example and burnt them all." The episode emphasized both Smith's honesty and the bizarre reach of economic legislation.

Smith was seen wending his way to work wearing a broad-brimmed beaver hat and, wrote Rae, "smiling in rapt conversation with invisible companions." In his latter years he rejoiced in his library and took particular pleasure in rereading the Greek poets. His closest companions were the great scientists Joseph Black and James Hutton, seminal figures in the studies of chemistry and geology respectively. The friends took regular Friday night dinners in Edinburgh's Grass Market. Smith also presided over lively Sunday suppers at Panmure House. (More than 200 years later its refurbishment is tied up in the Edinburgh planning and Scottish Heritage bureaucracies.)

When Smith died in July 1790, there was little note of his passing. Two Edinburgh papers produced two-paragraph obituaries recounting the anecdote of his being abducted by gypsies as a child. The *Times* of London produced a mixture of unflattering anecdotes and barbed comments. The piece mentioned a fall by Smith into a Glasgow tanning pit. He was accused of having "converted the [Glasgow] chair of Moral Philosophy into a professorship of trade and finance."

This tone of sneering dismissal marked one aspect of Smith's multi-faceted public image. Nevertheless, his iconic status was confirmed by his appearance in 2007 on the British 20-pound banknote. In 2008, fans, led by the London-based Adam Smith Institute, raised a substantial statue of him on the Royal Mile.

However, the inner walls of Smith's Canongate grave must have been growing ever smoother from the spinning caused by constant misrepresentation. Bill Gates's suggestion that it might never have occurred to Smith to meld *The Wealth of Nations* with *The Theory of Moral Sentiments* so as to put business at the service of global salvationism must surely have caused a few more revolutions.

Smith's name continued to be controversial in the town of his birth. In 2005, Adam Smith College was created from the merger of Glenrothes College and Fife College. A students' association protested on the basis of the "values" that Smith was thought to represent. A student leader, Paul Muirhead, declared that Smith was associated with "socio-economic policies that work against the people, that were synonymous with Thatcherite and Reaganite governments."

It remains an open question what Smith might have thought of being associated with an educational institution that featured courses in hairdressing, upholstery and nail care, but he would surely have had reservations about the appointment of Gordon Brown as the college's chancellor. Brown, the son of a Kirkcaldy minister of the Church of Scotland and Britain's prime minister during the 2008 crisis, had spent more of his own youth absorbing *Das Kapital* than reading *The Wealth of Nations*. As a 24-year-old student socialist, he had written that "the private control of industry has become a hindrance to the further unfolding of the social forces of production." Faced with the collapse of his Utopian dreams, he had continued to promote the conventional parody of capitalism and sought to turn Smith into a critic of markets. In 1989, as a Labour Party politician, he had declared of Prime Minister Margaret Thatcher, "Her economic insights revolve around the naive yearning for the Arcadian simplicities of a marketplace untainted even by the sinister insights of Adam Smith."

Later, after state control of industry was thrown off the Labour Party's political platform, Brown, still clinging to

Smith's allegedly "sinister insights," sought to turn him into a supporter of the open-ended redistributionist state. In 2002, introducing a debate on Smith at the University of Edinburgh, Brown claimed that Smith had been the author of the "helping hand" as well as the Invisible Hand. By the time he was ejected from office, Brown's own "helping hand" policies had helped dig Britain into a major financial hole. In 2010 Brown released a book about the financial crisis, *Beyond the Crash: Overcoming the First Crisis of Globalization*, in which he claimed to have been front and centre in saving the world by promoting a trillion dollars' worth of government spending.

An annual Adam Smith Lecture had been inaugurated in Kirkcaldy in 1986. Under Brown's chancellorship of Adam Smith College, invitees tended to criticize and/or misinterpret Smith or attempted to turn him into a proto-socialist global governor. Even the allegedly market-friendly speakers might have set Smith spinning.

In 2005, the lecture was delivered by U.S. Federal Reserve chairman Alan Greenspan, who declared, "One could hardly imagine that today's awesome array of international transactions would produce the relative economic stability that we experience daily if they were not led by some international version of Smith's invisible hand." Smith would hardly have been happy at being cited as the progenitor of an international financial system riven with misregulation and moral hazard, and heading for a crisis.

In 2009, the lecturer was Kofi Annan, former secretary General of the United Nations. Annan took obviously relished shots at the alleged failings of the capitalist system. He ritually bemoaned inequality and implied a malign reach for the Invisible Hand. "Mortgage defaults in Florida and Fife," he said, "are linked to health services in Tanzania and Togo."

Annan suggested that when it came to the global meltdown, Smith must have been looking down and wondering where his beloved prudence had gone. Perhaps so, but he certainly wouldn't have found it either in the operations of the UN or in the workings of the governments that had precipitated the crisis with artificially cheap money, through misregulation or by "nudging" people to buy houses they couldn't afford. Indeed, for Annan – the man who had presided over the genocide in Rwanda, the Iraqi oil-for-food scandal, the stumbling of the Millennium Development Goals, the UN's failure to reform itself, the escalation of the climate policy fandango and numerous other policy disasters – to invoke prudence displayed extraordinary chutzpah.

The 2011 lecture was delivered, as noted earlier, by the husband-and-wife socialist tag team of Amartya Sen and Emma Rothschild. Rothschild, apart from misrepresenting Smith's views on the relationship between wealth and power, suggested that he might have been a fan of "global governance": the rule of "men of system" writ gargantuan.

The following year, Adam Smith College was rocked by accusations of mismanagement and fraud, which led to a sharply critical government audit, the removal of senior administrators and the forced repayment of millions of pounds of grants from the European Union. In 2013, the name of Adam Smith disappeared from the local educational scene as the result of yet another administrative reorganization. The college was merged with Carnegie College and became, again, Fife College. Among the courses now on offer was one on sustainable resource management.

Toward the end of 2011, the impact of the ongoing economic downturn hit Kirkcaldy in a symbolic way. Jimmy Patrick was forced to close his McDonald's franchise on the High Street opposite the site where Smith had written *The Wealth of Nations*. Still, Patrick's other outlets were doing well. Also on the bright side, the numbers of Chinese tourists now visiting Smith's birthplace were reportedly greater than those of Chinese visitors to Karl Marx's tomb in Highgate.

Smith's economic message may be one for the ages, but it is crucial to remember that he lived in very different times, and it wasn't just that he lacked electric light, a fridge, running water, flush toilets, air conditioning, a telephone and a car. Wealth in his day was still associated primarily with aristocratic land-holders, and religion was a much more potent social force. With regard to the role of religion, it is worth recording that the most controversial thing Smith ever wrote had nothing to do with political economy. It was his obituary for his friend David Hume.

Smith's encomium noted that Hume had approached death "not only without perturbation, but with a positive gaiety of spirits." Since Hume was a "Godless skeptic" (although also referred to as "the virtuous heathen"), many considered Smith's account tantamount to the promotion of atheism. It provoked outrage. "A single, and as, I thought a very harmless sheet of paper which I happened to write concerning the death of our late friend Mr. Hume," reflected Smith, "brought upon me ten times more abuse than the very violent attack I had made on the whole commercial system of Great Britain."

That religion is a much less serious matter today was brought home during one of my trips to Kirkcaldy, where the Adam Smith Theatre was playing host to a spoof of the Bible. Presented by the Reduced Shakespeare Company (which had a smash hit with its production of the entire works of the Bard in 97 minutes), the manic, slapstick performance thankfully stopped short of a comic crucifixion but poked fun at the virgin birth and portrayed the resurrected Christ as the Easter Bunny. The audience laughed uproariously.

I reflected how inconceivable such a performance would have been in Smith's time, even to Smith, who was no fan of orga-nized religion. I also reflected that the Reduced Shakespeare Company would almost certainly be performing no spoofs of the Koran; it was a reminder — if any is needed — that some people still take their religion very seriously.

Religious extremism tends to flourish in areas that have underdeveloped commercial societies, but a flourishing commercial society still does not indicate general appreciation of the forces that made it that way. It was to pursue this issue — which had been nagging at me for years — that I had first set out, in 1993, to visit Smith's birthplace and resting place. Why do we bite the Invisible Hand? Why are people not more aware, or concerned, that attempts to replace the market system have led to repression, murder and poverty on a mammoth scale, while attempts to tame it, fine-tune it or give it a "human face" have so often ended in tears and unintended results?

My conclusion was that capitalism is underappreciated because it is fundamentally counterintuitive and in many ways morally objectionable to minds that were overwhelmingly formed in the very different environment of the Pleistocene, and that are still inclined toward a zero-sum view of resources and wealth, and disposed to see market relationships and their results as being all about power. More fundamentally, we are designed to feel and express gratitude to individuals, not systemic abstractions.

Although we are born with what Smith called the "propensity to truck, barter, and exchange," and with the drive in recent millennia to "better our condition" by specializing our labour — tendencies that are the bedrock of the towering complexities of Smith's natural order — we have no "natural" ability to appreciate what has sprung up in the mere blink of a biological eye. Equally important, we don't have to understand it to benefit from it. However, that fact led to the other — more problematic — part of my conclusion. There was indeed an "Adam Smith problem," but it wasn't that Smith might have changed his mind about human motivation between *Moral Sentiments* and *The Wealth of Nations*. It was the conflict between the complex human nature outlined in the first book and the emergent commercial environment outlined in the second, which its enemies would dub "capitalism."

The rapid changes of capitalist society — while providing stunning material benefits — not only have placed novel stresses on our understanding and our moral faculties, they have provided opportunities for power seekers to exploit the resultant confusion. What makes this situation so complex is that the urge to power — like morality, to which it is closely connected — is as reflexive and unconscious as it is clever at rationalizing itself.

Almost 300 years ago, that acute observer and great cynic Bernard Mandeville spotlighted the gap between people's behaviour and their professed morality in nascent commercial society. Such morality — which for most was embodied in religion — had evolved over eons to control anti-social behaviour, enable group living and facilitate the demonization and eradication of enemies. However, the emergence of the market order rendered some previously morally questionable activities — such as the pursuit of self-interest and the accumulation of wealth — socially beneficial.

Moralists continued to condemn the successful pursuit of self-interest in the market because they still reflexively equated it with selfishness: the pursuit of one's own interests *at the expense of others*. The spread of commercial society led to a heightening of Mandevillean hypocrisy at the same time that it rendered such hypocrisy arguably unnecessary. There was no shame in commercial success, because it could be achieved only by serving others.

Mandeville was a better moral psychologist than he was an economist. He concentrated on the alleged benefits to society of the decadent rich, but these prodigals were the scions of that hereditary landed aristocracy, which would decline into insignificance. In an expanding meritocratic commercial society it was possible for more and more people to better their condition by helping others achieve their own objectives, while facilitating a broader, more systemic good that was "no part of their intention." It was that startling fact that was at the root of Smithian analysis and the capitalist revolution.

However, the moralistic joys of condemning alleged greed and promoting self-sacrifice — primarily for others — died hard, as did the satisfactions of pretending not to be interested in material goods, or power. Hence, more than 200 years into the Industrial Revolution, Morrie Schwartz's anti-materialist hypocrisy could still receive wide praise from those who thrived in a system they condemned without understanding.

The widening comprehension gap was highlighted by Karl Popper in *The Open Society and Its Enemies*, and by Friedrich Hayek in his assertion that modern humans had to learn to live in "two worlds." Hayek also identified the "fatal conceit" of "rationalist constructivism" as the prevailing flaw of policy wonks, who believe that "the answer" is always more central planning, regulation and macro oversight. Since they have on their side both evolutionary mental shortcomings and the propaganda machinery of the state, it is no wonder that the public is easily persuaded that governments manage economies to beneficial effect.

While, as Hayek noted, the thing that intellectuals tend most to overestimate is the power of intelligence, it is misguided to see such attitudes simply as overweening "error." Socialism and its more subtle modern variants, such as sustainable development and the external monitoring of corporate social responsibility, are less errors than political strategies, stoked by real or manufactured moral outrage against a demonized ideological foe.

Reservations about capitalism — and the exploitation of those reservations — run across the political spectrum. People remain "unreflecting centralists," just as they are easily persuaded of the "fairness" of forced redistribution, particularly if they are its beneficiaries. As Popper pointed out, this led to many of the recommendations of *The Communist Manifesto* being adopted within democratic societies by the middle of the 20th century. Ironically, this was possible only because capitalism produced the wealth to facilitate communitarian ideals of sharing and security. But in the process it also enabled the hypertrophic growth of the self-serving tax-and-spend state that has promoted dependency and potentially crushing debt obligations, but that constantly seeks new rationales for its own expansion — most recently the alleged threat of man-made global warming.

Our use of language reveals our erroneous assumptions about the workings of the Invisible Hand, as well as skill in rhetorical manipulation in pursuit of power. If "social" has been the traditional weasel word of "progressives" — those who seek an ever larger role for the state — the new weasel word is "sustainable," which is in reality shorthand for yet more government control on the basis of alleged market imperfections. Tellingly, those who promote sustainable development rarely if ever address the unsustainability of the intrusive and expansive state, which had reached an existential crisis in Europe by 2010 and was still struggling three years later.

It was not merely economies that were under threat, but freedom. Indeed, the health of the former is closely linked to the preservation of the latter. The post-Communist, UN-centric, global salvationist thrust of the new nexus of sustainable development, corporate social responsibility and green global governance was designed to override national governments both from below and from above, and to ditch ballot-box democracy.

The great advantage of democracy is that it provides the opportunity to "throw the rascals out" and thus permit a broader evolutionary process under which policy errors may, eventually, be recognized and corrected. This is by no means guaranteed, however. Indeed, during the economic crisis that started in 2008, politicians were — out of a combination of ignorance, self-preservation and sheer desperation — universally returning to policies, such as Keynesianism, that had failed before and were bound to fail again.

As this book goes to press, if anything threatens the world with retarded growth and high unemployment, it is the confluence of the return of Keynesianism, the unsustainability of overgenerous welfare states, the delusions of regulatory financial "macroprudence" and the conceit of managing the global economy so as to control the weather, while aspiring to solve the problems of global poverty through tried-and-failed top-down methods.

And yet capitalism continues to work its wonders, both spectacular and mundane.

—⁊⁊—

I couldn't be in Moscow for the 20th anniversary of McDonald's Pushkin Square restaurant in 2010, but I spoke by phone to the head of McDonald's Russian and East European operation, Khamzat Khasbulatov. Khasbulatov had been one of the four young managers at the restaurant when I was there in 1991.

By almost any measure, McDonald's in Russia had been a great success. The company now had 245 outlets serving some 800,000 people daily. Pushkin Square alone had served some 130 million meals. The company had 25,000 employees and was responsible for another 100,000 jobs among its suppliers. Its parent, meanwhile, had cemented its position as the globe's leading food service company, with more than 31,000 restaurants in 118 countries.

Khasbulatov reminisced about how McDonald's had taken on post-Soviet entropy and won. To deal with the problems of an inconvertible currency, the company had hit on the strategy of plowing its rubles into local real estate. Since the company was allowed to take part of the rents from its foreign tenants in hard currency, it was thus able to import supplies that it couldn't source locally.

Eventually, the ruble had become convertible, although that certainly hadn't been the end of Russia's currency problems. Still, said Khasbulatov, given the harrowing experiences of its early years, it had been relatively easy to cope with the 1998 Russian financial crisis, when the ruble had again undergone major devaluation. Many other foreign investors had left at that time. McDonald's had hung in, continuing to build a management team tempered in the fires of business adversity. Khasbulatov said that most of his executives came from among those eager young Russians applauding customers and serving "Beeg Maks" at Pushkin Square in 1991.

McDonald's success in Russia was all the more remarkable because, although the country had changed immeasurably in the 20 years following the collapse of the Soviet Union, there were still cold winds blowing from the Kremlin. When Soviet Communism had imploded, a naive belief had emerged that capitalism would somehow "break out" spontaneously amidst the rubble. But how could the Russian people be expected to welcome a system not only that they were naturally inclined to distrust, but that had been demonized for 70 years? They also did not understand the importance of sound legal and political institutions and, equally important, the cultural characteristics of trust and cooperation. These were taken for granted in the West but had taken literally centuries to develop.

Under President Boris Yeltsin, who succeeded Mikhail Gorbachev, one of the strategies of post-Communist "shock therapy" had been to get government-controlled assets as quickly as possible into private hands. These assets were grabbed by a group of former Communist apparatchiks known as the "oligarchs," who were inevitably deeply resented.

In 2000, Yeltsin had been succeeded by Vladimir Putin, a former head of the KGB. Putin concentrated on bringing the Russian oil and gas industry back under state control as a means of securing revenue for his main purpose, which was to make Russia respected and feared again on the world stage. This process was made much easier by resentment against the oligarchs. The best-known example of Putin's shrewd move against them was the expropriation of the oil company Yukos and the show trial and imprisonment of its head, Mikhail Khodorkovsky. Khodorkovsky had proved a consummately skillful businessman, but he had been rash enough also to express interest in promoting political reform. Putin's regime was also marked by the unsolved murders of numerous businessmen and journalists.

The fate of these journalists had provided a point of reflection. When I returned to Toronto from Moscow in 1991, I went to see George Cohon, whose brainchild Moscow McDonald's had been. Cohon hadn't liked my questions and had threatened the magazine that was to publish my article with a lawsuit, even though he hadn't seen the article.

The article was published. There was no lawsuit. However, I wondered what might have happened if I had been trying to publish my story in a Russian magazine and a truly "powerful" figure — that is, a businessman with political influence — had decided to stop it. The failure of Cohon's threats in fact exemplified the much-to-be-desired *lack* of corporate power in the West.

Under capitalism, Cohon's considerable personal drive was channelled into positive activities. Could anybody deny that ambitious men are infinitely preferable as capitalists rather than as commissars? The oligarchs had almost all been stars in the Communist system, so their "success" in the subsequent privatization free-for-all was a stark reminder of the importance of the institutional environment for what people do with their lives and how, and how much, they contribute to society.

Adam Smith's great concern, as the scholar Jerry Z. Muller wrote, was "to take man as he is and to make him more like what he is capable of becoming, not by exerting government power and not primarily by preaching, but by discovering the institutions that make man tolerably decent and may make him more so."

Communism had channelled talented people who might have become capitalists into careers as commissars. After the fall of the Soviet Union, outrage was expressed when former commissars turned into capitalists, but this could hardly be laid at the door of capitalism. However, the unfairness of the privatization process provided an attractive political platform.

Vladimir Putin's approach was regarded as a model in at least one foreign capital, Havana, where the geriatric Castro brothers saw *putinismo*, with business under the thumb of a powerful state, as a possible escape hatch from any prospect of a "Havana Spring."

When Boris Yeltsin died in April 2007, obituaries across the Western media suggested that his regime had been most significant not for negotiating through the wreckage created by Communism but for unleashing "Wild West" capitalism, "buccaneer" capitalism or "crony" capitalism. The *Guardian* doubled up on the negative epithets by invoking "crony robber capitalism." The *Times* of London noted that Yeltsin's regime marked the lurch to the "barely regulated chaos of primitive capitalism." Even the *Wall Street Journal* claimed that it was his attempts to introduce capitalism that had "impoverished tens of millions, while enriching a handful, triggering a wrenching financial crisis in 1998." At least the *Journal* acknowledged that this process had given capitalism a "bad name," as if a worse name were possible. What these assessments confirmed above all was that capitalism remained a catch-all term for everything from criminality to fascism. Faced with the consequences of the collapse of Communism, both Russian autocrats and Western pundits reflexively blamed capitalism.

Putin was obliged by the Russian constitution to stand down as president in 2008 after two terms, but he continued to hold power as prime minister while his successor, Dmitry Medvedev, kept his chair warm. In 2012, Putin became president again. Under these circumstances, it paid for investors and businesses in Russia to keep mum about politics. McDonald's was happy to oblige.

The McDonald's experience in Russia represented an astonishing triumph of capitalist enterprise. The company stood for much more than simply fast food. That's why it had to keep its head down. Khamzat Khasbulatov took obvious pride when he said that McDonald's had become "part of Russian life, and a big part of the change in the country as well."

He admitted that the company still had problems with bureaucracy, the legal system and infrastructure, but he was understandably reluctant to discuss broader political issues. "My policy is to serve customers," he said.

Adam Smith would approve.

—m—

When the history of recent millennial times is written, there will be few more intriguing questions than why the majority of the global scientific community was so naturally inclined, or easily persuaded, or bullied, to support a draconian extension of political control in the name of managing the weather and securing a more "sustainable" future. The alleged "consensus" about the threat of catastrophic man-made global warming was a major factor in gaining widespread media and popular support for the notion that climate science was "settled."

Such beliefs could never have been successfully peddled if they had not fitted so easily into the anti-capitalist moral compost that had been accumulating since the Industrial Revolution. However, by 2013, both the climate policy and sustainable development juggernauts were coming off the rails. Not only had the Kyoto process collapsed, but the UN's Rio+20 conference, in June 2012, which was meant to celebrate progress toward sustainability, descended into farce — not least because nobody was quite sure what sustainable success looked like. Rio+20, which was very different from Maurice Strong's 1992 must-attend event, featured mostly B-list world leaders. (No Barack Obama. No David Cameron. No Stephen Harper. No Angela Merkel.) An umbrella group of NGOs bemoaned the 283-point official text's lack of mention of "planetary boundaries, tipping points or planetary carrying capacity," the very shibboleths of radical environmentalism's catastrophic assumptions.

The Rio+20 text had originally been sold as promoting "The Future We Want." However, the "we" in question had always been a self-selected group of aspiring global governors, UN bureaucrats, alarmist NGOs and corporate trendies, subsidy seekers and main-chancers whose interests were at odds with those of ordinary people. Rio+20's fizzling failure should be celebrated as "The Future We Avoided."

The grand UN-based system conceived by the likes of Maurice Strong to coordinate the activities of all mankind had proved utterly unsustainable, a dysfunctional mess that continued to generate nothing but endless meetings, agendas and reports. That sustainable development would inevitably collapse under its own contradictions was inevitable. What was fascinating was why every government on earth had earnestly committed itself to a concept hatched by ardent confessed socialists. Equally fascinating was the almost universal reluctance to acknowledge the extent of the organizational mess that had ensued.

Utopian fantasy had turned — yet again — into bureaucratic nightmare. The notion that the world could be weaned off fossil fuels by bureaucratic edict had proven a costly disaster. Green industrial strategies — which focused on the subsidy of technologies such as wind and solar power and the promotion of electric vehicles — were everywhere in crisis.

The UN-based institutional structure that was meant to control the great transformation had descended into Kafkaesque confusion. The process had three masters: the UN Environment Program (UNEP), which had been set up after Stockholm in 1972; the Commission on Sustainable Development (CSD), which had been created after Rio in 1992; and the UN's Economic and Social Council (ECOSOC), to which the CSD theoretically reported.

A 2011 report from Stakeholder Forum, a UK-based UN agency, and the Commonwealth Secretariat found these bureaucracies to be ill-coordinated and increasingly disconnected from the proliferating group of UN secretariats formed to deal with ever-multiplying multinational environmental agreements. Indeed, nobody had a handle on just how many programs, projects and organizations there were within the UN's exploding eco-regulatory universe. The report also found that this unwieldy system, which was meant to impose a god-like "balance," contained no mechanism for assessing whether the environmental benefits of agreements were actually greater than the costs of their implementation.

The "limits to growth"–style thinking that was at the heart of the sustainability project was also having trouble with the constant ability of capitalist ingenuity to breach those alleged limits. In October 2011, Dennis Meadows — the lead author of *The Limits to Growth*, the book that had been so influential in confirming the primitive prejudices of those who rejected the Invisible Hand — gave a speech in Ottawa in which he declared that it was "too late for sustainable development." He suggested, however, that there still might be some hope for salvation if people could just learn to "modify" their behaviour. It might be no more difficult than simply learning to fold your arms the opposite way. (He invited the audience to join him in this hokey exercise.)

During the question period, somebody was impolite enough to point out that Meadows had claimed a decade earlier that Canadian natural gas production had peaked. In fact, the application of sophisticated technologies such as horizontal drilling and hydraulic fracturing had made vast new reserves of shale gas economic to produce. Meadows squirmed to evade the latest example of human ingenuity exploding predictions of doom.

The authoritarian aspirations of sustainability were put on display again in 2012 by another co-author of *The Limits to Growth*, Jorgen Randers, in a book titled *2052: A Global Forecast for the Next Forty Years.* The root cause of all present and future woes, according to Randers, was the "short-termism" not just of capitalism but of democracy, against which he set the benign potential rule of "supranational bodies." Given the UN's disorganization and corruption, his claim seemed almost satirical. However, according to Randers, rejection of rule by the UN and its satellites was due merely to irrationality.

Randers projected a survivable world for the lucky few, such as himself, even though his vision sounded like something out of *Blade Runner*. He reluctantly acknowledged that water, food and fossil fuels would be available in 2052, but only "for those who can pay." Obviously he preferred a system in which access to water, food and energy was dictated by those who had power. There would even be some successes, according to Randers. He singled out China, but only if it could avoid "counterrevolution" against its "harmonious" authoritarian approach.

His praise for the Chinese model was in distinct contrast to his condemnation of the United States, for which he harboured hopes of revolution. "I believe such revolution in the United States would have exactly the opposite effect of counterrevolution in China," he wrote. "It would accelerate GDP growth and increase the effort to make the country more climate-friendly. If the revolution were associated with the election of a strong government, one would get the additional advantage of an increase in the planned investments necessary to boost well-being and postpone climate change."

Of the private sector, Randers projected that "it will become increasingly dangerous for high-profile corporations to deviate from acceptable behaviour — as defined by civil society." That is, business would have to kowtow to activist NGO thuggery, or else. However, he looked to "progressive heads of multinational corporations," presumably the kind of useful idiots who congregated annually at Davos, to join the coalition against free markets that would be orchestrated by the alphabet soup of international bureaucracies and NGOs, from the IPCC and UNEP to the WWF and Greenpeace.

Randers channelled his inner Mrs. Jellyby — the character from Dickens's *Bleak House* who neglects her children while obsessing over salvationist (but ultimately failed) plans for Africa — by suggesting that his own daughter was "dangerous" because her ecological footprint was 10 times that of an Indian girl. One might be tempted to write off Meadows and Randers as crackpots — the term so often used to denigrate climate "deniers" — if their thinking had not come to permeate the international agenda in the previous 20 years.

History meanwhile seemed to have proved Smith right in spades, but most people still didn't seem to get it. Was there any likelihood that they might? Does it matter?

—∞—

Some think that Smith's reflections on self-deceit in *The Theory of Moral Sentiments* inspired Robert Burns's poem "To a Louse":

> O wad some Power the giftie gie us
> To see oursels as others see us.
> It wad frae monie a blunder free us
> An' foolish notion.

The study of economics harboured a good many foolish — not to mention deadly — notions in the two centuries after Smith's death and continues to do so. I have suggested that the route to better understanding those "notions" lies in the study of human nature and the evolved — or unevolved — psyche, of which self-deception is a basic element. But it would be naive to be too optimistic.

Evolutionary psychology promises to be a valuable contributor to the "science of man" project originally pursued by

Hume and Smith. In particular, it can help us understand the conflict between the moral sentiments and the Invisible Hand. This clash has been at the root of political conflict for more than a hundred years. Ironically, however, evolutionary psychology is itself permeated by many of the anti-capitalist assumptions that I believe it should be examining, as is social science more generally.

As the former OECD chief economist David Henderson has pointed out, when it comes to economics, people do not know what they do not know, so they are unaware of what economics can teach them. Similarly, nobody wants to see himself as moralistic rather than moral. People want to believe that their ideas of right and wrong are based on eternal verities rather than on an imperfect, emotionally driven evolved faculty rooted in tribal utility and subject to social evolution and current fashion.

It would thus be naive to suggest that "we must" try to understand ourselves better, to learn about and appreciate the nature of economic markets and to be ever mindful of the fact that the moral sentiments can lead us astray. I hope that my attempt to plumb the psychology of Invisible Hand-biting may at least help those who support freedom and free markets to understand better why their opponents often see them merely as the peddlers of ideological "dirty pictures."

One of the weaknesses of promoters of free markets is that they imagine that pointing out policy failures might actually undermine their interventionist opponents' bedrock beliefs. Central planners tend to interpret failure not as *fundamental and inevitable* to their approach, but as merely indicating the need for more assiduous program tinkering and policy innovation. Policy inaction is inconceivable because it is considered morally inexcusable. The policy wonk's perpetual question, when faced with policy failure, is "Would you have us do nothing?" I have tried to suggest that the appropriate answer in many — if not the vast majority of — cases is "Yes."

"Doing nothing" sounds irresponsible, but what it really means is *government* doing nothing. People facing genuine problems do not "do nothing." They address them individually and by collective action without any need for policy guidance.

People are designed by evolution not to recognize themselves as power-hungry in order to be all the better at pursuing coercive power. They see themselves as being concerned only for bringing benefits to others, which will be achieved by expropriating commercial "oppressors," controlling market "exploiters" and "speaking up" for the consumer and the little guy.

This is certainly not to recommend *no* government, or to suggest there are no good reasons for going into politics. But I hope it is not too cynical to suggest that those who go into politics might be broadly divided into two groups: those who want to do good, and those who want to make sure that those who want to do good do not do too much harm.

It would be most naive of all to imagine that reflexive anti-capitalist power seekers would suddenly declare, "Oh, silly us. Here we are being driven by self-serving subconscious Machiavellian tendencies fed by unevolved Malthusian assumptions and primitive moralism. All this time we've been demonizing our opponents while of course they have a very good point. Just look objectively at history." People are obviously reluctant to be educated out of their emotional satisfactions, particularly when those satisfactions come attached not merely to moral self-inflation but to the exercise of power over others.

So, if capitalism functions, more or less, despite being fettered, and although people misunderstand, distrust or even hate it, does that matter? Ultimately it does, because misapprehensions will always be used for political purposes that undermine both wealth and freedom.

Capitalism has never promised to eradicate folly, or bad judgment, or criminality. Indeed, since it is not an articulated ideology, it has never promised anything. But it tends naturally to discourage such behaviours. It is not an anarchic system. It requires property rights and laws to ensure the enforcement of contracts and the punishment of crime. It promotes and rewards honesty and prudence. It facilitates charity.

One of the greatest misunderstandings about the 2008-09 financial crisis was that it represented "market failure." On the contrary, markets do not fail, only people do. It is markets that mete out the punishment. Markets are not perfect but then neither are they perfectible, except through their own ongoing evolution. Meanwhile human irrationality in no way justifies more government intervention, however subtle those new "nudges" may claim to be, unless such intervention is accompanied by a thorough examination of the irrationality that motivates the urge to power and leads it to seize upon any rationalization that serves its purposes. When it comes to academic analysis, this critical area appears to be almost a black hole.

The 2008-09 crisis was rooted at least partly in the belief that governments were minding the store — but in fact they were looting it. When it came to the human flaws that lay behind the private sector's contribution to the crisis, greed was perhaps less important than the hubris of financial engineers, along with people's natural deference to authority, and simple trust, which is so essential to the functioning of society but can wind up misplaced. Just look at all the bright people and institutions who invested with Bernie Madoff.

All that governments' best and brightest did to "save" the world from crisis was — like Gordon Brown — to clumsily throw huge amounts of taxpayers' money, and taxpayers' obligations in the form of government debt, at the problem; organize panicky bailouts; and recommend more and bigger oversight, thus not merely delaying dealing with underlying issues, but expanding the moral hazard that would ensure future crises. Government could only "bail out" capitalism because it knew — or desperately hoped — that capitalism would bail out government.

Politicians who had any knowledge of Adam Smith were no doubt praying that he was right in suggesting that private effort and initiative would compensate for "absurd" policy prescriptions. What made many of those prescriptions absurd was their failure to grasp both that the Invisible Hand is perhaps the most powerful and beneficent systemic force in human history, and that when you bite it, it always bites back.

Acknowledgements

It would be comforting, but inaccurate, to say that the list of those who encouraged me to write this book is long. My initial proposal, which started life as "In Search of Capitalism," met with underwhelming interest in the publishing community. I decided to write the book anyway. Eventually, I found an editor who was prepared to read it. Jonathan Schmidt of Key Porter was enthusiastic to publish, but Key Porter promptly went bankrupt. I thank Jonathan for his continued support, and for introducing me to Don Bastian, who planted the seed of self-publication, even though I did not in the end use his services.

I owe a great debt to Jan Walter, with whom, when she was a principal of Macfarlane Walter & Ross, I had published two previous books. I had not seen Jan for 10 years but somehow persuaded her to read the manuscript. She sent a wonderful note: "What a ride! This is exhilarating, heady, provocative, and infuriating reading." No word could have been more encouraging than "infuriating."

Jan provided me with another great gift by putting me back in touch with Barbara Czarnecki, who had worked on some of my previous books. Barbara agreed to be my editor and not merely displayed meticulous skill and consummate professionalism but offered me sound advice throughout a journey that was novel for both of us. I am profoundly grateful to her.

I also thank Donna Laframboise, who had gone through the self-publishing process, and her husband, Alan Dean, for their insights. Professor Filip Palda, too, was kind enough to share his experiences and frustrations.

I thank all those I interviewed in the course of my research, although I sometimes deal with them critically. One man to whom I refer several times but want to acknowledge again is David Henderson. Not only did two of his books provide inspiration, but he was kind enough to give me his time in London.

My Toronto friends have had to put up for a long time with references to "the book." First among them I thank Jim Doak. Jim at times seemed to know where I was going better than I did. The other long-term supporter of this project is Bob Lamond, who not merely shared an interest in Adam Smith but came from his home town of Kirkcaldy. Bob, a successful Calgary petroleum entrepreneur, provided me with some financial support early on, although only because he thought I was writing a completely different book. My thanks to him for not asking for his money back.

During most of the time I was writing this book, I was also producing a twice-weekly column for the *Financial Post* editorial page in the *National Post*. That column enabled me to delve into many of the issues covered in this book. I thank the *FP*'s editor, Terry Corcoran, for his support. I also thank Terry's wife, Claudia Krawchuk, for allowing me to inflict an early version of the manuscript upon her, to which she responded with valuable comments. Another prominent contributor to the *FP*'s editorial page, Larry Solomon, provided inspiration in many ways without going so far as to actually read the manuscript! Another gift from the *Post* was its graphics editor Rich Johnson, who was just transferring to the *Washington Post* when I persuaded him to design the book's cover.

One institution that I have to thank — although the thanks have been a long time coming — is the British Tourist Authority, which provided assistance in setting up that seminal trip between the tombs of Adam Smith and Karl Marx in 1993. I hope this book may inspire some readers to retrace that fascinating journey.

Another seminal piece of research, although I didn't realize it at the time, was the trip I took to Moscow and Helsinki in 1991 to write on Moscow McDonald's for *Canadian Business* magazine. That article not only formed the basis for the Moscow McDonald's chapter but raised questions that are at the heart of this book. I have to thank in particular the magazine's editor at the time, Randy Litchfield, who is still a good friend. When I speculate in the book about donating a kidney, he was the thought experiment's potential recipient (fortunately he has never needed it).

I also thank John Macfarlane at the *Walrus* magazine for commissioning me to write "What Would Smith Say?," an article on what the Sage of Kirkcaldy might have thought about the 2008 financial crisis. My association with John goes back a long way, through *Saturday Night* magazine and *Toronto Life,* and his time as another of the principals of Macfarlane Walter & Ross.

Among others who have helped, from providing information, advice or support to reading all or parts of the manuscript, I have to thank Michael Walker, Dirk Schlimm and Jennifer Clement, Halsey Bradford, Roger Best, Jim O'Malley, Patrick Luciani, Ron Moore, Gerry Nicholls, Garrett Herman and Chris Turney. In England, I especially have to thank Andrew Turnbull, Benny Peiser, Nigel Lawson, David Norman, Mike Lodwig, Alan Hunt and Ian Martin.

I was lucky enough to be invited to several symposia put on by the Liberty Fund. These exposed me to some extremely bright and thoughtful individuals who shared my enthusiasm for free markets. I also found the conferences of the Human Behavior and Evolution Society that I attended fascinating and useful, although I very much doubt that the HBES would want to be associated with all, or perhaps any of, my conclusions.

Again, I greatly benefited from meeting with and reading the works of Steven Pinker, David Livingston Smith and Ullica Segerstrale, but I doubt that they would support all my speculations. Jonathan Haidt was also kind enough to correspond with me, although I disagree with him on many points.

I encountered many fascinating and helpful people in and around Kirkcaldy, Glasgow and Edinburgh. Most are mentioned in the manuscript. Two who are not are Ann Watters and Douglas Mason. Ann Watters was chairwoman of the Kirkcaldy Civic Society when I met her. Douglas Mason was influential in the policies of Margaret Thatcher (especially the controversial poll tax, which arguably led to her downfall) until a tragic illness sidelined him and left him in straitened circumstances. Both were generous with their time. Both have since died.

Finally, I want to thank my daughter, Laurel. Laurel arrived on earth two years after my first trip to Kirkcaldy, accompanied me on a later visit to that hallowed (but less than touristy) place, suffered through road trips to both New Lanark and New Harmony, and has always provided me with inspiration.

Errors in this book are, of course, entirely my own.

Select Bibliography

Akerlof, George A., and Robert J. Shiller. *Animal Spirits: How Human Psychology Drives the Economy, and Why It Matters for Global Capitalism*. Princeton University Press, 2009.

Albom, Mitch. *Tuesdays with Morrie*. Broadway Books, 1997.

Anderson, Ray C. *Mid-Course Correction*. Chelsea Green Publishing, 1998.

Anderson, Ray, Charlie Eitel and J. Zink. *Face It: A Spiritual Journey of Leadership*. Peregrinzilla Press, 1996.

Arnhart, Larry. *Darwinian Conservatism*. Imprint Academic, 2005.

Baechler, Jean. *The Origins of Capitalism*. Translated by Barry Cooper. Basil Blackwell, 1976. Originally published as *Les Origines du capitalisme*, Editions Gallimard, 1971.

Bagehot, Walter. "Adam Smith as a Person: An Essay." 1876. http://oll.libertyfund.org/?option=com_staticxt&staticfile=show.php%3Ftitle=2165&chapter=200839&layout=html&Itemid=27

Bakan, Joel. *The Corporation: The Pathological Pursuit of Profit and Power*. Penguin, 2004.

Barkow, Jerome H., Leda Cosmides and John Tooby. *The Adapted Mind: Evolutionary Psychology and the Generation of Culture*. Oxford University Press, 1992.

Bast, Joseph, Peter Hill and Richard Rue. *Eco-Sanity: A Common Sense Guide to Environmentalism*. Heartland Institute, 1994.

Bastiat, Frédéric. *The Law*. Foundation for Economic Education, 1998. First published in 1850. Online at Bastiat.org.

Beckerman, Wilfred. *A Poverty of Reason: Sustainable Development and Economic Growth*. Independent Institute, 2004.

Boswell, James. *The Life of Samuel Johnson, LL.D*. Wordsworth Classics of World Literature, 1999.

Bramwell, Anna. *Ecology in the 20th Century: A History*. Yale University Press, 1989.

——. *The Fading of the Greens: The Decline of Environmental Politics in the West*. Yale University Press, 1994.

Branden, Barbara. *The Passion of Ayn Rand*. Doubleday, 1986.

Brown, Andrew. *The Darwin Wars: The Scientific Battle for the Soul of Man*. Touchstone, 2000.

Brown, Gordon. *Beyond the Crash: Overcoming the First Crisis of Globalization*. Free Press, 2010.

Buchan, James. *The Authentic Adam Smith*. Atlas Books, 2007. Published in Great Britain as *Adam Smith and the Pursuit of Perfect Liberty*.

Buchanan, James M. *Better Than Plowing and Other Personal Essays*. University of Chicago Press, 1992.

———. *What Should Economists Do?* Liberty Press, 1979.

Buchanan, James M., and Richard E. Wagner. *Democracy in Deficit: The Political Legacy of Lord Keynes*. Academic Press, 1977.

Cairncross, Frances. *Costing the Earth: The Challenge for Governments, the Opportunities for Business*. Harvard Business School Press, 1992.

Caplan, Bryan. *The Myth of the Rational Voter: Why Democracies Choose Bad Policies*. Princeton University Press, 2007.

Chagnon, Napoleon. *Noble Savages: My Life Among Two Dangerous Tribes – the Yanomamo and the Anthropologists*. Simon & Schuster, 2013.

———. *Yanomamo: The Fierce People*. Holt, Rinehart and Winston, 1977.

Chambers, Whittaker. *Witness*. Random House, 1952.

Cohan, William D. *House of Cards: A Tale of Hubris and Wretched Excess on Wall Street*. Doubleday, 2009.

Confer, Jaime C., Judith A. Easton, Diana S. Fleischman, Cari D. Goetz, David M. G. Lewis, Carin Perilloux, and David M. Buss. "Evolutionary Psychology: Controversies, Questions, Prospects, and Limitations." *American Psychologist*, February-March 2010.

Cosmides, Leda, and John Tooby. "Better Than Rational: Evolutionary Psychology and the Invisible Hand." *American Economic Review* 84, no. 2 (May 1994): 327-332.

Damasio, Antonio. *Descartes' Error: Emotion, Reason, and the Human Brain*. Penguin, 1994.

Darwall, Rupert. *The Age of Global Warming: A History*. Quartet Books, 2013.

Darwin, Charles. *The Descent of Man*. Penguin Classics, 2004.

———. *The Origin of Species*. Edited with an introduction by J.W. Burrow. Penguin Classics, 1985.

Dawkins, Richard. *The Blind Watchmaker: Why the Evidence of Evolution Reveals a Universe Without Design*. W.W. Norton, 1987.

———. *The Selfish Gene*. Oxford University Press, 2006.

de Waal, Frans. *Chimpanzee Politics: Power and Sex Among Apes*. Rev. ed. John Hopkins University Press, 1998.

———. *Good Natured: The Origins of Right and Wrong in Humans and Other Animals*. Harvard University Press, 1996.

Dennett, Daniel C. *Darwin's Dangerous Idea: Evolution and the Meanings of Life*. Touchstone, 1995.

Dewar, Elaine. *Cloak of Green: The Links Between Key Environmental Groups, Government and Big Business*. James Lorimer, 1995.

Donnachie, Ian. *Robert Owen: Owen of New Lanark and New Harmony*. Tuckwell Press, 2000.

Drucker, Peter F. *Post-Capitalist Society*. Harper Business, 1993.

Durant, Will. *The Story of Philosophy*. Pocket Books, 1953.

Easterly, William. *The White Man's Burden: Why the West's Efforts to Aid the Rest Have Done So Much Ill and So Little Good*. Penguin, 2006.

Ebenstein, Lanny. *Milton Friedman: A Biography*. Palgrave Macmillan, 2007.

Essex, Christopher, and Ross McKitrick. *Taken by Storm: The Troubled Science, Policy and Politics of Global Warming*. Rev. ed. Key Porter Books, 2007.

Ferguson, Niall. *The Ascent of Money: A Financial History of the World*. Penguin Press, 2008.

Ferguson, Niall. *The Cash Nexus: Money and Power in the Modern World, 1700-2000*. Penguin Press, 2001.

Frank, Robert. *Passions Within Reason: The Strategic Role of the Emotions*. W.W. Norton, 1988.

Friedman, Milton. "Champion of Economic Freedom." Interview by Academy of Achievement, January 31,1991. http://www.achievement.org/autodoc/page/fri0int-1

Fukuyama, Francis. *The End of History and the Last Man*. Free Press, 1992.

Gladwell, Malcolm. *Blink: The Power of Thinking Without Thinking*. Little, Brown, 2005.

Gore, Al. *The Assault on Reason*. Penguin Press, 2007.

———. *Earth in the Balance: Ecology and the Human Spirit*. Houghton Mifflin, 1992.

Haidt, Jonathan. *The Righteous Mind: Why Good People Are Divided by Politics and Religion*. Pantheon, 2012.

Harman, Oren. *The Price of Altruism: George Price and the Search for the Origins of Kindness*. W.W. Norton, 2010.

Harris, Sam. *The Moral Landscape*. Free Press, 2010.

Hauser, Marc D. *Moral Minds: How Nature Designed Our Universal Sense of Right and Wrong*. Ecco/HarperCollins, 2006.

Hawken, Paul. *The Ecology of Commerce: A Declaration of Sustainability*. HarperBusiness, 1993.

Hayek, Friedrich A., ed. *Capitalism and the Historians*. University of Chicago Press, 1954.

———. *The Constitution of Liberty*. University of Chicago Press, 1978.

———. *The Fatal Conceit: The Errors of Socialism*. Edited by W.W. Bartley III. Vol. 1 of *The Collected Works of F.A. Hayek*. University of Chicago Press, 1988.

———. *Hayek on Hayek: An Autobiographical Dialogue*. Edited by Stephen Kresge and Leif Wenar. University of Chicago Press, 1994.

———. "The Intellectuals and Socialism." *University of Chicago Law Review*, Spring 1949.

———. *The Road to Serfdom.* Edited by Bruce Caldwell. Vol. 2 of *The Collected Works of F.A. Hayek.* University of Chicago Press, 2007.

Hazlitt, Henry. *Economics in One Lesson.* Crown, 1979.

———. *The Failure of the "New Economics": An Analysis of the Keynesian Fallacies.* Ludwig von Mises Institute, 2007. First published by Van Nostrand in 1959.

Heilbroner, Robert. *Twenty-First Century Capitalism.* House of Anansi Press, 1992.

Henderson, David. *Innocence and Design: The Influence of Economic Ideas on Policy.* The 1985 BBC Reith Lectures. Basil Blackwell. 1986.

———. *The Role of Business in the Modern World: Progress, Pressures, and Prospects for the Market Economy.* Competitive Enterprise Institute, 2004.

Herman, Arthur. *How the Scots Invented the Modern World: The True Story of How Western Europe's Poorest Nation Created Our World and Everything in It.* Crown, 2001.

Hosle, Vittorio, and Christian Illies, eds. *Darwinism & Philosophy.* University of Notre Dame Press, 2005.

Hume, David. *A Treatise of Human Nature.* Penguin Classics, 1969. First published in 1739 and 1740.

Johnson, Paul. *The Birth of the Modern: World Society, 1815-1830*. HarperCollins, 1991.

——. "Blessing Capitalism." *Commentary*, May 1993.

——. *Modern Times: The World from the Twenties to the Eighties*. Harper Colophon, 1985.

Kahneman, Daniel. *Thinking, Fast and Slow*. Farrar, Straus and Giroux, 2011.

Kaletsky, Anatole. *Capitalism 4.0: The Birth of a New Economy in the Aftermath of a Crisis*. Public Affairs, 2010.

Kealey, Terence. *Sex, Science & Profits*. William Heinemann, 2008.

Klaus, Vaclav. *Blue Planet in Green Shackles: What Is Endangered: Climate or Freedom?* Competitive Enterprise Institute. 2007.

Kohn, Marek. *A Reason for Everything: Natural Selection and the English Imagination*. Faber and Faber, 2004.

Kuhn, Thomas S. *The Structure of Scientific Revolutions*. 3rd ed. University of Chicago Press. 1996.

Laframboise, Donna. *The Delinquent Teenager Who Was Mistaken for the World's Top Climate Expert*. Ivy Avenue Press. 2011.

Lawson, Nigel. *An Appeal to Reason: A Cool Look at Global Warming*. Duckworth Overlook, 2008.

——. "Five Myths and a Menace." Inaugural Adam Smith Lecture, Pembroke College, Cambridge, November 22, 2010.

Lemieux, Pierre. *Somebody in Charge: A Solution to Recession*. Palgrave Macmillan, 2011.

Lewis, Bernard. *What Went Wrong: The Clash Between Islam and Modernity in the Middle East*. Perennial, 2002.

Lindsey, Brink. *Against the Dead Hand: The Uncertain Struggle for Global Capitalism*. John Wiley & Sons, 2002.

Lloyd, John. *The Protest Ethic: How the Anti-Globalization Movement Challenges Social Democracy*. Demos, 2001.

Lomborg, Bjørn. *The Skeptical Environmentalist: Measuring the Real State of the World*. Cambridge University Press, 2001. First published in Danish in 1998.

Love, John F. *McDonald's: Behind the Arches*. Bantam, 1986.

Machiavelli, Niccolo. *The Prince*. Penguin Classics, 2003.

Mackay, Charles. *Memoirs of Extraordinary Popular Delusions and the Madness of Crowds*. 1885. Reprint: Coles, 1980.

Magee, Brian. *Confessions of a Philosopher*. Phoenix, 1998.

Mandeville, Bernard. *The Fable of the Bees: Or, Private Vices, Publick Benefits*. 1714. Reprint: Penguin Classics, 1989.

Marx, Karl, and Friedrich Engels. *The Communist Manifesto*. 1848.

Mayer, Colin. *Firm Commitment*. Oxford University Press, 2013.

Meadows, Donella H., Dennis L. Meadows, Jorgen Randers, and William W. Behrens III. *The Limits to Growth: A Report for the Club of Rome's Project on the Predicament of Mankind*. Potomac Associates, 1972.

Michaels, Patrick, ed. *Climate Coup: Global Warming's Invasion of Our Government and Our Lives*. Cato Institute, 2011.

Milloy, Steve. *Green Hell: How Environmentalists Plan to Control Your Life and What You Can Do to Stop Them*. Regnery Publishing, 2009.

Mises, Ludwig von. *The Anti-Capitalistic Mentality*. Libertarian Press, 1972. First published by Van Nostrand in 1956.

———. *Human Action: A Treatise on Economics*. 3rd ed. Henry Regnery, 1966.

Montford, A.W. *Hiding the Decline: A History of the Climategate Affair*. Anglosphere Books, 2012.

———. *The Hockey Stick Illusion: Climategate and the Corruption of Science*. Stacey International, 2010.

Muller, Jerry Z. *Adam Smith in His Time and Ours: Designing the Decent Society*. Free Press, 1993.

———. *The Mind and the Market: Capitalism in Modern European Thought*. Alfred A. Knopf, 2002.

Munk, Nina. *The Idealist: Jeffrey Sachs and the Quest to End Poverty*. Doubleday, 2013.

Muravchik, Joshua. *Heaven on Earth: The Rise and Fall of Socialism*. Encounter Books, 2002.

Nasar, Sylvia. *A Beautiful Mind*. Simon & Schuster, 1998.

———. *Grand Pursuit: The Story of Economic Genius*. Simon & Schuster, 2011.

Nowak, Roger, with Martin Highfield. *SuperCooperators: Altruism, Evolution, and Why We Need Each Other to Succeed*. Free Press, 2011.

O'Rourke, P.J. *On the Wealth of Nations*. Douglas & McIntyre, 2006.

Orwell, George. *Nineteen Eighty-Four*. Penguin, 1983. First published by Martin Secker & Warburg in 1949.

Phillipson, Nicholas. *Adam Smith: An Enlightened Life*. Allen Lane, 2010.

Pinker, Steven. *The Better Angels of Our Nature: Why Violence Has Declined*. Viking, 2011.

———. *The Blank Slate: The Modern Denial of Human Nature*. Viking Penguin, 2002.

———. *How the Mind Works*. Norton, 1999.

———. "The Moral Instinct." *New York Times Magazine*, January 13, 2008.

——. *The Stuff of Thought: Language as a Window into Human Nature*. Viking Penguin, 2007.

Pipes, Richard. *Property and Freedom*. Alfred A. Knopf, 1999.

Popper, Karl. *The Open Society and Its Enemies*. 2 vols. Princeton University Press, 1971.

Posner, Richard A. *A Failure of Capitalism*. Harvard University Press, 2009.

Proceedings. Symposium organized by Kirkcaldy Town Council to celebrate the 250th anniversary of Adam Smith's birth, June 5-6, 1973. Kirkcaldy Library, Kirkcaldy, Scotland.

Radcliffe Richards, Janet. *The Ethics of Transplants: Why Careless Thought Costs Lives*. Oxford University Press, 2012.

Rae, John. *Life of Adam Smith*. 1895. Reprint: Thoemmes Antiquarian Books, 1990.

Rand, Ayn. *Atlas Shrugged*. Signet, n.d. First published in 1957.

——. *Capitalism: The Unknown Ideal*. Signet, 1967.

——. *The Fountainhead*. Bobbs Merrill, 1943.

——. *The New Left: The Anti-Industrial Revolution*. 2nd ed. Signet, 1975.

Randers, Jorgen. *2052: A Global Forecast for the Next Forty Years*. Chelsea Green, 2012.

Raphael, D.D. *Adam Smith*. Past Masters series. Oxford University Press, 1985.

Read, Leonard E. *I, Pencil*. Foundation for Economic Education, 1999. First published in 1958.

Reisman, George. *Capitalism: A Treatise on Economics*. Jameson Books, 1996.

Ridley, Matt. "Adam Darwin: Emergent Order in Biology and Economics." The Adam Smith Lecture, London, November 13, 2012.

———. *The Origins of Virtue: Human Instincts and the Evolution of Cooperation*. Penguin, 1996.

———. *The Rational Optimist*. HarperCollins, 2010.

Rosenberg, Nathan, and L.E. Birdzell, Jr. *How the West Grew Rich: The Economic Transformation of the Industrial World*. Basic Books, 1986.

Ross, Ian Simpson. *The Life of Adam Smith*. Oxford University Press, 1995.

Rothbard, Murray N. *An Austrian Perspective on the History of Economic Thought*. Vol. 1, *Economic Thought Before Adam Smith*. Vol. 2, *Classical Economics*. Edward Elgar, 1995.

Rothman, Stanley, S. Robert Lichter and Neil Nevitte. "Politics and Professional Advancement Among College Faculty." *The Forum* 3, no. 1 (2005).

Rothschild, Emma. *Economic Sentiments: Adam Smith, Condorcet, and the Enlightenment*. Harvard University Press, 2001.

Rubin, Jeff. *Why Your World Is About to Get a Whole Lot Smaller: Oil and the End of Globalization*. Random House Canada, 2009.

Rubin, Paul H. *Darwinian Politics: The Evolutionary Origin of Freedom*. Rutgers University Press, 2002.

Rubinstein, W.D. *Capitalism, Culture, and Decline in Britain, 1750-1990*. Routledge, 1993.

Schumpeter, Joseph. *Capitalism, Socialism and Democracy*. Harper Torchbooks, 1976. First published in 1942 by Harper & Brothers.

Sciabarra, Chris Matthew. *Ayn Rand: The Russian Radical*. Pennsylvania State University Press, 1995.

Seabright, Paul. *The Company of Strangers: A Natural History of Economic Life*. Princeton University Press, 2004.

Segerstrale, Ullica. *Defenders of the Truth: The Sociobiology Debate*. Oxford University Press, 2000.

——. *Nature's Oracle*. Oxford University Press, 2013.

Seldon, Arthur. *Capitalism*. Basil Blackwell, 1990.

Shabecoff, Philip. *A New Name for Peace: International Environmentalism, Sustainable Development, and Democracy*. University Press of New England, 1996.

Shlaes, Amity. *The Forgotten Man: A New History of the Great Depression*. HarperCollins, 2007.

Singer, Peter. *A Darwinian Left: Politics, Evolution and Cooperation*. Yale University Press, 2000.

Skinner, Andrew. Introduction to *The Wealth of Nations*, books 1-3, by Adam Smith. Penguin Classics, 1986.

Skousen, Mark. *Making Modern Economics: The Lives and Ideas of the Great Thinkers*. M.E. Sharpe, 2001.

Smith, Adam. *The Theory of Moral Sentiments*. Edited by D.D. Raphael and A.L. Macfie. Clarendon Press, 1976.

———. *The Wealth of Nations*. Edited by Edward Cannan. Methuen, 1904. http://www.econlib.org/library/Smith/smWN-Cover.html

Smith, David Livingston. *The Most Dangerous Animal: Human Nature and the Origins of War*. St. Martin's Press, 2007.

———. *Why We Lie: The Evolutionary Roots of Deception and the Unconscious Mind*. St. Martin's Press, 2004.

Solomon, Lawrence. *The Deniers: The World-Renowned Scientists Who Stood Up Against Global Warming Hysteria, Political Persecution, and Fraud (And Those Who Are Too Fearful to Do So)*. Richard Vigilante Books, 2008.

Sowell, Thomas. *A Conflict of Visions: Ideological Origins of Political Struggles*. Rev. ed. Perseus Books, 2007.

Strong, Maurice. *Where on Earth Are We Going?* Texere, 2001.

Sunstein, Cass. *Simpler: The Future of Government*. Simon & Schuster, 2013.

Swift, Jonathan. *Gulliver's Travels*. Penguin Classics, 2001.

Tarbell, Ida. *The History of the Standard Oil Company*. Briefer version, edited by David M. Chalmers. W.W. Norton, 1969.

Tett, Gillian. *Fool's Gold: How the Bold Dream of a Small Tribe at J.P. Morgan Was Corrupted by Wall Street Greed and Unleashed Catastrophe*. Free Press, 2009.

Thaler, Richard C., and Cass R. Sunstein. *Nudge: Improving Decisions About Health, Wealth, and Happiness*. Yale University Press, 2008.

Thatcher, Margaret. *The Downing Street Years*. HarperCollins, 1993.

Thucydides. *History of the Peloponnesian War*. Penguin Classics, 1972.

Trevelyan, G.M. *Illustrated English Social History*. Vol. 4, *The Nineteenth Century*. Longmans, Green, 1942.

Trivers, Robert. *The Folly of Fools: The Logic of Deceit and Self-Deception in Human Life*. Basic Books, 2011.

Uglow, Jenny. *The Lunar Men: The Friends Who Made the Future, 1730-1810*. Faber and Faber, 2002.

Viner, Jacob. "Adam Smith and Laissez Faire." Lecture delivered at the University of Chicago on January 21, 1927, in a series commemorative of the 150th anniversary of the publication of *The Wealth of Nations*.

Wright, Robert. *The Moral Animal: Why We Are the Way We Are; The New Science of Evolutionary Psychology*. Vintage Books, 1995.

Index